CULTURE AND THE STATE IN SPAIN: 1550-1850

HISPANIC ISSUES
VOLUME 20
GARLAND REFERENCE LIBRARY OF THE HUMANITIES
VOLUME 2169

Hispanic Issues

Volume 20	*Culture and the State in Spain: 1550-1850* Edited by Tom Lewis and Francisco J. Sánchez
Volume 19.	*Modernism and its Margins: Reinscribing Cultural Modernity from Spain and Latin America* Edited by Anthony L. Geist and José B. Monleón
Volume 18.	*A Revisionary History of Portuguese Literature* Edited by Miguel Tamen and Helena C. Buescu
Volume 17.	*Cervantes and his Postmodern Constituencies* Edited by Anne Cruz and Carroll B. Johnson
Volume 16.	*Modes of Representation in Spanish Cinema* Edited by Jenaro Talens and Santos Zunzunegui
Volume 15.	*Framing Latin American Cinema: Contemporary Critical Perspectives* Edited by Anne Marie Stock
Volume 14.	*Rhetoric and Politics: Baltasar Gracián and the New World Order* Edited by Nicholas Spadaccini and Jenaro Talens
Volume 13.	*Bodies and Biases: Sexualities in Hispanic Cultures and Literatures* Edited by David W. Foster and Roberto Reis
Volume 12.	*The Picaresque: Tradition and Displacement* Edited by Giancarlo Maiorino
Volume 11.	*Critical Practices in Post-Franco Spain* Edited by Silvia L. López, Jenaro Talens, and Dario Villanueva
Volume 10.	*Latin American Identity and Constructions of Difference* Edited by Amaryll Chanady
Volume 9.	*Amerindian Images and the Legacy of Columbus* Edited by René Jara and Nicholas Spadaccini
Volume 8.	*The Politics of Editing* Edited by Nicholas Spadaccini and Jenaro Talens
Volume 7.	*Culture and Control in Counter-Reformation Spain* Edited by Anne J. Cruz and Mary Elizabeth Perry
Volume 6.	*Cervantes's Exemplary Novels and the Adventure of Writing* Edited by Michael Nerlich and Nicholas Spadaccini
Volume 5.	*Ortega y Gasset and the Question of Modernity* Edited by Patrick H. Dust
Volume 4.	*1492-1992: Re/Discovering Colonial Writing* Edited by René Jara and Nicholas Spadaccini
Volume 3.	*The Crisis of Institutionalized Literature in Spain* Edited by Wlad Godzich and Nicholas Spadaccini
Volume 2.	*Autobiography in Early Modern Spain* Edited by Nicholas Spadaccini and Jenaro Talens
Volume 1.	*The Institutionalization of Literature in Spain* Edited by Wlad Godzich and Nicholas Spadaccini

HISPANIC ISSUES
VOLUME 20

CULTURE AND THE STATE IN SPAIN: 1550-1850

TOM LEWIS AND FRANCISCO J. SÁNCHEZ
◆
EDITORS

GARLAND PUBLISHING, INC.
A MEMBER OF THE TAYLOR & FRANCIS GROUP
NEW YORK AND LONDON
1999

The editors gratefully acknowledge assistance from the Program for Cultural Cooperation between Spain's Ministry of Culture and United States' Universities; the College of Liberal Arts and the Department of Spanish and Portuguese at the University of Minnesota; and the University of Iowa.

Published in 1999 by
Garland Publishing Inc.
A Member of the Taylor & Francis Group
19 Union Square West
New York, NY 10003

10 9 8 7 6 5 4 3 2 1

Library of Congress Cataloging-in-Publication Data

Culture and the state in Spain, 1550–1850 / Tom Lewis and Francisco J. Sánchez, editors.
p. cm. — (Hispanic issues ; v. 20) (Garland reference library of the humanitites; v. 2169)
Includes index.
ISBN 0-8153-3484-2 (alk. paper)
1. Spain—Civilization—1516–1700. 2. Spain—Civilization—18th century. 3. Spain—Civilization—19th century. 4. Spanish literature—Political aspects. 5. Literature and state—Spain. I. Lewis, Tom, 1950– . II. Sánchez, Francisco J., 1959– . III. Series: Garland reference library of the humanities. Hispanic issues ; v. 20. IV. Series : Garland reference library of the humanities ; vol. 2169.
DP171.5.C85 1999
946'.04—dc21 99-16669
CIP

Printed on acid-free, 250-year-life paper
Manufactured in the United States of America

Hispanic Issues

Contents

Introduction

Tom Lewis and Francisco J. Sánchez

This volume represents an attempt to understand relationships between subjectivity and the state in Spain from the earliest articulations of the "subject" during the Renaissance to the consolidation of an array of bourgeois subjectivities in the mid-nineteenth century. The major argument running throughout the volume is that "literary discourse," from the time it emerges in the sixteenth century to the time it coheres within a wholly modern concept of the "aesthetic," actively develops forms of subjectivity in relation to institutions of class power. Whether we are concerned with the spread of mercantile social relations within waning feudalism or with the cultural "naturalization" of fully capitalist social relations, "literature" reflects the emergence of sensibilities which seek to coordinate and unify the economic, linguistic, political, and social conditions for individual experience. The overall picture of subject formation and state formation presented in this volume, therefore, starts from the initial "autonomy" of "literature" as a sphere of subjectivity for early modern political elites and moves toward the nineteenth-century generalization of the "aesthetic" as a bourgeois sphere in which both state-imposed and self-conferred forms of political subjectivity are realized.

What recent scholarship considers as "cultural discourse" is here conceptualized as involving, on the one hand, the articulation of the sphere of politics as the sphere of power relations and, on the other hand, the sphere of the "aesthetic" as the sphere in which subjects imagine their mode of subjection to or ideal participation in the social order. Cultural discourse in this sense both engages a reality and sets in motion a process of self-reflection, which itself may be conscious or unconscious. Anthony Cascardi, for example, discerns in seventeenth-century Spain "a self that had not yet come to conceive of itself in abstract terms as detachable from a social context in the manner of the Cartesian, Lockean, or Humean subject" (256). Thus his work rightly emphasizes the contradictory role of the "aesthetic" as an attempt to recuperate emancipatory energies in the very act of helping to institutionalize modern forms of subjectivity (subjection). Cascardi's otherwise insightful analysis, however, takes into account only the philosophical and psychological effects of the various fractures in aristocratic ideology. We think that it is necessary to add that this crisis, in which one model of consciousness eventually displaces another, also involves the emergence of the "literary" and, eventually, the "aesthetic." The "literary" and the other cultural discourses comprising the "aesthetic" serve as mediations enabling the subject to understand or to accept that the detachment of his or her individual self from specific social contexts is the requirement for her or his subjection to the state. This is a phenomenon which is no doubt important to consider at our contemporary juncture where some postmodern versions of culture seem to do away with the role of the state.

Inspired by a conviction of the inseparability of state and subject representations, the studies included in this volume adopt a critical stance toward literary, symbolic, and ideological representations of the various ways in which individuals and groups conceived of their contradictory relation to new economic and political realities. During the Renaissance and baroque periods, it is evident that the production of symbols and ideas concerning individual identities is shaped by the manner in which and the extent to which the state produces its own discourses of knowledge, ethnicity, sexuality, and values. The state subsequently succeeds in recruiting literature into its direct service in the second half of the eighteenth century, thus creating conditions in which the "aesthetic" can acquire a fully public engagement. By the nineteenth century, however, "literature" has become a commodity, circulating on the market and forcing authors to consider their potential publics as well as their potential patrons. In these circumstances, the "aesthetic"—now defined as a specific practice of writing concerned to shape a world of inner feelings and to adapt them to changing realities—regains a certain autonomy from direct state control. While the relationship between the state and the aesthetic thereby becomes more indirect, it paradoxically gains new strength by having the aesthetic begin to function "all on its own."

Discourses of Differentiation: "Literature" and the "Subject"

In the sixteenth and seventeenth centuries, Spanish economic and political developments are not supported by a culture imbued with a spirit of religious tolerance, scientific discovery, and philosophical inquiry. The formation of a "literary" culture, however, remains an important mediation conditioning the emergence of new, self-focusing conceptions of class as well as the group differences they entail. The research carried out by Wlad Godzich and Nicholas Spadaccini on the origin and functions of "literature" in Spain, for example, shares with Cascardi's work on the problem of "detaching" subjects from specific social contexts an explicitly Weberian emphasis on the history of institutions.

Nevertheless, Godzich and Spadaccini manage to tie the development of the "literary" more closely to the development of the state than does Cascardi. They explain the birth of "literature" in Spain precisely as the result of the rise of a specific practice of writing out of the confluence of a number of separate discourses in the sixteenth century, especially those of popular culture (*Literature Among Discourses* 41-61). This explanation subsequently undergirds their argument in favor of a homology between the novel as a new literary form—in particular, *Don Quijote*, with its unifying subsumption into one textual body of a variety of Renaissance and medieval genres and languages—and the role of the more highly centralized Habsburg state.

By means of this process of confluence and differentiation at a higher level, "literature" becomes a cultural product in its own right. As such, it enables, first, the formation of a cultural field in which "cultivated" individuals begin to develop a sense of "taste" or "distinction" on the basis of the distribution, reading, and discussion of literary works. Second, it permits individual acts of self-reflection on one's own position in a social arena increasingly perceived as opposed, and sometimes in contradiction, to one's private and intimate realms. This is the reason why baroque literature remains saturated with ideas of the "falsehood" or "subterfuge" of "reality." These constitute so many strategies for making sense of the growing distance between social transactions, which are determined by the attainment of success, and a realm of intimacy, which is still articulated around moral (and religious) conceptions of the self. Since the Renaissance, literary discourses have attempted to articulate a secular understanding of the human being as an entity that is shaped by political, nontheological forces.

Machiavelli's writing and its legacy in Spain, of course, represent one of the clearest expressions of the growing awareness of the subject's determination by political (state) forces. Machiavelli's discursive world surfaces as one in which all questions of truth, including the "truth" of state power, have a relative status. This status depends heavily on the subject's ability to make correct calculations to achieve objective ends. According to Machiavelli's legacy, therefore, the highest goal becomes the attainment of power and its perpetuation in one's hands. Catholic thinkers reject this notion for several reasons, among them, because they consider it to be atheistic, and because it explicitly undermines the existing power of the church. Yet Machiavelli's legacy also exercises a powerful impact within the newly established literary field. It is here that notions of epistemological relativism and of self-calculation as the supreme value become discursive weapons in the ideological battle to ground the modern self on a secular as opposed to religious basis.

Indeed, picaresque literature is above all concerned with the way in which discrete individuals emerge from and grow on the basis of a relationship between the knowledge that reality is devoid of truth and the intuition that, to the moral or religious dimensions of selfhood, there has now been added an economic dimension represented by the acquisition of "cultural" or "symbolic" capital. Literature thus becomes a major intellectual practice of the "hombre de letras" and Spanish Humanism because it constitutes an effective vehicle for transmitting and reflecting upon a new form of general knowledge which places "Man" at its center. Within Humanist literature, human beings begin to comprise a social and anthropological concern. Hence, this writing represents the first sustained effort in Spain to think about the role of "culture" in the formation of individuals. The propagation of secularized knowledges and a conception of self which included the attribute of "symbolic wealth" can be identified with specific sectors of the cultural elite in the late sixteenth century and the first half of the seventeenth century: bureaucrats, writers, lawyers, "letrados," "hombres cultos," and others.

Yet Maravall has shown how the modernizing impulse of the Renaissance suffers a historical setback when economic stagnation results from the fiscal policies of a ruling power comprised by a seigniorial-ecclesiastical block in the mid-seventeeth century. Recent historiography indeed confirms the advent of economic paralysis owing to the primary importance of a seigniorial (rent and imports) economy and financial capital (monetary speculation) (see Yun Casalilla). By the first half of the seventeenth century, the Spanish economy displays the easily recognized symptoms of underdevelopment: generalized unemployment, wide-spread poverty, political fragmentation, and minimal national levels of accumulation of commercial and industrial capital. Maravall himself tentatively situates the beginning of the crisis in conjunction with the defeat of the Comuneros Revolt. The internationalization of imperial policy thus coincides with the growing decapitalization of Castille, the concentration of wealth upon foreign speculation in American metals, and the victory of the Church against Reform. In the view of Cervantes as well as others, seventeenth-century Spain becomes a "república de hombres encantados" which has lost the direction of which the minority of "hombres de letras" once dreamt.

The period is also one, however, in which "papeles" appear everywhere, as Cervantes himself mentions, and in which the production of "letras" reaches grotesque proportions, at least in Saavedra Fajardo's opinion. We can still detect in these "papeles escritos" an important reflection of Tierno Galván's insight years ago regarding the picaresque: "En ningún país ha habido tan clara conciencia del proceso capitalista, sus elementos y sus consecuencias" (88). It is quite obvious that *pícaros* share with many other types of characters the same perspective on their social milieu: society does not function on the basis of the moral standards officially proclaimed in aristocratic ideology, but rather by means of self-affirmation—that is, the search for economic advantages at any price and a relativization of notions such as "virtud" and "honor" in light of individual circumstances.

When analyzing Quevedo's complex interplay of political reaction and critical writing, for example, George Mariscal points out that traditional notions such as *pureza de sangre* undergo a transformation to become the place where "the voice of marginalized groups [grafted] into aristocratic literary discourse . . . produced a subject that shared many of the elements at work in the configurations of subjectivity emerging in Spanish culture" (Mariscal 152). The awareness of moral relativism indeed may constitute one of the first moments of the production of a modern subject. This is something that Brownlee and Gumbrecht perceive, too, in what they conceptualize as relations between cultural continuities, which seek to maintain an established authority, and simultaneous explosions of heterogeneous discourses, which challenge that authority (Brownlee and Gumbrecht ix-xvii). Picaresque narratives, as well as many of the books of manners and advising, aim to make educated people participate in this knowledge on the relative status of inherited ideas, and seek to generate means of how to profit from it.

At the same time as individual self-interest begins to provide the primary context within which to assess ideas and values, however, the emerging subjects of modernity also discover their absolute submission to the state, which has become the primary entity capable of producing truth, whether by means of ideology or brute force. In other words, individuals become subjects through the belief that the state is the higher guarantor of certainty over and against the moral relativism of social transactions. Literature creates for the cultural elite a sense of participation in a way of looking at things which does not necessarily enjoy a rational status. By bringing the official conceptions of moral authority, religious ideas, sexual norms, ethnic classifications, and literary authority into the new realm of literary representation, and by showing individuals engaged in a conflict involving self-definition or self-assertion, literature makes possible in the seventeenth century the subject's sense of differentiation from excluded groups. At the same time, moreover, literature permits an understanding of self in relation to social reality in which the subject recognizes its absolute subjection to political power even as she or he attempts to negotiate the extent to which he or she will be able to develop a private sphere of economic and cultural profits.

In that regard, it may be said that literature establishes the conditions for thinking (about) the self as an entity directly dependent on the state, insofar as the state, above and beyond its embodiment as a set of juridical, political, and military institutions, is *also* a structured web of symbolic discourses.

Ironically, however, those discourses are frequently recognized as having only a relative status despite their claim to substantive truth-value, thus leaving a clear trace of the interchangeability of the sphere of individual growth with the "economic." Such is the case, for instance, with the status of *conversos*, who were often able to acquire nobiliary titles with money and good contacts; or with picaresque literature, in which "honor" and other virtues are described using the language of accounting; or with the writings of Gracián, for whom knowledge of how to conduct oneself constitutes an investment from which the individual may profit.

State, Culture, and Class

In the eighteenth century, and, indeed, throughout the Spanish Enlightenment, the absolutist state arguably becomes a "machine of culture," in which literary and symbolic production is conceived as relevant politically to the public representation of both the subject and the state. Jovellanos's views on the role of theater in the production of good citizens remains a well-known case: dramas should develop an awareness in citizens that individual destinies are intertwined with the destiny of the state. Literature of this period in fact evolves rapidly to the point of serving to attract to the domain of the state not only various circles of readers but also the intellectual world in general. This ability provides the state yet another means through which to legitimate its power ideologically, beyond the traditional means of religion and violence.

Godzich and Spadaccini, for example, have analyzed the institutionalization of literature within the state as part of the *ilustrados* program of cultural reforms. Under the absolutist state, they argue, literature serves "to mediate the gap between . . . traditional values that require they be seen as immutable if social identity and cohesion are to be preserved, and the immediate lived experience of the inadequacy or superfluousness of these values" (*Institutionalization* 34). A "crisis" of the young literary institution, however, is said to supervene during the first third of the nineteenth century in relation to the liberal revolution. Godzich and Spadaccini claim that the new political elites of Spanish liberalism no longer perceive literature as a useful vehicle through which to interpellate subjects within the state.

Our approach attempts rather to understand the interactions among literature, the state, and subjects within the context of social classes and class conflicts. We believe that it is important to underscore the class dynamics informing the processes of state and subject formation as we are describing them.

According to recent historiography, there is a steady growth of the Spanish economy throughout the eighteenth and nineteenth centuries which leads to the creation of important core-areas—fundamentally town centers—of capitalist development, as occurs in the rest of Western Europe. Ringrose demonstrates, for example, that "underlying economic variables show Spain following a path of gradual, accelerating economic expansion throughout the eighteenth and nineteenth centuries. The dynamic sometimes shifted from one region to another, but even in the troubled first half of the nineteenth century there is evidence of expanding population, commercial activity and per capital income" (390). Economic growth also facilitates the formation of a capitalist class composed of merchants, bureaucrats and landowners.

Much is made of the tendency of these groups to assimilate themselves as quickly as possible into aristocratic circles and lifestyles. This, however, is not a phenomenon unique to Spain, but rather a permanent option and even propensity of the members of the European bourgeoisie from the fifteenth century onward. The constant risk of bankruptcies under the complex system of credit throughout the whole period of trade and manufacturing—owing to the permanent monetary crisis resulting from the lack or excess of cash flow—obligates capitalist groups to ensure their profits by transferring the bulk of their activity from commercial and industrial capital to rent.

At the level of cultural forms, there should exist a way to discover conflicts between the sensibilities of at least some fractions of this new bourgeois class and the official or public culture emanating from the state's machine. This possibility is discounted by those researchers who, like Jesús Cruz, claim that the Spanish *clases medias* of the early nineteenth century do not define their social identities in opposition to the aristocracy and therefore do not succeed in establishing a distinctly bourgeois culture or "habitus." Yet in one arena—aesthetic practices—such a perspective clearly falls short. It is true, of course, that the emerging discourse of aesthetics is allied with state projects of modernization beginning with the reign of Charles III, and thus that in the eighteenth century aesthetic practices still compete primarily with official ecclesiastical discourses for the formation of subjects. In the later neoclassical (1814-35) and romantic periods (1835-50), however, aesthetics itself surfaces as a terrain of possible conflicts with the state.

Aesthetics and Politics

In the latter part of the eighteenth century, the existence of officially sanctioned *cafés* and literary magazines permits the development of a particular sensibility or "taste" through which a differentiated notion of the "aesthetic" can take shape. The cultural activity of the absolutist state, moreover, marks the beginnings of "aesthetics" as a particular dimension of politics. Nevertheless, it is not until politics becomes an actual, possible, and realistic means through which the new Spanish bourgeoisie can lay claim to a direct participation in the organization and direction of the state that "aesthetics" is transformed into a relatively autonomous sphere capable of conveying—whether in a straightforward or critical manner—bourgeois goals, expectations, and desires.

Paradoxically, the first attempt to introduce European romanticism into Spain is rejected by the more progressive intellectuals. The new aesthetic ideas are associated rather with Fernandine reaction because early proponents, such as Nicholas Böhl de Faber, share the Schlegel brothers' view of Calderón's ideologically conservative theater as embodying the essence of Spanish national character. Not until neoclassical writers encounter the frequently more liberal formulations of romantic sensibility circulating in England and France (Byron, Shelly, Hugo, and Dumas) are Spanish *progresistas* able to embrace the new aesthetics as culturally conducive to political transformation in the 1830s.

The bulk of Spanish romantic production, of course, appears in the form of historico-nationalist romanticism, which develops gradually out of Spanish neoclassicism and a sustained tradition of indigenous literary criticism, including Agustín Durán's *Discurso*. Historico-nationalist romanticism indeed finds itself quickly enlisted as an aesthetic ideology into the ranks of political *moderantismo* during the 1830s. With figures such as José de Espronceda, Mariano José de Larra, and the young Patricio de la Escosura, however, there emerges side by side with historico-nationalist romanticism a liberal or "social" romanticism. This minoritarian yet influential form of romanticism is to be distinguished from its *moderado* counterpart by its primary focus on the present, its committment to *progresista* politics, and its desire to affect the politics of state through the agency of an independent aesthetic discourse.

Such an attempt to create a discourse relating romantic aesthetics and progressive politics elicits a swift backlash. As early as 1837, for example, Spanish essayist and literary critic Jacinto de Salas y Quiroga begins to decry "romantic excess" in the same breath as he vituperates against anarchy and immorality. Along with several other leading literary and art critics of his day, he attempts to inflect the new aesthetics away from a progressive milieu and toward serving the political ends of an emerging *moderantismo*: "Es preciso que el escritor público se revista de toda su dignidad para oponerse al torrente que lo va todo arrasando y que lejos de adular las pasiones populares se alce tremendo como sacerdote de paz que es a predicar una religión de fraternidad" (qtd. in Flitter 5). Salas y Quiroga in fact retains those elements of Romantic ideology that contribute legitimacy to the new liberal state by means of its construction of a national past. Furthermore, he countenances a Romantic focus on the present insofar as the aesthetic is subordinated to bourgeois morality and an integral sense of the nation. By attempting to reign in the disruptive energies of an aesthetics linked to *progresismo*, therefore, Salas y Quiroga helps to establish the relative autonomy of the new aesthetic practices in Spain as a sphere of ideological confrontation.

From this moment on in nineteenth-century Spain, literature and literary criticism always constitute forms of cultural intervention into politics, although this sometimes occurs in spite of the expressed wishes of individual authors and texts. Aesthetic practices now act in this manner independently of direct state control and on the relatively autonomous basis of a new process of institutionalization. What we are claiming here is that the development of the aesthetic sphere in Spain follows the general patterns of cultural and historical development of particular areas of social practice in a capitalist society. Ideally, many social practices under capitalism—from economics to aesthetics—are viewed as differentiated from the activities of the state. In reality, however, they maintain concrete relations to the state at any given point of their development since the eighteenth century.

The Essays

The essays included in the present volume attempt both to describe and to analyze key aspects of the trajectory of "literature" and the "aesthetic" in relation to the formation of political subjects between 1550-1850. The historical scope of the essays has been chosen to coincide with the building and dismantling of the absolutist state in Spain. Indeed, it is in the context of the rise and fall of Spanish absolutism that literature receives both its early modern and modern institutionalizations. Taken as a whole, the volume is thus concerned to investigate the role of literature in the articulation of cultural notions of "state," "nation," "subject," and "citizen"—notions which together work to comprise specific spheres or spaces of subjectivity in which certain social identities can be realized and others are marginalized or excluded.

Malcolm K. Read opens the volume by arguing that the absolutist state supports not only an embryonic notion of the "people" but also a territorial notion of the "nation." In this context, language is viewed by early modern elites as far too important to be surrendered to public whim. By the mid-decades of the sixteenth century, it is felt that public usage no longer constitutes an adequate mechanism of control and needs to be replaced by a more personalized authoritarian presence, one which operates from the private sector. Read explores the association of the state, education, and grammatical law through an analysis of the works of Villalón, who develops certain notions and processes indispensable to the functioning of mercantilism. Villalón's work describing the "alma bella" demonstrates the need of the incipient bourgeoisie to function via a "dialogic," ultimately contractual, subject. The essay also situates this form of subjectivity in the context of the debate between what Juan Carlos Rodríguez has termed "animism" and "substantialism."

Mary Elizabeth Perry discovers one of the cultural processes at work in the formation of the modern state in the distribution of a discourse of sexual and ethnic differences. The permanent "sexualization" of minorities, such as Jewish and Muslim populations, results in the construction of a Spanish "national" identity conceived as the suppression of all "deviances." In many ways, colonization and oppression of minority groups involve rituals of separation that hold in relationship the "key-stone, boundaries, margins and internal lines" of the "total structure of thought." Golden Age literature justifies such rituals through emphasizing the deceit of these peoples and their proclivity for witchcraft.

Francisco J. Sánchez then analyzes the emergence of a literary discourse of wealth in the context of Castilian socioeconomic and cultural underdevelopment in the sixteenth and seventeenth centuries. This literary discourse shares many of the concerns of political and theological economists regarding the cultural consequences of decapitalization in Castile. The way in which money and wealth establish the conditions for the emergence of a world of social uncertainty reflects the constitution of selves grounded on a structure of mercantile values. In the case of Alemán's picaresque novel, *Guzmán de Alfarache* (1599-1604), this description also entails a meditation upon a self that is constructed by and through the contradictions between traditional and capitalist conceptions of religious values and socioeconomic expectations as materialized within the context of the decline of Castilian and Spanish economy.

In a seminal essay, Edward Baker argues that what today we understand as literature, as well as the complex forms of authorial and readerly subjectivity that are inseparable from the way we conceive of "literature," scarcely exist in the Spain of the 1600s. The patronage system of the period comprises a set of social practices that condition all areas of aristocratic and ecclesiastical existence. The authorial subject, whom contemporary readers associate with literary creation, thus must be seen as having its roots in the market for recreational books that begins to emerge over the course of the seventeenth century. In *Don Quijote*, the effects of this market are registered in the narrator's concern to arrogate to himself a high degree of authorial autonomy and to his narrative a discursive legitimacy that the dominant culture did not afford.

Sara Nalle takes us into the world of printing, selling, and reading books of popular Catholicism, which give rise to a unique market in religious literature. Though this literature is neither heretical nor subversive, it does permit access to religious debates on the part of poorly educated and often independent-minded readers. Such access can result in unpredictable interpretations, and Nalle demonstrates this through the study of the inventories of five sixteenth-century book shops in Cuenca and Burgos. Subsequently, the case of one Sánchez is analyzed. Sánchez fell into the hands of the Inquisition after developing a highly personal and heretical interpretation of the Virgin Mary on the basis of his reading of popular religious texts.

Bradley J. Nelson analyzes the ideological implications of the *emblem* He argues that there is an "aesthetic" project directly related to the consolidation of a political hegemony. Nelson notices that the iconography of emblems takes the reading subject to an allegorical level in which this subject actualizes the cultural superstructure of the baroque. Following Bourdieu's characterization of cultural and symbolic capitals, Nelson argues for understanding emblematic literature in cultural and sociopolitical terms. On the one hand, emblems configure a "common base" in order to integrate a diversity of educated individuals, while, on the other hand, these individuals may "differentiate themselves" according to the degree of knowledge provided in the emblematic literature. The emblem becomes one of the cultural objects aimed at producing an experience of unity between the individual and the ideological objectives of the "guided culture" of the baroque, in Maravall's characterization.

José Valero follows recent historiography in suggesting that the political revolution of the 1830s in Spain is not accompanied by a corresponding social revolution. The continuity of informal institutions of local patronage and clientelism tends to blur, as alien to oligarchic practice, the liberal distinction between public and private affairs. Valero sees as one of the causes of this "failure of rationalization" the weak development of civil society and, more concretely, of a public sphere which could exist outside the direct control of the state. This failure in turn is related to the specific structural causes which, from the eighteenth century on, impede reformist intellectuals from becoming "floating" intellectuals, that is, intellectuals who are free from state or aristocratic patronage. The contradictions of the public position of reformist intellectuals is exemplified by their "ambiguous" reactions to the phenomenon of "public opinion," which arises over the course of the eighteenth century and throughout the first third of the nineteenth century as a superior authority to which all other opinions must bow, including those opinions emanating from positions of power.

Susan Kirkpatrick analyzes the lines of exclusion signaled by Carolina Coronado's commentary, made in response to Larra's declared enthusiasm for Spain's new "liberties," that women are not part of the "nation" in the 1830s. A highly charged term of liberal discourse, "nation" denotes a hypothetically unified aggregate of the Spanish population, one undifferentiated by estate or class. Yet differentiations among kinds of national subjectitivies are built into the emerging discursive system which comes to represent the relationship between the liberal state and its subjects. Kirkpatrick's essay thus examines two forms of symbolic representation of the "nation": one in legislative texts, specifically the Constitutions of 1812 and 1837, and one in theater, specifically Zorilla's *Don Juan Tenorio*. Kirpatrick demonstrates that, for theatrical as well as constitutional representations, the national subject always dissolves into a hierarchy of differentiated subjectivities.

Finally, Tom Lewis's essay examines some of the specific problems encountered in conceptualizing the relation between literature, the state, and subject formation in nineteenth-century Spain. Lewis argues that literature becomes a key site of symbolic negotiations among competing political discourses in the process of imagining what "Spain" should or would be. Throughout the 1840s, and especially during the years which Raymond Carr describes as "the extended revolutionary period of 1844-1848," aesthetic transformations of religious forms and sensibilities into secular or quasi-secular forms and sensibilities contribute to the emerging *moderado* hegemony defining the nation. This mode of symbolic resolution of political disputes between moderates and progressives contributes to the process of consolidating bourgeois class rule in Spain in the aftermath of the revolutions of 1848.

There remains much that is controversial and still unresolved in our field regarding the emergence and function of literature across distinct modes of production, state formations, and hegemonic cultures from early modernity to the mid-nineteenth century. We hope our volume can contribute to clarifying some of the central problems and issues. We also hope that the volume might help to keep open a debate on the long process through which literature and the aesthetic come to be constituted as a complex arena in which—sometimes directly, more often indirectly—the struggle for state power unfolds.

Works Cited

Brownlee, Marina S., and Hans Ulrich Gumbrecht. "Introduction." *Cultural Authority in Golden Age Spain*. Eds. Marina S. Brownlee and Hans Ulrich Gumbrecht. Baltimore: Johns Hopkins UP, 1995. ix-xii.

Cascardi, Anthony. *The Subject of Modernity*. Cambridge: Cambridge UP, 1992.

Flitter, Derek. "Zorrilla, the Critics, and the Direction of Spanish Romanticism." *José Zorrilla (1893-1993): Centenial Reading*. Nottingham: University of Nottingham Monographs in the Humanities, 1993.

Godzich, Wlad, and Nicholas Spadaccini. "Popular Culture and Spanish Literary History." *Literature Among Discourses. The Spanish Golden Age*. Eds. Wlad Godzich and Nicholas Spadaccini. Minneapolis: U of Minnesota P, 1986.

_____. "From Discourse to Institution." *The Institutionalization of Literature in Spain*. Eds. Wlad Godzich and Nicholas Spadaccini. Minneapolis: The Prisma Institute, 1987.

_____. "The Course of Literature in Nineteenth-Century Spain." *The Crisis of Institutionalized Literature in Spain*. Minneapolis: The Prisma Institute, 1988.

Maravall, José Antonio. *Las comunidades de castilla. Una primera revolución moderna*. Madrid: Alianza, 1979.

_____. *La Cultura del Barroco*. Barcelona: Ariel, 1980.

Mariscal, George. *Contradictory Subjects. Quevedo, Cervantes and Seventeenth-Century Spanish Culture*. Ithaca: Cornell UP, 1991.

Ringrose, David R. *Spain, Europe, and the 'Spanish miracle,' 1700-1990*. Cambridge: Cambridge UP, 1996.

Tierno Galván, Enrique. *Sobre la novela picaresca y otros ensayos*. Madrid: Tecnos, 1973.

Yun Casalilla, Bartolomé. *Sobre la transición al capitalismo en Castilla*. Salamanca: Junta de Castilla y León, 1987.

Works Cited

[illegible]

Chapter 1

Cristóbal de Villalón: Language, Education, and the Absolutist State

Malcolm K. Read

It has often been pointed out that the publication of Nebrija's Spanish grammar in 1492 coincides with the beginnings of Spanish overseas imperialism and, in close association, the rise of Spain's Absolutist State. At the same time, attention has been drawn to the strategic role of the educational apparatus within these historical processes. Such gestures, indeed, are in danger of becoming a commonplace: Nebrija himself was aware of the relevant interconnections and the fact of their existence gains nothing from its mechanical repetition. However, it will be my claim in what follows that the association between the state, education, and grammatical law has not been thought through systematically. The omission is surprising since all three domains converge on similar issues of legitimation, which cry out for comparative analysis. By way of initiating the latter, the present paper proposes a common framework of discussion, respecting the autonomy (in the last instance) of the different levels involved, but demonstrating how each needs to be understood within the broader context of the transition from feudalism to capitalism.

My goals are both modest and quite ambitious. Modest to the extent that attention will be limited to a number of works attributed to the Renaissance scholar, writer, and humanist Cristóbal de Villalón (c.1505-58). Not a great deal is known about Villalón's life, and his identity and authorship have been the focus of intense scholarly debate. Indeed, it has been suggested that his name conceals the identities of three or possibly four writers. Disagreements have been fueled no doubt by the thematic and generic diversity of Villalón's oeuvre, which at one time included *Viaje a Turquía* and even *Lazarillo de Tormes.*[1] While the works discussed below can confidently be attributed to Villalón, it is of no great consequence, theoretically speaking, whether they can finally be "grounded" in a single author. Genealogically, their ideological interconnections, offset against an apparent diversity of form, would still call for comment and explanation. How precisely, as discursive practices, do they interrelate within the context of a single social formation? Which of them, if any, is dominant? and so on. This brings me to the more ambitious aspects of my paper, namely, an attempt to theorize the interrelationships between the economic, political, and ideological levels. The Althusserian outlines of this project should immediately be obvious. Let us begin to fill in the details.[2]

With the implosion of Stalinism and the alleged failure of Marxism, it became fashionable to relegate Althusser to the status of mere theoretical curiosity, as scholars turned to questions of meaning, identity, representation, and difference. The nature of the failure of Althusserianism has now been extensively analyzed and assessed (see Elliott), as have the reasons for the rejection of "older" preoccupations with social structures, production, and reproduction (see Callinicos 1993). It is becoming increasingly apparent that the abandonment of the Althusserian heuristic was premature and that, in the absence of broader Marxist perspectives, the "new" social movements are running aground for reasons that Marxists have always believed to be of fundamental importance (see Resch). Within the discipline of Hispanism, stubbornly conservative, anti-theoretical, and intellectually shallow, it was perhaps inevitable that the brilliantly executed and ongoing research program of the Althusserian Juan Carlos Rodríguez was destined to be ignored and silenced.[3] One of my aims in this essay is to illustrate something of the power and range of Rodríguez's work, and to urge the need for its continuation.

The Language of Mercantilism

We will begin our study of Villalón with his *Provechoso tratado de cambios y contrataciones de mercaderes y reprobación de la usura* (1546), a work which, while an ideological product, lies in greatest proximity to economic practice. As the first part of its title indicates, what we have, in essence, is a mercantilist tract, characteristic of the painful transition from the self-sufficient natural economy of feudalism to the commodity-money economy of capitalism. As such, mercantilism marks a stage in the primitive accumulation of capital, when profit-bearing money was converted into capital and when, accordingly, professional commerce, formerly viewed as a sin, was increasingly looked upon as the main source of a nation's wealth, at least by the nascent bourgeoisie and the crown. The best way to augment this wealth, according to the Mercantilists, was by increasing the number of products capable of being converted into money, so as to stimulate a growth in exchange values. Predictably, they confused the latter with the physical form of that product which functions as money, namely, gold and silver. The result was the obsessive quest for precious metals that drove the Spanish imperialist enterprise.[4]

Necessarily, Villalón is constrained by these conceptual horizons. His attention remains naively fixated on the sphere of money circulation. By implication, money constitutes the principal component of the nation's wealth. However, the second part of the title of his thesis, roundly condemning usury, alerts us to the fact that, while a mercantilist text, Villalón's is a peculiarly Spanish variety thereof. One is struck in particular by the enormous disparity between the intricacy of the early European banking system, both national and international, to which Villalón proves to be a singularly instructive guide, and the author's manifest conviction that so much of the activity that he is attempting to regulate is, simply and quite literally, the work of the Devil. To explain this disparity, it is important to recall that the *Provechoso tratado* is a typical product of the Transition. In economic terms, this means that it is overdetermined both by a passionate capitalist thirst for money and by the prejudices and practices of slave and feudal economies. For the latter, the economic ideal was the self-sufficient, consumer economy, where exchange was confined to surpluses produced by individual economies and was carried out *in natura.*

It is this attachment to "nature" which explains the profoundly conservative tenor of Villalón's treatise, and the pre-eminence it accords to ethical values: "Que no es licito el usurar segun ley divina, humana ni natural" (Villalón 1546: fol. II [verso]) ("The fact is that it is not licit to practice usury, according to divine, human or natural law"). The virtues of maintaining proper distinctions, quintessentially those between the human and the divine, will not be lost upon subsequent capitalist ideologues. Without them, nonequivalent exchange and profit upon alienation, indispensable though they may be to the proper functioning of mercantilism, pose a moral dilemma. Equally insoluble and, on moral grounds, inexcusable is the distinction between reasonable and inflated prices (fol. xxiv [recto]). We will note in passing how Villalón's presupposition in the gradual devolution of society, from a state of natural perfection, contaminates his attitude toward the "natural" meaning of words. The aim is clearly to restore this natural meaning (e.g., fol. ix [verso]), and so to reconnect the exchange value of words with their use value or, as Villalón describes it elsewhere, with "la sustancia de las palabras" (1966: 166) ("the substance of words").

The visible anxieties regarding both kinds of currency, verbal and economic, is understandable. Just as ornate poetic fashions were allegedly debasing poetic idiom, and thereby raising insuperable barriers to popular participation in public affairs, so also was coinage being adversely affected by the huge quantities of metals being shipped into Europe. Such inflationary practices, on both accounts, were benefiting the commercial bourgeoisie as they impoverished the peasantry, craftsmen, and workers. Literary artisan *par excellence,* Villalón identifies with the latter, many of whom had been so ravaged as to be reduced to begging.

Of course, in no sense was Villalón a Physiocrat *avant la lettre*, persuaded that prices should be allowed to find their own natural level. On the contrary, he was simply continuing an established tradition: during the latter half of the Middle Ages a number of church decrees were issued which totally proscribed the levying of interest on loans, and which threatened usurers with excommunication. Suspicion attached to money to the extent that it became an end, rather than a means: ". . . el dinero no engendra de si algun fructo como todas las naturales mientes, pero produce de si ganancia mediante la buena industria de aquel que lo trata. Pues cosa injusta es que alguno goze interesse de industria y trabajo ajeno" (fol. v [recto]) (". . . in itself, money does not engender any fruit, in the way that natural minds do, but only produces profit through the good industry of whoever deals in it. For it is an unjust thing that anyone should enjoy the interest of another's work and industry"). Such statements should not be confused with the physiocratic preoccupation with production, sustained by a labor theory of value. Villalón's concern with use values, like that of his scholastic predecessor, is that of a person who remembers an organic community, in which individuals helped each other "freely" and spontaneously, that is to say, without "interest." The particular ferocity of his resistance is symptomatic of the rapid decline in the regional or town economy in the sixteenth century, occasioned by the expansion of the market and the growth of merchant capital.

The importance of distinguishing between the ideas of the Physiocrats and those of emergent Mercantilists such as Villalón is apparent when we consider their respective attitudes to the state. The former were advocates of free trade, arguing that the circulation of money (like that of words) regulates itself, and that the market is determined spontaneously, without state intervention. The latter were practical men who sought to influence the course of economic life through the control of money, to which end they enlisted the active assistance of an increasingly centralized state, bolstered by its own bureaucracy, army, and navy. In the struggle for domination over the world market, mercantilism stood for protectionism. It went hand in hand with regulation of all aspects of national economic life, imposing fixed prices and granting monopoly rights. In the end, it would elicit violent opposition from the rising and newly consolidated industrial bourgeoisie, which stood to benefit from free trade.

We might have expected that, in his one work dedicated to economic exchange, Villalón would have opted for the generic form that foregrounds verbal exchange, otherwise the *dialogue*. It was, after all, the genre that he preferred in his more "literary" texts. However, he chose instead a more formal exposition. One possible explanation is that he operated in terms of a fundamental generic distinction between "theory" and "literature." If this were true, it would explain why his grammatical treatise, reviewed below, likewise avoided the dialogic genre. Be that as it may, commercial activity required its appropriate thematization. To begin with, economic exchange presupposes the existence of subjects of a particular kind, the ideological production of which fell to discursive theory and practice. In this respect, it is worth recalling the nonchalance and notorious unreliability of the feudal nobility over contractual issues. While as good as his word, upon which his name and honor depended, the feudal lord was not above treating agreements in a cavalier manner. A word, freely given, could also be freely withdrawn (see Mariscal 80-81). Such an attitude, needless to say, was entirely at odds with the world of international finance described in Villalón's treatise, which could only function if contractual obligations were rigorously respected. For this to happen, important ideological battles needed to be fought and won, as elsewhere Villalón showed every sign of realizing.

From "Serfs" to "Subjects"

Villalón's *Provechoso tratado* is an exercise rooted in the interior of the economic level, intent upon spelling out conditions indispensable to mercantilist exchange. However, it was within a context more ideologically remote from actual economic practice that the Spanish humanist produced certain other key notions and processes indispensable to the functioning of mercantilism. I have in mind *El scholástico* (c. 1540), a work which stands midway between Villalón's theoretical texts and his more ostensibly imaginative works. It consists basically of a dialogue between a number of distinguished academics and humanists, attached to the University of Salamanca, who retire to the country estate of the Duke of Alba, there to discuss issues of national importance regarding education. In effect they constitute what would today be understood as a governmental "think tank."

While seemingly removed from the economic level as such, the work's generic structure locks it into the process of *exchange*. Throughout its history, the bourgeoisie needs to operate via a "dialogic," ultimately contractual subject. True, at this stage, it is a Platonic soul, still mired in a discourse adapted to the transition, whose "fullness" contrasts with the emptiness of the classic bourgeois subject. It is, in the most literal sense, divinely inspired, by the god of friendship. But it already exhibits a mobility that will be subsequently put to good use socially: "Y afirmava [Acibiades] que a ningun hombre tocava este dios con su deidad, que no hiziesse del una metamorphosi: porque le secava de si y le transformava en la cosa en que el mas ponia su amor" (Villalón 1966: 22) ("And [Alcibiades] affirmed that this god, in its divinity, did not touch any man in whom it did not bring about a metamorphosis; because it drew him out from within himself and transformed him into the thing which was the object of his love"). In this respect, the "beautiful soul" stands opposed to the medieval "serf," "vassal," or "lord," which explains why Bonifacio, the estate manager, welcomes the guests with a lament on his role as palace servant. The visitors agree that serfs (*siervos*) are no longer appropriate in a Christian age: ". . . porque por qualquier ierro nos remuerde interiormente nuesta conciencia como reconozca ser contra nuestro buen natural" (29) (". . . because we are gnawed by our conscience, inwardly, for any mistake [we commit] that it recognizes as going against our innate moral sense"). They thereby alert us to the origins of the beautiful soul in the *free* Christian conscience, notably in the mystical traditions of the late Middle Ages, of which the whole phenomenon of knightly service—one free soul in the service of another—constitutes a more secular variant (see Rodríguez 1990: 78-81).

However, while medieval precedents certainly exist, it is also important to recognize the qualitatively distinct function of the beautiful soul during the sixteenth century. In a society characterized by increasing social (and geographical) mobility, the Absolutist State will seek to impose itself through impersonal but *internalized* values, as opposed to the personal violence that prevailed in medieval society. In other words, the individual conscience will constitute the social controlling mechanism that will gradually take the place of feudal "honor." One of the goals that *El scholástico* patently sets itself is to negotiate the process of substitution. Hernán Pérez de Oliva (1492?-1533), possibly the leading dialoguist of Villalón's text, dominates what is a key exchange in this respect, concerning the true nature of nobility. Not surprisingly—as the author of a distinguished dialogue on the dignity of man—Oliva's contribution to the debate in *El scholástico* was both lucid and precise. For some, he explains, nobility is dependent upon lineage, for others, upon deeds performed in war, whereas others see it as conditional upon achievements in learning, "porque no toma la gloria por ajenos hechos" (118) ("because it is not parasitic upon the glory of others"). The first two criteria clearly privilege the aristocracy—the martial arts, of course, were traditionally associated with the nobility—doubtless for which reason Oliva makes no secret of his own preference for the third. As evidence he adduces examples of ancient civilizations which set particular store by the ennobling power of letters, irrespective of claims regarding individual ancestry (120). The message is clear: individual merit counts for far more than honors socially conferred.

Here, at least, positions are unambiguously defined. But during the transition the question of ideological allegiance was rarely so simple and straightforward. For example, it is Oliva who objects to the use of slaves as teachers for the young, somewhat surprisingly, given his position on the inherent nobility of the human spirit. To his credit, the schoolmaster is quick to spot the contradiction, posing the obvious question: if, as Oliva claimed earlier, all men are equal and made of the same elements, where exactly does their inequality lie? It is a bitter irony that finds the famous humanist accused of attaching excessive importance to clothing: ". . . asi es mas loco el que juzga al hombre por los vestidos y capa con que cubre el cuerpo, no mirando su ser interior" (129) (". . . thus, it is madness to judge a man by the clothes and cloak that cover his body, without taking his inner being into account"). For clothing, as indicative of an individual's natural status, figures prominently in what we will argue below to be a quintessentially "substantialist" or feudal ideology. By inclination an exponent of "animist" doctrines, Oliva does his best to defend himself. He was, he protests, only speaking metaphorically on the issue of slavery. But his excuses ring hollow. In truth, his problem lies with the "dignity of man," a concept which was never intended to encompass civil equality. Understood in this broad sense, it lands Oliva in a contradiction that is destined to plague the bourgeoisie throughout it long history, between its promotion of political liberties and the profoundly undemocratic nature of its productive relations. It is an issue to which we will return below.

Public versus Private

El scholástico is a text typical of a period of transition between, in its own case, feudalism and capitalism, to the extent that it embodies a clash between two different ideological matrices, a feudal ideology based upon the concept of the "serf" and a bourgeois ideology based upon that of the "subject." The latter is to be understood in strictly historical terms. As Rodríguez explains—and I am going to be following him closely through this part of the discussion—it would be a fatal error to universalize the notion of the subject, by extracting it from its place within the interior of a particular historical matrix. In other words, every effort needs to made to avoid narrativizing the "serf"/"subject" along liberal lines, whereby the free individual finally emerges from the bonds of freedom into the realm of liberty. Rodríguez is adamant: "tal oposición únicamente significa el paso desde unas relaciones sociales a otras (*siervo* es sólo un término que nos indica la especial—y necesaria—inscripción de los individuos en las relaciones de clase características del feudalismo; *sujeto* es sólo un término que nos indica la especial—y similarmente necesaria—inscripción de los individuos en las relaciones de clase caracteristicas del capitalismo, tanto en su primera fase como en las fases posteriores, etc.)" (1990: 11-12) ("On the contrary, such an opposition only signifies the transition from one set of social relations to another [*serf* is only a term that indicates the special—and necessary—inscription of individuals in class relations characteristic of feudalism; *subject* is only a term that indicates the special—and similarly necessary—inscription of individuals in class relations characteristic of capitalism, both in its early phase and in its later phases, etc.]").

The aim—let us be very clear about this—is not to deny that the transition from servitude to feudalism, and thence to capitalism, was in some degree liberating, nor to reject the conceptual or theoretical validity of historical progress *per se*. Clearly, any such move would jeopardize the core of Marxism, as a research program. Indispensable to the latter is the idea that individual freedom, as a political ideal, can be more effectively achieved under capitalism than under feudalism. Rodríguez's point is that such notions as "serf" and "subject" are not effective realities in themselves, but simply privileged categories through which are expressed and objectified the basic functional processes of the feudal or bourgeois ideological matrix. What this implies is that capitalist freedom represents only formal emancipation, since, lacking access to the means of production, the worker is still forced to sell her labor power. On this basis, the contradiction between the formal equality of citizens and their real, socioeconomic inequality remains to be resolved.

Fundamental to Rodríguez's position is a theoretical distinction between *notions,* through which an ideology exhibits itself, and the internal mechanisms of ideology:

> Cuando decimos que el "siervo" y el "sujeto" no existen realmente nunca, no queremos decir que no existan "sólo" en el nivel económico o en el político (niveles ambos a los que una cierta tradición marxista mecanista—la inversión hegeliana—ha solido atribuir por antonomasia la esencia de la realidad, los ha considerado como los "únicamente reales"—*sic*-: la ideología—el nivel ideológico objetivo de una formación social—es, sin embargo, una realidad tan plena, sabemos hoy, como cualquiera de los otros niveles sociales y el hecho de que el nivel económico sea siempre, por supuesto, el determinante, no quiere decir que los demás niveles no sean tan "reales" como él), sino que lo que queremos decir es que siervo y sujeto no existen (como valores plenos y en sí) tampoco en el enterior mismo de sus respectivos niveles ideológicos. (12)

> (When we say that the "serf" or the "subject" never actually exists, we do not mean "only" on the economic level or on the political level, as the case may be. (Both of these are levels which a certain mechanistic tradition within Marxism, by simply inverting the Hegelian dialectic, has commonly seen as constituting the essence of reality *par excellence,* has considered them as the "only real"—*sic*. Nevertheless, as we know today, ideology—the objective ideological level of a particular social formation—is a reality as full as any other social level, and the fact that the economic level is, of course, always the one that determines does not mean that the other levels are not just as "real." Rather we mean that the serf and the subject do not actually exist *either* (as

full values in themselves) within their respective ideological instances.)

Sociological processes, the implication is, operate "behind the backs" of subjects and are not to be confused with consciousness or awareness of change, individual or otherwise. Feudal ideology "says" that man is essentially a "serf" or "servant" of a "Lord" (with and without a capital letter), whereas the bourgeois ideological matrix will "say" that "man" is essentially "free." Such notions are the visible signs of internal necessity exclusive to a specific ideological matrix and to no other; they are *lived* as unalterable elements of reality, experienced at the level of everyday life as "the way things are." And an ideological matrix "no es otra cosa que la reproducción, en el nivel de la ideología, de la contradicción básica de clases que constituye cada tipo de relaciones sociales: la 'contradicción' entre 'siervos/señores' en el feudalismo, la contradicción entre 'burgueses/proletarios' en el capitalismo, etcétera" (14) ("is nothing other than the reproduction, at the level of ideology, of the basic class contradiction that constitutes each type of social relations: the 'contradiction' between 'serfs/lords' in feudalism, the contradiction between 'bourgeoisie/proletariat' in capitalism, et cetera").

The social formations of the transition, let us remind ourselves, are characterized by a struggle between bourgeois and feudal relations, in which the political level necessarily becomes dominant. Versions of Marxism, particularly those emanating from the Second International, have commonly assumed the progressive development of productive forces. In the face of such teleological narratives, Spanish history of the sixteenth century suggests the importance of allowing for, and theorizing, an element of irreducible contingency, insofar as it exemplifies an instance when the fettering of the productive forces by the social relations is resolved in favor of stagnation and regression.[5] At the same time, it is important to recognize that not everything was lost:

> La matriz ideológica de las relaciones sociales de transición segrega directamente una temática política en el siguiente sentido: ese efecto objetivo que el funcionamiento absolutista supone en tanto que tendencialmente liquidor de las relaciones feudales y

> estructurador de los límites favorables a la producción plena de las relaciones burguesas se presenta, en el nivel de la ideología, como la estructuración de las esferas de *lo privado y lo público*. (33)
>
> (The ideological matrix of transitional social relations secretes directly a political thematics in the following sense: the objective effect that absolutism supposes in its functioning—notably its tendency to liquidate feudal relations and to impose limits favorable to the full production of bourgeois relations—manifests itself, on the level of ideology, as the structuration of the *private* and *public* spheres.)

The dialoguists of *El scholástico,* let us reminds ourselves, retire to a place of privacy, in which to "hablar sus negoçios publicos y pribados" (13) ("discuss their public and private affairs"). The autonomy of the political sphere presupposes a willingness on the part of the Absolutist State not to interfere in the sphere of the private (although the activities of the Inquisition illustrate the distinctive nature of the Spanish case). Theoretically, what is required to explain this situation is not simply a theory of the public, but a theory of the relation between the public and private, "considerando siempre al otro elemento como su sombra o como su inversión necesaria" (Rodríguez 1990: 34) ("always considering one element to be the shadow and necessary inversion of the other"). This structure is tendentially favorable to the bourgeoisie to the extent that this class will seek to intervene in the public sphere from a position within the private. Again, close consideration of *El scholástico* is in this sense richly rewarding, insofar as the dialoguists are at pains to emphasize that the love which animates their private discourse functions to bind together the body politic: "con quanta seguridad viven los príncipes que rigen sus republicas y reinos con amor: y en quanto peligro tiene el estado y la vida aquel que la gobierna con temor y crueldad" (13) ("how great is the security of rulers who govern their republics and kingdoms with love; and how precarious is the state and the life of whoever governs through fear and cruelty"). While its repressive apparatuses are always on hand, in case of emergency, the new Absolutist State prefers to secure its stability via the ideological apparatuses, operating through internalized self-discipline at the level of subjectivity.

Absolutism, then, is a compromise formation, the result of a struggle, within the public sphere. In Spain, the relative strength of the nobility, vis-à-vis bourgeois capitalist interests, is manifest in the dominance of bureaucratic officialdom, to the detriment of commerce and trade. Yet the possibility could never arise where a return to feudalism was possible. Within the bureaucratic apparatus, new fractions, not least that made up of "writers," will use the new structures to further their professional interests. Likewise, the army will henceforth function as a national force, no longer made up of separate retinues, owing their allegiance primarily to their own feudal lord. Internally, the day of the solo knight has passed, and that of massed professional infantrymen arrived. Yet when it came to materializing images derived from the public sphere, it was perhaps the Spanish language itself which best embodied the idea of the "nation" and the "people." And understandably so, insofar as, if the notion of the subject was to prevail ideologically, it had also to be produced linguistically, a claim we will substantiate by turning to Villalón's *Gramática castellana.*

The Subject of Language

Throughout Absolutism's first stage, down to the mid-sixteenth century, the question of public representation as such simply did not arise. While entry into the public sphere was open to negotiation, the emphasis upon "merit" as opposed to "blood" only ever concerned the possible integration of the lower nobility and middling fraction of bureaucrats and artists. And needless to say, it would be quite anachronistic to think in terms of "democracy." Pereira explains: "Se trata más bien de una esfera pública encargada de representar el poder absoluto del rey *ante* los súbditos, con un límite de intermedio que separa el círculo burocrático cortesano del resto de la población" (48-49) ("It is rather a question of a public sphere charged with representing the absolute power of the king before his subjects, with an intermediary zone separating the bureaucratic, courtly circle from the rest of the population"). Political involvement for the mass of the population did not extend beyond the rapt contemplation of the spectacle of government.

Social divisions are most effective when marked and reinforced by language. In the sixteenth century, relevant barriers divided the literate from the illiterate, Latinists from non-Latinists, and those who controlled relevant dialects, registers, and styles from those that did not. Such linguistic differences were exploited by different classes and class fractions to establish and preserve basic social divisions. Of these, the most salient implied the coexistence of what Pereira has called two "circuits of information," consisting of a state and a civil circuit (49). Only the courtiers and bureaucrats had direct access to the former, whereas the lower orders and women were restricted to the latter. In this way, a knowledge of Latin became indispensable to the socially mobile. In a world of literal transubstantiation, as portrayed in Villalón's *El crotalón* (1559), "grammar" in this sense remained a key to professional success: "Ya yo era buen mozo de quince años; y entendía que para yo no ser tan asno como mi amo, que debía de saber algún latín. Y ansí me fue a Zamora a estudiar alguna gramática" (Villalón 1973: 61) ("I was already a young lad of fifteen, and I understood that, in order not to end up a bigger ass than my master, I should know a little Latin. And so I set off for Zamora to study grammar"). Not surprisingly, the vernacular also became a key site in the struggle between those excluded from the public sphere or seeking greater participation, and those seeking to maintain its exclusivity. To this extent, Vallalón's *Gramática castellana* (1971 [1558]), far from being the marginal text that literary critics usually take it to be, is central to an understanding of his whole oeuvre.

As Villalón indicates on the very first page of this work, issues of authority and value are never more keenly felt than over language: "Todos cuantos hazen cuenta de las lenguas y de su autoridad dizen, que la perfection y valor de la lengua se deve tomar y deduçir de poder ser reducida a arte" (Villalón 1971: 5) ("All those who concern themselves with languages and with their authority say that the perfection and worth of language should be based on and deduced from its capacity to be reduced to art"). Languages, that is to say, are to be evaluated precisely to the extent that they lend themselves to discipline and control. The authority of the Absolutist State needs to be brought to bear on a linguistic community which, until Villalón's day, "ha andado suelta sin subjetarse a regla, ni ley" (7) ("has wandered around freely, without being subjected to rule or law"). However, once fully established, the public sphere inevitably becomes a contested arena, in which the "public" or "people" offers itself as a possible norm. When it pays, as in the case of the theater, it will indeed be difficult to resist its logic, which, as we know, Lope exploited to telling effect. While the same forces threaten to prevail in matters of linguistic usage, language was finally far too important to be surrendered to public whim. At this point the effectiveness of interventions from the private sphere becomes apparent. The relevant criterion of authority, we are informed, is the "usage" of the well spoken (52), redefined later as "la costumbre de los mas cuerdos y mas avisados en el hablar" (73) ("the habits of those most learned and most informed in matters of language"). Clearly, Villalón has in mind those charismatic individuals who, while operating within radically transformed social structures, were still able to ground their authority naturalistically. This normative emphasis suggests that, by the mid-decades, it was felt that public usage was no longer an adequate mechanism of control and needed to be replaced, or at least eked out, by a more personalized authoritarian presence, operating from the private sector.

The Absolutist State sustains not only an embryonic notion of the "people" but also the territorial notion of the "nation." The first glimmerings of a "national" language policy can be traced to the practical impetus given to Castilian by the literary activity of Alfonso el Sabio, who assumed the burden of official name giver. What strikes one most is the limited nature of state control at that time, in accordance with the still rudimentary nature of Absolutism. Alfonso's very notion of "language" ("lingua") was far more abstract than our corresponding concept, in the sense that it allowed for the inclusion of what would be for us distinctly heterogeneous elements (see Niederehe 96-103, 114-15). Historically, the late Middle Ages witnesses the consolidation of Castilian's hegemony, through the completion of the Reconquest and the elimination of the other languages and dialects of the Peninsula, as part of Castile's expansionist policy (see Entwistle 159). While Villalón's grammar is emphatically a grammar of *Castilian,* not of *Spanish,* the extent of his patriotism is clear: "Y ansi ahora yo como siempre procuré engrandecer la cosas de mi nación" (8) ("And so now, and always, I have tried to promote the interests of my homeland"). Indications are that the grammarian is as much concerned with the linguistic consequence of Spain's continuing imperial expansion overseas as with the internal process of centralization. His grammar was, after all, published overseas and, symptomatically, celebrates Charles V's victories at Lansgrave and his subjection of Saxony and the German principalities. The linguistic correlate of Spain's newfound political confidence is a grammar or "art" of Castilian "desasido del Latin" (11) ("disengaged from Latin"). The language's independence is further bolstered, diachronically, by a reconstituted version of the history of Castilian, whose origins are no longer to be found in Latin but in the time of the early kings of Castile and Leon (7; see Read 1990: 19-20).

Particularly significant in the light of our preceding discussion of animism is the emergence in the *Gramatica* of the "subject" as a more or less clearly defined category of discourse. The theoretical innovation involved is one that historians of linguistics have noted (see Peñalver Castillo 85-91), but have failed to explain. It concerns a distinction between, on the one hand, the grammatical subject of a phrase such as "Yo amo a Dios" ("I love God")—the example is Villalón's—in which an agent ("la persona que haze esta obra de amar" ["the person who does the loving"]) stands opposed to the verb and object ("la persona que padece" [the person receiving the action"]); and, on the other hand, a speaker who constitutes a binding presence with respect to one or more phrases, "las quales todas juntas espresan y manifiestan cumplidamente el conçibimiento del hombre en el proposito que tiene tomado para hablar" (85) ("all of which, taken together, duly express and exteriorize the conceptual processes of the man whose aim it is to speak"). In the latter case, Villalón is obviously concerned with acts of enunciation, emanating from a source in subjectivity.

It is my belief that with this second kind of subject Villalón is registering, within the realm of grammatical studies, the impact of the "beautiful soul" that was elaborated in *El scholástico*. The latter attaches great importance to pupils' inner lives and to the habit of silence: "la lengua no ha de ser libre ni soltera mas muy captiva y atada al pecho y coraçon: de manera que lo que hablare, este primero muy rumiado en las entrañas" (1966: 143) ("a person's tongue should not be free or loose, but captive and tied to his breast and heart, so that what he says is first carefully thought out within"). On the strength of classical precedents, Villalón advises that learned men not speak in public, at least without having prepared themselves thoroughly beforehand (143). Such vigilance over levels of verbosity prefigures the morbid pretensions and excessive concern with the niceties of social etiquette which characterize the socially mobile petty bourgeoisie in capitalism's more advanced stages. This, however, will be a future development: during the first (Mercantilist) stage of capitalist development, the attitude in question is a global feature of the bourgeoisie.

As linguistic historians have described (see Peñalver Castillo 81), Villalón innovates theoretically in a second important respect, that is, in his reduction of the parts of speech to three (1971: 13). The importance of this innovation will be apparent later in the century in Francisco Sánchez el Brocense and Gonzalo Correas and the wholesale attempt to reduce language to "reason" (see Padley 201). In the present context, we will simply note how the threefold division reasserts the role of nature, in the guise of universal features of languages. This linguistic equivalent of "natural law" marks a transition from an early phase, in which scholars refined a notion of "usage," in conjunction with a proto-subject or beautiful soul, to a subsequent period, during which linguistic legitimation took a "rational" form. The difference between "usage" and "reason," however, should not be exaggerated: throughout the transition, words circulate in the form of a conventional currency (exchange values) that are ultimately grounded in nature (use values).

Types of usage based upon conventional norms and rational discourse have other features in common: notably, both posit a subject that is still underwritten by the transcendental authority of religion. The resurgence of neofeudalism in Spain in the second half of the sixteenth century doubtless contributed, in part, to the move to root syntactic structures in the *formal spirit* of reason. It will be followed, around the turn of the century, by attempts to assert the *substance* or *essence* of language, as constituted by its syntax or lexicon (see Read 1983: chs. 6 and 7; 1990: ch. 1). Pérez Oliva gives us a foretaste of the lexical variety of substantialism when he gestures nostalgically toward the pristine substance of words (Villalón 1966: 166). In this way, grammatical and linguistic studies act out the opposition between form and matter, spirit and body. The compromise discourses to which this conflict gives rise lie outside the range of the present study (see Read 1983). More relevant to our own concerns is how this broadly ideological opposition was rehearsed and first formulated in the work of Villalón.

Animism and Substantialism

The first part of the sixteenth century, we have argued, witnessed the emergence of a homogeneous, centralized court society, straddling a newly created divide between the private and public sectors. In the process, a system in which social relations were secured on the basis of elementary forms of domination, such as personal loyalty and allegiance, gradually gave way to one characterized by objective, impersonal mechanisms. Whereas the feudal lord was obliged to work, on a daily basis, to produce and reproduce prevailing, but always precarious, conditions of domination, his successor could simply let the system take its own course.

Nevertheless, while it facilitated the working of power on one level, the impersonality of the new structures posed problems when translated into market mechanisms, whose "neutrality" spelt the loss of seigniorial control over the sphere of economic relations. It is not by chance, Oscar Pereira reasonably argues, that political relations are affirmed, in the form of the divine right of kings, precisely at the moment when the economic sphere is becoming autonomous. In effect, the personalized relations characteristic of feudalism "se irán transformando en unas relaciones *abstractas* que ligarán de manera directa pero imaginaria al individuo con el estado" (Pereira 39) ("will gradually be transformed into *abstract* relations that will bind the individual to the state in a direct but imaginary way"). In the process of transformation, these relations are internalized by the individual or, as he has now become, an "alma bella" or "súbdito." If this soul is, in an important sense, "free," it is also subjected by the prince to the principles of true prudence and virtue, in the interests of the peace and tranquillity of the republic.

The subjectivity in play in such dialogues as *El scholástico,* Rodríguez has been at pains to explain, should not be confused with its subsequent Kantian, empirical, romantic, or phenomenological variants (1990: 129 ff). It is a "soul" with features that distinguish it even from "reason," the next stage in its transmogrification. In order to subsist effectively, it requires a second interlocutor, with whom to engage in dialogue. Animism itself remains, more generally, a transitional discourse, serving basically to facilitate coexistence with feudalism. Literary production in the Golden Age, it stands repeating, is the result of a battle between two modes of production, a battle that determines the configuration of the Absolutist State. The basic structure, as Juan Carlos Rodríguez explains, is not the result of one determination: "Al contrario, puede ser vista desde dos ópticas; es de hecho *elaborada* por dos sistemas ideológicos distintos, sistemas que expresan el efecto que esa única estructura privado/público ejerce bien sobre la nobleza . . . , bien sobre la burguesía" (1990: 55-56) ("On the contrary, it can be seen from the standpoint of two distinct optics; in point of fact it is *elaborated* via two distinct ideological systems, systems that express the effect that the single private/public structure exercises both over the nobility . . . and over the bourgeoisie"). Thus, in *El scholástico,* an animist *dialogue*, individuals continue to *dispute,* after the medieval fashion, within a space which, while confessedly private, is owned by a local dignitary. Moreover, animist positions continue to be hotly contested by substantialism. Let us consider, by way of illustration, the question of the social role of women.

Dialoguists Francisco de la Vega and Alberto de Benavides present women as the threatening embodiment of sin, responsible for most of the woes which afflict men and which threaten to undermine civilization. This brand of misogyny is only too familiar from late medieval texts. Ideologically, it is one of the purest expressions of substantialism, and broadly serves the interests of a feudalism promoting the virtues of "blood" and "honor." It presupposes the absolute baseness of matter, the weight of the organic, and the corruption of the body which contaminates the soul. In contrast, the position assumed by Alonso Osorio and Hernán Pérez de Oliva is rather more problematic in that they discover in antiquity evidence of sexual equalities, under primitive matriarchies, not to mention examples of individual women who knew how to die "varonilmente" (Villalón 1966: 202). Spain, let us remind ourselves, appeared to allow women a significant place in public life: for example, in contrast to Puritan England, it allowed women to play female roles in the theater and on a quintessentially public stage. We should be in no hurry, however, to interpret this as evidence of the progressive pressures of animism. Appearances are deceptive, in both the case of Osorio and Oliva, and of Spain. It is rather that substantialism which, insofar as it views women as a combination of spirit *and* matter, can find no grounds on which to exclude women, as women, from the public sector (see Rodríguez 1990: 103).

The distinctively animist card is only finally played by Francisco de Bobadilla, when he questions the very terms of reference of the debate. What all the previous dialoguists have in common, he points out, whether they have criticized or praised women, is their antagonism to love itself.

> Tiene por objeto y fundamento este amor celestial a la hermosura del anima: la qual es un resplandor del vulto divino que en ella dios infundio al principio de su creacion, como en naturales hijos suyos. Y esta hermosura es aquella inclinaçion de obrar virtud: la qual aunque dios la imprima en todas las criaturas que son capaçes de amor, mas perfectamente la infunde en las animas, y mas en los angeles: porque son criados para gozar de dios, y hechos a su semejança. Y aunque se pueden dezir hermosas las plantas, y ervas y piedras, estrellas planetas y sol y otras muchas cosas materiales, no se dizen hermosas por que tengan expresada esta divina hermosura: pero mientras mas rastro y semejança della tuviere en si tanto mas partiçipara deste amore celestial y sera mas capaz del. Preguntar me ha alguno como la cosa que no tiene anima se puede dezir tener esta hermosura que dezis que es inclinaçion de hacer bien? Esto façil mente se puede entender por exemplo: los arboles que no dan mas flores, como alelies, açuçenas, lilios y jazmines con que graçiosa mente complazemos al sentido del olor, quien me negara que por aquella obra buena que nos hazen, con ser poca no los amemos y deseemos . . . ? (Villalón 1966: 204)
>
> (This celestial love has as its object and basis the beauty of the soul, which is the radiance of the divine form that God infused in it at the dawn of its creation, as if they were His own children. And this beauty is the inclination

of love to act virtuously, which, although God imprints it on all creatures that are capable of love, he infuses it to greater perfection in souls, and particularly in angels, insofar as they are created to rejoice in God, and are made in His image. And although it can be said that plants are beautiful, along with herbs and stones, stars, planets and the sun and many other material things, yet they are not said to be beautiful in the sense of expressing this divine beauty; but the more they share in this beauty, and the greater their resemblance to it, the more they will participate in this celestial love and be capable of it. Someone will ask me how the thing that has no soul can be said to have this beauty, since in your view it is an inclination to do good. This can best be understood through examples: the plants that produce nothing but flowers, such as wall-flowers, white lilies, lilies and jasmines, [but] which delight us with their perfume. Who could possibly suggest, in view of this service, although small, that we should not love them and desire them?)

A little later, we are treated to a celebration of the disciplinary status of music, and in particular of its contribution to the harmony not simply of the state but of the universe: "por que despues de ser sciençia que engrandeçe los animos y los esfuerza a comprender cosas altas, escriven que todo el mundo el cielo y la tierra se conservaba y rigen conforme a musica y armonia ordenada" (209) ("because in addition to being a science that ennobles souls and strengthens them in the understanding of spiritual things, they write that the whole world, heavens and earth, are maintained and ruled by conformity to music and ordered harmony").

I have quoted the above passages at length because they encapsulate the animist, neo-Platonic concern with erotic love that drives *El scholástico.* Love not only figures prominently in the work's content but also shapes its dialogic form. Its formative influence does not escape the attention of the dialoguists themselves, who, at the very commencement of their journey, observe explicitly that love, in the form of friendship, animates their conversation. What is significant about animist love, as Bobadilla's description of it perfectly demonstrates, is that it *transforms* the whole material world,

and thereby renders the whole of creation beautiful and worthy of love and admiration:

> Y desta manera los cuerpos humanos son capaces del por causa de las animas que en si posen: por que rellena el anima desta hermosura comunicala con el cuerpo en aparencia exterior, mostrandonosla con una graciosa piedad en los ojos, con buenos colores en el rostro, con apuestos y meneos bien comedidos: con lo qual todo junto muestra el cuerpo de fuera la bondad que el anima tiene dentro en si: y de aqui los venimos ambos a amar. (205)
>
> (And in this way human bodies are capable of it on account of the soul that they carry within them; because the soul fills the body with beauty, transfers [this beauty] to the body's outward form, revealing it, with gracious piety to our eyes, in the face's good complexion, in elegance and refinement of gesture; as a result of which the body shows on the outside all the goodness taken together that the soul has within; and thus we come to love both.)

It is this ideology, needless to say, that will serve the new Galilean science. A medieval cosmos, within whose terrestrial realm of corruption objects strove to achieve stasis, is replaced by a unified cosmos in which movement is the norm.

It is not simply women's issues that demonstrate the difficulty of weighing the respective claims of feudalism and modernity, of substantialism and animism. Let us consider, by way of further illustration, the exchange in *El scholástico* over the supernatural power of words. I have in mind the discussion generated by the old woman who deploys her "signos, palabras y figuras" (99) ("signs, words and figures") in the interests of curing a sick patient. It is tempting to see in dailoguists' magical attitudes a residual element of substantialism, to the extent that they presuppose a seemingly substantialist belief in the capacity of words to "put matter in motion." Words, on this naturalistic basis, are not simply an abstract currency (exchange values) but a potent force (use value). Such a view, however, would be, at most, only partially valid. The condemnation of miracles by Don Quixote, Juan Huarte, and others is not necessarily indicative of a progressive rationalism. On the contrary, it exhibits a substantialist inability to entertain the possibility of radical, that is to say, substantial transformation (cf. Rodríguez 1990: 261-63). It is interesting to note that the incident concerning the old woman is immediately followed by a tale about a necromancer, which, while it concedes the transformatory potential of his science, also celebrates the protagonist's downfall (99-100). Clearly, we are in the presence of a radically fragmented, contradictory text.

Disciplining the Body Politic

The ideological confusion and incoherence evident in *El scholástico* needs constantly to be kept in view. In particular, the continuing impact of substantialism should never be underestimated, as the ideological counterpart to the political success of the nobility in blocking and reversing the gains made by the bourgeoisie in the early decades of the sixteenth century. For while the nobility adapts with difficulty to a public/private functioning detrimental to it own dynamics, it can nevertheless use its superior political leverage to impose its own ideological concerns upon the public sector.

The extent to which *El scholástico* compromises with feudalism is apparent even as the dialoguists settle into their idyllic surroundings. The discussion focuses initially on theology, traditionally the Queen of the sciences, a reminder that religion still played a vital social function. The medieval university was one of the key sites for the reproduction of religious ideology, which responded to the needs of the nobility and helped to make its hegemony possible. And while Villalón's dialoguists soon transfer their attention to legal studies, in accordance with the dominance of politics during the Transition, it is significant that they find a common point of convergence in the concept of natural law: "Veneravan tanto los antiguos las leyes y estimavanlas en tanto por su nescesidad: que las honrravan en los lugares donde las tenian como a cosas vivas: y las hazian sacrifiçio como a verdaderos dioses" ("The Ancients so venerated laws and held them in such esteem because of their necessity, so much so that, in the places where they [i.e., the laws] were kept, they were honored as living things, and sacrifices were made to them, as to real gods"). By grounding laws naturalistically in this way, the problem of their legitimation is avoided: "Asi desta manera todos los otros que dieron leyes a sus pueblos afirmaron averlas recibido de algun dios por se las hazer mas venerar" (74) ("In this way, all those others who provided their people with laws claimed to have received them from some god, so that they [the laws] would be venerated more").

"Natural law" proves definitive of the transition. According to this ultimately Stoic thesis, man is by nature a social animal, disturbed by passional disorders which are the consequence of a fall from grace. It was normal to conceive the latter in historical rather than mythical terms, laying due stress upon the struggle for ascendancy in the ensuing period between the forces of civil progress and those of war and poverty. Life in the community, on this basis, "is only possible within the structure of society where the precepts of natural law become officially specified and proclaimed, and where the coercive power of the State guarantees and reestablishes the primitive order" (Noreña 212-13). The activity of the ruler is similarly constrained. His role is to deploy the power invested in him to (re)impose and defend the inalienable moral values of the community.

While the importance of legal studies to the proper functioning of the state cannot be sufficiently emphasized, it would be very easy to miss the comparable role of medicine. It has often been pointed out, by Foucault among others (Foucault 1981: 116-17), that medical practitioners, from the sixteenth century onward, are notable for their reformist social ambitions. The obvious example, in the case of Spain, is Juan Huarte de San Juan, author of *Examen de los ingenios para las ciencias* (1575). Significantly, *El scholástico* recommends that the state provide a salaried body of medical officials, charged with the care of the body politic: "Por çierto muy mas que felice se puede llamar aquella republica que esta proveida de doctos medicos: porque no ay cosa que sea de mas provecho a la çiudad, ni mas nescesaria para la conservaçion de sus amigos y para triumphar de sus enemigos que la salud" (76) ("To be sure, happy is the republic that is provided with learned doctors, because there is nothing more useful to a city, or more necessary for the well-being of its inhabitants, if they are to triumph over their enemies, than [good] health [care]").

Ideologically, medical texts are as complex and contradictory as any others in the transition, and certainly one would not wish to deny, particularly in the case of Huarte, the obvious influence of animism. However, it is equally important to emphasize the extent to which their terms of reference, namely, the body's proportions and harmony, its humors and temperaments, and so on, fall strictly within the ambit of organicist thinking (see Rodríguez 1990: 330 ff). In this respect, *El scholástico* is a typical product of its time:

> Porque le parescio a [Galeno] que las pasiones del anima por la mayor parte nascian de las indispusiçiones del cuerpo: por lo qual dezia que para volverla en su natural era nescesaria primero la medicina del cuerpo: y que luego se sosegaria el anima. Dieron [los antiguos philosophos] por final subjecto a esta nuestra sciençia la salud del cuerpo por la qual la estimavan en mas: porque tenian gran consideraçion a la perfeçion de un tan proporçionado compuesto, y a la armonia de sus miembros y dispusiçion. Consideravan tambien ser arca donde se reservaba el anima. (75)

> (Because it seemed to [Galen] that the passions of the soul, for the most part, are a result of bodily indispositions, for which reason he claimed that in order to return it to its natural state of well-being, medicine was above all else indispensable to the body. Only then would the soul be at peace. [The Ancient philosophers] considered the goal of this science of ours to be the health of the body, for which reason they esteemed it highly, because they attributed great importance to a well-balanced compound and to the harmony of its members and to its disposition. They also looked upon it as a container in which the soul was kept.)

It would be only too easy to mistake this brand of materialism, essentially of classical extraction, for some modern counterpart. The insistence that the body politic needs to be "cleansed" and "bled"—note the obsession with blood—is a radically substantialist construct.

Educating the Beautiful Soul

We have grown accustomed to references to the ongoing "crisis" or, to quote Chitty and Benn's recent formulation, "debilitating and long-standing contradiction" (Benn and Chitty, 469) that lies at the heart of the Western education system.[6] Yet perhaps it is only too easy to speak in these terms. It bears considering to what extent our current problems are best accounted for by the *absence of crisis.* I intend this as more than a playful paradox, for certainly a casual perusal of the history of Spanish education, at least, reveals a marked continuity of purpose and design. As is evident from the *Siete Partidas,* the basic functional and structural components of Western education are already in place in Alfonso el Sabio's day, including a body of salaried specialists or professionals who derive their authority from the university (see Lerena 120).

At the same time, during the transition, significant changes did occur. The bourgeoisie increasingly contested aristocratic hegemony and, crucially, from within the educational apparatus, as opposed to the Church. Villalón set out to negotiate the passage from a scholastic to a humanistic curriculum. He shared with others, notably Juan Luis Vives, his eminent compatriot and predecessor, the conviction that the state was obliged to provide a modern system of secular education. (A preoccupation with educational issues will remain the hallmark of the bourgeoisie throughout its history.) While dominated by scholasticism, with its characteristic horror of experimentation, even a university as traditional and conservative as Salamanca—on the evidence at least of Villalón's *El scholástico*—felt under pressure to provide the army of judges, accountants, scribes, and bureaucrats required to man the burgeoning state apparatuses.

It is at this point that the vital contribution of the bourgeoisie to Absolutism needs to be re-asserted. For, as Rodríguez insists, the fact is that, while it dominates the concrete state site, the nobility cannot control the impact of the bourgeoisie, "impacto que fuerza la formación no sólo del Estado absolutista, sino también de [las] formas de transición" (56) ("an impact that forces the formation not only of the Absolutist State, but also the forms of transition"). The newly created public/private dichotomy is ultimately advantageous to the bourgeoisie, whose members prefer to intervene in public affairs from their position within the private sphere. Indications are that the substantialist anxieties attending the discussion of word magic derive from the animist association between transubstantiation and social mobility. The transformative potential of the beautiful soul, as we emphasized earlier, included its capacity to ascend to more socially prestigious positions. Indeed, animism proposes as the goal of education the production of a universal man distinguished by his mobility: "Asi que aquellos antiguos varones procuraron de se enseñar de gran diversidad de sciençias por se mostrar sabios y universales en todo: ninguno se contentó con saber una sola. En cuya imitaçion quiero yo que el nuestro discipulo se procure enseñar en todas; y trabaje saber de todas para su mayor perfeçion" (93) ("Thus, the Ancients tried to master a great diversity of disciplines in order to appear learned and universal in all things. No one was content to learn just one. In imitation of which I want our pupil to try and learn all [the sciences], to his greater perfection"). "Failure to achieve," Oliva explicitly argues, can in no way be attributed to one's nature. He is opposed by the Rector, who insists, from a substantialist standpoint, that the individual is, or should be, constrained by the limitations of his body: "Ni aun la debemos consentir [al anima] subtilizar tanto, y vagar por tantas sciençias que como Icaro subiendo mucho se queme las halas y caiga" (93) ("Furthermore, we should not allow it [the soul] to be over subtle, nor to wander through so many disciplines that, like Icarus, by flying so high, it burns its wings and falls"). The logical outcome of this view is a conservative emphasis on the virtues of specialization.

The characterization of animism needs to be exact and carefully nuanced. We are moving very much within the domain of natural law, not of contractual association. On this basis, education served to (re)kindle within the individual a set of innate moral values. The egalitarian principles which these values presuppose are those of Renaissance humanism, not of an Enlightened liberalism. What was actually involved was the rejection of an elitism of blood in favor of one based on merit, itself indelibly stamped upon nature. However, by the same token it would be equally wrong to underplay animism's radical implications. The prominence it accords pedagogically to individual subjectivity helps to explain that self-assertive tendency so characteristic of its advocates. Politically, the transcendental perspective of "universal man" embraces the workings of the Absolutist State, in the sense that it licenses the individual's participation in the public sphere. At its most brazen, self-assertion constitutes a self-authenticating process, which, eventually, will be extended to the liberal state itself. In contrast, the effect of the bodily limitations that preoccupied the substantialist is to disenfranchise large sections of the population. By implication, most people, certainly the lower orders, are simply unable to grasp the mechanisms of the state in all their complexity.

Debate over the freedom of the "beautiful soul" was never more heated than when it concerned the rights of the reader. Hence the aggression with which Pérez Oliva confronts his opponents' attempts to base their arguments on the authority of the Bible: "Y para corroboraçion y fundamento desta su herrada y ignorante opinion, procuran haber auctoridades y exemplos de la sagrada escriptura: los quales torcidos, y como traydos por los cabellos les paresce que vienen a concluir" (133) ("And to corroborate and support this erroneous, ignorant opinion, they try to find authorities and examples from the Scriptures, which, when twisted and forced, seem to them to confirm their views"). The logic of his argument should be obvious: the soul's freedom extends to reading; within the realm of the private, subjects should feel quintessentially free as readers to interpret, for themselves, the words on the page. Yet it was a curious feature of animist literalism that, like its Protestant counterpart, it gave rise to a new brand of authoritarianism. In this respect, few gestures are more revealing and, within the context of sixteenth-century culture, more subversive, than Oliva's simple insistence that conservative readers of the Bible are guilty of *misreadings*. And few questions more disquieting that those which he subsequently poses: if people think the apostles are worthy models, why do they not imitate them in their simplicity? how do these same people reconcile their position with their conspicuous (aristocratic) consumption? and, furthermore, how do they reconcile the squandering of Church rents with imitation of the Church's founding Fathers? But perhaps even more disquieting than these questions is the attitude to authority which they presuppose. Oliva makes a point of flaunting his own irreverence: "Y pues tanto nos va en seguir a los apostoles en su rusticidad, pesquemos todos" (136) ("And since so much rests on our emulating the apostles in their rusticity, let us all become fishermen"). The time was rapidly approaching in Spain, if it had not already arrived, when it would not be possible to take such liberties with impunity.

Conclusion

Educationally, the bourgeoisie is driven in Spain to contest aristocratic rule not primarily through the state university, which, down to the twentieth century, will remain a stronghold of conservatism, but through private schools and academies, the first of which appear in the mid-sixteenth century. Neofeudal influences continue to block further development until the nineteenth century, when the Ley Moyano of 1857 marks a transition to a humanist pedagogical ideology (see Lerena 169-76). While the first part of the twentieth century in Spain (as elsewhere in Europe) saw the caretaker state gradually replaced by an interventionist state, this country enters belatedly into the stage of monopoly capitalism, from the late 1960s to the early 1970s (261), at a point when humanist educational ideology began to be contested by a technicist ideology (278 ff). The rise of the latter corresponds with the neoliberal revolt against "big government," with its emphasis on privatization and deregulation—evidence of an undiminished intervention on the part of the state, but now in the interests of international capital. Although the impact of technicist ideology has been felt throughout the Western world, Spain is distinguished by its own special nuances. Significantly, the Royal Academy, as a quasi state body, has come under increasing attack as an obstacle to technological development, along with the traditional teaching of philology in the state universities. Ideologues in the private sector have not been slow to discern parallels between the present communications revolution and the invention of printing in the Renaissance:

> el paso del papel a la electrónica . . . ha generado cambios, que recuerdan los que provocó, en su momento, el descubrimiento de la imprenta: las lenguas que no consiguieron uniformar su ortografía y su gramática desaparecieron o quedaron relegadas a meras hablas locales; en la actualidad, las lenguas que no consigan

desarrollar medios informáticos que garanticen su posibilidad de ser manipuladas electrónicamente perderán su importancia económica y política. (Subirats)

(the passage from paper to electronics . . . has generated changes that recall those once caused by the discovery of printing: the languages that were unable to standardize their orthography and grammar disappeared or were relegated to mere local dialects; today, the languages that are unable to develop informatic media that guarantee the possibility of their being manipulated electronically will lose their economic and political importance.)

One is bound to wonder, even so, whether this is the correct way to frame the problem, in the sense that, while systemic contradictions are clearly at issue, it is not so clear whether the productive forces play the central role that some people would like us believe. Capitalism, it is true, requires workers with technical expertise, and increasingly looks to education to nurture them. But whether the immediate requirements of economic life are, or can be, the prime consideration in educational practice is another matter. For as Althusser insisted long ago, imparting technical know-how is only part of the task of educational institutions, the other being to reproduce relations of production, by way of disciplining pupils for entry into the workforce. If he is correct, schools and universities are not, and cannot function as, factories. It is a curious kind of technological fetishism, one might add, that attributes the fate of regional languages to their failure to modernize, and omits to mention that their very marginality is the consequence of crimes perpetrated by centralized powers in their imperialistic drive to dominate the globe. But again, the blind spot of bourgeois linguists has always been ideology, along with the role that language plays in the maintenance, and subversion, of prevailing relations of production. And so these same linguists are condemned endlessly to re-enact a confrontation, which is ideological through and through, between an increasingly residual, conservative elite, housed in the Royal Academy ("limpia, fija y da esplendor") and Spain's emergent, newly self-assertive, professional petty bourgeoisie.

Notes

1. For a general introduction to the work of Villalón, see Kincaid.

2. Since I will be arguing below, in the strongest terms, that the category of the subject is always an ideological notion, not the source of economic and political forces impinging, more or less directly, upon texts, it could reasonably be argued that I have ridden rough-shod over the issue of Villalón's identity, the theoretical complexities of which needed to be teased out far more. The suspicion may linger that "Villalón" is but the means whereby, having been ejected through the front door, the category of the subject is re-admitted through the back. Subjectivity, needless to say, is an issue fraught with difficulties, particularly for anyone intent on continuing the Althusserian project, since this category marks precisely the point at which Althusserianism began to unwind (see Locke). In the present context, I would simply argue, with Leonard Jackson, that "there is a great deal of difference between the subjectivity—that is, the total personality—of a real person, which is something that survives and develops throughout life, . . . which is so incredibly tough and enduring that you can normally dissipate it only by physically destroying the body in which it operates, and the temporary illusion of partial consciousness which lasts while you read a book" (Jackson 227). Post-structuralists, we know, have been notoriously reluctant to make such discriminations (see Foucault 1977), but with regrettable consequences regarding the issue of agency. On the question of the unconscious, I will follow Juan Carlos Rodríguez in indicating "la diferencia entre *inconsciente ideológico* (que es el único que vale para estos planteamientos) y el inconsciente *tout court,* esto es, lo que supone como objeto *saber-no saber* del sicoanálisis freudiano" ("the difference between the *ideological unconscious* (which is the only unconscious relevant to the present context) and the unconscious *tout court,* that is, what presupposes as an object the *knowing-not knowing* of Freudian psychoanalysis"). The latter concerns the transhistorical—not ahistorical—process of transition from animal to human, from child to adult. "Me interesaría," Rodríguez adds, "recalcar esa diferencia básica entre *transhistórico* y *ahistórico,* la diferencia que establecería el objeto del saber del sicoanálisis. Pero delimitando a la vez la realidad del *otro* inconsciente, radicalamente histórico, del que partimos, esto es, el *incosciente ideológico*" (Rodríguez 1994: 33) ("I believe it important to emphasize the difference between *transhistorical* and *ahistorical,* the difference that would establish the object of psychoanalytic knowledge. But at the same time delimiting the reality of the *other* unconscious, radically historical, from which we are beginning here, that is, the *ideological unconscious*").

3. Within the North-American academy, the one notable exception was Mariscal (1991), although this work in itself was greeted with a certain amount of puzzlement and incomprehension, not to say outright hostility.

4. For a useful summary of the economic thought of the period, see Rubin, part I. The literature on the transition from feudalism to capitalism is vast. For a good summary of that indebted to Althusser, focusing on Pierre-

Philippe Rey, Guy Bois, Peter Kriedte, and Perry Anderson, see Resch 131-57. For a useful discussion of the work of Robert Brenner, see Callinicos 1995: 122-25; 131-34.

5. For an excellence summary of the Spanish Absolutist State, in the European context, see Anderson.

6. See Carnoy.

Works Cited

Anderson, Perry. *Lineages of the Absolutist State.* London: NLB, 1974.

Benn, Caroline, and Clyde Chitty. *Thirty Years On: Is Comprehensive Education Alive or Well or Struggling to Survive?* Harmondsworth: Penguin Books, 1997.

Callari, Antonio, and David F. Ruccio. *Postmodern Materialism and the Future of Marxist Theory.* Hanover, London: Wesleyan UP, 1996.

Callinicos, Alex. "What Is Living and What Is Dead in the Philosophy of Althusser. *The Althusserian Legacy.*" Eds. E. Ann Kaplan and Michael Sprinker. London, New York: Verso, 1993. 39-49.

______.*Theories and Narratives: Reflections on the Philosophy of History.* Durham: Duke UP, 1995.

Carnoy, Martin, 1982. "Education, Economy and the State." *Cultural and Economic Reproduction in Education: Essays on Class, Ideology and the State.* Ed. Michael W. Apple. London: Routledge & Kegan Paul., 1982. 79-126.

Elliott, Gregory. *Althusser: The Detour of Theory.* London, New York: Verso, 1987.

Entwistle, William James. *The Spanish Language, Together with Portuguese, Catalan and Basque.* London: Faber and Faber, 1962 [1936].

Foucault, Michel. "What Is an Author?"*Language, Counter-Memory, Practice: Selected Essays and Interviews.* Trans. Donald F. Bouchard and Sherry Simon. London, New York: Longman, 1977.

______.*The History of Sexuality. Volume I. An Introduction.* Trans. Robert Hurley. Harmondsworth: Penguin Books, 1981.

Jackson, Leonard. *The Dematerialisation of Karl Marx: Literature and Marxist Theory.* London, New York: Longman, 1984.

Kincaid, Joseph J. *Cristóbal de Villalón.* New York: Twayne, 1973.

Lerena Alesón, Carlos. *Escuela, ideología y clases sociales en España.* Barcelona: Ariel, 1976.

Locke, Grahame. 1996. "Subject, Interpellation, and Ideology." *Postmodern Materialism and the Future of Marxist Theory.* Eds. Antonio Callari and David F. Ruccio. London: Hanover: Wesleyan UP, 1996. 69-90.

Mariscal, George. *Contradictory Subjects: Quevedo, Cervantes, and Seventeenth-Century Spanish Culture.* Ithaca: Cornell UP, 1991.

Niederehe, Hans J. *Alfonso X el Sabio y la lingüística de su tiempo.* Trans. Carlos Melches. Madrid: Sociedad General Española de Librería, 1987.

Noreña, Carlos G.*Juan Luis Vives*. The Hague: Martinus Nijhoff, 1970.

Padley, G. A. *Grammatical Theory in Western Europe: 1500-1700. Trends in Vernacular Grammar II*. Cambridge: Cambridge UP, 1988.

Peñalver Castillo, Manuel. *Estudios de historia de la lingüística española*. Granada: Instituto de Estudios Almerienses, 1993.

Pereira, Oscar. *Arte, literatura y subjetividad en la primera modernidad*. Unpublished MS.

Read, Malcolm K. *Visions in Exile: The Body in Spanish Literature and Linguistics: 1500-1700*. Amsterdam/Philadelphia: John Benjamins, 1990.

_____. *The Birth and Death of Language: Spanish Literature and Linguistics: 1300-1700*. Madrid: Porrúa, 1983.

Resch, Robert Paul. *Althusser and the Renewal of Marxist Social Theory*. Berkeley: California UP, 1992.

Rodríguez, Juan Carlos. *Teoría e historia de la producción ideológica: Las primeras literaturas burguesas (siglo XVI)*. Madrid: Akal, 1990.

_____. *La norma literaria*. Granada: Biblioteca de Bolsillo, 1994.

_____. *Lorca y el sentido: un inconsciente para una historia*. Madrid: Akal, 1994.

Rubin, Isaac Ilyich. *A History of Economic Thought*. Trans. and ed. Donald Filtzer. London: Pluto Press, 1979.

Subirats, Carlos Rüggeberg. "La lengua española ante el reto de las nuevas tecnologías." *El mundo*. May 23, 1996.

Villalón, Cristóbal de. *Provechoso tratado de cambios y contrataciones de mercaderes y reprobación de la usura*. Valladolid: Francisco Fernández de Córdoba, 1546.

_____. *El scholástico*. [c. 1550] Ed. Richard Kerr. Madrid: Consejo Superior de Investigaciones Científicas, 1966.

_____. *Gramática castellana*. [1558] Fac. ed. and study by Constantino García. Madrid: CSIC., 1971.

_____. *El crotalón*. [1559] Madrid: Espasa-Calpe, 1973.

◆ Chapter 2

The Politics of Race, Ethnicity, and Gender in the Making of the Spanish State

Mary Elizabeth Perry

"The King of the Three Religions," Alfonso X called himself in late thirteenth-century Castile. In assuming this title, he not only emphasized the deep and complex cultural roots of Spanish identity; he also acknowledged that Christians, Muslims, and Jews all lived in the kingdom of Castile, and he implied that he would continue the system of *convivencia*, or coexistence, in which Christians, Jews, and Muslims lived in relative harmony. Religious minorities freely practiced their own beliefs and traditions in this system, but they had to pay for that freedom through special taxes. And they sometimes had to live in particular quarters, dependent on the ruler's protection. Within two centuries of the reign of Alfonso X, however, any pretense of protection or harmonious coexistence crumbled under waves of increasing intolerance. Jews and Muslims had to convert to Christianity in order to remain in their homes, and a Spanish identity began to emerge along with a fledgling central state.

Minorities played a major role in the making of the Spanish state, for around them developed a politics of race, ethnicity, and gender. Spanish Christians constructed an identity in the medieval and early modern periods as they responded to Jews and Muslims, two groups that differ very markedly and had different experiences in the Iberian Peninsula. Moreover, Christianized subgroups developed from both Jews and

Muslims, which also differed from one another and from their parent groups. Despite the diversity among these several minorities, they played a similar political role as counter-identities essential to the unification of diverse Christians and to the development of their consciousness as Spaniards.

Anthropologists, sociologists, cultural critics, feminists, literary critics, and political theorists provide interpretative assistance in an analysis of this political role, which can be seen as a process involving three overlapping stages. First, the difference of these minority groups became transformed into deviance, particularly through racialization and an inscription of the body. Second, Christians increasingly perceived the pollution of these deviant groups as a threat to their social order. And third, Christian authorities expelled both groups in response to the political imperatives of a developing central state.

The Transformation of Difference into Deviance

Diversity did not suddenly appear in late medieval Spain, nor did the deviance subsequently associated with minority groups. Jews, for example, had lived in the Iberian Peninsula since pre-Roman times, and they had their own history, language, religion, and traditions that gave them a well-defined identity. Yet others, who resented their differences, regarded them less as the Chosen People than as a devious group that maintained its own identity in a position of ambiguity. Outside centers of power, yet vulnerable to maintaining good relations with those who held power, Jews sometimes had to ally themselves with victorious invaders. Hatred of the Jews goes back at least to the sixth century B.C.E. when Persian conquerors of ancient Egypt began to enlist the Jews as allies, establishing a pattern that would be repeated many times.[1] Some historians of medieval Europe believe that anti-Semitism intensified in the eleventh and twelfth centuries, when many European communities began a transition from segmentary societies to more centralized states (Moore 151). The persecution of Jews reached a climax in England in 1291 with the decision to expel the Jews, and in the following century with a similar expulsion in France.

On the Iberian Peninsula a pattern of Christian anti-Semitism intensified after the Muslim invasion of 711 when

Sephardic Jews who had suffered oppression under the Christian Visigoths appeared to welcome the Muslim conquerors.[2] Muslims, in fact, selected some Jewish leaders to govern several important cities under their rule, and they often designated Jews to be mediators between Muslims and Christians because of the Jews' education and linguistic abilities. During the tenth and eleventh centuries the culture of Sephardic Jews blossomed into a Golden Age of philosophy, science, and poetry in the Muslim kingdom of al-Andalus.

With time, however, Muslim officials began to regard Jews less as helpful allies and more as a minority that had gained too much influence and ought to be persecuted. During the twelfth century, then, Jews migrated from Muslim-ruled al-Andalus and went northward where Christian kings seemed to welcome them, granting some of the wealthier Jews tax exemptions so they would share their knowledge of Muslim politics. Yet most Jews paid taxes, and many acted as financial advisors and as tax-farmers for Christian rulers, who used their wealth and expertise and also deflected onto Jews popular resentment about rising taxes.

Because Jews played important roles for Christian rulers, anti-Semitism also became useful as a weapon for opponents of their authority. The series of succession crises in the Kingdom of Castile that occurred throughout the thirteenth and fourteenth centuries finally erupted in a civil war in which Henry of Trastámara accused Pedro the Cruel of allowing the royal govenment to be mortgaged to the Jews. After winning the support of nobles and commoners resentful of paying taxes for a growing central monarchy, Henry murdered Pedro, his rival for the throne, and declared an end to the civil war. Then, in a pattern seen throughout Europe, the new regime established its legitimacy, discredited its enemies, and strengthened its hold on the instruments of power through a campaign of moral repression that included attempts to control marginal groups such as prostitutes and Jews. (Moore 135-36)

Developments within the Church in the Iberian Peninsula also encouraged the rise of anti-Semitism in the thirteenth and fourteenth centuries. As Christians took over more and more land from the Muslims in their "Reconquest," the Church grew in both wealth and influence. It made stronger demands for orthodoxy, particularly with the rise of the mendicant orders and with the crusade against the Albigensians, who lived in southern France and spilled over the Pyrenees into Iberia. Facing internal problems such as imposing the Roman rite on those who favored the old Visigothic rite of worship, the Church also sought unity through orthodoxy and in campaigns to convert the Jews. Friars organized public disputations in which they would debate rabbis, and when a rabbi appeared to be too successful they would close the disputation, ostensibly because of the threat of mob violence.

Anti-Semitism flourished in the fourteenth century not only as a weapon for those in power, but also as an expression of popular fears and resentments born of economic problems and fed by secular and ecclesiastical authorities. In the massive dislocations following the Black Death, for example, many people blamed the Jews for poisoning wells and otherwise causing the epidemic that decimated the population throughout Europe (Gerber 111-12). Popular beliefs that Jews profited from the misfortunes of others provided ready tinder in 1390 for the violently anti-Semitic sermons of Ferrant Martínez, who urged the faithful to destroy all synagogues and expel Jews from Seville and its surrounding villages. This pogrom, which began in 1391, spread throughout the peninsula. Thousands of Jews were killed outright, and thousands of Jewish women and children were sold into slavery, their bodies branded with the marks of slavery. Probably 200,000 Jews converted out of fear in the 1390s, and more than half of the remaining Jews converted in the next generation.

Baptized Jews became another deviant minority group. Called by Christians "Conversos" or "*marranos*," a derogatory term meaning pigs, these former Jews remained suspect as false converts. Some, in fact, became sincere Christians, but others retained their Jewish beliefs and traditions, which they attempted to maintain in secrecy. These crypto-Jews hid scrolls and sacred writings, memorized the important prayers of Judaism, and passed them on to their children.[3] Ironically, the Inquisition helped to perpetuate Jewish beliefs and traditions by the public proclamation of edicts of grace that listed offending beliefs and traditions, and also through the diligent questioning of Conversos suspected as false converts.

In Toledo, once the principal Jewish city on the Iberian Peninsula where some 12,000 Jews lived in the twelfth century, a major riot broke out in 1449, aimed against wealthy

Conversos. After days of killing and sacking, town officials regained control and then passed the first of what would be called purity-of-blood statutes, laws that excluded from any municipal office people of Jewish ancestry. Significantly, these laws institutionalized a belief that difference inherited with the blood at birth was so deviant that it could not be changed or tolerated.[4] "We declare," said the preamble to the Toledo ordinance, "the so-called Conversos, offspring of perverse Jewish ancestors, must be held by law to be infamous and ignominious, unfit, and unworthy to hold any public office or any benefice within the city of Toledo, or land within its jurisdiction . . ." (qtd. in Gerber 127). Note that this law did not focus on religious practices or beliefs; in targeting difference as an inherited quality, purity-of-blood laws racialized difference, inscribing deviance on the body. Purity-of-blood laws would spread throughout the peninsula, and later they would be applied to another religious minority, the Moriscos, those people or their descendants who had converted from Islam to Christianity.

Sentiment to expel the Jews grew as inquisitors uncovered thousands of false converts. Conversos would never completely convert until their fellow Jews were gone, the argument went. But Ferdinand and Isabel needed the tax revenue of Jews while they were fighting the Muslims. Finally in 1492, with the defeat of Granada, the last Muslim stronghold on the peninsula, the Catholic kings called for the expulsion of the Jews. About 175,000 Jews left their kingdoms, the majority to settle for a while in Portugal. But another 100,000 Jews converted so that they could remain in their homes. The expulsion thus enlarged the group of Conversos remaining in the Spanish kingdoms, and it exacerbated Christians' suspicion of them. Despite the exodus of the Jews, then, persecution of Conversos increased, fed by both popular resentments and a racialist belief that they had inherited their difference from Old Christians through tainted blood.

At the same time, dominant Christians were transforming another religious minority into a deviant group. The Catholic Kings' promise of religious tolerance made to their newly acquired Muslim subjects at the capitulation of Granada in 1492 lasted less than a decade before the Crown issued a series of decrees that Muslims must convert to Christianity or leave the Iberian peninsula.[5] Christians and Muslims had known about their cultural and religious differences from centuries of living together, but in the sixteenth century Muslim differences became Morisco deviance as Christians required Muslims to convert. The dominant Christians imposed their power to name this group, calling them "Moriscos," and applied to them racialist beliefs and purity-of-blood laws that hindered their integration into the dominant culture.

In addition, Christians transformed Moriscos into a deviant group by inscribing the body through a process of sexualization which had already begun against the Jews. Both Jews and Muslims circumcised their sons, a practice that Christians prohibited as a ritual mutilation that marked their bodies forever.[6] In many ways, however, Christian actions against Jews and Muslims also mutilated their bodies, from branding them as slaves to subjecting them to questioning under torture. Seeking to discredit minorities by associating them with sexual perversions, Christians marked their bodies through rhetoric, laws, and institutions that sought to define them. During the sixteenth century this process became especially evident against the Moriscos.

Bathing and ritual washing, for example, had long been recognized as a difference between Jews and Christians and between Muslims and Christians.[7] In Castile, Christian contempt for bathing as "effeminate" had resulted in the destruction of most Muslim and Jewish bath buildings by the end of the fifteenth century (Jiménez Lozano 100). Moreover, one chronicler attributed Christian military victories to Muslim baths, which, he declared, "were the cause of a certain softness in their bodies, and of excessive pleasure, from which there proceeded idleness and other deceits and evil dealings which they inflicted on one another in order to sustain their customary ease" (Pulgar qtd. in Harvey 271). In the following century, this sexualized rhetoric took on the legal form of directives from the Crown which told local authorities that among those things they must do to "instruct" and Christianize Moriscos was to enter their homes and remove any baths or bathing vessels.[8]

As the Inquisition began to prosecute Moriscos who continued their Muslim traditions, it aimed its institutional power against such practices as bathing. The "edicts of faith" by which the Holy Office called on the faithful to denounce themselves listed a variety of forbidden acts, and they usually included baths and washing as evidence of Morisco apostasy.

Inquisitors used sexualized language in their edicts as they condemned the washing of the arms, the hands, face, mouth, nose, ears, legs and "shameful parts."[9] And witnesses used the same language as they denounced Moriscos for "washing like a Muslim," including their "shameful parts."[10]

Christians also sexualized Muslim differences in marriage rituals and practices. They imputed to Moriscos a lack of sexual restraint because they married cousins within forbidden degrees of relatedness, thus breaking the Christian taboo. Moriscos continued to marry in the Muslim manner, Christians said, and asked for the rites of holy matrimony only after carrying out the Muslim wedding—a ritual of Koranic readings, dowry agreements, dying red with henna parts of the bride's body, and singing and dancing the leilas and zambras that secular instructions and inquisitorial prosecution repeatedly forbade.[11]

Polygamy appeared to be even more depraved to Christians who were scandalized by evidences that Muslim men and, to a lesser extent, Jewish men took more than one wife. This practice, Christians believed, not only violated a moral order, but could overturn an entire social order based on divine law and the distribution of women through monogamous unions.[12] Even though few Moriscos took more than one wife except in times of crises, Christians declared that the Koran provided for polygamy, giving "a very great license so that a man can have many women, young ones and as many as he can take in battle and can maintain, and not only single women," one writer added significantly, "but even those belonging to others."[13] To people critical of Moriscos, polygamy could destroy a social order in which women belonged to triumphant or privileged men.

Christians condemned polygamy and other Morisco marriage traditions that increased their birth rate, declaring that these people multiplied like "bad weeds."[14] Complaining that Moriscos married at a very early age, even as young as 10 or 11 years, Christians implied that Moriscos engaged in more and earlier sexual activity. In fact, recent scholars have found very little difference in age at first marriage. Bernard Vincent, for example, found that in sixteenth-century Granada the average age for marriage for all men was 24-25 years and for women 18-19 years, with Moriscas marrying approximately 12 to 14 months earlier than Old Christian women (Vincent, *Minorías* 49).[15] Yet Christians repeatedly voiced fears about the fertility of Moriscos, their fears not only fueled by real evidence of population increase among Moriscos, but also confirmed by the fact that most Moriscos married, undeterred by a Christian veneration of virginity and celibacy (Domínguez Ortiz and Vincent 83-84). Morisco differences became perceived as increasingly dangerous deviance as the Morisco population grew. Not surprisingly, proposals for solutions to the "Morisco problem" frequently included enslavement or high marriage taxes as ways to discourage marriage. Some proposals even called for castration.[16]

Sexualizing minorities cannot be reduced to the single concern about high fertility, however, for Christians accused Jews and Muslims of sodomy and other nonreproductive sexual activity that they strongly condemned. To Christians such as Pedro Aznar Cardona, Mohammed had "injured" marriage by approving polygamy, marriage within prohibited degrees, and sodomy (Aznar 96-114). Asserting that the Koran invited both men and women to engage in sodomy, Christians passed secular laws against it, and in Aragon the Inquisition prosecuted this "nefarious sin."[17] Although authorities condemned many Moriscos for sodomy, they prosecuted many Christian clerics, as well. Since this "sin" was almost exclusively a male offense, some of the accused purportedly took the passive role prescribed for women in heterosexual relations, thus inverting the gender order and subverting the order of "nature." Christian critics who defined religious minorities as sodomites inscribed their bodies as the site of deviance (Vincent, *Minorías* 66).

Increasing Structural Danger Through Pollution

Racialized and sexualized, Jews and Conversos, Muslims and Moriscos became perceived as groups that threatened the very structure of society. Christians used their dominant position to exercise what cultural critic bell hooks has called the "political power of representations," a power that cannot be ignored (hooks 57, 72). In their speech and writings, Christians seized the power to say who these people were and what they represented, and the message was clear: Moriscos and Conversos, descendants from Muslims and Jews, represented the impure, the lewd, and the nefarious—in a word, pollution. Christians had not only a right, but a duty, to defend themselves against this pollution.

Yet anthropologist Mary Douglas has reminded us to look for deeper meanings of pollution, which is never an isolated phenomenon and makes sense only "in reference to a total structure of thought" (Douglas 41). This "total structure of thought" provides a gendered view of the world and the basic conceptualization necessary to any society, for it legitimates hierarchy and authority, establishes rules for inclusion, and justifies exclusion—qualities also essential for a political state. In early modern Spain, the Christian rulers used religion to legitimize their authority, and they used pollution to justify exclusion. Purity-of-blood statutes, for example, which excluded people of Muslim or Jewish descent from certain offices, from many professions, and from attending university, implied the pollution of "pure" Christians through mixture with the "tainted" blood of others.

As they distinguished themselves from Jews, Muslims, and their descendants, Spanish Christians developed a conceptualization of their society that had a form with external boundaries, margins, and internal structure. Douglas has noted that such images of society contain the power to reward conformity and to repulse attack (114). With energy even in its margins and unstructured areas, an image of society has the power to control people or to stir them to action. In sixteenth-century Spain rituals of exclusion and abhorrence enabled Christians to define their society, express its inherent power, and create the reality of a Spanish identity.

In many ways, colonization and oppression of minority groups involved rituals of separation that Douglas noted would hold in relationship the "key-stone, boundaries, margins and internal lines" of the "total structure of thought" (41). Through the solemn public announcements and ceremonies of sheriffs and clerics, Christians separated Conversos and Moriscos from their religious buildings and bath-houses, their religious leaders and language, their music and dance, their family traditions of birth, marriage, and death, their customary ways of preparing and consuming food. To forbid such aspects of their culture, authorities believed, could neutralize Moriscos' and Conversos'—the New Christians'—powers of pollution. Old Christians also divorced themselves from Jews and Muslims through rituals of public decree and expulsion; from Conversos and Moriscos, they dissociated themselves through rituals of genealogical accounting required by purity-of-blood statutes that strongly discouraged intermarriage, and through inquisitorial rites, such as the public edicts of grace and the autos-de-fé, that prosecuted and punished Conversos and Moriscos for apostasy.

Golden Age literature justified such rituals through emphasizing the deceit of these people and their proclivity for witchcraft. The Morisca witch appeared in *La pícara Justina*, *Guzmán de Alfarache*, and Cervantes's "El coloquio de los perros," to name just a few examples.[18] In reality, Moriscos and Jews—like Christians—had traditions of witchcraft, most notably that of love magic through which women in particular sought to control the object of their affection.[19] Note here the sexual basis for Christian fears of Jewish and Morisco pollution through witchcraft, not only through giving women power over men and thus inverting gender power positions, but also through threatening to control male sexuality.

Morisco love magic beliefs appear in *aljamiado* literature, that is, writings of Castilian dialect in Arabic script which became prohibited in the sixteenth century. The manuscript *Libro de dichox marabilloxox*, for example, includes formulae for capturing the person one loves, cabalistic signs for love affairs, and recipes for the man who hates his wife and another to make a man love a particular woman (Ribera and Asín 99-101). Several cases before the Inquisition demonstrate the persistence of love magic traditions, such as that of one Morisca who asked another for a piece of paper containing a formula that would restore peace between her husband and herself (Fournel Guérin 536). Such formulae not only used the forbidden language, *aljamía*, but also assumed the ability of women to know and use supernatural powers to control others.

In addition, Christians saw sexual menace in Moriscos inversion of the gender prescriptions by which Christians attempted to order their world. Traditional Morisco costumes, for example, featured "trousers" for women and a long robe or "skirts" for men. Morisco women performed heavy physical work and agricultural labor that Christians usually left to men.[20] And Morisco men engaged in the commerce or manual labor that Christians considered base. As Christian oppression increased during the sixteenth century, Morisco women assumed roles that men usually carried out, particularly as religious teachers, and as leaders of an opposition to Christian attempts to obliterate their culture.[21] Reports from the battlefields of the rebellion of 1568-70 described Moriscas fighting alongside the men, although they had no weapons and used stones and roasting spits against the Christian soldiers and their horses.[22]

To Christian authorities, Moriscos represented a foreign group, not only because they were believed to be spies for the Turks, but also because their very presence symbolized the disorder that Spanish Christians feared throughout their society. In gendered form, this disorder became a sexual menace that seemed especially dangerous.[23] It unleashed a gender inversion in which women sought to control the sexuality of men and assumed male dress and many male roles. Reputed to encourage juvenile sexual activity in both early marriages and liaisons between boys and older men, Moriscos and Conversos were also accused of engaging in nonreproductive heterosexual behavior and "unnatural" homosexual acts of sodomy.

Christians distorted and exaggerated Converso and Morisco differences into stereotypes that further marginalized and demonized them; but ironically, the more that Christians marginalized and demonized their enemy, the more menacing and resistant and polluting this enemy seemed to become.[24] Using their power of representation, Christians portrayed Morisco men as flabby and effeminate sodomites and pedaphiles, and Morisco women as obstinant, lewd, and treacherous, slyly hiding behind a veil. Their policies of increasing oppression served not to enforce assimilation, but to further alienate Moriscos and ensure their marginality, which, in the words of bell hooks, is "much more than a site of deprivation," for "it is also the site of radical possibility, a space of resistance" (hooks 149). In early modern Spain, the women especially of the crypto-Jewish and Morisco communities carried out this resistance in their everyday lives, covertly continuing, despite proscription, Jewish or Muslim traditions of preparing and consuming food, speaking Hebrew or Ladino, Arabic or *aljamía* to their children, and teaching them to pray in the Jewish or Muslim manner. As Christians discovered the extent of this resistance, they hardened their resolve to rid themselves of their internal enemies, these people of pollution.

Political Imperatives

In fact, Christian perceptions and policies created two demonized minorities that played a critical role in a major political imperative for the infant Spanish state, the development of national identity. As Anne Norton points out in her recent book, *Reflections on Political Identity*, subcultures, minority groups, the alienated, and the dissident hold ambiguous positions "between identities." Politically, they act as liminars, which "serve as mirrors for nations. At once other and like, they provide the occasion for the nation to constitute itself in reflection upon its identity. Their likeness permits contemplation and recognition, their difference the abstraction of those ideal traits that will henceforth define the nation" (Norton 53). For Norton, nations determine what they signify and what they will become through what they reject. In the case of Spain, Christian rulers saw Jews and also Muslims as so different that they identified them with the foreign that had to be expelled.

Ironically, Moriscos, Conversos, and crypto-Jews who had ostensibly chosen to convert to Christianity became counter-identities against which Christians could unify and define themselves. "As more generally in early modern Europe," Peter Sahlins has pointed out in his important study of the boundaries between France and Spain, "national identities were frequently defined by counter-identities" (Sahlins 107). Moreover, the sense of difference that Sahlins finds "so critical in defining an identity" could be expressed through religion, which provided both metaphors and a language of resistance (Sahlins 9, 123). It is no accident that Christians increasingly oppressed Conversos and Moriscos during the sixteenth century, for this was a critical time for a developing Spanish state in search of a unifying identity; and it is not surprising that racialization and sexualization increased the potency of this counter-identity, for sexual and biological menace derived its power from taboos intertwined with religious beliefs.

A sexualized counter-identity promoted the need for a state that could carry out certain ethical functions which Antonio Gramsci identified as very significant in state-building. In his words, "every State is ethical in as much as one of its most important functions is to raise the great mass of the population to a particular cultural and moral level, a level (or type) which corresponds to the needs of the productive forces for development, and hence to the interests of the ruling classes" (258). Although the fledgling Spanish state lacked an apparatus of its own to carry out this ethical program, it could call upon the support of a Church, Inquisition, secular justice, and schools—all participants in the "civil society" that Gramsci saw as the real power that supports a state and its ruling class. Using a metaphor from the trench warfare of World War I, Gramsci wrote that civil society was a "powerful system of fortresses and earthworks" buttressing the state, which to him was only an "outer ditch" for a ruling class attempting to maintain power (238).

The presence of Conversos and Moriscos in sixteenth-century Spain provided two deviant groups that helped the ruling Christians to define their social, as well as political, boundaries. These social boundaries, according to sociologist Kai Erikson, are constantly shifting, and they "remain a meaningful point of reference only so long as they are repeatedly tested by persons on the fringes of the group and repeatedly defended by persons chosen to represent the group's inner morality" (13). Their experience with Conversos and Moriscos enabled Spanish Christians not only to better define their own socio-sexual norms, but to know how to control any group that might deviate from these norms. Moreover, they could call on a unified Inquisition that could act throughout the Spanish Empire to defend the boundaries set by these norms.

In addition, the deviancy myths used to identify Conversos and Moriscos in sixteenth-century Spain provided a continuing justification for granting the state power to control these groups. Anthropologists such as David Sibley have noted that such myths generate "deviancy amplification," for they filter information, create and exploit stereotypes, which then provoke a reaction that leads to increased deviance, a polarization of attitudes, confirmation of stereotypes, and intensified oppression (Sibley 29; Cohen 29). Clearly, the Inquisition's persecution of Conversos and Moriscos provided a continuing and intensifying policy of control, a rationale for a unified effort to control these groups not only in the Spanish kingdoms, but also in the Netherlands, the Italian possessions, and vast areas of the Western Hemisphere.

Rituals to control Conversos and Moriscos ensured their permanence as deviant groups. Public proclamations of the edicts of grace that listed offensive behaviors of suspected apostates reminded all those who heard them of how Christian authorities had defined what was to be abhorred. Once arrested, Conversos and Moriscos had to participate in more rituals that demonstrated their own vulnerability before the power of the Inquisition. At a public auto-de-fe, the faithful gathered, unified against those found guilty by inquisitors, who would read aloud for all to hear their names, crimes, and punishments. Frequently penitents had to wear the sanbenito, a sack-like garment, marked with symbols of their offenses, which held their criminality up to public scorn. Even after death, the penitent's sanbenito with his family name and crimes was suspended from the beams of the parish church so that the family would be forever branded with his deviance. Notably missing from these ceremonies of deviance is a ritual to integrate the penitent into society once the punishment had been completed (Erikson 16-17).

As groups identified as enemies by Spanish Christians, crypto-Jews and Moriscos promoted not only a unifying identity that could cover over the great class and regional differences among the people of this realm; they also prompted the growth of a central bureaucracy, a central army, and the imposition of central authority over local governance. What the Crown lacked in bureacracy, the Church and Inquisition provided because they had assumed the task of Christianizing Conversos and Moriscos, enforcing compulsory schools on their children, and prosecuting them for apostasy. The rebellions of Moriscos in Granada in both 1500 and 1568 justified the raising of armies to serve the king, and the dispersion of the defeated Moriscos from Granada in 1570 removed tens of thousands of them from the traditional control of local nobles. In this dispersion, Philip II not only reduced the power of certain nobles; he also ignored the protests of towns and cities that opposed the loss of their Morisco populations and from those that did not want to welcome relocated Moriscos into their jurisdictions.[25] Resettlement of the Moriscos throughout Castile provided a rationale for further royal intrusion into municipal affairs, sometimes by crown-appointed corregidores, but usually carried out by clerics. In 1581, for example, archbishops and bishops complied with royal instructions and directed their parish priests to carry out a census of their Morisco populations.[26]

Christian authorities used Conversos and Moriscos to rationalize the need to scrutinize private lives and invade their homes. When the Inquisition proclaimed an edict of grace, it called on the faithful not only to examine and denounce themselves, but to denounce their neighbors and family members for acts such as changing into clean clothing on Fridays, for circumcising their sons, for washing their bodies, for speaking or reading Arabic, *aljamía*, Hebrew or Ladino. Sheriffs, both secular and employed by the Inquisition, had the authority to enter homes to discover whether people were engaging in prohibited acts, and they received instruction to enter unexpectedly at mealtime to see whether people were eating seated on the ground in the Muslim manner, or preparing food with oil rather than with animal fat. Under such scrutiny, Converso and Morisco homes became transformed into a primary arena of cultural conflict, particularly when Conversos and Moriscos attempted to resist the oppression directed against them by propagating oppositional sentiments and by preserving cultural traditions in their homes (Johnston 49; hooks 45, 214). Such developments seemed to feed the small and fledgling central state, which depended so heavily on the Church to set and enforce social boundaries.

Finally, demonizing Conversos and Moriscos as a racialized and sexualized Other provided a myth for the infant state that sacralized its origin in the crusades of the Reconquest. This myth claimed continuity with the Reconquest, which Christians saw as a holy war against the infidel, culminating with the expulsion of the Jews and the defeat of the Muslims. Christians perceived Conversos as biological descendants of the Jews they had expelled, and they saw Moriscos as direct descendants of those Muslims whom they and their ancestors had defeated in a seven-centuries-long series of wars and skirmishes. Christian authorities claimed the glory and legitimacy of Reconquest heroes who had defeated the Muslims, and those who wanted to flatter the king would call upon this myth.

Damián Fonseca, who wrote a justification for the expulsion of the Moriscos, provides a fine example of the use of heroic myth. "And although most kings of Spain have been brave Hercules who struggle against this beast of so many heads, and have won glorious victories," he declared, "most notable is the most illustrious King Philip III, taking for his singular enterprise to break the most pernicious head of this dragon, which is Mohammed" (Fonseca *Prologue*). Fonseca thus legitimized Philip III as one of a long line of victorious Reconquest kings, and his imagery served to justify a royal decision to expel the Moriscos and override local concerns and opposition from nobles who relied on Morisco vassals. In 1609 Philip III finally issued a decree expelling Moriscos, declaring that conscience bound him to excise "the things that cause scandal and damage to good subjects, and danger to the State, and especially offense and disservice to God our Lord."[27] Obedient to the political imperatives of a developing Spanish state, Philip III, like Ferdinand and Isabel before him, decided to expel a minority group whose difference had been transformed into racialized and sexualized deviance, abhorrent and unacceptable to the developing national identity.

Notes

1. See Benzion Netanyahu, *The Origins of the Inquisition in Fifteenth-Century Spain*. I would like to thank members of the Southwestern Consortium in Spanish History for their helpful discussion of an earlier version of this essay.

2. For more on the Jews in Iberia, see Yitzhak Baer, *A History of the Jews in Christian Spain.*

3. See Moshe Lazar, "Scorched Parchments and Tortured Memories: The 'Jewishness' of the Anussim (Crypto-Jews)."

4. Note that these statutes were not without critics; for more discussion, see Henry Kamen, *Inquisition and Society in Spain*, esp. 114-33.

5. These decrees began in Granada in 1501; for more discussion, see Mark D. Meyerson, *The Muslims of Valencia in the Age of Fernando and Isabel: Between Coexistence and Crusade*, 90-95.

6. See Bernard Vincent, "The *Moriscos* and Circumcision."

7. Jews, of course, do not follow the same ritual bathing as Muslims; for Jews, the most important example is the *mikveh*, the ritual bath for women following the menstrual period or giving birth. See Renée Levine Melammed, "Sephardi Women in the Medieval and Early Modern Periods," 120.

8. See the *Informe* from Madrid to Valencia quoted in Mercedes García Arenal, *Los moriscos*, 116-25.

9. Archivo Histórico Nacional (hereafter AHN), Inquisición, libro 1244, 107.

10. An excellent example is the case of Madalena Morisca, reported to the tribunal of the Inquisition in Seville in 1609, in AHN, Inquisición, legajo 2075, no. 19.

11. Damián Fonseca, *Justa expulsion de los moriscos de España: con la instruccion, apostasia, y traycion dellos: y respuesta á las dudas que se ofrecieron acerca desta materia* (Rome, 1612), ms R 11918 in the Biblioteca Nacional (hereafter BN), 110-11; See Bernard Vincent, *Minorías y marginados en la España del siglo XVI* , 55-70.

12. A few Jews followed the Muslim practice of polygamy, also; see Melammed, "Sephardi Women," 118-19.

13. Ricoldo de Montecrucio, *Reprobación del Alcoran*, BN, Raros 4.037, n.p., Chapter 1.

14. *Informe* of Don Alonso Gutiérrez, reprinted in Pascual Boronat y Barrachina, *Los moriscos expañoles y su expulsión: Estudio histórico-crítico* I, 635; Padre Aznar Cardona, quoted in García Arenal, *Los moriscos*, 233.

15. See also James Casey and Bernard Vincent, "Casa y familia en Granada"; Margarita María Birriel Salcedo, "Mujeres y familia, fuentes y metodología"; and Margarita María Birriel Salcedo, "La experiencia silenciada, las mujeres en la historia de Andalucía. Andalucía moderna."

16. See the *Informe* of D. Alonso Gutiérrez reprinted in Pascual Boronat y Barrachina I, 637; see also Domínguez Ortiz and Vincent, 71.

17. Often called "pecado nefando," sodomy cases were prosecuted by the Inquisition in Aragon and by secular justice in Castile. For Inquisition prosecution of sodomy, see Rafael Carrasco, *Historia de los sodomitas. Inquisición y represión sexual en Valencia*; Ricardo García Cárcel, *Herejía y sociedad en el siglo XVI: La inquisición en Valencia 1530-1609* , 288; and E.W. Monter, *Frontiers of Heresy: The Spanish Inquisition from the Basque Lands to Sicily*, 276-302. In Castile secular law rather than the Inquisition prosecuted sodomy; see Mary Elizabeth Perry, "The 'Nefarious Sin' in Early Modern Seville," and in Kent Gerard and Gert Hekma, eds.*The Pursuit of Sodomy: Male Homosexuality in Renaissance and Enlightenment Europe*. An example of Christian rhetoric pointing to the Koran as the basis for Muslim and Morisco sodomy is in Montecrucio, *Reprobación,* n.p., Chapter 1.

18. Julio Caro Baroja (*Los moriscos del Reino de Granada (Ensayo de Historia Social)* 229-30) discusses the old Morisca witch in *La pícara Justina* and the fame of Moriscas as witches in *Guzmán de Alfarache*. See José María Delgado Gallego, ("Maurofilia y maurofobia, ¿dos caras de la misma moneda?" 22-30) esp. for discussion of Cervantes's *El coloquio de los perros.*

19. Caro Baroja, *Los moriscos*, 113, makes this point and says there was not much difference in the love magic of these different groups. For more on women and love magic, see María Helena Sánchez Ortega, *La mujer y la sexualidad en el antiguo régimen: La perspectiva inquisitorial* , 138-53; and María Helena Sánchez Ortega, "Sorcery and Eroticism in Love Magic"; for love magic and Jewish women, see John Edwards, "Male and Female Religion Among Spanish New Christians," unpublished paper presented at the University of California at Davis, April 1992, 7; and John Edwards,

"Religious Faith and Doubt in Late Medieval Spain: Soria *circa* 1450-1500."

20. For example, see the response of the town of San Clemente, quoted in Domínguez Ortiz and Vincent 40; and Antonio Collantes de Terán Sánchez, *Sevilla en la baja edad media: La ciudad y sus hombres* 335.

21. Inquisition cases abound with evidence of women's roles as religious leaders, teachers, and opposition leaders. For the tribunal of Seville, see AHN, Inquisición, legajo 2075. See also Juan Aranda Doncel, "Las prácticas musulmanas de los moriscos andaluces a través de las relaciones de causas del tribunal de la inquisición de Córdoba"; and Ricardo García Cárcel, 229.

22. "Relación muy verdadera sacada de una carta que al Illustre Cabildo y regimiento desta ciudad," Sevilla: Alonso de la Bar, 1569, n.p., BN ms R31.736.

23. R.I. Moore makes this point very clearly as he discusses the political applications of Douglas's theory of pollution in his book, *The Formation of a Persecuting Society*, 100.

24. David Sibley, *Outsiders in Urban Societies* 29, describes the process of polarization that increases and confirms stereotypes.

25. See, for example, the letter from the Duke of Alva to Philip II, Archivo General de Simancas (hereafter AGS), Cámara de Castilla, legajo 2171; legajo 2166, "Proceso contra algunos cristianos que retienen moros en el Reyno de Granada contra lo ordenado"; and legajo 2187 for protests from the towns of Antequera, Loja, and Guadix.

26. AGS, Cámara de Castilla, legajo 2183.

27. *Traslado de la cédula real que se publicó en la ciudad de Córdova a diez y siete días del mes de Enero* (Córdova, 1610), n.p., BN, ms. V.E. 36-4. This document is also available in the Archivo Municipal de Sevilla, Sección 4, Tomo 23, No. 35.

Works Cited

Aranda Doncel, Juan. "Las prácticas musulmanas de los moriscos andaluces a través de las relaciones de causas del tribunal de la inquisición de Córdoba." *Las prácticas musulmanas de los moriscos andaluces (1492-1609), Actas del III Simposio Internacional de Estudios Moriscos.* Ed. Abdejelil Temini. Zaghouan: Centre d'Etudes et de Recherches Ottomanes, Morisques, de Documentation et d'Information, 1989. 11-26.

Aznar Cardona, Pedro. *Expulsion justificada de los moriscos españoles.* Huesca: Pedro Cabarte, 1612.

Baer, Yitzhak. *A History of the Jews in Christian Spain.* Philadelphia: Jewish Publication Society of America, 1966. 2 vols.

Birriel Salcedo, Margarita M. "Mujeres y familia, fuentes y metodología." *Conceptos y metodología en los estudios sobre la mujer.* Ed. Barbara Ozieblo. Málaga: Universidad de Málaga, 1993. 43-69.

_____. "La experiencia silenciada, las mujeres en la historia de Andalucía. Andalucía moderna." *Las mujeres en la historia de Andalucía. Actas del II Congreso de Historia de Andalucía* . Córdoba: Junta de Andalucía, 1994.

Boronat y Barrachina, Pascual. *Los moriscos expañoles y su expulsión: Estudio histórico-crítico.* Valencia: Francisco Vives y Mora, 1901. 2 vols.

Caro Baroja, Julio. *Los moriscos del Reino de Granada (Ensayo de Historia Social).* Madrid: Artes Gráficas, 1957.

Carrasco, Rafael. *Historia de los sodomitas. Inquisición y represión sexual en Valencia.* Barcelona: Laertes Editorial, 1986.

Casey, James, and Bernard Vincent. "Casa y familia en Granada." *La familia en la España mediterránea (siglos XV-XIX).* Ed. Francisco Chacón. Barcelona: Crítica, 1987. 172-211.

Cohen, S. *Folk Devils and Moral Panics.* St. Albans: Paladin, 1973.

Collantes de Terán Sánchez, Antonio. *Sevilla en la baja edad media: La ciudad y sus hombres.* Sevilla: Ayuntamiento, 1977.

Delgado Gallego, José María. "Maurofilia y maurofobia, ¿dos caras de la misma moneda?" *Narraciones moriscas.* Sevilla: Editoriales Andaluzas Unidas, 1986. 22-30.

Domínguez Ortiz, Antonio and Bernard Vincent. *Historia de los moriscos: Vida y tragedia de una minoria* Madrid: Biblioteca de la Revista de Occidente, 1978.

Douglas, Mary. *Purity and Danger: An Analysis of Concepts of Pollution and Taboo.* New York and Washington: Frederick A. Praeger, 1966.

Edwards, John. "Religious Faith and Doubt in Late Medieval Spain: Soria *circa* 1450-1500." *Past and Present* 120 (1988): 3-25.

_____. "Male and Female Religion Among Spanish New Christians." Unpublished paper presented at the University of California at Davis, April 1992.

Erikson, Kai T.*Wayward Puritans: A Study in the Sociology of Deviance.* New York: John Wiley and Sons, 1966.

Fonseca, Damian. *Justa expulsion de los moriscos de España: con la instruccion, apostasia, y traycion dellos: y respuesta á las dudas que se ofrecieron acerca desta materia* . Rome: Iacomo Mascardo, 1612.

Fournel Guérin, Jacqueline. "La femme morisque en Aragon." *Les Morisques et leur temps* Paris: Centre National de la Recherche Scientifique, 1983.

García Arenal, Mercedes. *Los moriscos.* Madrid: Editora Nacional, 1975.

García Cárcel, Ricardo. *Herejía y sociedad en el siglo XVI: La inquisición en Valencia 1530-1609.* Barcelona: Ediciones Península, 1980.

Gerard, Kent and Gert Hekma, eds.*The Pursuit of Sodomy: Male Homosexuality in Renaissance and Enlightenment Europe.* New York and London: Haworth Press, 1988.

Gerber, Jane S. *The Jews of Spain: A History of the Sephardic Experience.* New York: The Free Press, 1992.

Gramsci, Antonio. *Selections from the Prison Notebooks.* Eds. and trans. Quintin Hoare and Geoffrey Nowell Smith. New York: International Publishers, 1972.

Harvey, L.P. *Islamic Spain 1250 to 1500.* Chicago: U of Chicago P, 1990.

hooks, bell. *Yearning: Race, Gender, and Cultural Politics.* Boston: South End Press, 1990.

Jiménez Lozano, José. *Judíos, moriscos y conversos.* Valladolid: Ambito, 1982.

Johnston, Hank. *Tales of Nationalism, Catalonia, 1939-1979.* New Brunswick, N.J.: Rutgers UP, 1991.

Kamen, Henry. *Inquisition and Society in Spain.* Bloomington: Indiana UP, 1985.

Lazar, Moshe. "Scorched Parchments and Tortured Memories: The 'Jewishness' of the Anussim (Crypto-Jews)." *Cultural Encounters: The Impact of the Inquisition in Spain and the New World.* Eds. Mary Elizabeth Perry and Anne J. Cruz. Berkeley and Los Angeles: U of California P, 1991. 176-206.

Melammed, Renée Levine. "Sephardi Women in the Medieval and Early Modern Periods."*Jewish Women in Historical Perspective.* Ed. Judith R. Baskin. Detroit: Wayne State UP, 1991. 115-34.

Meyerson, Mark D. *The Muslims of Valencia in the Age of Fernando and Isabel: Between Coexistence and Crusade.* Berkeley: U of California P, 1991.

Monter, E.W. *Frontiers of Heresy: The Spanish Inquisition from the Basque Lands to Sicily.* Cambridge and New York: Cambridge UP, 1990.

Moore, R.I. *The Formation of a Persecuting Society: Power and Deviance in Western Europe, 950-1250.* Oxford: Basil Blackwell, 1987.

Netanyahu, Benzion.*The Origins of the Inquisition in Fifteenth-Century Spain.* New York: Random House, 1995.

Norton, Anne. *Reflections on Political Identity.* Baltimore: The Johns Hopkins UP, 1988.

Perry, Mary Elizabeth. "The 'Nefarious Sin' in Early Modern Seville." *Journal of Homosexuality* 25. 3-4 (Spring 1988): 63-84.

Ribera, Julián, and Miguel Asín. *Manuscritos árabes y aljamiados de la biblioteca de la junta.* Madrid: Junta para Amplicación de Estudios é Investigaciones Científicas, 1912.

Sahlins, Peter. *Boundaries: The Making of France and Spain in the Pyrenees.* Berkeley: U of California P, 1989.

Sánchez Ortega, María Helena. "Sorcery and Eroticism in Love Magic." *Cultural Encounters: The Impact of the Inquisition in Spain and the New World.* Eds. Mary Elizabeth Perry and Anne Cruz. Berkeley and Los Angeles: U of California P, 1991. 58-92.

_____. *La mujer y la sexualidad en el antiguo régimen: La perspectiva inquisitorial.* Madrid: Ediciones Akal, 1992.

Sibley, David. *Outsiders in Urban Societies.* New York: St. Martin's Press, 1981.

Vincent, Bernard. *Minorías y marginados en la España del siglo XVI.* Granada: Diputación Provincial de Granada, 1987.

_____. "The *Moriscos* and Circumcision." *Culture and Control in Counter-Reformation Spain*. Eds. Anne Cruz and Mary E. Perry. Minneapolis: U of Minnesota P, 1992. 78-92.

◆ Chapter 3

A Discourse on Wealth in Golden Age Literature

Francisco J. Sánchez

During the sixteenth and seventeenth centuries in Spain there emerged a literary discourse that describes human relations in terms of wealth. This literary discourse shared many of the concerns of political and theological economists regarding the cultural consequences of the lack of capitalization in Castile: poverty, unemployment, overvaluation of money, lack of productivity, the so-called aristocratization of society, and the general downfall of the *república*. Moreover, these phenomena were brought about in relation to the status of a modern subject within the conditions of dispossession of individuals and the general feeling that an "unreal" world was taking over society by means of a warlike situation among individuals.

This essay will attempt to show in some representative works the way in which literature reflected of a self constituted by a mercantile structure of values, the means of realizing the transition from traditional morality into a practical activity toward economic gains. This mercantile self is the bearer of a theatrical sensibility, a structure of feelings that depicts the subject as conscious of the distance that separates the ideas and beliefs of a traditional, originally feudal society, from a contemporary reflection upon an individual, economic-oriented action. This sensibility discloses, I believe, a split in the ontological constitution of the self which is something other than merely the depiction of roles according to social functions.

The individual thus conceived in his or her social characterization as an actor experiences a duality, looking toward a society founded on a mercantile exchange, while remaining anchored in a kind of a moral intimacy. That is, the external motivation for action is clearly the attainment of economic benefits at the expense of other individuals, even while the self reflects upon the moral contractions of the social world. In this sense, the individual may be said to "present" himself or herself, along theatrical lines in the struggle for survival, growth, and defense. In the case of Alemán's picaresque novel *Guzmán de Alfarache* (1599-1604), for example, this description also entailed a reflection upon a self constructed by and through the contradictions between feudal and capitalist conceptions of religion, moral values, and social expectations within the context of the decline of Castilian and Spanish economy.

A Discourse on Wealth

González de Cellorigo's esoteric *dictum*, cast in the middle of his description of the causes of Spain's economic and political crises around 1610, has become a common place in contemporary historical research:

> Y llega a tanto que, por las constituciones de las órdenes militares, no puede tener hábito mercader ni tratante, que no parece sino que se han querido reducir estos Reinos a una República de hombres encantados que viven fuera del orden natural. (González de Cellorigo 79)
>
> (And it gets to the point where, by the decrees of the military orders, merchant nor dealer can join them, it does not seem as though but rather they have wanted to reduce these Kingdoms to a Republic of enchanted men who live outside the natural order.)[1]

González de Cellorigo is criticizing the excessive value people place on "honra"—honor—and the low social esteem given to work, specifically agricultural work and commerce. It is worthwhile to note that Cellorigo situates his arguments within the context of the devastating human and economic consequences of the plague of 1596. Recently, Pérez Moreda has observed that:

> The plague of 1596-1602 resulted, therefore, in a socially selective rise in mortality. It was as if the rats and fleas had held back in the face of wealth and social standing. (Pérez Moreda 39)

Within the context of pauperization and economic decline, Cellorigo pointed at some specifics for the stagnation of labor and industry. Pierre Vilar, some years ago, undertook a socioeconomic interpretation of the "time" of *Quixote* in which he related don Quijote's madness to González de Cellorigo's concerns with the evils of idleness, socio-psychological attempts of aristocratization, and disregard for productive activities at the threshold of Spain's seventeenth century.[2] In another place, González de Cellorigo states something that is even more illuminating, namely, that Spain has reached the nadir of bankruptcy:

> A muchos del Reino da que mirar el ver lo que las cosas de España señalan con tan contrarios efectos de lo que ellas en sí prometen, porque vemos al Rey más rico, más poderoso en todas suertes de riqueza y de grandeza, que España ni otra monarquía tuvieron y los vasallos en las mayores ocasiones de ser ricos, poderosos, hacendados, que ningún estado de República pudo alcanzar . . . y con todo ello no se halla en las historias que España haya llegado a mayor quiebra de la en que se ve. (González de Cellorigo 89)

> (To many in the Kingdom seeing what the affairs of Spain point out with results so contrary to what they promise is grounds for suspicion, because we see the King richer, more powerful in all fortunes of wealth and grandeur, that Spain nor any other monarchy had and the vassals the most opportunities to be rich, powerful, landed, which no Republic state could achieve . . . yet in spite of all that it is not found in the histories that Spain has ever fallen into a deeper bankruptcy than the one in which it now finds itself.)

The major responsibility for having arrived at such a situation is, paradoxically, Spain's wealth: "lo que más ha hecho daño a estos Reinos es que las mismas riquezas que les han entrado son las que los han empobrecido" (ibid.) ("What has most hurt these Kingdoms is that the same riches which have entered them are the very things which have impoverished them").

Spain is poor because it is rich.[3] Too much wealth in monetary terms has produced too much poverty. The people have given most of their energies to the trade of American gold and silver, for the exclusive purpose of accumulating values in the "censos"—investments in private debt—(50-51) with the result that differences between rich and poor have grown out of "proportion" (88-89), while commerce has been jeopardized:

> Y es que el mercader por el dulzor del seguro provecho de los censos deja sus tratos, el oficial desprecia su oficio, el labrador deja su labranza, el pastor su ganado, el noble vende sus tierras por trocar ciento que le valían por quinientos de juro, sin considerar que habiendo dado todos en este trato la renta firme de la heredad se acaba y el dinero se va en humo. Porque uno que labra ha de sustentar a sí y al señor de la heredad y al señor de la renta, y al cogedor del diezmo y al recaudador del censo y a los demas que piden, y de ahí arriba se puede hacer cuenta que de la poca gente que trabaja a la que huelga sale a razón de uno por treinta. (72)
>
> (And it's that the merchant because of the sweetness of the sure profit of the "censos" abandons his business, the official looks down on his office, the farmer abandons his farm, the shepherd his flock, the nobleman sells his lands so as to exchange for a hundred what was certainly worth five hundred, without considering that having given all in the deal the steady income from the property ends and the money evaporates in airs. Because one who farms has to support oneself and the landowner and the taxgatherer, and the tithe taker, and the debt collector and the rest who solicit, and in this way upwards it can be calculated that the ratio between the few people who work and the idle is one in thirty.)

He complains that the economy is driven by financial speculation and that working people are overburden by heavy taxation. In the same fashion, a few years later López Bravo was to link poverty to this speculation with rent,[4] Sancho de Moncada was to say that the poor paid more than the rich;[5] and Fernández de Navarrete blamed the plight of farmers and peasants to financial speculation, taxation, usury, and artificial overpricing:

> todo lo que adquieren con sudor [peasants and farmers], lo consumen en la voraz polilla de los censos y en la paga de las mohatras y usuras, a que les compele las necesidades . . . para que con sus vejaciones se enriquezcan los escribanos y procuradores. (Fernández de Navarrete 532-33)

> (All which the [peasants and farmers] acquire through sweat they consume on the voracious clothes moth that is the "censos" and in paying for fraudulent sales and usuries, which necessity requiries of them, so that by their maltreatment the notaries and attorneys enrich themselves.)

Though the specific arguments varied, these political economists were all committed to articulating a defense of mercantilist policies, that is, a defense of protectionist measures against imports in order to favor the development of "internal," so to speak "national" (essentially Castilian) commerce and industry. Sancho de Moncada, after exposing racist and xenophobic justifications against gypsies and other ethnic minorities, says that foreign monarchies and people are growing at the expense of Spain's people,[6] citing it as the reason for the lack of employment, increased imports, and social and economic idleness and speculation in Castile.[7] Still in 1630, Caxa de Leruela continues to see the relationship between financial speculation and economic dependency on foreign goods:

> La ociosidad . . . ha llamado en su favor a la industria, y negociación de extranjeros, que le cuida las inteligencias, le ajusta los tiempos, previene las ocasiones y todo lo dispone diestramente para el beneficio, y que ha abierto la puerta a las mercaderías de fuera, y defraudando al

comercio los caudales de marca mayor, embebiéndolos en los censos, juros, vínculos y mayorazgos (reclinatorio de esta holgazanería). (Caxa de Leruela 54-55)

(Slothfulness . . . has summoned industry to its aid, and the business of foreign people, which looks after its abilities, adjusts the seasons, foresees the risks and dexterously disposes everything for a profit, and which has opened the doors to outside merchandise, and defrauding to commerce the best fortunes, enthralling them to the "censos," perpetuities, entailments and "mayorazgos" [the couch of this idleness].)[8]

It is well known that the battle against imports as the first step toward a viable national industry dates back to the first half of the sixteenth century. During the first dacades of the seventeenth century, the *arbitrista* Fernández de Navarrete asks for the prohibition on the import of wheat,[9] while Sancho de Moncada insists on the enforcement of laws which encourage the retention of raw materials in the country.[10] Both of them believe that these measures will curtail speculation by the idle classes, reduce unproductive expenditures, and lessen vagrancy, poverty, and even the breakdown of marriages.

However, the relation between speculation and poverty was something that Luis Ortiz already had pointed to around 1557. His memorandum is a petition for the implementation of protectionist policies aimed at increasing Castilian manufacturing. Arguing for his proposals, Ortiz says that the source of "world money" is Spain: "Lo primero se a de considerar que la prinçipal fuente del dinero del mundo es España, así por lo que en ella naze como por lo que biene de Indias" (*Memorial del contador Luis Ortiz* 127) ("The first thing to be considered is that the principal source of money in the world is Spain, both because of how much is from here and because of how much comes from the Indies").

The money in the world comes to Europe from America. It does it through Spain, but it leaves her as Spain is decapitalized by the defeat of local industries. Ortiz has the clear understanding that competition among nations insures the circulation of money and argues that the king must provide for the increase of money in the kingdom and for the acquisition of foreign money: "no sólo se da rremedio que no salgan dineros del rreyno, mas se probee que entre él de otros rreynos, todo o la mayor parte de lo que en ellos obiere" (146) ("Not only is it prescribed as a cure that money should not leave the kingdom, but also that money from other kingdoms enter in it, all or the greater part of what in them existed").

It may be said, in general terms, that seventeenth-century *arbitristas* were concerned, above all, with the lack of productivity of Spain, while certain contemporaries of Ortiz, such as Vives, had in mind, first and foremost, how to get rid of poverty in order to drive the economy. In both cases, however, all they were describing the progressive decapitalization of the Spanish monarchy.

The symptoms of this decapitalization appeared to be highly contradictory, since on the one hand, Spain was the first to receive in its ports and cities America's metals, and on the other these metals seemed to be somehow related to the spread of poverty and the stagnation of Castilian commerce. Hamilton argued that American metals caused a "revolution of prices" that, in turn, made possible a rapid increase of benefits for the capitalists by way of permanent decreases in salaries.[11] Pierre Vilar, however, rather understood that the flow of gold and silver confronted the specific relations of production in Spain and in other parts of Europe, with the former becaming dependent on the industrial centers of the latter.[12] Some years before Vilar, Carande identified this decapitalization as the result of the state's debt first to German banks, then to Italian, which could only be alleviated by constant confiscation and increasing taxation.[13] More recently, Felipe Ruiz Martín has shown the devastating consequences of these policies on the Castilian bourgeoisie.[14] Also, Vassberg gives us a good account of this tax burden on Castilian peasants,[15] while for his part Artola has pointed out that the complex system of taxation, especially with regard to collections, resulted in a permanent creation of intermediaries who sought significant profits from the rent and investment of taxes, that is, with the private investment of the state's incomes. By the second half of the seventeenth century: "[se] permite descubrir la presencia de una burguesía financiera con importantes recursos económicos y amplio crédito" (Artola 211) ("we see the existence of a financial bourgeoisie with important economic resources and ample credit").

Increasing taxation, increased poverty, and increasing overvaluation of aristocratic ideals, such as honor, are reported by González de Cellorigo, Sancho de Moncada, Fernández de Navarrete, and López Bravo, who says:

> el dueño de un censo, el poseedor de un mayorazgo, el contertulio de la ociosidad literaria, el que fomenta el ocio ajeno o, lo que es peor, el sembrador o protagonista de pleitos o el maestro o ministro de cualquier tipo de engaño o desvergüenza, bien comido y vestido y acaso con lujo—puede alcanzar todos los honores. (López Bravo 261-62)

> (the owner of a "censo," the holder of a "mayorazgo," the fellow member of a useless literary circle, the one who encourages sloth in his neighbors, or, what is worse, the sower of or protagonist in disputes or the teacher or minister of whatever kind of trickery or shamelessness, well fed and dressed and perhaps living in luxury—can obtain all the positions.)

In his study on the transition to capitalism in Castile, Yun Casalilla qualifies the overall significance of the interrelation between debt and a "seigniorial figure" of this type of capitalist interested exclusively in financial speculation:

> la nobleza local, las oligarquías rectoras de las ciudades, los mercaderes y banqueros y los funcionarios enriquecidos a la sombra del Estado dedicaron una parte creciente de sus capitales a la constitución de censos sobre las rentas de mayorazgos y de juros sobre la Hacienda real. (643)

> (The local nobility, the ruling oligarchics in the cities, the merchants and the bankers and the functionaries prospering in the shade of the State dedicated a growing part of their capital to the establishment of "censos" on the revenues of "mayorazgos" and on perpetuities on the Royal Hacienda.)

The so-called aristocratization, the strengthening of seigniorial and ecclesiastical power in Spain, was reported in the *Relaciones Topográficas* of 1575-1580, where at one point people complained about the "diezmos"—the Church's taxation—: "ya no se sabe si el estado es una forma de Iglesia o la Iglesia una forma de estado" ("It is no longer known whether the state is a kind of church or the church a kind of state").[16] Salomon notes that the *Relaciones* mention expropriations of communal lands and small properties and that large landowners, both noblemen and churchmen, lived solely on land rents from the area of New Castile.[17] More recently, Francis Brumont has concluded similar socioeconomic consequences for the area of Old Castile; though the structure of ownership differed, the result of the crisis was: "enriquecimieto de ricos, emprobrecimiento de los más, aparición de más jornaleros y de más pobres" (Brumont 225-31) ("The enrichment of the rich, the impoverishment of the majority, the appearance of more day laborers and more poor people").

The increasing empowerment of the Church is the very reason why writers such as Fernández de Navarrate, López Bravo and, still in 1630, Caxa de Leruela warn against the extraordinary number of people choosing an ecclesiastical career, and against the opening of new convents.[18]

The crisis of Castilian commerce in the 1530s, the rapid spread of poverty, and the so-called "typical" Spanish obsession with "honor" led Cavillac to conclude that it was "the victory of financial capital" ("el triunfo del capitalismo financiero") (Cavillac, "La problemática . . ." cxx). According to Wallerstein, this financial capital, grounded on monetary speculation, was the consequence of a larger dynamic in which the Spanish—and Portuguese—empires were immersed in the development of capitalism, of the "new world-system."

In Wallerstein's analysis, Spain and Portugal took the first steps into the new system during the "short" sixteenth century, but they fell back during the "long" sixteenth century and finally they survived the seventeenth as a peripheries of the core centers of capital accumulation in central Europe. In other words, their decadence was the result of a reorganization of capitalism that must break through any imperial conception of sovereignty, in favor of an economic system composed of free nations.[19]

Concerns with the circulation of wealth were closely connected with the debates on poverty and proposals to eradicate and/or control it.[20] Writers developed extensive views on the role of money. During the same period of time that initiates the collapse of the Spanish economy (the second half of the sixteenth century), major works appear on the question of money, profit, and monetary investments.

Of course, the *memorialistas*—writers of "memorials," essays addressed to the King or some other political institution—and the *arbitristas* in general also write on money. Ortiz's *Memorial* analyzes the relation between imports and circulation of money, and later López Bravo shows a clear understanding of its function in trade:

> el verdadero valor del dinero depende de su peso y calidad natural, sí; pero también de las mercancías que balancea, y tanto más vale el dinero, cuanto mayor es el número de mercancías que balancea, y tantas más balacea cuantas más afluyen. (López Bravo 332)

> (The true value of money depends on its weight and natural quality, yes; but also on the commodities which it balances, and the value of the money increases when it balances a greater number of commodities, and it balances more the more the commodities flow.)

As we have seen, however, Ortiz, López Bravo, Sancho de Moncada, González de Cellorigo, Fernández de Navarrete, and Caxa de Leruela intended to promote mercantilist policies to ignite "national" production. They had in mind, loosely speaking, an *idearium* grounded in Castilian mercantile capital which was jeopardized by the decapitalization brought about by Spain's dependency on European manufacturers and the permanent increase of private and public debts.[21] These political economists paid attention to what Marx later saw as the rule of primitive accumulation in the relation between monetary speculation and the negative appearance of wealth in debt:

> The only part of the so-called national wealth that actually enters into the collective possession of a modern nation is the national debt. . . . Public credit becomes the *credo* of Capital. . . . The public debt becomes one of the most powerful levers of primitive accumulation. As with the stroke of a enchanter's wand, it endows unproductive money with the power of creation and it turns it into

> capital, without forcing it to expose itself to the trouble and risks inseparable from its employment in industry or even usury. The state's creditors actually give nothing away, for the sum lent is transformed into public bonds, easily negotiable, which go on functioning in their hands just as so much hard cash would. But furthermore, and quite apart from the class of idle *rentiers* thus created, the improvised wealth of the financiers who play the role of middlemen between the government and the nation . . . the national debt has given rise to joint-stock companies, to dealings in negotiable effects of all kinds, and to speculation: in a word, it has given rise to stock-exchange gambling and the modern bankocracy. (Marx 1, 919)

Moreover, there were moral economists who, following basically Scholastic doctrine, were able to give a very broad and complete picture of the circulation and accumulation of money and, therefore, unintentionally, of the accumulation of capital. Following well-established interpretations of Aristotle's idea of money, Tomás de Mercado writes around 1569:

> En ninguna parte, en ninguna ocasión, se apreció jamás cosa según su natural, sino por nuestra necesidad y uso. Hasta en los metales y en la misma moneda, el oro, plata, piedras y perlas, que es lo sumo de todo oriente y Occidente de este viejo mundo, en ninguna provincia ni reino del nuevo que llamamos Indias tuvo tanta reputación, y en muchos de ellos no tiene aún el día de hoy ninguna. (Mercado 96)

> (Never, at no time, was a thing ever valued according to its nature, rather as a result of our needs and uses. Even with the metals and in the coin itself, gold, silver, stones and pearls, which are the sum of all the Orient and Occident of this old world, and in no province or kingdom of the new which we call Indies had it ever so great a reputation, and in many parts of them it still does not have any today.)

The question is not just that Spain can extract gold and silver and take them to Europe; the question, obviously, is that the value of money is a specific social value. Since its value is socially determined, the issue that follows is to question how and why there is a real variation of that value. Tomás de Mercado, as well as many of the other economists of the "School of Salamanca," were trained theologians and their concerns were preceptive in nature: "De arte que la justicia que en todos los contratos es la igualdad que en ellos se ha de hacer, a lo cual—como extensamente probamos—nos obliga no sólo la ley divina, sino también la misma ley natural" (ibid. 55) ("What is just is equality in the contracts, to which—as we extensivley prove—not only divine law but also natural law itself obligates us").

This preceptive and Thomistic consideration was related to a interest against foreign intervention in internal trade: "cuando quisiere por buenos respectos traer de fuera y vender alguna mercadería, no venda ni dé en ninguna manera a ningún particular este privilegio . . . sino ponga sus oficiales [of the state] que lo tengan y ejerciten" (ibid. 95)[22] ("When you would like for good reasons to bring from outside and sell some merchandise, do not by any means sell this privilege to just anyone . . . but have your officials set it and apply it").

Looking after justice and equality in economic dealings has been the official theological position. It was supposedly based on an interpretation of Aristotle's writings on money, or "chrematistics," the search for the principle of proportion in the economic (originally household business). However, though being theological or moral, the intent of these economists was to give a general and sometimes very specific description of the market, as well as the first modern analysis of the formation of value in exchange.

Pierre Vilar noted that both groups of writers, the political economists and the moral economists, shared the same view of the problem, though with a difference in approach:

> No se puede confudir el camino intelectual recorrido por los doctores-confesores con el recorrido por los "políticos" autores de "memoriales." Los primeros esbozan una teoría de los precios tras meditar sobre los cambios, ya que se plantean el problema individual de la legitimidad de las ganancias; entran de lleno en la vía del subjetivismo psicológico, del análisis microeconómico, del equilibrio. Los segundos se plantean preguntas sobre la economía global, sobre la hacienda real; están en la vía de la "contabilidad nacional."[23]

(The intellectual path travelled by father confessors cannot be confused with the one traveled by the "political" authors of "memoriales." The former outline a theory of prices after pondering about exchange rates, since they pose the individual problem of the legitimacy of profits, they enter entirely on the route to psychological subjectivism, and microeconomic analysis, of balance. The latter pose questions concerning the global economy, concerning the Royal *hacienda*; they are on the route of "national accountancy.")

Mercado, for example, describes the increase in value of some commodities in American trade as a result of these commodities being paid for in the colonies, though the sale is realized in Spain:

Por lo cual es injusto que, vendiéndose aquí la mercadería o vino, se pague como vale en Nueva España por remitirse allá la paga, porque realmente sólo tiene en cuenta con la necesidad presente del que compra. Y así excede muchas veces no solamente al doble y tres doble al precio verdadero y corriente, más aun al de las Indias. (Mercado 194)

(Because of this it is unfair that, selling here [in Spain] the merchandise or wine, one pays what it is worth in New Spain so as to remit the pay there, because really this only takes into account the needs of the one who buys. And in this way the price exceeds many times over not only double and treble the real and current price, but still more that of the Indies.)

We do not care, as Tomás de Mercado did, whether this trade is fair or not. We can see here the creation of a value in circulation which has to do with the increase of price, that is, as Marx would put it, with merely an increase in the form or the "name" of the universal equivalent of exchange, money.[24]

These ghostly fluctuations of value corresponded to the concrete circumstances of the local markets, of course, and the need of many entrepreneurs to have rapid access to cash. For example, another transaction that these moralists considered to be wrong was the "barata"—the selling by credit, at a higher price, to someone who, because of his financial needs, will have to resell in cash at a lower price.[25]

This debt chain will be the standard situation of Spain's capital as well as of the state's treasury, because, at the level of large-scale trade, it was mainly foreign banks and financial companies which were the only ones able to afford large sums of money. The internationalization of the financial system is already described by Mercado:

> Tienen contratación en todas las partes de la cristiandad y aun en Berbería. A Flandes cargan lanas, aceites y bastardos; de allá traen todo género de mercería, tapicería, librería. A Florencia envían cochinilla, cueros; traen oro hilado, brocados, seda y, de todas aquellas partes, gran multitud de lienzos. En Cabo Verde tienen el trato de los negros, negocio de gran caudal y mucho interés. A todas las Indias envían grandes cargazones de toda suerte de ropa; traen de allá oro, plata, perlas, grana y cueros, en grandísima cantidad. Item, para asegurar lo que cargan, que son millones de valor, tienen necesidad de asegurar [receive payments] en Lisboa, en Burgos,en Lyon de Francia, Flandes, porque es tan gran cantidad la que cargan que no bastan los de Sevilla, ni de veinte Sevillas, a asegurarlo. Los de Burgos tienen aquí sus factores que o cargan en su nombre o aseguran a los cargadores, o reciben o venden lo que de Flandes les traen. Los de Italia también han menester a los de aquí para los mismos efectos. De modo que cualquier mercader caudaloso trata el día de hoy en todas las partes del mundo y tiene personas que en todas ellas les correspondan, den crédito y fe a sus letras [bills of payments] y las paguen, porque han menester dineros en todas ellas . . . De modo que cualquiera de éstos . . . tiene necesidad de tener dineros en todas partes o para comprar o pagar o cobrar, porque en todas deben y les deben. (Mercado 374-75)
>
> (They trade in every corner of Christendom and even in Barbary. To Flanders they carry wools, oils, and sails; from there they bring all sorts of wares, tapestries, books. To Florence they send cochineal, skins, they bring gold thread, brocades, silk, and from all those regions, a great many linens. In Cape Verde they have the slave trade, a business of great profit and benefit. To all parts of the

> Indies they send great cargos of all sorts of clothes; they bring from there gold, silver, pearls, grain and skins, in the greatest quantity. Furthermore, to insure what they carry, which is worth millions, they have necessity to recieve payments in Lisbon, Burgos, Lyons in France, Flanders, because the quantity which they carry is so great that the ones of Seville are not enough, nor of twenty Sevilles, to insure it. Those from Burgos have here their agents who either carry in their name or insure the shippers, or recieve or sell what they are brought from Flanders. Those from Italy also have need of those from here for the same money. So that any wealthy merchant trades today in all parts of the world and has people who in all of them correspond with them, give credit and attest to their bills of payment and pay them, because they have need of money in all of them . . . so that any of these . . . has reason to have money in all parts or to buy or pay or charge, because everywhere they owe and are owed.)

After Mercado, and around 1590, the Jesuit Luis de Molina more than any other writes with greater specificity on the nature and circumstances of monetary dealings. Like Mercado, Molina is a moralist in the sense that, being also a theologian, his economic analysis is for him only a means to establish a moral justification for profit. He was concerned rather with the welfare of the *república*, and thus he emphasized, for instance, the intentions of people involved in any transaction in order to see whether those intentions were theologically correct. Following these assumptions, Molina investigated the transformation in value of money and capital, particularly in operations of credit, in order to distinguish "usury," the lending of money with the intention of acquiring profit—morally condemned—from the rightful acquisition of gains. Like everyone in the Scholastic tradition, Molina is also looking for parity and equality in transactions, and thus a gain would be correct only as a payment for service and to pay back a possible economic injury that the lender would have by loaning out his money.[26]

In the same vein as that of the political economists, these Scholastic economists considered money to be a measure of value, and, precisely because of that, an unproductive commodity. And like the *memorialistas*, the moralists related their concerns with financial speculation, rent, commodity imports, and idleness to a sociopolitical interpretation of the state of society.

I have mentioned these few writings to point out that the sixteenth- and seventeenth-century intellectual horizon represents an effort to map the major transformations in the foundations of the socioeconomic structure. My comments do not exhaust all the economic issues brought forward in these writings, nor do they encompass all the writers. My point is that this horizon concretized a discourse in which decapitalization and debt were the major junctures of social analysis. To mention again Yun Casalilla, the emergence of capitalism was founded in:

> un sistema hacendístico y fiscal que, esto es lo importante, se convirtió al mismo tiempo en un pesado engranaje de extracción y distribución del producto social entre los poderosos . . . todo ello era fruto de un sistema que difícilmente podía generar riqueza y que se había convertido en una maquinaría de creación de pobres y de diferenciación social y económica. (Yun Casalilla 448)

> (an economic and fiscal system which, this is the important thing, was converted at the same time into a heavy gear of extraction and distribution of the social product between the powerful . . . all of that was the fruit of a system which with difficulty could generate wealth and which had changed into a machine creating poverty and social and economic differentiation.)

A Mercantile Self in Theatrical Clothes

These were also the themes upon which a whole segment of the literary field built its inquiry into the new forms of social aggression and individual self-interest. Literary works became the instrument of a larger circle of writers and readers to reflect on the way individuals acted according to their access to wealth or their aspirations to acquire it. This reflection had moral, religious, and to a certain degree political overtones. Decapitalization and debt, the way that Castile faced its position in the European capitalist system, produced a sometimes bitter reflection on the nature of this system. Is the world upside-down? some people asked, is the world ruled by evil? some others whispered, why is there no ground, no firm base in human relations? It is tempting to say that Early Modern Spain understood the subtle mechanisms of power and social marginalization; but it is also tempting to say that the literature of that society focused its productivity along the path of money. Is it real? it questioned, and by this questioning, literature engaged in the enterprise of making sense of the confrontational nature of society.

This enterprise attempted to articulate a representational dimension of society; this is a nonsubstantialist characterization of social interaction that I will call a theatrical sensibility. This theatrical sensibility, this "structure of feelings" to use Raymond Williams's terminology, is the literary or aesthetic perception that the transformations in the socioeconomic structure of society had as a consequence the production of "unreal" or apparent forms of social and individual beings.

At the end of this period, there is a somewhat obscure work that, nevertheless, exemplifies the historical connection between financial capital and this theatrical sensibility. *Confusión de confusiones* is a work in the tradition of the Renaissance's dialogues in which José de la Vega describes the settings and the functioning of a stock market.[27] The text begins by stating that the intention is to assess "el estado de la India, la disposición de la Europa, y el juego de los accionistas" (de la Vega 66) ("the state of the Indies, the disposition of Europe and the game of stockbrokers").

There are many literary references throughout the work. At one point it mentions Don Quixote as a comic—"gracioso"—hero, and the third dialogue starts with Segismundo's words, from Calderón's *La vida es sueño*—"mísero de mí. Ay infelize"—to continue the monologue in a comic mood: "que si pago muriendo" ("if I pay while I die"). The idea is to describe the movement of the stock market as "comedias"—the contemporary word for plays.

The "acciones" ("the stocks") function as plays because in the market:

> campean con inimitables realces las trazas, las entradas y salidas, los escondidos, las tapadas, las contiendas, los desafíos, las burlas, los dislates, los empeños, el apagarse las luces, el refinarse los engaños, las traiciones, los embustes, las tragedias. (de la Vega 156)

(The schemes, the entrances and exits, the hideouts, the cover-ups, the disputes, the challenges, the gibes, the absurdities, the pledges, the appeasements, the news, the refinement of the swindles, the betrayals, the fibs, the tragedies, all campaign with inimitable splendor.)

This tragical-comical expression seeks to cover all possible outcomes of the movement of stocks. Moreover, theatrical elements become constitutive elements of the way this movement is perceived and acted upon by different actors. This theatrical feeling is also the consequence of a state of things in which the individual must be on the lookout out for the action of other people: "Mirad que no deve [sic] dormir quien tiene enemigos" (61) ("Remember that you must not sleep if you have enemies"). This is advice that could be read in many literary texts from 1600 onward.

To be awake is, then, to see the movement of people in their apparent disguise, with their apparent intentions, as Gracián further elucidated. "Acciones tienen algo de divinas" ("stocks have something of a divine aspect") it is said at one point; it means that they appear everywhere, nobody knows how they arrive, where they come from, how they dress, and so on. It is the whole theatrical movement that produces the perception of something, the image of an activity.

This dialogue continues a tradition that stems from the Renaissance; it is, however, revealing a literary-economic connection. Yet this fusion is only an explicit aspect of the way the literary field has acquired its autonomy from other writing practices, while underlining its debt to the intellectual horizon on the discourse on wealth, that is to say, the horizon of capitalist relations.

It was at the end of the fifteenth century with *La Celestina* that the depiction of capitalist relations began to shape an important segment of Spanish literature. It did so by showing the specific nature of social confrontation resulting from economic wealth, and by constituting the individual's interiority upon self-awareness of the distance between ideas of love and friendship and their use in the pursuit of goals and success.[28]

This distance corresponds to the epistemological break from a teleological conception of the individual and the world, as well as to the primacy of the acquisition of economic gains in the representation of individual self-assertion. Self-assertion is also accomplished by the transformation of the ideals of friendship and love into the means for the acquisition of goods for oneself—whether those goods are sexual satisfaction or money. Friendship and love do not bind people together but rather they are instruments of a social practice directed to private ends.

It is precisely the change in the conception of such ideas as friendship that Alasdair MacIntyre situates the beginning of "modern" morality, a morality blended with relativistic and "emotivistic" notions of virtues that broke with the "classical," fundamentally Aristotelian, conception of morality based on "a shared recognition of and pursuit of a good."[29] In the case of *La Celestina* it is quite clear that all understanding of community, shared values, and higher and collective goals configure the material reality of a discourse of private interests. The whole story is the constitution of a business by the investment in ideas and desires, by the articulation of mutual dependency, and by the submission of speech and thought to the production of profits. In this sense, what MacIntyre understands as the emergence of modern, relativistic morality must be anchored as well in the constitution of the mercantile structure of values. Only on the basis of this structure do individuals realize their social role as economic entities in the modern world—that is, as self-valorizing individuals whose values cannot but be exchange values, whose ideas are nothing but what they produce for individual growth.

As a consequence, this self-assertion also responds to a logic of its own which, in its turn, makes possible the constitution of a sphere of social interaction described in representational terms. This sphere is deceptive, devoid of truthfulness, and so on; it is a space that I call theatrical in order to think of it in nonmoral terms.

I believe this is the way the work seeks to depict social confrontation and individual self-constitution, beyond whatever intentions Fernando de Rojas had in mind. The result of the dialogues is to reach either a momentary and, in most of the cases, strategic agreement, or a victory over the other. This is a kind of victory which, to Celestina and the servants, means a concretization of things which can eventually or potentially be transformed into gold or money.

As opposed to this dialogization, the individual faces himself or herself in the monologues in a state of confusion or alienation or, in the case of the old woman and Sempronio, in a state of reconsideration of what to do and how to get the most out of the next dialogue. Every dialogue becomes the discursive space of a business-oriented action which was previously a diffused and formless theme in the monologue. This discursive space, in turn, acquires the predominant role in the understanding of desires, motives, and goals of individuals.

This will be the sphere of literature. This will be the field of the awareness of the autonomy of the individual and, therefore, the means for its self-constitution. In relation to the general discourse on wealth, literature had to be also witness to one of the primary consequences of the primitive accumulation of capital, namely, poverty. It is not original to say that *Lazarillo de Tormes* talks, among other things, about poverty, the place of honor in the lower echelons of the nobility, and a somewhat distorted conception of humanist fame. Lázaro de Tormes possesses a very pragmatic idea of fame, an idea publicly seen as something infamous. Whatever the author's intentions were, the case is, too, that the novel emerged at the time that debates on poverty were a familiar issue for a circle of readers, be those readers of an Erasmian mood seeking reform in the Church, of a more feudal-oriented conception of poverty, or of a more urban, secular persuasion. In the last instance, the work tells how social drives for economic improvement introduce changes in the perception of moral and cultural beliefs which, in turn, affected the very constitution of the individual self. In this sense, Juan Carlos Rodríguez argues that *Lazarillo de Tormes* opens literature to the world of capitalism.[30] Lázaro de Tormes, after leaving behind the scarcity of rural poverty and the daily uncertainties his mother must pass through as a worker, learns about hunger. He also experiences the hypocrisy of laymen and clergy, which inflict on him a suffering that somehow he will manage to transform into social and practical knowledge to attain a "good puerto," "cumbre de toda buena fortuna" ("a safe harbor, peak of all fortunes").

By way of representing the different aspects of this poverty, the transition from the childhood of ignorance to a cynical accommodation which is free, according to Lázaro, of moral requirements, *Lazarillo de Tormes* is on the way to disclosing a world of marginal human beings under the original conditions of capitalism.[31] It is a marginal world, then, that enters into the "literary," converting or rather making literature into an intellectual enterprise on the marginal.[32] The modern world becomes "disenchanted," to use a Weberian notion that Cascardi elaborates in order to describe social integration by means of a traumatic knowledge. On the one hand, such knowledge paves the way for expectations and social aspirations,[33] and, on the other hand, it clearly establishes the final relativity of all individual efforts in the face of the possession or dispossession of things. In fact, we are dealing with the relativity of all moral precepts and systems of belief in the construction of this modern, individualized self.

This is why *Lazarillo de Tormes* is constructed as an episodic articulation of moments of life, which are also sequential points that condense several discursive realities in the actual concretization of the struggle for oneself. Whether those realities are religion, social status, or repressed sexuality, it is absolutely true that *Lazarillo* is the result of a "point of view," in the sense that all possible interpretations of reality become a world with a coherent meaning only if one acquires the key to grow. This may be an irregular, pathological, or immoral growth, but in order to judge it, there must be a superior entity, beyond the concreteness of life, able to evaluate it according to standards other that the sphere of struggle.

Gómez-Moriana sees this higher entity in the formation of a structure of discursive domination emerging from the exposition of Lazarillo's voice to "vuesa merced," the addressee to whom Lázaro writes his life after "vuesa merced" has, for some unknown reasons, become inquisitive regarding the "case."[34] Even in this case, this superior entity acquires a power to control the discourse, a power to shape individual lives that, in the last instance, is a political-ideological construction. But it is not an entity able to erase the radical reality which Lázaro articulates as the only perspective available to make sense of the transformations in oneself and the world.[35]

A moral-religious discourse thus will have to be inserted in order to channel the intellectual reality of a world without judgments about the value of actions, a discourse to counteract the emergence of the value of things, means to acquire them, and ultimate goals of a society structured according to rich (people with money) and poor (people with nothing). Analyzing the "modern" understanding of this dichotomy, Maravall told us that being poor is not only an economic definition. The poor man makes his appearence in the middle of a culture that states either the poor are a threat or a natural consequence of the social order. Even Vives, the exemplary defender of the secular and the urban, productivist solution to poverty, thought that "deben considerar (los pobres) primeramente que la pobreza se la envía Dios justísimo por un oculto juicio, aun para ellos muy sutil, pue les quita la ocasión de pecar" (*Del socorro de los pobres* 267) ("they [the poor] should consider first that poverty is sent by the most just God for an undisclosed reason, still for them very subtle, for it takes away the chance to sin").

Indeed, this hidden plan of God must be a very subtle one for Lazarillo to understand it. He knows, however, the ironic nature of moral reality and, by extension, the ironic dimension of many of the signs of social distinction. His mother advised him to be on the side of the "good people," and that is exactly what he has always intended: to be on the side of the means of acquiring money. To have money and to be good is part of Lázaro's description of his infamous life and, we know, of the way a decent man must live. His great discovery, the discovery of the modern self, is to remain silent in the face of the apparent contradiction between a moral value and the conditions for accomplishing it; or rather to keep on with the irony, with that negative space between meaning and expression.

Lázaro's self-affirmation is the confirmation of the surplus of signification of the negative dynamics of irony, especially regarding moral assumptions, and "todo va de esta manera" ("everything else goes the same way"). It is at the intersection of the irony that the reader may understand the conundrum of Lazarillo and the impossibility of finding a solution to the contradiction. The double meaning of irony is the double meaning of hypocrisy, mercantile morality, and self-deception. His final infamy, his seeming known acceptance of his wife's adultery with his protector, the archpriest, is nevertheless his good fame, since "quien presta atención nunca medrará" ("if you care about what they say, you will never climb up in society"). It might be a moral injunction, but it is also a statement on the conditions for social success.

In fact, the reinforcement of a traditional mentality brought about in matters of religion by the Counter-Reformation will consolidate the aristocratic point of view regarding social inequalities; though, I want to argue that through this reaction there persists still the reality of a mercantile intellectual life. In Mateo Alemán's *Guzmán de Alfarache*, this intellectual life shows a high level of maturity which cannot at all be confused with a straightforward endorsement of a state of mind of the nobility.

Like many, if not all, political and moral economists, Felipe de Carrizales, in Cervantes's *El celoso extremeño*, wonders about the value of his silver bullion. He has become a rich man in America with the "inquieto trato de las mercancías" ("the troublesome dealings with commodities") where he went after he spent his "hacienda y juventud en Europa" ("his capital and youth in Europe"). He ponders, however, what the value of his metal really is, since he does not see any profitable activity in trade anymore. Carrizales has a moment of intimate reflection:

> Contemplaba Carrizales en sus barras, no por miserable, porque en algunos años que fue soldado aprendió a ser liberal, sino en lo que había de hacer de ellas, a causa que tenerlas en ser era cosa infructuosa, y tenerlas en casa, cebo para los codiciosos y despertador para ladrones. . . . Por otra parte, consideraba que la estrecheza de su patria era mucha y la gente muy pobre, y que el irse a vivir a ella era ponerse por blanco de todas las importunidades que los pobres suelen dar al rico. (Cervantes 2, 101-02)
>
> (Carrizales contemplated his bars [silver bullion], not out of miserliness, because in the years that he was a soldier he learned to be liberal, rather because of what to do with them, because having them in themselves was an unfruitful thing, and having them at home, bait for the covetous and an arousement to thieves. . . . On the other hand, he considered that his country was in dire straits and the people very poor, and thus to move there was to become a target for all the importunities which the poor tend to give the rich.)

Carrizales does not see a way to keep his wealth safe, since in themselves, "en ser," his bullion bars were worth nothing;

moreover, being now a rich man he will become a target for the poor. Carrizales "contemplaba"; that is, he meditated upon his silver, but he does not do so because he was a "miserable" ("miser"), a cheap lover of silver. Rather he is reflecting on his silver and by means of that meditation he describes for himself the social state of his country. Not surprisingly, Carrizales decides to diversify his silver in a "censo"—monetary investment in private debt—in a bank in order to live on rents and to build a magnificent house:

> Compró un rico menaje para adornar la casa, de modo que por tapicerías, estrados, y doseles ricos mostraba ser de un gran señor; compró, asimismo, cuatro esclavas blancas, y herrólas en el rostro, y otras dos negras bozales . . . dio parte de su hacienda a censo, sitada en diversas y buenas partes, otra puso en el banco, y quedóse con alguna, para lo que se ofreciese. (Cervantes 2, 104)
>
> (He bought a rich set of furniture to adorn the house, so that with tapestries, furniture, rich curtains, he presented himself as an important nobleman; he bought, likewise, four white slaves . . . he invested part of his hacienda in a "censo," placed in diverse and good areas, another he put in the bank, and he kept some, for whatever came up.)

In his youth he wasted his capital, and now being an old man, he is one of those rich people living on money and flaunting it as an important nobleman. To round out his economic meditation, he decides to get married in order to secure his capital.[36]

If *La Celestina* is written in the context of the emergence of a general mercantilization of social relations, and *Lazarillo* is the ironical response to individual dispossession, the literary field during the transition between the sixteenth and seventeenth centuries focuses prominently on the consequences that the general state of economic insecurity had in the formation of the inner space of the individual self. This is an inner space that not only relativizes moral and religious values, but that also is buried in the fragmentary patches of a dark and deep place from where the individual observes the socioeconomic struggles outside himself. In other words, the question the literary field explores during the period of clear and acute decapitalization is not only, as was the case during the first half of the sixteenth century, the representation of moral relativism, but also and together with it the broader issue of the constitution of the self in negative terms, that is, as the entity which is not the drive for the acquisition or defense of personal assets.

Guzmán de Alfarache is, at one point in his life, a merchant. He becomes a merchant through marriage and his father-in-law urges him to undertake a transaction to increase his capital. This is the episode of the "escrituras and contraescrituras" ("letters and counter-letters of payments") where Guzmán agrees to be involved in fictitious loans of money in order to increase the amount of his capital and to attract patrons. At the time his payments fall due, he does not have the cash, and he ends in bankruptcy. He bitterly complains:

> Y en Castilla, donde se contrata la máquina del mundo sin hacienda, sin fianzas ni abonos, más de con solo buena maña para saber engañar a los que se fian de ellos, toman tratos para que sería necesario en otras partes mucho caudal con que comenzarlos y muy mayor para el puesto que ponen. (Alemán 771-72)
>
> (And in Castile, where the machine of the world is engaged without wealth, without bonds, or payments, but with only good strategy for knowing how to decieve those who trust them, they take out contracts which in other parts much wealth would be required for starting them and even more for the bid which they place.)

Guzmán painfully finds out that economic competition is a struggle among individuals who will use any means necessary to deceive, that is, to attain money. But also Guzmán says that there is a relation between this individual struggle and the "máquina del mundo" ("the state of the monarchy") which follows the same course, only with "buena maña" ("a good trick"). At this time, the pícaro, the deceiver being now deceived, expresses a moral and social concern that is a reflection, or meditation, upon his individual and concrete life, in this case, regarding his life as a merchant.

Before having this experience, Guzmán has discovered that "no hay otra cordura ni otra ciencia en el mundo, sino mucho tener y más tener" (679) ("there is no other wisdom or plan of study than to have more and much more"). Monetary wealth replaces all other attributes and virtues of people. This conception of the world, this new reality is, it goes without saying, the consequence of the social and economic relations that capitalism has brought about during the Renaissance. Money and gold as a means of enrichment are possible in *La Celestina* because individuals, especially in cities, are breaking with traditional means of subjection and dependency, and organizing their lives in terms of self-interest. Yet Guzmán stresses a moral component that has to do with the structuration of his writing within the symbolic sphere of his society.

Guzmán decides later on to study theology in order to make a living. As is the case for many people in literature and in reality, a scholastic career is a way to escape poverty or to secure a privileged socioeconomic position. I have quoted some political economists who saw the dangerous increase in the number of these people and its impact in the stagnation of production. Kagan has shown as well the stagnation of the schooling system and the university as a whole, a consequence of both the seigniorial political reaction and the occupation by so-called orthodox Church doctrines of all areas of formal knowledge.[37] Tomás Rodaja, in Cervantes's *El licenciado Vidriera*, confesses that he wants to study at the university level because he has heard that "de los hombres se hacen los obispos" ("men may become bishops") but, tragically, he dies fighting as a soldier in an imperial war in Flandes where he goes to make a living.[38]

The economic consideration of all Guzmán's social roles is also elaborated on in relation to marriage. Guzmán's two marriages are essentially businesses; the second one is even an economic enterprise, using his wife as a sexual commodity. As Rodríguez Matos has nicely analyzed, it is precisely Gracia, his wife, that becomes the means for his enrichment after he realizes that the Church is not a profitable place for him. "Grace" is what the Christian soul is supposed to receive as a gift from God.[39]

I am not here arguing whether the book is a moralistic condemnation of a bad Christian pícaro, of a robber or a criminal. I am saying that the intervention of literature within the discourse of the symbolic sphere of the author's society has by necessity to fuse the economic and the moral in its own configuration. Marriage was a concern of theologians, of course, but we saw that it was a matter of state for some political economists who were discussing wealth. Having repeated many times that the decrease in population in Spain was one of the reasons of the economic downfall, González de Cellorigo goes on to advise on the proper marriage because:

> la tierra es muy aparejada para producir cuanto conviene a la vida civil y a sustentar más de lo que sustenta. A lo cual no es de poco estorbo estar las mujeres de España en tan poca estimación de los hombres, que huyendo del matrimonio desamparan la procreación y dan en extremos viciosos. . . . Procede también esto porque las mujeres son gravemente costosas según el estado presente . . . y doncellas muy virtuosas, por faltarles las dotes, se están arrinconadas. (González de Cellorigo 58)

> (The earth is too well suited for producing as much as is convenient for civil life and for sustaining more than what it sustains. Thus, it is no small bother that men in Spain esteem women so little, fleeing from wedlock they foresake procreation and take to extreme vices. . . . This also occurs because women are terribly expensive according to the present time . . . and maidens, too virtuous, lacking dowries, are neglected.)

Here we can read many of the issues around which many picaresque texts are built: deception in marriage, prostitution, money. Guzmán takes the lead, transforming his home into a brothel, so representing as well the particular relationship that men and women establish in the symbolic fusion between the economic and the moral. His house becomes the meeting place of rich people who pay to sexually use his Gracia. Everything goes well and Guzmán is able to afford the life of a "prince":

> Yo me trataba como un príncipe. Rodaban por la casa las piezas de plata, en los cofres no cabían las bordaduras y vestidos de varias telas de oro y seda, los escritorios abundaban de joyas preciosísimas. Nunca me faltó qué jugar, siempre me sobró con qué triunfar. Y con eso gozaban de su libertad. (Alemán 840)

(I treated myself like a prince. The pieces of silver rolled around the house, the clothes and embroideries of various fabrics of gold and silk did not fit into the coffers, the desks abounded in terrifically precious jewels. I never lacked [money] to play, I always had enough in order to win. And they enjoyed their freedom [the people paying for Gracia].)

Like Felipe de Carrizales, Guzmán is spending money to live the way a nobleman would. His activity is reduced to playing cards and he now has enough money to win the game. True, Guzmán is a player; he has been a player and, before becoming a merchant, he did quite well with gambling. This is a social reality, but for Guzmán it is also the way he describes the confrontation of individuals over wealth. This is a confrontation on the representational level in which the players play with what the others might or might not know concerning the owner's wealth.

Gambling is thus essentially to play with the other's cards. The poor Ensign Campuzano, one of the characters of Cervantes's *El casamiento engañoso*, also attempts to become rich by marrying Estefanía, because he has seen her wearing some apparently very valuable rings. She is however just another rogue like him, ready to deceive, rob him, and run. Campuzano himself confesses to his friend Peralta that the chain he was wearing did not have much worth either. In any case, during the time they are married, Campuzano says: "almorzaba en la cama, levantábame a las once, comía a las doce, y a las dos sesteaba en el estrado" (Cervantes 2, 286) ("I had breakfast in bed, I got up at eleven, ate at twelve, and at two I took a nap in the drawing room"). In other words, he was living the life of an idle rentier.

These texts deal with the question of wealth by showing the representational status that money permits people to acquire. Then, those transformations in social structure, those new perceptions of being a society divided into rich and poor, are elaborated on, in works like *Guzmán de Alfarache* in such a way as to describe not merely the possession or dispossession of goods, but also the acquisition of a value of a different sort. Guzmán says: "Es el pobre moneda que no corre" (354) ("A pauper is a coin which does not circulate"). The brutal alienation of people that the sentence implies is somehow of less interest than the implicit conceptualization of society from the point of view of money. Poor people do not flow the way money does. In what sense do they not flow? They do not flow in the sense that poor people do not produce symbolic values—those values that establish differences in status which, in turn, are the means of defining the social self of the individual as a natural attribute.

The poor person:

> Come más tarde, lo peor y más caro. Su real no vale medio, su sentencia es necedad, su discrección locura, su voto escarnio, su hacienda del común; ultrajado de muchos y aborrecido de todos. (ibid.)
>
> (Eats later, the worst and the most expensive. His "real" [coin] is not worth half, his judgment is foolish, his discretion madness, his curse scorn, his wealth public property, outraged by many and abhorred by all.)

The poor person eats later because he must let the rich eat first; he eats the worst part, because the best is for the rich; the poor eats what is the most expensive because the poor has nothing. And therefore nothing of what he has is worth anything: his talk is considered stupid, his capital belongs to everybody, he is injured by many and hated by everybody. We can see an economic-cultural figure emerging from eating bad to being rejected, from not having rational discourse to being completely dispossessed. But the rich man:

> ¡Qué viento en popa! ¡Con qué tranquilo mar navega! ¡Qué bonanza de cuidado! ¡Qué descuido de necesidades ajenas! . . . De todos es bien recibido. Sus locuras son caballerías, sus necedades sentencias. Si es malicioso, lo llaman astuto; si pródigo, liberal; si avariento, reglado y sabio; si murmurador, gracioso; si atrevido, desenvuelto; si desvergozado, alegre; si mordaz, cortesano; si incorregible, burlón; si hablador, conversable; si vicioso, afable; si tirano, poderoso . . . Todos le tiemblan, que ninguno se le atreve; todos cuelgan el oído de su lengua, para satisfacer a su gusto . . . Con lo que quiere sale. Es parte, juez y testigo. Acreditando la mentira, su poder la hace parecer verdad y, cual si lo fuese, pasan por ella . . . ¡Cómo lo festejan! ¡Cómo lo engrandecen! (354-55)

> (What wind on the stern! On what a calm sea he sails! How care-free! How little he worries about others' necessities! . . . He is well recieved by all. His madness is chivalrous undertaking, his foolish is judgment. If he is malicious they call him astute, if prodigal liberal, if avaricious moderate and wise, if grumbling charming, if impudent assured, if shameless happy, if mordant courtly, if incorrigible funny, if gossipy sociable, if vicious affable, if tyrranical powerful . . . All fear him, let no one dare him; all stand by his everyword, to satisfy his pleasure . . . He gets away with anything. He is party, judge and witness. Accrediting lies, his power makes it seem true and, as if they were, they pass for it . . . How they the court him! How they exalt him!)

For Guzmán, to be rich is to acquire the capacity for transforming the reality of some attributes, to obtain an additional meaning in the characterization of the individual. This transformation is possible because money introduces its evaluating mechanism even into the constitution of the body: "Porque el dinero calienta la sangre y la vivifica; y así, el que no lo tiene, es un cuerpo muerto que camina entre los vivos" (ibid.) ("Because money warms the blood and revives it, and so, he who does not have it, is a dead body which walks among the living").

Blood, "sangre," refers here to the physical element of the body and also to the symbolic value of nobility. Guzmán plays with both meanings to establish the common denominator between nature and society, since he tells us that the only wisdom is "tener." As in all texts of the picaresque, Guzmán considers the values of lineage and nobility to be merely illusions that can only fulfill their pretensions through wealth. For that reason, the life of an individual must be fed, must be heated ("calienta, vivifica") by the all-powerful element that money is. Otherwise, like the Squire in *Lazarillo de Tormes*, the individual becomes a dead body wandering around in search of vital food. Guzmán goes on to say:

> Que ninguno se afrenta de tener por pariente a un rico, aunque sea vicioso, y todos huyen del virtuoso, si hiede a pobre. La riqueza es como el fuego, que, aunque asiste en lugar diferente, cuantos a él se acercan se calientan, aunque no saquen brasa, y a más fuego, más calor. (684)

(That no one should be insulted by having a rich relative even if he is vicious, and everyone flees from the virtuous, if he stinks like a poor person . . . Wealth is like fire, which, even though it assists in a different place, those who approach are warmed, even if they do not take live coals, and the hotter the fire, the greater the warmth.)

The poor person stinks and the rich man, regardless of how immoral he might be, is fire, heat, the element of human survival. These, and many other discursive digressions that sometimes have been seen as sermonary, are Guzmán's moral-economic meditations. They introduce a mercantile dimension through which the text inquires into the nature of a society officially subsumed within traditional notions, but which, at the same time, is a society pervaded by the reality of economic struggle.

Mateo Alemán wrote on many different topics, including a hagiography and an orthography. He was also commissioned to report on the living conditions of galley prisoners working in the Almadén's mercury mines under the control of the German bankers.[40] He was a close friend of Pérez de Herrera, in whose circle of social reformers concerned with poverty he spent a good deal of his time. In a letter to his friend dated October 1597, Alemán reacts to all the efforts being made by people like Pérez de Herrera

Muchas veces me puse a considerar (O amigo Máximo) y muchas noches, aun cansado de negocios, dejé de pagar el censo a naturaleza, desveládome en el amparo de los pobres, tanto por el bien común cuanto por mi propio interés que, habiendo de tratar su causa, no pudiera excusar la mía. Pero como semejante trato requería más acción y mayor poder, siempre lo temí, viéndome falto del caudal que pide tan alta mercadería y matería tratada de tan doctos varones que, cuando quisiese decir algo, sería reiterar lo que ellos tiene dicho y estampado y a todos es notorio. (Cros, *Protée et le gueux* 436)

(Many times I have began to consider [O friend Máximo] and many nights, although tired of business, I stopped paying the rent to nature, suffering sleepless nights in the aid of the poor, as much as for the public good as well as for my own benefit which, having to treat their cause, could not excuse mine. But since such a trade required more action and greater force, I always feared it, seeing myself as lacking the wealth which such a commodity requires and which has been studied by people so wise, that it would be to reiterate what they have said and published and which is well-known to all.)

I want to emphasize the consideration of intellectual work as "caudal"—wealth, capital—and the subject of his study as "mercancía"—commodity. I only want here to point out that Alemán's concerns for the state of the poor are an integral component of his intellectual life. These concerns show the moral implications both of his intellectual work as well of the state of society. Moreover, in another letter a few days later, he seems to write in a more personal mood, showing gratitude for Máximo's friendship to him; at some point he goes on to talk about his own life:

> Ya sabes mi soledad, mi flaca substancia, ya me ves por oprobio reputado. Los que de mí recibieron bien me dejaron, los que alegremente comieron a mi mesa, con rostros triste y enfado me despiden de su puerta, negándome su conversación y compañía, que es por la ingratitud; más me duelen los que me halagaban y consolaban; querían despeñarme muchos en mi mocedad . . . burlé, reí, jugué . . . volví la cabeza, no los hallé, pasaron adelante por la posta, dejáronme atrás, y nunca más los vi. Otros volaron tan alto que se olvidaron de mí . . . estimábalos más que oro ni plata; faltó la plata, gastóse el oro y ellos con ello; por amigos los tuve . . . los granjeé con dineros. (ibid. 442-43)

> (You already know my solitude, my weakness, you already see me made famous by opprobrium. Those who received good by me have left, those who joyfully ate at my table, with sad countenances and anger dismiss me from their door, denying me their conversation and company, that because of ingratitude; I am hurt more by those who flattered and consoled me. Many wanted to bring me down in my youth. I joked, laughed, played . . . turned my head, and did not see them, they passed in front by the post, they left me behind, and I never saw

them again. Others flew so high they forgot about me . . . I valued them more than gold or silver; the silver was lacking, the gold was wasted and they with it; I had them as friends . . . I won them with money.)

Can we not see here the same mood, even the same stylistic composition, that we find in Guzmán's meditations? I am not at all saying that Guzmán is any kind of alter-ego of Alemán; rather, I am saying that Alemán's writing intervenes in the discourse on wealth by means of this permanent fusion of moral-mercantile meditations. Through this fusion, Alemán uncovers the reality of insolidarity that emerges from the circulation of gold and money and the explicit consideration of values such as friendship, as being immersed in the process of mercantilization. It also points to an increasing conceptualization of human interrelations in terms of violence, from deception or robbery to a general state of war among nations and individuals.

It is under these conditions that we may assess as well the crucial question of the illegitimacy of Guzmán and its effects on his life and his own writing. Guzmán was born as the consequence of a debt; he is the byproduct of the financial connection between Seville and Genoa. His father goes to Seville in order to obtain his part of a share paid by his partner; in the process he has sex with an old man's wife. Guzmán is born. It is this event that gives birth to the story of this individual between Italy and Spain, as well as to the transformation of his original negative value in the process of interpreting his society as a field in which individuals increase their credit, reputation, their "haber" ("assets") in the general bookkeeping of life.[41]

His illegitimacy, his own person, must circulate among two seemingly related conceptions of property, the feudal understanding of legitimate property according to lineage, and the capitalist legitimation according to his own free valorization. His own self-valorization is one of negative origin. In this sense, everything appears to be artificial, the product of a fundamental and original lack, of a real beginning.

So Guzmán begins over and over again to make use of his negative value to increase his individual potential as well as to reflect on the way moral precepts smoothly change to a description of the artificiality of social life. In other words, his social self is a mercantilized entity to the same degree that his intellectual perceptions of society are grounded in the break from feudal legitimization and, thus, in the capitalist conception of free-moral growth.

Guzmán circulates through accounts, credits, petitions, robberies, usuries, and "mohatras" (fictitious sales to increase artificially the price). His purpose is to concretize his dealings in cash, to show a growth of his self by a constant consumption of his credit, to make real, from the point of view of feudal property, his unreal legitimacy. I suspect this is why Juan Carlos Rodríguez considered *Guzmán* an example of a "substantialist" ideological matrix, that is of an aristocratic, feudal conception of a world degraded by capitalist relations.[42] But to read Alemán this way, one cannot appreciate the complex description of a mercantile self, whatever the "ideological" matrix we want to suppose in it. It does miss the point of the functional and monetary value of all discourses, including moral and religious ones, in the description of symbolic forms of capital.

Moreover, Juan Carlos Rodríguez considers that the implication of Guzmán sermonary discourses is to "to show the inevitability of appearances."[43] They are inevitable, I want to add, precisely because these appearances are elements of the presentation of the social being in a world turned into a theater of deceptions. These appearances are unavoidable as they are the mechanisms to produce a positive mark of signification, an additional value grounded in credit, in the valorization of the momentary and negative, or false, toward a future and positive profit.

"O te digo verdades o mentiras" ("I am telling you either truths or lies") says Guzmán to the reader, which is a concise and simple way of telling us that he is talking about a radical truth which does not leave room for discussion: take it or leave it. He is lying if you think the world functions according to feudal legitimacy and religious precepts. He is telling the truth if you, like him, observe the function of negative values as instruments of economic increase. And this is because, as Guzmán shows in his writing, there is a fundamental contradiction between moral precepts and negative values—between what Guzmán sermonizes and what Guzmán does—which, nevertheless, is the very justification of the self's own interests.

The most obvious example of this contradiction as justification of the self is Guzmán's informing authorities about Soto and other galley-fellows of a pending rebellion. His companions have told him of the rebellion and ask him for advice on how to proceed; they think that above all considerations, Guzmán will be on their side against the authority that keeps them imprisoned. But Guzmán thinks differently: "hice mi consideración, y como siempre tuve propósito firme de no hacer cosa infame ni mala" (*Guzmán* 904) ("I made my deliberation, and . . . I never wanted to do any bad action nor any infamy").

Ironically, Guzmán says that, since he has intended to avoid bad action, he places himself under His Majesty, under the state, to become an informer againts his galley-mates. The question is not whether to believe him or not; the question is to see the transition from morality to the personal justification for an action, namely, his own profit. Has Guzmán always intended to do good? Of course not. In what sense, then, is he acting according to any morality? In the sense of the very negation of morality to the benefit of his self-interest, which is nothing other than his individualized signification of freedom and economic value. This consideration is his reason to tell authority about the conspiracy. Not surprisingly, he is able to perceive at this moment the relation between his self and the superior political form, the state.

This total lack of coherence reflects the same circumstances arisen from Lazarillo's ironic understanding of the good people and the good fame. It is the feeling of a radical break between the inner and the outer in the individual that modernity is supposed to have brought by its rupture with the teleological, feudal world. It is, however, the prerequisite of the modern individual *per se*. MacIntyre argues that these are the features of the problem of morality, once secularization and modernity have broken with a "functional conception of man" in which moral values depends on a telos.

Curiously, MacIntyre places this break during the wave of anti-Aristotelism from the Late Middle Ages to the seventeenth century. Scholasticism was, however, the official intellectual authority in Spain, and it remained so in Spanish universities until much later. MacIntyre's argument is nevertheless valid in a broader sense, especially if we do not conflate Aristotelism with Scholastic doctrines and if we remember that the Spanish moral economists never disengaged the analysis of economic behavior from ethical questions. In any case, the moral self is in *Guzmán* too an entity devoid of meaning unless it is in relation to this irreconcilable break.

Guzmán's self-creation is the expression of the working of capitalist relations in the constitution of this "outer" reality where signification has to do with self-interest. It is perceived as an artificial reality, a reality devoid of substance and, in this sense, it is a reality that can be read as possessing theatrical features.

Guzmán's outer world is his social being, an either pragmatical, cynical, or deceptive being; moreover, I would say that this being is in the same strain as Gracián's reconsideration of the political dimension of appearances. These appearances become the realm of a theorization of the individual self-constitution by aesthetic means which are charged with symbolic forms of capital.

The conception of individual confrontation as a confrontation between actors is the basis of most literary works of the first three decades of the seventeenth century in Spain. The idea that the defense of oneself depends on the proper evaluation of the other's intentions (something that Gracián will theorize at a socio-poetic level) informs the literature of the period. The individual becomes an actor in the sense that he or she adopts economic interest as the field in which to acquire a social definition—a definition that, in turn, is the result of a deeper understanding of a war of all against all. The representation of this war, however, is given in individual terms and, thus, in the way the self-constitution is nothing but the means to deceive the other.

Several texts come one after the other to reiterate, throughout the crisis of the Spanish economy, the state of a general, individual-oriented suspicion of society as the place where the self can be dissolved by decreasing its economic definition. We have all the attacks by *pícaros* and *pícaras*, all those other texts to moralize on the degraded nature of society, those collections to warn about the dangers of any interaction between individuals. This was, I believe, the manner in which the literary field finally discovered its position within writing, namely, to depict the individuality of social activity, an activity conceived as a ghostly play of economic intentions.

In 1620 Juan de Luna gives in a *Segunda parte de la vida de Lazarillo* a more dramatic picture of dispossession and of social aggression than in its original. There is no hope for socioeconomic improvement throughout his story and, much less, any notion of social accommodation when, at the end Lázaro, badly beaten and in absolute poverty, decides to wait in a church for his death:

> Púseme en un rincón considerando los reveses de la fortuna, y que por dondequiera hay tres leguas de mal camino; y así determiné quedarme en aquella iglesia para acabar allí mi vida, que según los males pasados no podía ser muy larga, y para escusar el trabajo a los clérigos que no me fuesen a buscar a otra parte después de muerto. (Luna 387-88)
>
> (I put myself in a corner considering the reversals of fortune, and every which way there are three leagues of bad paths; and in that way I determined to stay in that church so as to end there my life, which it could not be too long because of my past sufferings, and so as to excuse the work for the clerics, that they would not look for me elsewhere after death.)

In 1620 too, Cortés de Tolosa relates in *Lazarillo de Manzanares* the story of a boy who goes from the orphanage to a family of criminals, and who at the end hopes to make a living in America. Also in 1620, Carlos García publishes in Paris his novel *La desordenada codicia de los bienes ajenos*, where from beginning to end the text takes us to a world of persistent deception, criminality, and, particularly, robbery. The representation of society as being "possessed" by thieves at all levels acquires a dark satirical twist that seems to point to the belief that the world surrendered to Satan. But this seventeenth-century Satan is only the final step in the insatiable search for another's wealth:

> De aquí infiero el engaño notable en que vive hoy el mundo, creyendo que la pobreza fue inventora del hurto, no siendo otro que la riqueza y prosperidad; porque el amor y deseo de la honra crece, cuando ella mesma se aumenta . . . De aquí entenderá vuestra merced que el hurtar es naturaleza en el hombre y no artificio, y que va por herencia y propagación en todo el linaje humano. (García 73)

> (From here I infer the notable deception in which the world lives today, believing that poverty was the inventor of robbery when, on the contrary, it was wealth and prosperity: because the love and the wish for honor grows when that itself grows. Thus, you may understand that robbery is in the nature of man and not something acquired, and that it goes by heritage through all of humankind.)

This depiction of social violence in individual terms is also the theme of many of the tales included in the collection *Guía y aviso de forasteros que vienen a esta corte* published in 1620 by Liñán y Verdugo. The narrative frame of the book involves two friends in Madrid, "el uno pleiteante y el otro pretendiente" ("one was a plaintiff, the other was a public office-seeker") who, at the Palace's door, meet a man coming from Granada to resolve a question regarding an inheritance. The friends advise the newcomer on the dangers that he will face in the city-court. The first advice is to find an inn

> de gente que viva bien, y en buena vecindad, que sea en calle de barrio, y población honrada: de lo cual suele ser indicativo el estar adornada de casas y edificios altos, ricos y bien labrados, donde de ordinario vive gente noble y principal, rica y poderosa. (Liñán y Verdugo 61-62)

> (of people who live well, and in good company, that it be in the street of a barrio, and honorable population; the indicators of which tend to be that it is adorned with houses and high buildings, which are rich and well bricked, where noble, rich and powerful normally live.)

This is the best way to avoid criminals, thieves, and poor people in general. It is, however, a clear expression of a cultural dimension of class awareness. Most of the stories follow the pattern of *pícaros* and *pícaras* ready to attack any imprudent man in order to extract from him an economic benefit. What the friends, however, want to say is that noble and well-bred people are the target of the lower class, that there is always the threat of economic ruin because of them.

Society as a theater of deceptions, individually oriented and economically grounded—this is intervention of literature into the discourse on wealth. The elaboration of a self under a mercantile structure of values is, then, the first level of the autonomy of literature, through which a proper literary culture emerges. This culture, this theatrical aspect of life, becomes conceptualized by the very same process of literary perception to the point that material wealth and ideas compress into the symbolic constitution of the self.

We must not forget, however, that dispossession and war are the landmarks of the origins of the modern world. This is the picture that in 1646, *Estebanillo González* radically offers in all parts of Europe during the Thirty Years' War. Estebanillo is clearly a nationless individual who runs from one place to another in order to survive; the work is a clear example of dispossession at the international level at the time that the European states fought the first large-scale war of capitalism.[44] Estebanillo travels throughout the empire and allied kingdoms, changing nations, armies, and occupations. He becomes a mercenary, then abandons the battle-field; he spends a good deal of his time in the taverns and bears the jeering and maltreatment of the powerful people, hoping that one of them will finally protect him. *Estebanillo González* is a literary work, but it is in many important aspects a historical document.[45] The literary writing and the general discourse on the formation of values through wealth have even here a historical referent in the reality of war.

Estebanillo is, above all, a buffoon, a being without any moral intimacy, absolutely immersed in his theatrical dimension. He is at all times an external presentation of an individual with no other goal than to survive. His only intimacy, his only interior world is to acknowledge his cowardice and his complete refusal to accept any moral principle. Almost at the end of the period under consideration, the literary Estebanillo establishes the primary determination of money in the construction of selves in the new world, the modern world of economic value.[46]

Notes

1. Quotations have been translated from Spanish by Luis Marxuach.

2. Vilar says: "Así en el declive de una sociedad gastada por la historia, en un país que ha llevado al punto más extremo sus contradicciones . . . en aquel momento surge una obra maestra que fija en imágenes el contraste tragicómico entre las superestructuras míticas y la realidad de las relaciones humanas." (*El tiempo del Quijote* 345) ("In a country which has taken to the most extreme point its contradictions . . . in that moment a masterpiece appears which fixes to images the tragicomic contrast between the mythic superstructures and the reality of human relationships").

3. The economic paradoxes go on: "nunca tantos vasallos vio ricos como ahora hay, nunca tanta pobreza entre ellos, ni jamas Rey tan poderoso, ni de tantas rentas y Reinos, ni le ha habido hasta aquí que haya entrado a reinar que hallase tan dismiuidos empeñados estados" (89-90) ("At no time had so many rich subjects been seen as there are now, and at no time amid them so much poverty, nor a King so powerful, nor so many revenues and Kingdoms, nor until now soveriegn who beginning his reign discovered so diminished and debt-ridden states").

4. López Bravo 340.

5. Moncada 179.

6. He says: "con los frutos del reino se sustentan extranjeros, y fuera justo se sustentaran nacionales" (Moncada 102) ("the fruits of the kingdom enrich foreigners; national people are the one who rightfully must be enriched").

7. Ibid. 108-09.

8. Caxa even will go as far as to ask for a more explicit intervention of the state to reduce "bienes vinculados," that is, the system of "mayorazgos" that blocked the selling of lands: "se deberían facilitar las licencias para enajenar bienes vinculados, hasta que se redujeran a cantidad, y número congruente a la razón de Estado de estos reinos" (ibid. 56) ("permits must be given to alienate them in order to reduce them to the amount and number fitting the reason of the State of these kingdoms"). The fight for the abolition of "mayorazgos," we know, will be a lost cause until the nineteenth century. True, Caxa is here defending the owners grouped in the Mesta, who have seen their wood trade going down as a result of the crisis of Castilian wood industry, which in turn was the consequence of the consolidation of the financial-industrial complex of the United Provinces. Thus, his position against agricultural rent.

9. Fernández de Navarrete 535.

10. Moncada 105.

11. See for example, his *American Treasure and the Price Revolution in Spain*.

12. See "Problems of the Formation of Capitalism," where he contested Hamilton's "inflationary" conception of the rise of capitalism and advanced the idea of understanding Spain's stagnation as the result of its role in incorporating the American labor force within the European economy. See also his *History of Gold and Money* for a larger picture of the movement of metals.

13. See *Carlos V y sus banqueros*, especially vol. 3, *Los caminos del oro y de la plata.*

14. *Pequeño capitalismo: Gran capitalismo*, where he describes Castilia's dependency on Genoese interests.

15. *Land and Society in Golden Age Castile*, especially pp. 190-230.

16. In Noël Salomon, *La vida rural castellana en tiempos de Felipe II*, 223. Also Vassberg, in *La venta de tierras baldías* . . . follows up some cases of land confiscation and dispossession of small owners and the obligation imposed on some peasants to buy the lands in which they had been working for generations under communal or municipal ownership.

17. Ibid. 268 ff. and 320.

18. López Bravo 233-34; Férnandez de Navarrete 537. Caxa de Leruela says: "La retirada que han hecho muchos a los claustros y sacerdocio en España ha sido ocasionada de las miserias, trabajo, y necesidad del siglo. . . . El quedarse muchísimos acobardados sin estado, es efecto de la misma causa, en que no tiene poca parte la vanidad, reconociendo las dificultades que oprimen al matrimonio" (Caxa de Leruela, 61-62) ("The retirement which many in Spain have made to the cloisters and the priesthood has been occasioned by the century's misery, toil, and hardship. . . . the unwed state of many is an effect of the same cause, in which vanity has played no small part, recognizing the difficulties which oppress matrimony").

19. See *The Modern World-System.* During the seventeenth century, what Spain faces is the loss of the struggle for political hegemony in Europe, the economic hegemony having already been lost during the "long" sixteenth century.

20. See Linda Martz, *Poverty and Welfare in Habsburg Spain: The Example of Toledo* for a description of these debates in the sixteenth century, particularly pp. 7-91. Also Maravall's first two chapters of his *La literatura picaresca desde la historia social*, where he traces the changes in the conception of poverty, from the Medieval idea of the "religious" role of the poor, to the modern, secular, and urban-centered, understanding of poverty as a social disease. Cavillac's essay, mentioned, is a seminal work on the issue.

21."Pues cuanto oro, y plata, entra de las Indias parece tesoro de duendes, y que el mismo viento, que lo trae, lo lleva" (Caxa de Leruela 38) ("Because all the gold, and silver, which enters from the Indies seems like an enchanted treasure, and that the same wind which brings it in, takes it out").

22. It is worth noting that Castilian trade with America is considered by Mercado to be part of the "internal" as opposed to the foreign trade.

23. "Los primitivos españoles del pensamiento económico. 'Cuantitativismo' y 'bullonismo'" 145. In this study, Vilar shows how these writers argued against the export of metals because it was the consequence of the lack of national wealth, and not because their monetary thinking was founded on the idea that wealth was equivalent to the amount of money in circulation. See also Grice-Hutchinson, "Contributions of the School of Salamanca to Monetary Theory as a Result of the Discovery of the New World."

24. See *Capital* 1, 162-63; 195-98.

25. Tomás de Mercado, ibid., 240. The question of the cash-flow as one of the determinant circumstances in the accumulation of continental financial capital through American trade is analyzed by Wallerstein, cited, and before him by Ferdinand Braudel, in *Civilization and Capitalism*, more extensively in vol. 2, *The Wheels of Commerce.*

26. For a discussion of this issue, see Francisco Gómez-Camacho, Introduction to his edition of Molina's *Tratado sobre los préstamos y la usura* (c. 1597); for a broader analysis of Molina's nominalism in the measure of value in "time," see also Gómez Camacho's Introduction to Molina's *Tratado sobre los cambios*, mentioned, and Vilar's "Los primitivos españoles del pensamiento económico," also mentioned. For a discussion on the question of economic welfare in the Scholastic tradition and the "public good" based in natural law, see Schumpeter, *History of Economic Analysis*, particularly pp. 96-115. For a study of the origins of the Scholastic interpretation of Aristotle's position on money, see Odd Langholm, *Wealth and Money in the Aristotelian Tradition.*

27. The complete title accomplishes the idea of portraying the stock market in literary, theatrical terms: *Diálogos curiosos entre un filósofo, un mercader discreto y un accionista erudito: Describiendo el negocio de las acciones, su origen, su etimología, su realidad, su juego y su enredo.*

28. Maravall understood the representation of class conflict in this text in relation to the emergence of new relations of dependency between masters and servants. Rodríguez-Puértolas saw the class conflict around the depiction of social resentment. In any case, the social confrontation is centered on economic wealth, which is for González-Echeverría the ground for the elaboration on sexual symbolism in terms of the "structures of commerce." Deyermond, too, accepted the primary importance of class division in the conception of the work.

29.*After Virtue* 155. MacIntyre argues that modern morality and so-called secularization is the result of the rejection of Aristotelism, which for him means the rejection of a possibility of a rational justification of a moral order.

30. Juan Carlos Rodríguez, in *La literatura del pobre*, argues about *Lazarillo* being a genuine product of the new ideological "matrix" of capitalist relations, since its character is given as essentially free from feudal sociocultural dependencies. Rodríguez goes on to say that only the poor could represent this new conception of absolute freedom of the self, as required by capitalism.

31. "El *Lazarillo* es la primera novela moderna porque es el primer texto literario que muestra, tanto en su forma como en su contenido anecdótico, la presencia en la vida humana de las fuerzas que el modo de producción capitalista conjura" (Beverley 63) ("*Lazarillo* is the first modern novel because it is the first literary text that shows, in form and content, the presence in human life of forces that the capitalistic mode of production contrives").

32. See Maiorino's Introduction to*The Picaresque: Tradition and Displacement.*

33. See *The Subject of Modernity*, where Cascardi argues that modernity suffers in its very modernity a sort of break with a teleological understanding of the place of individuals in society and the beginning of longing for restoration through processes of self-abstraction.

34. See *Dicourse Analysis as Sociocriticism.* Gómez-Moriana argues that Lázaro is "the vicar of the true subject," (65) accommodating his voice to dominant discourses. On the other hand, we do not know, exactly, what the case is. As a matter of general agreement, most of the scholarship and readers of this novel think that it refers to Lazarillo's acceptance of a triangular sexual relation between his wife and the "arcipreste de San Salvador," his protector and for whom Lázaro sells wine. The final chapter is, in any case, full of linguistic ambiguities, because as a matter of fact, why is this powerful person going to ask Lázaro, a nobody, about a sexual scandal? Ferrer-Chivite has proposed another interpretation, that the writer and the person involved in the "case" are not the same person ("El Lázaro de Tormes ¿caso o casos?").

35. Years ago, Gilman saw that "Lazarillo not only eats, he also judges; and his story from the beginning involves a process of discovery, estimation and rejection" ("The Death of Lazarillo de Tormes" 159).

36. I have analyzed the relation between this unfortuned marriage and the old man's economic fortune in *Lectura y representación: Análisis cultural de las "novelas ejemplares,"* pp. 112-31.

37. See *Students and Society in Early Modern Spain.* Kagan gives an account of the decrease of financial support to popular literacy, which goes hand in hand with the economic decline.

38. See my analysis of this novel in *Lectura y representación*, cited above, where I argued that Cervantes is questioning in this novel the social function of reading and of formal education.

39. Carlos Rodríguez Matos in *El narrador pícaro: Guzmán de Alfarache*, proposes to read Guzmán's whole narration as the way that the picaro-writer takes on different roles as a means to seduce his audience in order to obtain a benefit.

40. This is a report that Alemán could not carry out until two years after the assignment because of the many obstacles laid down by the mine's administration. He was eventually even removed from the commission following apparently strong pressures from the bankers to the King. See Edmond Cros, *Mateo Alemán.*

41. "[Guzmán] ha hecho de la convivencia un libro mayor en el que escrupulosamente anota las partidas económicas y espirituales, como corresponde a quien quiere estar a buenas con Dios y con los hombres" (Montalvo 132) ("[Guzmán] has transformed social relationship into an account book where he scrupulously annotates economic and spiritual entries, as the proper thing for someone who wants to be in God's favor and in men's favor").

42. See his *La literature del pobre*, pp. 226-37.

43. Ibid. 218.

44. That is why Juan Goytisolo said that *Estebanillo* probably represents one of the first antiwar testimonies ("*Estebanillo González, hombre de buen humor.*") Nicholas Spadaccini and Anthony Zahareas analyzed the contribution that the novel made to the picaresque: "Es *Estebanillo* la 'Vida' picaresca que lleva a su fin lógico la definición del pícaro como hombre sin profesión alguna" (Sapadaccini and Zahareas 34) ("*Estebanillo* is the picaresque "life" that takes to a logical end the definition of the "pícaro" as a man without any employment"). This is, in other words, the depiction of individuals left alone and absolutly propertyless.

45. Spadaccini and Zahareas's mentioned essay studies this issue in detail.

46. I want to acknowledge the time, work, and talent that Helen Ryan has devoted to this essay throughout the editing process.

Works Cited

Alemán, Mateo. *Guzmán de Alfarache*. Ed. Francisco Rico. Barcelona: Planeta, 1983.

Artola, Miguel. *La Hacienda del Antiguo Régimen*. Madrid: Alianza Editorial, Banco de España, 1982.

Beverley, John. "El *Lazarillo* y la acumulación originaria." *Del Lazarillo al Sandinismo: Estudios sobre la función ideológica de la literatura española e hispanoamericana*. Minneapolis: The Prisma Institute, 1987. 47-64.

Braudel, Ferdinand. *The Wheels of Commerce*. Vol. 2 of *Civilization and Capitalism*. Trans. Sian Reynolds. Berkeley: U of California P, 1992.

Brumont, Francis. *Campo y campesinos de Castilla la Vieja en tiempos de Felipe II*. Madrid: Siglo XXI, 1984.

Carande, Ramón. *Los caminos del oro y de la plata*. Vol. 3 of *Carlos V y sus banqueros*. Madrid: Sociedad de estudios y publicaciones, 1967.

Cascardi, Anthony J. *The Subject of Modernity*. Cambridge: Cambridge UP, 1992.

Cavillac, Michel. "La problemática de los pobres en el siglo XVI." Introduction to his edition of *Amparo de pobres* by Cristóbal Pérez de Herrera. Madrid: Espasa Calpe, 1975. lxxv-cciv.

_____. *Pícaros y Mercaderes en el Guzmán de Alfarache*. Trans. by Juan Azpitarte. Granada: Universidad de Granada, 1994.

Caxa de Leruela, Miguel. *Restauración de la abundancia de España*. (c. 1630). Ed. Jean Paul Le Flem. Madrid: Instituto de Estudios Fiscales, 1975.

Cervantes, Miguel de. *Novelas ejemplares*. Ed. Harry Sieber. Madrid: Cátedra, 1986. 2 vols.

Cortes de Tolosa, Juan. *Lazarillo de Manzanares*. Ed. Giuseppe E. Sansone. Madrid: Espasa-Calpe, 1974.

Cros, Edmond. *Protée et le gueux. Researches sur les origines et la nature du recit picaresque dans Guzmán de Alfarache*. Paris: Didier, 1967.

_____. *Mateo Alemán: Introducción a su vida y a su obra*. Salamanca: Anaya, 1971.

Deyermond, Alan. "Divisiones socio-económicas, nexos sexuales: La sociedad de *Celestina*." *Celestinesca* 8.2 (1984): 3-10.

Estebanillo González. Eds. Nicholas Spadaccini and Anthony Zahareas. Madrid: Castalia, 1978. 2 vols.

Fernández de Navarrete, Pedro. *Conservación de Monarquías y discursos políticos sobre la gran consulta que el consejo . . .* (1619). Ed. de *BAE*. v. 25. Madrid: Rivadeneyra, 1861. 449-546.

Ferrer-Chivite, Manuel. "El Lázaro de tormes, ¿caso o casos?" *Actas del X congreso de la Asociación Internacional de Hispanistas*. Barcelona: PPU, 1992, tomo I. 425-31.

García, Carlos. *La desordenada codicia de los bienes ajenos*. Ed. Giulio Massano. Madrid: José Porrua Turanzas, 1977.

Gilman, Stephen. "The Death of Lazarillo de Tormes." *PMLA* 81.3 (1966): 149-66.

Gómez-Camacho, Francisco. "Introducción" to his edition of Luis de Molina's *Tratado sobre los préstamos y la usura*. Madrid: Instituto de Estudios Fiscalas, Instituto de Cooperación Iberoamericana, 1989.

_____. "Introducción" to his edition of Luis de Molina's *Tratado sobre los cambios*. Madrid: Instituto de Estudios Fiscalas, Instituto de Cooperación Iberoamericana, 1990.

Gómez-Moriana, Antonio. *Discourse Analysis as Sociocriticism: The Spanish Golden Age*. Minneapolis: U of Minnesota P, 1993.

González de Cellorigo, Martín. *Memorial de la política necesaria y útil restauración a la república de España.* (1600) Ed. José L. Pérez de Ayala. Madrid: Instituto de Estudios Fiscales, Instituto de Cooperación Iberoamericana, 1991.

González Echeverría, Roberto. *Celestina's Brood. Continuities of the Baroque in Spanish and Latin-American Literature*. Durham: Duke UP, 1993.

Goytisolo, Juan. "*Estebanillo González, hombre de buen humor.*" *Ruedo Ibérico* 8 (August-September 1966): 78-86.

Grice-Hutchinson, Marjorie. "Contributions of the School of Salamanca to Monetary Theory as a Result of the Discovery of the New World." *Economic Thought in Spain*. Eds. Laurence S. Moss and Christopher K. Ryan. Vermont: Elgar, 1993.

Hamilton, Earl J. *American Treasure and the Price Revolution in Spain. 1501-1650*. New York: Octagon Books, 1970.

Kagan, Richard L. *Students and Society in Early Modern Spain*. Berkeley: U of California P, 1974.

Langholm, Odd. *Wealth and Money in the Aristotelian Tradition. A Study in Scholastic Economic Sources*. Oslo: Universitetsforlaget, 1983.

Lazarillo de Tormes. Ed. Joseph V. Ricapito. Madrid: Cátedra, 1983.

Liñán y Verdugo, Antonio. *Guía y aviso de forasteros que vienen a esta corte*. Ed. Edisons Simons. Madrid: Editora Nacional, 1980.
López Bravo, Mateo. *Del rey y la raçón de governar*. (1616-1627). In Henry Mechoulan, *Mateo López Bravo. Un socialista español del siglo XVII*. Madrid. Editora Nacional, 1977. 97-343.
Luna, Juan de. *Segunda parte de la vida de Lazarillo de Tormes. Sacada de las crónicas de Toledo*. Ed. Pedro M. Piñero. Madrid: Cátedra, 1988.
MacIntyre, Alasdair. *After Virtue. A Study in Moral Theory*. Notre Dame: U of Notre Dame P, 1984.
Maiorino, Giancarlo. "Picaresque Econopoetics: At the Watershed of Living Standards." *The Picaresque: Tradition and Displacement*. Ed. Giancarlo Maiorino. Minneapolis: U of Minnesota P, 1996. 1-39.
Maravall, José Antonio. *El mundo social de La Celestina*. Madrid: Gredos, 1964.
_____. *La literatura picaresca desde la historia social*. Madrid: Taurus, 1986.
Martz, Linda. *Poverty and Welfare in Habsburg Spain. The Example of Toledo*. Cambridge: Cambridge UP, 1983.
Marx, Karl. *Capital*. Vol. 1. Trans. by Ben Fowkes. New York: Penguin Classics, 1990.
Mercado, Tomás de. *Suma de tratos y contratos*. (1569-1571). Ed. Nicolás Sánchez-Albornoz. Madrid: Instituto de Estudios Fiscales, 1977. 2 vols.
Molina, Luis de. *Tratado sobre los préstamos y la usura*. (1597). Ed. Francisco Gómez-Camacho. Madrid: Instituto de Estudios Fiscales, Instituto de Cooperación Iberoamericana, 1989.
_____. *Tratado sobre los cambios*. (1597). Ed. Francisco Gómez-Camacho. Madrid: Instituto de Estudios Fiscales, Instituto de Cooperación Iberoamericana, 1990.
Moncada, Sancho de. *Restauración política de España*. (1619). Ed. Jean Vilar. Madrid: Instituto de Estudios Fiscales, 1974.
Montalvo, Manuel. "La crisis del siglo XVII desde la atalaya de Mateo Alemán." *Revista de Occidente* 112 (September 1990): 116-35.
Ortiz, Luis. *Memorial del Contador Luis de Ortiz a Felipe II*. (1558) Ed. Manuel Fernández Alvarez. *Anales de Economía* XVII (1957).
Pérez Moreda, Vicente. "The Plague in Castile at the end of the Sixteenth Century and Its Consequences." *The Castilian Crisis of the Seventeenth Century. New Perspectives on the Economic and Social History of Seventeenth-Century Spain*. Eds. I.A.A. Thompson and Bartolomé Yun Casalilla. Cambridge: Cambridge UP, 1994. 32-59.
Rojas, Fernando de. *La Celestina*. Ed. Dorothy S. Severin. Madrid: Cátedra, 1995.
Rodríguez, Juan Carlos. *La literatura del pobre*. Granada: Comares, 1994.
Rodríguez Matos, Carlos. *El narrador pícaro: Guzmán de* Alfarache. Madison: The Hispanic Seminary of Medieval Studies, 1985.
Rodríguez Puértolas, Julio. "*La Celestina* o la negación de la negación." *Literatura, Historia, Alienación*. Barcelona: Labor, 1976. 147-71.
Ruiz Martín, Felipe. *Pequeño capitalismo: Gran capitalismo: Simón Ruiz y sus negocios en Florencia*. Barcelona: Crítica, 1990.

Salomon, Nöel. *La vida rural castellana en tiempos de Felipe II*. Trans. Frances Espinet. Barcelona: Ariel, 1982.

Sánchez, Francisco J. *Lectura y representación: Análisis cultural de las "Novelas ejemplares" de Cervantes*. New York: Peter Lang, 1993.

Schumpeter, Joseph A. *History of Economic Analysis*. New York: Oxford UP, 1954.

Spadaccini, N., and A. Zahareas. "Introducción crítica" to their edition of *Estebanillo González*. Madrid: Castalia, 1978. Vol. 1, 9-120.

Vassberg, David E. *La venta de tierras baldías, el comunitarismo agrario y la corona de Castilla durante el siglo XVI*. Madrid: Servicio de Publicaciones Agrarias, 1983.

_____. *Land and Society in Golden Age Castile*. Cambridge: Cambridge UP, 1984.

Vega, José de la. *Confusión de confusiones. Diálogos curiosos entre un filósofo agudo, un mercader discreto y un accionista erudito . . .* (1688) Ed. facsimile. Madrid: Sociedad Española de Publicaciones, 1958.

Vilar, Pierre. *A History of Gold and Money. 1450-1920*. Trans. Judith White. London: New Left Books, 1976.

_____. "Los primitivos españoles del pensamiento económico. 'Cuantitativismo' y 'bullonismo.'"*Crecimiento y desarrollo*. Barcelona: 1976. 135-62.

_____. "El problema de la formación del capitalismo." Ibid. 106-34.

_____. "El tiempo del *Quijote*." Ibid. 332-46.

Vives, Juan Luis. *Del socorro de los pobres, o de las necesidades humanas* (1526). Ed. *Biblioteca de Autores Españoles*. Vol. 35. Madrid: Rivadeneyra. 261-91.

Wallerstein, Immanuel. *The Modern World-System*. New York: Academic Press, 1974, 1980. 2 vols.

Yun Casalilla, Bartolomé. *Sobre la transición al capitalismo en Castilla*. Salamanca: Juanta de Castilla y León, 1987.

Chapter 4

Patronage, the Parody of an Institution in *Don Quijote*

Edward Baker

Don Quijote is a book of questionable paternity. We know this for we are told so by the first authorial voice we encounter on fiction's uncertain border, the narrator of the 1605 prologue: ". . . aunque parezco padre soy padrastro de don Quijote." ("But I, though in appearance Don Quixote's father, am really his step-father") (25).[1] The border is unclear because the prologue unfolds in the terrain where fiction and nonfiction meet. It is simultaneously text and paratext, and so it stands both within and without fiction's space, which in 1600 is an unsteady demarcation for writers and readers alike. This is not the place to take up the quarrel over whether the prologue's voice belongs to the empirical author, Miguel de Cervantes Saavedra, or is one of a series of authorial positions constructed and/or deconstructed throughout the course of the fiction, although I think that in *Don Quixote: An Anatomy of Subversive Discourse*, James Parr has made a reasonably faithful description of the formal mechanisms of authorship and, in general, of the metafiction contained in the early chapters of the *Quijote*. My concern here is to broaden the notion of paternity, and thus of authorship, to include the institution of patronage.

There is a very great deal of recent critical and scholarly literature on the general theme of patronage in early modern Europe, beginning with Sir Francis Haskell's work dating from the 1960s, and in general its quality is very high. Unfortunately for literary scholars, the bulk of that work, and by and large the best of it, has been done by and for art historians. What is true of Europe in general can also be said of Spain in particular. Historical work on patronage in early modern Spanish art has allowed no less an authority than Jonathan Brown to state in his prologue to Fernando Checa's superb work, *Felipe II. mecenas de las artes*, that "durante los últimos veinte años han sido muchos los estudios que se han dedicado al mecenazgo artístico de la rama española de los Habsburgo, y ello ha tenido como resultado una percepción mucho mas clara de su papel preponderante en el escenario del arte europeo." This is so because in the period that immediately interests me, roughly the twenty or so years surrounding the writing and publication of the first part of *Don Quixote*, artistic patronage is somewhat more evolved than is its literary analogue, and for good reasons. Costly artistic projects in early modern Europe left behind abundant documentation, including the contractual arrangements whereby those projects were undertaken.

Moreover, in the development of seigneurial societies in Catholic Europe, the channeling of sumptuary expenditures by both secular and ecclasiastical princes toward forms of self-representation is of great importance. Here a nuance is in order: by "self-representation" I do not quite mean what ordinarily we understand in the present-day academy by the construction of subjectivity, but something more like individual embodiments of rank and, especially, the ceremonial forms of its display. Early modern artistic patronage is part, and a very important part, of the orientation of vast, new, and concentrated wealth toward highly spectacular and costly forms of the representation of rank. The very materiality of the great architecture, sculpture, and painting of the time presupposes enormous expenditures, and the necessary growth of institutions that channel them. Consequently, the status of architects, sculptors, and painters and the institutionalization of that status, including the increasingly elaborate institution of patronage, is considerably more evolved than is the status of writers. By way of example, there is no Spanish writer in the time of the Austrian monarchy whose standing in the broad area where the links of culture and power are forged is remotely as elevated as that of Velázquez.

This is particularly true of authors of the works that most interest us—literary ones. This essay is not the place to discuss in any detailed way the historical process by which the discursive formation that today we call literature arose. In the Spain of 1600, what today we understand as literature enjoyed an extremely ambiguous status and the complex forms of authorial and readerly subjectivity that are inseparable from the way we conceive literature scarcely existed. Therefore, we should take great care not to read our own subjectivity back into a historical past in such a way that, almost inevitably, we will discover in the Spain of 1600 what is not necessarily there. Literature had not quite yet emerged as an integrated discursive field—what Bourdieu and the French sociologists of culture call "le champ littéraire"—and certain key components of it, notably the novel, barely exist at all from the standpoint of the dominant culture of the time. Narrative fiction scarcely makes an appearance in the poetics and the discursive taxonomies of sixteenth- and seventeenth-century Spain, the land where literary historiography is forever telling us that the novel was "born." And yet in the early seventeenth century it hardly exists not only because key works such as the bulk of picaresque narrative, Cervantes's *Quijote* and the *Novelas ejemplares,* the *novela cortesana,* and so on, have yet to be composed or else have not yet been printed. Although this is the case, it seems far more important that the very great number of those books that were in print by 1600 were not yet understood as a single generic enterprise: the *Amadises, Dianas, Lazarillos,* and *Patrañuelos* did not quite constitute distinct forms or thematic varieties of a discrete genre—narrative fiction. Further, to the degree that such a generic undertaking existed, it could not readily be considered both lovely and useful, the Horatian standard for judging these matters, or, in consequence, remotely as important, that is, as ennobled and ennobling, as poetry. Put another way, the kinds of works that Cervantes wrote, the *Galatea,* the *Quijote,* the *Novelas ejemplares,* and the *Persiles,* did not quite yet belong to a unified discursive field, but rather to four distinct though related ones.

Recreational reading, the sole category capable of containing them, was so governed by dispersion that today we are hardly able to recognize it as a category at all. Here, the problem for literary historiography is two-edged. On the one hand, recreational reading had no standing in the poetics or in the discursive taxonomies of early modern Spain, and there is no compelling reason why it should, since it neither is now nor was then a discursive category at all but a social and functional one. On the other, it has not received the kind of attention that it deserves from our own critics and historians, for we have been slow to describe and analyze actual reading practices of concretely historical readers belonging to diverse social classes, although starting in the 1970s, scholars as diverse as Eisenberg, Chevalier, Whinnom, Berger, Frenk, Ife, Bouza, and Nalle have made a very good beginning at bringing the question to our attention. Seen from the perspective of who read what as well as how and why they read it and what they made of it, the books that today we regard in their generic commonality as novels were bound together not so much by the thematic or formal unity that manifestly they did not possess as by a social function. They filled unoccupied time, that is, time not otherwise claimed by obligations to God or Man, and occasionally, though not always, filled it in ways that moralists did not consider excessively harmful.

Let us look very briefly at the consequences of that statement. It means that the *Celestina*, the *Diana, La Gitanilla,* and *Las harpías de Madrid* stood in roughly the same functional relation to readers of the time as collections of apothegmatic writings, miscellanies like the *Silva de varia lección*, jokebooks, travelogues mixing varying degrees of fantasy with equally varying degrees of reality, chronicles that did likewise, and a vast and diverse etcetera that merits far more attention than it has received. Finally, in 1600 there has not yet emerged anything like what we regard as the professional writer who lived or attempted to make a living producing literary commodities for what Bourdieu characterizes as the market of symbolic goods. The authorial subject, or rather the range of authorial subjects that we associate with literary creation, will be constructed by a culture that begins in the Enlightenment and reaches its culmination in the twentieth century, in the high modernism of the interwar period, although its roots can be found in the vastly expanded market for recreational books that in Spain emerged during the seventeenth century. One of them was the *Quijote,* and its author was sufficiently concerned with the status of authorship, with the authority or lack thereof invested in a certain kind of writing, to inscribe the problem in that book's fiction and metafiction, and to do so in ways that still puzzle us. It is also the case that roughly between the last quarter of the eighteenth and the first half of the nineteenth century, those emerging authorial subjects were projected historically upon the newly constructed field of a properly national literature and culture. Thus, by way of example, we have an historiography that speaks to us about the Spanish literature of the Middle Ages, referring to a social formation (Spain), an object of knowledge (literature), and an historical period (the Middle Ages), none of which really existed in the time of Berceo, Juan Ruiz, or Francisco Imperial. Moreover, this kind of literary historiography tends to homogenize notions of authorship, assimilating Santillana, Calderón, Galdós, and Lorca to roughly the same status in the long and transhistorically conceived march of Spanish literary history.

With this in mind, we can return to the question of patronage and the institutions that govern what in the last two centuries we have come to regard as literary authorship. There is a sense in which patronage, or rather the pairing of patronage-clientage, is simply the way of referring to a very broad range of early modern social practices in state and church affairs, as well as in the arts and letters. It is a term for one of the important ways in which the hierarchies of seigniorial society work, for what an art historian, Werner Gundersheimer, calls "virtually a permanent structure characteristic of all early European material high culture" (3). It was all-pervasive in early modern Europe and provoked the constant complaints of humanists and writers. The most serious questioning of it in the sixteenth century can be found in Thomas More's *Utopia*, precisely because it posits the abolition of the property relations upon which patronage rests. Gundersheimer observes: "The general point is evident: in eliminating hierarchy, More has at least theoretically annihilated political, religious and apparently artistic patronage, the very existence of which depends on differences of wealth, occupation and status" (8). So it is useful to keep in mind that patronage is a set of social practices that condition virtually all areas of nobiliary and ecclesiastical existence, and not only the immediate artistic, intellectual, and literary uses to which surplus will be put. Stated in the sociologese of Eisenstadt and Runiger, patron-client relations

> denote . . . a distinct mode of regulating crucial aspects of institutional order: the structuring of the flow of

> resources exchange and power relations and their legitimation in society. This implies that, while many organizational aspects of patron-client relations . . . can be found in many different societies, yet their full institutional implications and repercussions are seen only when they become a part or manifestation of the central mode of regulating the flow of resources and processes of interpersonal and institutional exchange and interaction in a society or a sector thereof. (49)

It should be clear from the foregoing that this mode of regulation was not merely individual in scope. In *Naissance de l'écrivain*, Alain Viala has pointed out that in France there was always a powerful personage or a political clan behind the literary academies, (51) and we could add that in the Europe of the time it is difficult to conceive of a powerful personage in the absence of a political clan. Patronage, then, for our immediate purposes, is the means whereby early modern European societies organize and regulate the dispensing of resources devoted to the arts and humanities, including, although mostly at the edges, the kind of writing we regard as literary. Thus, the patron-client relation stood at the very center of a writer's activity, for as Robert Evans puts it in his work on *Ben Johnson and the Poetics of Patronage*: "The connection between poetry and patronage, then, involved more than how writers were paid, the way they made their livings. It involved, more fundamentally, how they lived their lives" (23). Finally, we may add that patronage in all its forms was intensely patriarchal, even when dispensed by a matriarch.

We might ask, then, what happened to authors in the Spain of 1600 who stood outside the networks of patronage or had irregular access to them. They wrote for "the market," and I place those words in quotation marks because I would like to convey the idea that by simply evoking "the market" in connection with the print world of Cervantes's time we may be suggesting something more than is really there. This is especially the case if we look at the problem from the standpoint of literature and its ambiguous status in that world. Some twenty years ago, Maxime Chevalier pointed out in *Lectura y lectores en la Espana del siglo XVI y XVII* that in private libraries of the period there is relatively little of what we regard as literature (25). Careful reading of book lists would seem to confirm that observation, although not necessarily Chevalier's view that its cause was the low cultural level of readers, particularly among the nobility. Far more plausible are Laspéras' observations regarding the distortions produced by the sources, nearly always testamentary documents. He argues that relatively youthful readers favored recreational books and tended to discard them with the onset of old age (537). In an article on what was actually read or at least printed in sixteenth- and seventeenth-century Spain, Keith Whinnom made substantially the same point in a very effective way: if we examine the world of print in Cervantes's time, the Golden Age so-called, we find that it is dominated by devotional writings of one sort or another. There is not a single author whose work we value as great literature—not Quevedo, not even Lope, certainly not Cervantes—whose presence in the early modern Spanish world of print can even remotely be compared to that of Fray Luis de Granada, whose *Libro de la oración*, a prayer manual, was far and away the book most often reprinted in the sixteenth and seventeenth centuries, with more than one hundred appearances in print. Casting his gaze beyond the opposition between literary and devotional works, Whinnom remarks that if we are going to concentrate on "pure literature," which is an entirely justifiable and perfectly legitimate choice—we ought at least to remember that for every work of pure literature there was at least one other book which was more widely read. *Celestina* was outdone by the *Libro de la oración*, *Diana* was overshadowed by Fray Luis de Granada's *Guía de pecadores, Don Quijote* saw fewer editions than Pedro Mexia's *Silva de varia lección*. Lope's *Arcadia* does not match Guevara's *Epfstolas familiares* (Whinnom 194).

So, let us return to our question: what happens to the author—not necessarily one we regard as specifically literary, simply an author—without a patron, who stands outside or at the margins of the aristocratic and ecclesiastical institutions and their mechanisms for allocating resources and signaling approval? Cervantes himself satirized such an author in Part 2, Chapter 22 of the *Quijote:* he is the cousin of the "licenciado," the man who guides Don Quijote and Sancho to the Cave of Montesinos. Putting it in the best possible light we could say that the cousin is an independent scholar; in actuality he is an unattached scribbler, an out-of-control logorrheic whose profession, or so he avows, is that of humanist, and whose "ejercicio," he states, is "componer libros para dar a la estampa, todos de gran provecho y no menos entretenimiento para la república" ("compose books for the press, all of great profit and entertainment to the commonwealth") (610). One bears the title *el de las libreas*, "donde pinta setecientas y tres libreas, con sus colores, notas y cifras, de donde podían sacar y tomar las que quisiesen en tiempo de fiestas y regocijos los caballeros cortesanos sin andarlas mendigando de nadie, ni lambicando, como dicen, el cerbelo, por sacarlas conformes a sus deseos e intenciones" (2, 205-06) ("*The Book of Liveries*, in which he described seven hundred and three devices with their colours, mottoes and ciphers. From these the gentlemen of the court could extract and use whatever they pleased at festival times and celebrations, and would then have no need to beg their liveries from anybody, or to rack their brains, as they say, to invent them to suit their desires and purpose") (610). The cousin further elucidates his "ejercicio":

> Otro libro tengo también a quien he de llamar *Metamorfoseos. o Ovidio español*, de invención nueva y rara; porque en el, imitando a Ovidio a lo burlesco, pinto quien fue la Giralda de Sevilla y el Angel de la Madalena, quien el Caño de Vecinguerra, de Córdoba, quienes los Toros de Guisando, la Sierra Morena, las fuentes de Leganitos y Lavapiés, en Madrid, no olvidándome de la del Piojo, de la del Caño Dorado y de la Priora; y esto, con sus alegorías, metáforas y translaciones, de modo que alegran, suspenden y enseñan a un mismo punto. (2, 206)
>
> (I have another book as well, which I mean to call Metamorphoses, or the Spanish Ovid, a new and rare invention. In it, parodying Ovid, I give an account of the Giralda of Seville and the Angel of the Magdalen, the Gutter of Vecinguerra at Cordova and the Bulls of Guisano; the Sierra Morena; the fountains of Leganitos and Lavapies in Madrid, not omitting those of the Piojo, of the Golden Gutter, and the Priora; all this with such allegories, metaphors, and transformation as will delight, surprise and instruct at the same time.) (610)

He goes on in this vein, explaining the contents of another, similarly off-kilter and absurdly imitative, effort, the *Suplemento a Virgilio Polidoro*. However, his last remark on the *Ovidio*'s value is especially telling, because it virtually repeats the observation that Don Diego de Miranda, the Caballero del Verde Gabán, makes in Part 2, Chapter 16, regarding his tastes in reading:

> Tengo hasta seis docenas de libros, cuales de romance y cuales de latín, de historia algunos y de devoción otros; los de caballerías aun no han entrado por los umbrales de mis puertas. Hojeo más los que son profanos que los devotos, como sean de honesto entretenimiento, que deleiten con el lenguaje y admiren y suspendan con la invención, puesto que destos hay muy pocos en España. (2, 153)

> (I have about six dozen books, some in Spanish and some in Latin, some historical and some devotional, but books of chivalry have never so much as crossed the threshold of my door. I read profane books more than devotional, since they give me honest entertainment, delighting me by their language, and arresting and startling me by their inventions—though there are very few of this kind in Spain.) (566)

Don Diego de Miranda's and the cousin's views on recreational reading are remarkably similar, but it is not likely that Don Diego would agree that the cousin's efforts, should they see the light of day, might delight their readers with their language and astonish them with their inventiveness, thus increasing their number in Spain, where, Don Diego believes, there are few such works.

The cousin's conversation with Don Quijote and Sancho is very revealing of his abiding unreason and the knight's and squire's momentary reasonableness. Sancho asks him a question of the kind regularly found in the recreational books that collected jokes, games, questions, and answers and that were very popular at the time:

> Dígame señor, así Dios le de buena manderecha en la impresión de sus libros: sabríame decir, que sí sabrá, pues todo lo sabe, quién fue el primero que se rascó en la cabeza, que yo para mí tengo que debió de ser nuestro padre Adán? (2, 206-07)

(Tell me, sir—good luck to you with the printing of your books—but can you say—though I know you ca, for you know everything—who was the first man to scratch his head? For it's my opinion that it must have been our father Adam.) (611)

The series of questions and answers lead to Sancho's conclusion that "para preguntar necedades y responder disparates no he menester yo andar buscando ayuda de vecinos" ("if it's a matter of asking stupid questions and giving foolish answers I've no need to go looking for help from the neighbours") (611), and Don Quijote's agreement: "Más has dicho, Sancho, de lo que sabes . . . ; que hay algunos que se cansan en saber y averiguar cosas que, después de sabidas y averiguadas, no importan un ardite al entendimiento ni a la memoria" (2, 207) ("You have said more than you know, Sancho, said Don Quixote, for there are some who tire themselves out learning and proving things which, once learnt and proved, do not concern either the understanding or the memory a jot") (611). The humanist-cousin's relative, the "licenciado," describes him as a "famoso estudiante y muy aficionado a leer libros de caballerías." Famous he may or may not be, but we can easily believe that he is an avid reader of chivalric romance. The parallel with Don Quijote is sufficiently clear so that we need not insist on it in any detail: he is to writing what the knight errant is to reading.

What immediately concerns us is that in the figure of the improvised humanist we have, reduced to absurdity, the profession of "componer libros para dar a la estampa," writing for the market pure and simple. No more awful fate could befall an early modern writer and it is deeply revealing both that the cousin's effort have not yet seen the light of day, although he writes for that purpose alone, and that Cervantes never accepted his own fate as an author who wrote books "para dar a la estampa." Although it has been argued very convincingly that Cervantes was not the starveling of romantic legend (Eisenberg 1986), still it is clear that he failed miserably to build the sort of conventional career that he sought when he made his way to the Court upon his release from Algerian captivity in 1580. When, in 1585, Part 1 of the *Galatea* saw the light of day, it was the first of Cervantes's works to gain access to the world of print and—other than the occasional bit of encomiastic verse—the last to do so for twenty years. In the time separating the two books, Cervantes stood at the margins of the institutional circuits that provided some of those who wrote with a certain standing and income. Unlike the cousin, he did not "componer libros para la estampa," but for considerably more than the years separating the *Galatea* from the *Quijote*, no patron bestowed gifts upon him, including, as far as we call tell, the man to whom he dedicated the first volume of his masterpiece.

In the first of a series of three brilliant essays on early modern European print culture that make up *The Order of Books*, Roger Chartier has given us a reading of the *Quijote*'s title page in which Cervantes is positioned between a putative patron, don Alonso Diego López de Zuñiga y Sotomayor, seventh duke of Béjar, and the visible signs of the market—the "privilegio," the printer Juan de la Cuesta, the well-known Madrid bookseller Francisco de Robles. Chartier correctly emphasizes the dominance of patronage (43-46). Although there is compatibility between the two, in the semifeudal and seigneurial Castile of 1600, and indeed in seigneurial Europe in general, there is no equality between the market and the system of patronage, personified in this instance by the nobleman whose titles are spelled out for all to read. He is "duque de Béjar, marqués de Gibraleón, conde de Benalcáçar, y Bañares, vizconde de la Puebla de Alcozer, señor de las villas de Capilla, Curiel y Burguillos." Béjar was a personage of very high rank who was in a position to bestow great favor upon a writer or artist, should he choose to do so, as on occasion he did. But, as Alain Viala reminds us, patronage is a two-way street: "Le poète se divinise en divinisant le mécène" (70). The poet elevates the bestower of gifts to the heavens and in doing so is similarly elevated. In the system of rank and honor and the symbolic forms of expression that governed social esteem in Cervantes's world, divinization was not available to those who wrote solely for the market, who, like the cousin of the "licenciado," "componían libros para dar a la estampa," and whether or not Cervantes raised Béjar to the heavens, his troubles went unrewarded.

Cervantes's discomfort—of Béjar's we have no record—is visible in the dedication of the 1605 *Quijote,* beginning with the fact that much of it is lifted from another dedication, Herrera's to the marqués de Ayamonte in the 1580 annotated edition of Garcilaso's poetry. Vicente Gaos opportunely reminds us that from beginning to end the *Quijote* is seeded with other texts; indeed it is a veritable riot of intertextuality, and Gaos calls attention to the parodic aspects contained in those citations in general and those of the dedication in particular: "En vista de lo cual, calladamente acude a Herrera para que hable por él, en paradójico rasgo de humor, pues la dedicatoria, en este punto, es una humorada" (15) ("In light of which he silently goes to Herrera so that he may speak for him, in a paradoxical stroke of humor, for the dedication, at this point, is playful and humorous"). "Una humorada" which, like the rest of the *Quijote,* parodies the conventions of a remarkable range of discursive practices, and not just romances of chivalry.

Of all the targets of Cervantes's parodic wit, none is more purely conventional than the dedication, and I would like briefly to examine two related aspects of the genre's conventionality. In the symbolism attached to the early modern system governing writers' protection and their service to their protectors, the putative beneficiary of the dedication, the patron, is codified both as the father or patriarch of the book and its first or at least its privileged reader, and I suspect that the code retained its symbolic function whether or not the patron actually read the book. In *Ben Johnson and the Poetics of Patronage,* Robert C. Evans reminds us of the hierarchies of Elisabethan society: "With God the Father at the head of an enormous chain of subordinate relationships, with the monarch as God's vice-gerent on earth and as a father to his people, and with individual fathers as little sovereigns, minor masters of their own families and households, Renaissance culture formed a web of patriarchal relations" (24). The God of the Habsburgs may not have been identical in every regard to that of the Tudors, but if momentarily we leave aside theological niceties, Evans's characterization is fully applicable to Spain. The seigneurial sense of patriarchy is a key to understanding the very limited authority of authorship in European culture prior to the general crisis and eventual dissolution of the various *anciens régimes,* and we can see this reflected in dedicatory writing. Beginning in the nineteenth century, the closer we come to the present day, the more the dedication is an affair of the heart; most often it expresses affective relations of one kind or another. But even when it does express relations of subordination it tend toward the laconic. The modern dediction is a one- or two-line expression of gratitude, as distinct from the usually more elaborate paratexts of early modern print culture. The centered bourgeois author of modern times is, after all, the sovereign producer of a commodity, the book. In turn, the modern the bourgeois reader, the purchaser and consumer of that commodity, shares with him a measure of that sovereignty. Early modern authors were far more likely to aspire to some form of clientage, whether in the form of a relation of momentary favor or long-term servitude as a lord's secretary, his son's preceptor, or some similar arrangement. Whatever the relation, authorial authority in early modern print culture was substantially dependent upon the largesse of a nobleman or woman or, alternately, that of a prince of the Church.

Now we can turn our attention fully to the dual and related questions of patriarchy and household, in that order. If the 1605 prologue's voice belongs not to the father but to the stepfather of *El ingenioso hidalgo don Quixote de la Mancha*, it is not merely because he cannot be considered the sole author or be assimilated to the voice of the empirical author, Cervantes. The *Quijote* is a book whose metafiction parodically works through the multileveled question of origins and authorship of a certain kind of book, not exactly a "novel" but, more broadly and in a way that I would argue is more historically accurate, a work of recreational reading, a "libro de entretenimiento" whose nobility stands in an inverse relation to its commodification. It is a book that is centrally occupied with what for Cervantes was the infinitely prickly matter of the very limited authority granted the authors of such productions by the dominant cultural values of Counter-Reformation Spain: armed Christianity and latinate humanism.

Let us look at this hierarchic relation between that culture and recreational books in the light of the 1605 *Quijote*'s most important paratext, the prologue. The prologue is a defense of storytelling set against a series of paratextual straw men, including prologues themselves and the encomiastic verse that is the point of access to so many books of the time. The stepfather of Don *Quijote*—we may regard him as the stepauthor—states in the prologue that he needs none of this, and repeats the attack made on ornamental writing contained in the dedication: "Sólo quisiera dártela monda y desnuda, sin el ornato de prólogo, ni de la inumerabilidad y catálogo de los acostumbrados sonetos, epigramas y elogios que al principio de los libros suele ponerse" (1, 51) ("I would have wished to present it to you naked and unadorned, without the ornament of prologue or the countless train of customary sonnets, epigrams and eulogies it is the fashion to place at the beginnings of books") (26). But the most important thrust is directed at the scholarly apparatus of Christian and humanistic learning that literally surrounds certain fictional works. Here the allusion to Lope's *Arcadia* is clear but its interest is essentially anectodal. What counts is the dismantling of the archive of Christian humanism as the legitimating device of recreational reading: the quotes from Plato, Aristotle, and "toda la caterva de filósofos," as well as from Sacred Scripture, the marginalia, the endnotes, the index of authors at the beginning, listed alphabetically from A to Z. The learned apparatus of the sacred and humanist archive is obviously a legitimating device for books of the kind that Cervantes avowedly wrote and defended in the prologue to the *Novelas ejemplares*: recreational books. And they require a defense because unlike theological and devotional works and those of secular learning which conform to the *doxa,* unlike even poetry which has noble practitioners and, when written according to precept, is able to wed beauty to truth, narrative fiction does not come equipped with the halo of legitimacy. The apparatus of sacred and profane learning is intended to provide that legitimacy or at least its appearance, but it can also be read in a contrary way, as a frame that the dominant discursive practices built around frivolous books so that if they could not be entirely eliminated, they could at least be contained. In the dialogue between *Don Quijote*'s stepfather and the friend who so opportunely turns up to solve the problem—how can so unlearned a man write a suitable prologue?—the frame simultaneously is shattered through ridicule and enfolded into the story, so that the discourses that constitute the frame become raw textual material for the tale of authorial woe the stepauthor dialogically tells. Thus, the narrator arrogates to himself an authorial autonomy and to his narrative a discursive legitimacy that the dominant culture could not and would not provide.

Today and since the nineteenth century, that autonomy has been based on a fully constructed discursive formation, the one we call literature. Literature enjoys a prestige underpinned by both state and civil institutions—education, publishing, prizes and honors of every description—that, at least in the realm of high culture, provides, it with a legitimacy that rarely is questioned, and grants to successful authors a considerable measure of wealth and autonomy. Simultaneously, modern subjectivity finds its proper resting place in romantic and postromantic authorial subjects. In Cervantes's time this was not the case, and, as I have just suggested, of all the genres which today constitute literature, narrative fiction was held in the lowest regard in the seventeenth century; it was the one most lacking and immediately in need of the autonomy with which Cervantes attempts to endow it.

To my students who were about to embark upon a reading of the *Quijote,* I have on occasion explained in the following way this bid for the purely discursive autonomy of a mere fabulist and his fable in a world that denied him social autonomy as an author and the contrast between Cervantes's time and our own. In the seventeenth century, a teacher who in an institution of higher learning proposed a seminar on *Don Quijote*, or *La pícara Justina* or a work of apothegmatic writings, or some of the miscellanies of the period, or any other recreational books such as collections of proverbs, question-and-answer books, collections of *chascarrillos,* and the vast etcetera that made up the world of recreational reading would have been taken for a lunatic. True, philology could be used to comment upon certain contemporary texts—Herrera's *Garcilaso* is a stunning example, but the notion of turning that science to a reading of, let us say, the *Romancero* or *Marcos de Obregón*, much less doing so in, let us say, the University of Salamanca, would have been considered absurd. Yet this is precisely what Cervantes proposed in the dedication of the 1615 *Quijote* to don Pedro Fernández Ruiz de Castro, conde de Lemos. It is, I think, very difficult for us to appreciate fully the hilarity of his statement to Lemos that no less a personage than the Emperor of China has proposed to found a school to teach his subjects the Castillian language and that the text of those lessons is to be none other than the *Quijote,* whose author will be the college's rector. We cannot fully appreciate it because although the *Quijote* is a very funny book, it is also today, and for some two hundred years has been, the jewel in the crown of Spanish letters, the centerpiece of a national culture and an imperial language, itself an institution within the institution of literature.

Thus, it is difficult, indeed all but impossible, for us to grasp the deep hilarity of a proposition that recommends itself in 1615 for its sheer, utter outlandishness. Colleges taught the disciplines associated with catholic Christianity and latinity; they taught law, both canon and civil; they taught theology and scholastic philosophy. Unlike ourselves, they did not teach recreational readings nor were they run by the authors of such books. The paternity of this kind of book might be called into question, but why should anyone in a position of authority, whether civil or ecclesiastical, care one way or the other, unless the book's language and themes were contrary to the *doxa* and, therefore, belonged in the *Index librorum prohibitorum*? At least in this very important sense, the books that we classify as literary were not very different from other books that doctrinally were suspect, although from the standpoint of the moralists, the fact that they were also great fun was not exactly a palliative.

So it is in the field of discourse where the empirical author, Miguel de Cervantes Saavedra, an unattached writer of what at the time were properly regarded as mere fabulations, arrogated to himself a measure of the authority that *socially* was unavailable to him other than by way of transmission from above, through the subordination of the patron-client relation. But Cervantes also alluded to the space of that authority—the household. Here, in his house, the authorial voice of the prologue, the *Quijote*'s stepfather, is autonomous indeed. And so he argues, albeit in a backhanded way, when he addresses the reader, the "desocupado lector": ". . . y tienes tu alma y tu cuerpo y tu libre albedrío como el más pintado, y estás en tu casa, donde eres señor de ella" (51). The implication is clear: "estás en tu casa donde eres señor de ella," *and so am I*, for as he immediately demonstrates in the prologue, he, the stepwriter, is the lord both of his household and the tales that he tells when he is in it. Unlearned he may be, but he is lord of his unlearned home. That authorial autonomy is then replicated at the level of the reader, Don Quijote, in his own household. Within the space of his library, Don Quijote is a singular case of readerly autonomy, for he has forsaken his habitual occupations and alienated his patrimony in order to buy the books that fill it, and reading those exclusively recreational books has become his sole occupation (Baker 15-17), so that he is truly a reader for the writer—even if only a stepwriter—constructed in the prologue.

The passage in the prologue on the household not only echoes the allusion to households in the dedication, but, as we shall see, in the parody of patronage contained in Part 1, chapter 9, as well. As Gaos points out in the appendix to his edition of the *Quijote,* the dedication to Béjar, like most of his dedications, is an exercise in self-justification. "Hay que observar que en las dedicatorias de sus libros lo que suele hacer Cervantes, más que adular a los nobles a quienes los dirige, es autoelogiarse" (15) ("One must note that in the dedications to his books Cervantes engages in self-praise more than in the adulation of the nobles to whom they are directed"). In the dedication Cervantes eases into a falsely self-deprecatory tone. He solicits Béjar's protection of a book that is "desnudo de aquel precioso ornamento de elegancia y erudición de que suelen andar vestidas las obras que se componen en las casas de los hombres que saben" (49) ("naked of that precious adornment of elegance and erudition in which works composed in the houses of the learned usually go clothed") (23), deploying the anti-ornamentation motif that, as we have seen, is then repeated in the prologue. The *Quijote* is so obviously not a book composed in the house of a learned man, a man equipped to furnish the work with the necessary ornaments of refinement and erudition, that one such man, the stepauthor of the prologue, needs a friend to provide him with both an ornamental strategy and bits and snippets of ancient authors to carry it out. So he, the stepwriter, surely does not qualify as a man of learning and the book that he has stepwritten does not qualify as one composed in such a man's house, and the same reasoning may be applied to the empirical author. This being the case, what earthly reason would Béjar have to grant the work his protection and, in effect, to become its symbolic father and the reader who will confer upon it a legitimacy that manifestly it does not possess?

This disqualification of the book is further developed in the pages of Part 1, Chapter 9, in which the *Quijote*'s metafiction turns on a parody of patronage. In Chapter 8 there is a break in the plot. Don Quijote and the "vizcaino," swords raised on high, are about to cut one another in half, but what actually is cut in half is the story, so that the "fendientes" that the two swordsmen never discharge are objectified in the text, effecting the formal division between parts one and two. Each

of these parts has its author. Chapter 8 concludes with the narrator informing us that

> en este punto y término deja pendiente el autor desta historia esta batalla, disculpándose que no halló más escrito, destas hazañas de don Quijote, de las que deja referidas. Bien es verdad que el segundo autor desta obra no quiso creer que tan curiosa historia estuviese entregada a las leyes del olvido . . . y así no se desesperó de hallar el fin desta apacible historia, el cual, siéndole el cielo favorable, le halló del modo que se contará en la segunda parte. (1, 137-38)
>
> ("the author of this history left the battle in suspense at this critical point, with the excuse that he could find no more records of Don Quixote's exploits than those related here. It is true that the second author of this work would not believe that such a curious history could have been consigned to oblivion . . . so, he did not despair of finding the conclusion of this delightful story and, by the favour of Heaven, found it, as shall be told in our second part.") (74-75)

Here, a new narrative voice turns to the first person and recounts the tale of how the second author's manuscript was found and how he, the reader of the first manuscript, was instrumental in bringing the second one to light.

It is he who finds the second manuscript in the Alcaná de Toledo, purchases the papers that the boy has come to sell to a silk merchant, finds a "morisco aljamiado" to translate the Arabic manuscript into *aljamía*, that is, Castillian, and sets the translator up in his house. In sum, he acts not only as the anxiety-ridden reader of a mere fragment of a proven page turner but, more importantly, as the morisco's patron. Let us have a look at both these roles. They are very closely related, because, as I observed at the outset, symbolically the patron is the first or privileged reader of the text, and he discharges the obligations flowing from that privilege by gracing the work with his approval and the author with his protection (or not, according to his whim.) The model patron is noble, learned, wealthy, generous, and discerning, and he grants his largesse to works possessing similar characteristics, those enbellished with the noble trappings of humanistic learning, written in the houses of learned men. By contrast, the improvised patron of Chapter 9 of the *Quijote* is a not particularly discerning devourer of writing of just about any kind: "[Y]o soy aficionado a leer, aunque sean los papeles rotos de las calles" ("I have a taste for reading even torn papers lying in the streets") (76). These words, which so often have been read as Cervantes's self-congratulation at his insatiable intellectual curiosity, when seen in a parodic context, are not necessarily an effusion of praise. This indiscriminate reader can also be seen as a satire of the "desocupado lector" invoked in the prologue. Since to all appearances he has nothing better to do, he seems to have devoted himself fully to seeking out the continuation of the manuscript so that he might discover what happened to Don Quijote and the "vizcaino," and he tells us of "el trabajo y diligencia que puse en buscar el fin desta agradable historia" (1, 142) ("my toil and pains in searching for the end of this delightful history") (76). But of course he is the "desocupado lector" of what amounts to nothing more than a good read, or a fragment thereof. And so he goes to no end of trouble for a book that in his own words will provide almost a couple of hours' pleasure. This sounds about right for a recreational book, the kind that was read for surcease between occupations, demands, and obligations of a very serious kind, but not for the sort of writing that would justify the complete abandonment of those duties and exigencies.

And in this the reader/patron/author of Part 1, Chapter 9, is more like Don Quijote than are any of the characters in Cervantes's tale of madness and knight errantry, for this is precisely what Don Quijote has already done. When we analyzed the authorial voice in the 1605 prologue, we saw that Don Quijote's autonomy as a reader was similar to that voice's autonomy as a writer, for the hidalgo had abandoned his usual occupations and sold his patrimony to buy books. Following which, he did absolutely nothing but read chivalric romance day and night until his brain dried up, and so rather than a momenarily "desocupado lector" he becomes what I have called a full-time reader of part-time books (Baker 28). Now we can easily see the parallel between the mad hidalgo and the metafictional reader who even reads papers picked up in the street and drops everything in order to find the continuation to a tale of adventure. And we cannot know what everything is because he is not so much a character as a narratological function, and thus has no life, no fictional existence of his own. He sets out on a parodic quest for the sole purpose, like any reader of nineteenth-century *folletines* or any listener or viewer of their legitimate successors, the serialized, plot-driven radio soap operas and adventure movies of the thirties and forties, or the TV soaps of more recent times, of answering the all-important question that informs his metafictional existence: What happens next?

To add to his not terribly elevated taste in reading, our reader/patron is also something of a chiseler. He buys the entire packet of manuscripts from the boy for half a *real* when, by his own admission, it surely was worth six. And rather than money, he pays the morisco both on the cheap and in kind: two *arrobas* of raisins and two *fanegas* of wheat. In fact, this latter detail is a repetition of a motif that Cervantes had already employed. In Chapter 1, the hidalgo sells his land to buy books; what he actually sells are "muchas hanegas de tierra de sembradura," that is, wheat land, for the word "hanega" or "fanega" was used both as a measure of grain and the amount of land needed to produce it. So, the worth of the rest of *El ingenioso hidalgo don Quijote de la Mancha*, from Chapter 9 to the conclusion, can be measured both in time—a good way to kill two hours—and if not in money in produce—so many raisins and so much wheat. All of this is at a very great remove from the mutual sacralization ("le poète se divinise en divinisant le mécène") that Viala quite rightly sees at the symbolic core of the patron-client system in early modern European letters that sacralizes a pecuniary relationship which at bottom was a form of beggary that Samuel Johnson eschewed in his letter to Chesterfield. But that was in mideighteenth-century England, when a market for symbolic goods made it possible for some of those who produced for it to survive and then some. A century and a half earlier and in Spain, Lope made a living from the sort of thing that Viala describes. Cervantes wished that he could, was unable to do so, and wrote a parody for a world in which the noble birth of certain kinds of poetry, the Horatian art that is both sweet and useful, might be divinely inspired, but a commodity found in the street like the *Quijote* would have to make do with raisins and wheat, and with a morisco translator rather than Calliope.

Cervantes's frustration and his response to it are to be found not only in Part 1, Chapter 9, of the 1605 *Quijote* and in the dedication to Béjar but also, ten years hence, in the dedication of the 1615 *Quijote* to what for him was a far more important personage, Lemos. In Part 1, Chapter 9, to make certain that the translation is done right, the finder of the manuscript temporarily makes the morisco part of his household. He, as distinct from the man of learning and refinement whose house is invoked in the 1605 dedication, actually descends to reading papers found by sheer chance in the streets. The invitation of the morisco to the patron's house is particularly hilarious in view of the moriscos' standing in Spanish society, and also because one of the solutions to the economic problems of early modern writers was to become part of a lord's household, in effect a servant. This could be a desirable sinecure in a seigneurial society and a deeply patriarchal and clientelistic culture in which it was virtually impossible to survive, much less make a career, from the proceeds of writing, that is, to live off the sale to a printer of the "privilegio," the royal grant of the right to print the work in a certain place for a stipulated amount. He writes for the market, a somewhat degraded activity and a somewhat degraded place, for let us not forget that the market is also the city street, which is where our improvised patron found both the Arabic manuscript and the morisco translator in this parody of literary legitimation. The Alcaná, the Toledan street of, among others, Jewish merchants, was a far cry from the palaces of great lords and the homes of learned men. And lest we think that Cervantes disdained the patronage that he parodied, let us not forget that when, toward the end of his life, he did at last secure a patron, Lemos, he was bitterly disappointed when the great man journeyed to Italy as viceroy of Naples and failed to grant Cervantes's wish to be taken along as part of a brilliant literary court. Hence his jibe in the dedication to Lemos of the 1615 *Quijote* about the Emperor of China.

The metafictional voice in Part l, Chapter 9 that narrates the finding and translation of the second manuscript has multiple functions. He is both reader and patron, but he is also the author in a limited but still in the seventeenth century important sense that as patron he is responsible for the manuscript's reaching our hands and quite probably, as Parr argues, has editorial functions as well. And leaving aside the parodic qualities of the metafiction, there is nothing capricious or absurd about this, for in the symbolic system of literary patronage in seigniorial societies, the patron in effect becomes the lord of the book. Not, of course, in the serious sense, the politically and juridically binding sense, that Béjar was lord of the villages of Capilla, Curiel y Burguillos, as the title page of the 1605 *Quijote* informs us. As symbolic lord of the work dedicated to him, we have seen that he would be the privileged reader (whether or not he actually ready the work), but even more importantly he lent or refused to lend some of his social authority, a small portion of the weight of his rank, to an author who in most instances possessed very little of that all-important authoritative substance. Thus, it is not unreasonable to state that in a momentary and limited symbolic fashion, the patron was actually patron/reader/author. However, Cervantes's parody of patronage extends even further. It is inscribed in the *Quijote* as the fiction's metafictional instantiation, the tale's condition of possibility.

In sum, Cervantes rejected the institution of patronage at the level of discourse and wrote a hilarious parody of it. Nevertheless, in practice he both accepted and actively pursued it, although not nearly with the success that would have made a splendid conventional career for a writer of recreational books. Beginning with the prologue, he wrote a measure of authorial autonomy into the *Quijote,* but, not satisfied with the status of an unattached fabulist writing, like the *primo* in Part 2, Chapter 22, for *la estampa*, he cast about for patrons and at last found one, don Pedro Fernández de Castro, conde de Lemos, who seemingly failed to live up fully to Cervantes's not inconsiderable expectations. But that was after the 1605 *Quijote* and in no small measure due to its public acceptance. The *Quijote,* however, remained a fatherless book, but today it no longer requires seigneurial protection, for the institutional framework that governs its existence has changed radically. It is a key to the origins of a unified generic field, that of the novel, and is the centerpiece of a national literature. Both are unmistakably modern constructs. There is, however, a measure of continuity between us and the first internal reader, the first *lector in fabula* whose quest was not so much for Arthur, the Grail, or justice, as it was for the next episode. Now, as then, the *Quijote* commands the presence of reading subjects, albeit in ways that inevitably are vastly different from those of the seventeenth century, precisely because we come to it with the ideological furnishings of the last two hundred years. Nonetheless, for us, as for the metafictional reader/patron/author of Part 1, Chapter

9, to whom we still owe a debt of gratitude, it remains a very funny book and a proven page turner.

Notes

1. English translations of *Don Quijote* are from *The Adventures of Don Quixote*. Trans. J.M. Cohen. Baltimore: Penguin Books, 1950. Other translations are by the volume editors.

Works Cited

Baker, Edward. "Breaking the Frame: Don Quixote's Entertaining Books." *Cervantes* 16 (Spring 1996): 12-31.

Berger, Philippe. *Libro y lectura en la Valencia del Renacimiento*. Valencia: Edicions Alfons el Magnanim, 1987. 2 vols.

Bourdieu, Pierre. *Les règles de l'art.* Paris: Editions du Seuil, 1992.

Bouza Alvarez, Fernando J. *Del escribano a la biblioteca. La civilización escrita europea en la alta Edad Moderna (siglos XV-XVII.)* Madrid: Sintesis, 1992.

Carrascón, Guillermo. "En torno a la dedicatoria de la primera parte del *Quijote.*" *Anales Cervantinos* 29 (1991): 167-78.

Cervantes, Miguel de. *El ingenioso hidalgo don Quijote de la Mancha*. Ed. Luis Andrés Murillo. 3rd. ed. Madrid: Castalia, 1984. 3 vols.

Chartier, Roger. *The Order of Books*. Trans. Lydia G. Cochrane. Stanford: Stanford UP, 1994.

Checa, Fernando. *Felipe II mecenas de las artes*. Prologo de Jonathan Brown. 2d ed. Madrid: Nerea, 1993.

Chevalier, Maxime. *Lectura y lectores en la España del siglo XVI y XVII*. Madrid: Turner, 1976.

Eisenberg, Daniel. "Who Read the Romances of Chivalry?" *Kentucky Romance Quarterly* 20. 2 (1973). 209-33.

_____. "Did Cervantes Have a Library?" *Hispanic Studies in Honor of Alan D. Deyermond. A North American Tribute*. Ed. J.S. Miletic. Madison, Wis.: Hispanic Seminary of Medieval Studies, 1986. 93-106.

Eisenstadt, S.N, and Runiger, Louis. "Patron-Client Relations as a Model of Structuring Social Exchange."*Comparative Studies in Society and History* 22 (1980): 42-77.

Evans, Robert C. *Ben Jonson and the Poetics of Patronage*. Lewisburg: Bucknell UP, 1989.

Frenk, Margit. "Lectores y oidores. La difusion oral de la literatura en el Siglo de Oro." *Actas del Vll Congreso Internacional de Hispanistas*. Roma: Bulzoni, 1982. 101-23.

_____. "Ver, oír, leer. . . ."*Homenaje a Ana Maria Barrenechea.* Eds. Lía Schwartz Lerner and Isaías Lerner. Madrid: Castalia, 1984. 235-40.

Gaos, Vicente. "El duque de Béjar y la dedicatoria de la primera parte del *Quijote* de Miguel de Cervantes." *Don Quijote*. Tomo III. Apéndices, Gramática, Bibliografía e Índices. Edición crítica y comentario de Vicente Gaos. Madrid: 1987. 12-17.

Gundersheimer, Werner L. "Patronage in the Renaissance: An Exploratory Approach." *Patronage in the Renaissance*. Eds. Guy Fitch Lytle, and Stephen Orgel. Princeton: Princeton UP, 1981. 3-23.

Haskell, Francis. *Patrons and Painters: A Study in the Relation between Italian Art and Society in the Age of the Baroque*. [1963] 2nd. rev. ed. New Haven: Yale UP, 1980.

Ife, B.W. *Reading and Fiction in Golden-Age Spain. A Platonist Critique and Some Picaresque Replies*. Cambridge: Cambridge UP, 1985.

Laspéras, Jean Michel. "Chronique du livre espagnol. Inventaires de bibliothèques et documents de librairie dans le monde hispanique aux XVe, XVle, et XVlle siècles." *Revue Francaise d'Histoire du Livre* 28 (1980): 535-57.

Nalle, Sara. N. "Literacy and Culture in Early Modern Castile." *Past and Present* 125 (1989): 65-96.

Pardo Manuel de Villena, Alfonso. *Un mecenas español del siglo XVII. El conde de Lemos. Noticia de su vida y de su relación con Cervantes. Lope de Vega. los Argensola y demás literatos de la época*. Madrid: Imprenta de Jaime Rates Martfn, 1911.

Parr, James A. *Don Quixote: An Anatomy of Subversive Discourse*. Newark, Del.: Juan de la Cuesta, 1988.

Viala, Alain. *Naissance de l'écrivain. Sociologie de la littérature a l'âge classique*. Paris: Editions de Minuit, 1985.

Whinnom, Keith. "The problem of the 'Best-seller' in Spanish GoldenAge Literature." *Bulletin of Hispanic Studies* 57 (1980): 189-98.

◆ Chapter 5

Printing and Reading Popular Religious Texts in Sixteenth-Century Spain

Sara T. Nalle

Long ago, in his book *Erasmus and Spain*, the great Hispanist Marcel Bataillon described a whole class of Spanish religious literature, the devotional books written, translated, and published under the auspices of Cardinal Cisneros or during the reign of Charles V. Although it was clear from Bataillon's masterpiece that the printing press was absolutely crucial to the promotion of a new type of religiosity in sixteenth-century Spain, Bataillon himself was primarily interested in tracing the impact of Erasmian ideas on Spanish intellectual life. Consequently, he and those who have followed him have neglected to study many aspects of the popular religious press. Most fundamentally, for example, although we know that the Spanish church was deeply suspicious of religious books printed in the vernacular, we know very little about the market for these religious books—what was generally available and at what cost to the reader, and who the readers were. Just as importantly, although we also know that the church's fear of heresy led to the banning and censorship of many religious books in the vernacular, we do not know much about *how* they were read—what kind of reading would lead to the outright banning of so many texts? The books in question were not what we would call subversive. None advocated outright heresy, revolution, or social change, and yet they were treated as if they in fact could provoke such results.

In this article, I will take up both of these questions: the market for religious books, and the impact which these books could have on the public. While scholars have studied the history of printing in different Iberian cities, few have attempted either to analyze the actual business of selling books,[1] or to evaluate the ramifications of an expanded market in religious texts for potential readers.[2] As both of these topics are enormous, I will limit myself to suggesting how scholars may begin to evaluate the market for religious books, and to providing a case study of a lower class reader whose reading of seemingly innocent materials led to quite heretical results. Here I am not so much interested in the famous books of Spanish mysticism and Erasmianism which were read by well-educated laymen and nuns; their influence and prohibition has been the subject of much scholarly comment.[3] Rather, I hope to describe a world of books and readers which was considerably beneath the notice of the likes of Francisco de Osuna and Teresa de Avila: the work-a-day printed works and readers of popular Catholicism.

A great deal of ink has been spilt over the question of whether there was any market at all for books among lower class people during the Spanish Golden Age. The two arguing points have been literacy rates and the cost of books. In the past, Hispanists claimed that literacy was confined to the upper and middling classes of society, a tiny fraction of the population, who also were the only persons who could afford to purchase books. Such conclusions typically were based on studies of private libraries, usually inventoried at the time of death. We can easily appreciate the drawbacks to such an approach: only more valuable collections would be inventoried, and, only certain types of individuals (lawyers, ecclesiastics, noblemen, and merchants) were in a position to collect books. A number of years ago I showed that literacy rates were much higher than previously had been estimated (about half of Castilian males could read in the sixteenth century), and that the possession of books was rather more widespread than indicated by the evidence culled from testaments. As a consequence, the book market as a whole tended to reflect the relatively unsophisticated taste of middle and lower class readers, who were primarily interested in religious and didactic works (Nalle, 1989). Although we now know more about literacy and reading preferences than before, the second part of the question, the availability of books and pamphlets to readers of modest economic means, has never been answered in any systematic way. Because of the selective nature of the sources, information provided by testaments or in Inquisition interviews can only hint at the true range of the market. Rather than to rely on the fragmentary evidence which comes to us via consumers, in this article I will reverse the process, and begin with evidence which describes the activities of distributors: inventories from sixteenth-century printers and booksellers.

As a starting point, we can safely assume that printers and booksellers stocked their businesses with products which they expected to sell; printers who were also retailers particularly were well-positioned to know whether potential consumers would find their books' subject matter attractive and if their prices were a good value given the product's intended use. Printer-retailers' pricing and stocking strategies, in effect, can tell us a great deal about the likelihood of particular texts reaching the hands of lower class readers. If a significant portion of Castilian bookstores' inventories was priced at, for example, less than a laborer's wages for one day, then we may draw the conclusion that printers and retailers expected to sell at least part of their wares to a public of modest economic means. When using inventories to establish the availability of any particular kind of book, three aspects of the business must be determined: (1) the type and number of books in stock; (2) the internal pricing structure of the shop; and (3) the relationship between the pricing structure and wages. Inventories from functioning bookstores provide a snapshot of the industry as it operated in a determined historical setting. By contrast, most studies of early publishing rely on bibliographies of *surviving* editions, a strategy which omits all the titles which have been lost and moreover is insensitive to local variation.

Bookstore inventories usually were drawn up without any rationale of organization beyond perhaps alphabetical listing; before they can be used to answer any questions we may have about the overall structure of the book business, the information must be sorted into general categories of literature while retaining data about prices and quantity of items in stock. Once this is done, it quickly becomes apparent how important the trade in religious books was to printers and retailers. In five Castilian bookstores operating between 1528 and 1581, 47 percent to 58 percent of their stock was religious in nature. In four Barcelona printers' inventories dating from 1538 to 1595, anywhere from 46 percent to 73 percent of their stock was also religious (Nalle 1989, 84; Peña 1994, 91). In other parts of sixteenth-century Europe, particularly Italy, religious books may not have been as important to the trade as Renaissance production; but in Spain, the stocking strategies of printers and retailers indicate that they believed that the reading public was more interested in religious publications.

To reconstruct the market specifically in religious books, for this essay, five inventories were used. They are (1) the Cromberger shop in Seville (1528); (2) the Remón shop in Cuenca (1545); (3) Juan de Ayala's shop in Toledo (1556), (4) Juan de Junta's shop in Burgos (1556), and (5) Miguel Rodríguez's shop, also in Toledo (1581).[4] The first four inventories derive from businesses which combined all aspects of the market: printing, wholesaling, and retailing. Cromberger, Junta, and Ayala's establishments were large by Spanish standards, while Remón and Rodríguez's shops were smaller, chiefly retail establishments. To determine the overall structure of the market, each bookstore's inventory of religious books was sorted according to the total number of books in stock and their price. Although we perhaps are more familiar with the ducat, for ordinary expenses, sixteenth-century Castilians thought primarily in terms of reals, half reals, maravedis, and *blancas*. There were 2 *blancas* to a maravedi, 34 maravedis to a real, and 375 maravedis (11.03 reals) to a ducat. Book prices tended to mirror the currency: common prices were a half real, real, real and a half, and so on, with relatively few books being sold for an odd amount of maravedis. In Seville in 1528 (Figure 5.1), fully three-quarters of Cromberger's inventory of religious stock was priced at less than 5 maravedis (although this part of the inventory did not account for much of the *value* of the merchandise). In Cuenca and Toledo (1556), on the other hand, about 90 percent of the two booksellers' religious stock was valued at under 5 maravedis. Moreover, the pamphlets alone were worth a quarter of the combined value of religious books and pamphlets. Although it is somewhat misleading to mix truly cheap printed materials, which were produced in enormous quantities, with books, which were produced and stocked in limited quantities, it is important to realize that for Remón and Ayala, the market in broadsheets and pamphlets constituted a significant part of their total business in religious publications. If we remove the pamphlet literature from the inventories and just consider the books, for the first four businesses, between one-half to three-quarters of all of the religious books on offer were still priced at a real or below. (Rodríguez's shop shows a rather different pricing structure, some of which was a result of inflation.)

A more precise picture of the market can be drawn if we further distinguish between two broad categories of religious books, publications intended for use exclusively by priests and religious (mostly in Latin, but not always) and those which were meant for the devout reading public (clerical or lay). Devotional works included books of hours and prayers, hagiography, contemplative and ascetic texts, and miscellaneous treatises, almost all of them in the vernacular. In all of the stores, devotional texts accounted for 57 percent to 80 percent of the religious books for sale. When pamphlets, which were almost entirely devotional in nature, are added into the total, devotional materials accounted for nine tenths (89-93 percent) of the religious books and pamphlets in stock at four of the shops. Clearly, if these five businesses were typical, throughout the century one of the main emphases in the book trade was to supply devotional texts to readers, whoever they may have been, at popular prices.

Although trade in devotional books accounted for the larger portion of books sold, ecclesiastical books (Scripture and the church Fathers, works on theology, canon law, missals, sermons, and miscellaneous guides to church practice) were by far the more lucrative part of the business. Some of these books could be extraordinarily expensive. Such was the difference in cost between the two broad categories of religious books that a few handsomely bound Bibles and decretals could easily eclipse the value of all the rest of the religious books combined, as was the case in Seville, where less than 3 percent of the inventory, all ecclesiastical books, accounted for over 50 percent of the total value of the entire stock in religious books (Figure 5.2). Generally speaking, the higher the price, the more likelihood that a particular book was destined for the ecclesiastical market.

The five bookshops' inventories show that devotional books were on the average much cheaper than other religious books and that these formed a large majority of the stock. By comparing the bookstores' religious stock against the benchmark of one day's wages for an unskilled laborer, we may appreciate just how cheap these books could be.[5] In 1528, a laborer earned about 25 to 30 maravedis a day; at midcentury he was earning about 40 maravedis, and by 1581 his wage had gone up to about 85 maravedis. In all five of the businesses, the majority of their religious stock was priced well below the benchmark of one day's wages. Except for Junta, who carried no pamphlets or small books to speak of, and for Rodríguez, whose shop in 1581 clearly reflected the impact of the century's price revolution, the large majority of items kept in stock were valued at 5 or fewer maravedis. In this price range, one could buy single sheets of prayers, pamphlets, and chapbooks up to 20 pages in length. Importantly, the inventories suggest that during the first half of the century the price of various common religious pamphlets *declined* by about 15 percent at a time when the cost of living increased by one-third to a half and salaries more or less kept up with inflation. In other words, religious publications which were deliberately aimed at the poor actually got cheaper as the century wore on.

If we lay aside the pamphlet literature and concentrate just on the bona fide books, surprisingly, one day's wages will still buy almost any devotional book in the shops. For example, in Toledo where in 1556 a day's wages stood at about 40 maravedis, 8 maravedis bought Venegas's *Formula de orar*; half a real (17 maravedis) bought Miguel Pérez's *Vida de Nuestra Señora*, and 20 maravedis bought the ascetic classic, the *Contemptus Mundi*. In Guillermo Remón's shop in Cuenca, Juan de Cazalla's *Lumbre del alma,* which was banned in 1559, was valued at 15 maravedis; another book to be put on the 1559 Index was the *Despertador el alma*, available for one half real. Toward the end of the sixteenth century, a laborer's wages had risen from about 40 maravedis in 1550 to about 85 maravedis, but the price of the *Contemptus Mundi* in Toledo had risen by only 5.5 maravedis, to 25.5 maravedis. About four-fifths of the devotional books in Rodríguez's store were valued at 2 reales (64 maravedis) or less; the shop's wares reflected the impact of inflation, but as was the case elsewhere, the price of most religious books which were not meant specifically for priests remained below the benchmark of one day's wages.

The inventories also give us an idea of how commonplace some publications could be. Broadsheets, pamphlets, and the short plays known as *farsas* were printed or carried in stock by the tens of thousands; short books were often available by the thousands. Cromberger, one of Spain's largest printers, had in stock some 60,000 items priced at less than 5 maravedis, and 8,800 books for one half real (17 maravedis) or less (Figure 5.1). Ayala's publishing and retail business was similar to Cromberger's shop: he carried 78,000 items for less than 5 maravedis, and 5,000 books for one half real or less (Figure 5.5). The three retail shops' scale was far smaller and rather different in emphasis. Remón, located in the small textile-producing city of Cuenca, specialized in very inexpensive items (Figure 5.3), while Junta and Rodríguez (Figures 5.7-5.10), both located in archiepiscopal seats, put more of their inventory into expensive liturgical books and collections in theology and canon law. Still, all three retailers offered hundreds of religious books at prices well below the benchmark of one day's wages.

Taken together, the inventories confirm one of the truisms about the invention of printing, even in Spain, that the press put materials within the grasp of a far wider portion of the population than previously had been available. The question which immediately comes to mind, of course, is what kind of books and pamphlets? Popular religious publications were enormously diverse and occasionally innovative, particularly in the first half of the sixteenth century, before the Inquisition began to exert some control over the industry. Included in the inventories at popular prices were many of the books that Bataillon described as the important works of Spanish spirituality—not always the masterpieces, like Francisco de Osuna's *Abecedarium* (which at 85 maravedis for each installment was out of the reach of poorer readers), but very influential works nonetheless, such as Juan de Cazalla's *Lumbre del alma* or García de Cisneros's *Exercitatorio de la vida espiritual*.

One of the more surprising aspects of this early religious printing was the extent to which the church took advantage of the press to promote reforms. During the Pre-Reform of the late fifteenth and early sixteenth centuries, church leaders were quick to exploit the printing press not only for grandiose projects like the Polyglot Bible, or the first works of Spanish mysticism, but also to bring out inexpensive books which were meant to improve the lower clergy's training. These publications explained in Spanish how one could be a good priest or hear confessions, summed up liturgical practice, reprinted the diocesan constitutions, and taught plain song.[6] For laymen, church leaders immediately saw the advantages of using the press to aid in the catechization programs, which had begun in the late fifteenth century. The 1488 synodal constitutions of Toledo included for reference a version of the so-called *tabla moral*, or list of required prayers (Huerga). Almost immediately thereafter printers began to bring out pamphlet-sized catechisms based on the *tabla moral*. The first two examples seem to have been printed in Seville (1493), and then Toledo (1496).[7] Right on the heels of the pamphlet catechisms, or *doctrinas*, as they were called in Spanish, came the primers [*cartillas de leer*], which were nothing more than the alphabet and syllabic combinations of letters inserted before the prayers of the catechism. The first *cartilla* appears to have been Archbishop Hernando de Talavera's eight-page "Primer and Catechism in Spanish to Teach Children How to Read," printed in Granada and Salamanca around 1505.[8] The idea of the catechism-primer caught on, and soon they were being produced everywhere. At mid-sixteenth century the *cartillas* figured prominently in the missionary work of Juan de Avila and the Jesuits, who preferred Avila's *cartilla* to their own, written by Father Ripalda.

The *doctrinas* and *cartillas* always were among the cheapest and most abundant of the shops' offerings, with the exception of Junta, who seems to have eschewed that aspect of the trade altogether. For slightly more money, about 5 to 8 maravedis, one could pick up confession guides, the dance of death, and the short plays known as *farsas*. The *farsa*'s importance in the later development of the baroque theatrical form known as the *auto sacramental* is well known.[9] Instead, let us consider what the *farsa* meant in the context of the goals of the reformist church in the first half of the sixteenth century. In late medieval Castile, laymen often created their own mystery plays and put them on inside the churches on holidays. However, these popularly conceived skits were the bane of church officials, who complained that the *farsas* were often scandalous in nature and taught bad theology as well. Formal complaints about *farsas* appeared in the synodal constitutions of both Granada (1529) and Cuenca (1531).[10] The printing press could serve three purposes here. First, there was the well-established, although increasingly suspect, tradition of putting on the *farsas*. The audience was primed and ready to consume the product, either for its private entertainment or for public performances. For the printer-entrepreneur, producing the *farsas* very likely would be a successful investment, just as the *cartillas* had proved enormously successful. For church officials, the printed *farsa* offered an excellent opportunity to capitalize on people's interest in theology in order to offer them the correct doctrine, which they could teach to themselves through the performance of the plays. In eight simple-to-understand pages, the theology of the Incarnation or the Eucharist could be presented, or the play could bring to life the Seven Deadly Sins or the teachings of the Ten Commandments (Nalle 1992, 166-68).

If Cromberger's inventory is indicative of the general trend, by 1528 printers had already discovered that there was a market in these plays. Cromberger carried about 5,000 of them, although since Clive Griffin, who discovered this inventory, was able to identify only half of the titles, it is not clear if Cromberger favored religious over secular titles. Thirty years later, however, there was no doubt in Ayala's mind about which kinds of *farsas* to stock. Of the ten thousand or so in his inventory, 7,500 were religious in nature, such as the 1,010 copies of F. López de Yanguas, *Farsa del mundo, y moral del autor de la real* (quarto, 16 p., 1551); 952 *Autos del hijo pródigo* by Lope de Rueda (first known performance in Seville, 1559); and 962 *Farsas del sordo*, by the same author. As it turned out, like Lope de Rueda, the earliest known authors of the printed religious *farsas* were priests.

The *doctrinas, confesionarios, cartillas,* and *farsas* were orthodox publications, a reflection of the close ecclesiastical collaboration in their production. Very few examples of the above genres were placed on the Index of Prohibited Books.[11] However, not all of the very cheapest religious publications were printed as works of indoctrination. The two pre-Index printers' inventories reveal that unorthodox (although not Protestant) religious pamphlets were just another aspect of their business.[12] Highly questionable, for example, were the 9,200 *nóminas* and 21,000 sheets of unidentified prayers carried by Cromberger in 1528. *Nóminas* were written spells (in this case, printed) that were folded up into a small packet and worn as an amulet to ward off sickness, fever, and hemorrhoids. Most were created for use by Christians, but I have encountered references to *nóminas* which were used by *conversos* and Moriscos. The prayers, or *oraciones*, were very similar to the *nóminas*. These were prayers asking for favors from the saints. Traditionally, blind men had specialized in reciting them for charity, but now the faithful could buy printed versions, which could be kept for future reference. In 1545, the Conquense printer Guillermo Remón carried 750 prayers of St. Cyprian (condemned in 1581) and 1,000 *coplas de la Emperatriz*, which may have been a version of the Empress's Prayer, condemned in 1583 (Vílchez Díaz).

In this profoundly religious country, where one of the questions from Philip II's *Relaciones topográficas* concerned local miracles, the supernatural was the subject of endless curiosity—and curiosity sold books. Thus, from the beginning, an important component of the popular religious press were hagiographies and pamphlet accounts of miracles and new saints. The pamphlet literature dealing with miracles was so ephemeral that even less of it has survived than the *cartillas* and *farsas*. Take for example the publicity surrounding the creation of a new local saint, Julián, the second bishop of Cuenca. In 1518, his body was discovered incorrupted after three hundred years, which was certain proof of the bishop's saintly status. Early news of the discovery of the saint was spread in two editions of pamphlets published in Cuenca in 1527 and 1529, all examples of which seem to have been lost except for two copies in the Columbine library.[13] In 1551, the saint won a new holiday, which spurred more interest in him. In Ayala's 1556 inventory we find 12,000 *pliegos* entitled "Alegrías de Cuenca," which can only refer to the news of the saint and the miracles he caused, since nothing else of note happened in the city at that time. Of these 12,000 *pliegos*, not one seems to have survived (Nalle 1991).

In the higher price categories, the single most common publication for sale was the book of hours.[14] Given the history of these books, we might suspect that they would form an important part of the market for religious books. Although remembered today for their stunning illustrations, hours were developed in the fourteenth century in northwestern Europe to provide members of the growing literate middle class with a religious text in the vernacular which they could read during the Latin Mass or while at home during the course of the day. These texts were translations and summaries of the most important parts of the Bible—some of the psalms and parts of the four evangelists, plus prayers, instructions, and practical items, like calendars of moveable holy days. Almost all included special hours for the Virgin Mary. Books of hours satisfied individuals' desire to develop a more intense, personal religion, often focused on the Virgin, and gave them partial access to the same texts which priests used in their sermons and liturgy, indeed, to the very word of God. The books remained enormously popular through the late Middle Ages and well into the sixteenth century. The invention of the printing press made the books accessible to even a wider audience than before. Some editions were expensive, exquisite examples of the printers' craft, but as literacy and the vogue for personal religious devotions spread to the lower classes during the sixteenth century, printers brought out simplified, inexpensive editions meant for the popular market.

Just how popular was popular? It is easy enough to find out the pricing of such books from the inventories we have examined earlier. At midcentury, in Cuenca, they ranged in cost from 10 to 75 maravedis (mrs.) unbound, in Toledo, 25 to 55 mrs., and in Juan de Junta's shop in Burgos, from 6 to 85 mrs. unbound. Junta also offered some bound copies, which went for 34 to 119 mrs. (one to three-and-one-half reales) (Pettas 124, 160). Moreover, the available choice in types of books of hours was considerable. In Remón's shop in Cuenca there were small hours from Lyon for 12.5 maravedis, expensive bound hours from Toledo for 50 maravedis, hours from Venice and Portugal, hours in special fonts and sizes, hours in Latin or Spanish, special hours for women readers, or hours dedicated just to the Passion. In Toledo, Ayala had in stock 959 volumes of hours, listing 7 different editions in Spanish, while Juan de Junta carried 315 unbound hours representing 21 different editions, and 24 bound books representing several more editions. Nor was the passion for hours confined to Castile; in Barcelona, in the first half of the century, hours were an extremely important part of the trade in religious books, accounting for one-third of the stock in two shops (Peña 1994).[15] The enormous popularity of hours—abundantly available, cheaply priced, and widely diffused—presented churchmen with a true dilemma. On the one hand, hours encouraged piety and taught laymen more about their faith. On the other, hours tended to place more emphasis on private devotions and put large chunks of translated Scripture into circulation. Both aspects of the publications weakened the church's control over how the faith was to be practiced and understood.

In 1553, all of the church's fears were confirmed in the case which follows. A few years before, in 1551, a destitute woolcarder in a village of the Castilian diocese of Cuenca bought a book of hours from a neighbor. On opening his purchase, he found inside an illustration which profoundly upset him because it was an exact representation of a vision which the man had recently experienced. Motivated by his desire to understand what had happened to him, the man read and absorbed the contents of the book, to the extent that his speech took on the very flavor of the text. To the horror of everyone in his village, Sánchez, as the man was called, decided to use his new-found religious learning to construct an elaborate and very heretical personal rendering of Catholic eschatology. In Sánchez's case, we have the key elements of the wider problem: the easy accessibility of printed religious books on the one hand, and on the other, the unpredictable use to which they could be put, once in the possession of badly educated (and often independent-minded) readers.

Before attempting to identify the edition which Sánchez might have purchased, let us see what actually happened to him. One day in 1550, after working all day in the fields, Sánchez experienced a vision. Sánchez explained several years later to the inquisitors what happened to him.

> por San Juan de Junyo que abrá çinco o seys años venyendo este confesante de segar de la vega de Yémeda, que es junto a Cardenete, que puede aver asta media legua, en acabando de ençerrar el sol que avn no era anocheçido, allegando que allegó junto a vn hermyta que se dize San Sebastián, en el ayre se le representaron en figura de lumbre o de cleridán figuras de dos honbres y vna muger, y la muger se le figuró que estaba en medio de los honbres, y ençima de la dicha muger se le representó que estaba vna abe, que con la punta de vna ala tocaba del otro, y viendo esto se yncó de rodillas y rezó alli çinco pater nósteres con çinco ave marías, y después luego tres pater nósteres con tres ave marías y todo de rodillas, suplicando a dios que si aquello era cosa buena se lo declarase, y sy no se lo apartase y que en este medio se desapareçió aquello que vido y que le paresçió

que quedó su coraçon consolado y asy se fue a su casa y nunca lo dixo a nadie. (Archivo Diocesano de Cuenca, Secc. Inq., leg. 196, exp. 2216, f. 120v-121r)

(About five or six years ago, around St. John's feastday in June, I was coming back from reaping at the valley of Yémeda, which is next to Cardenete, no more than a half-league away. The sun had set, but it wasn't night yet. Just as I was approaching a chapel which is called St. Sebastian's, there appeared in the air in the form of a luminous image the figures of two men and a woman. The woman appeared to me to be in-between the two men, and above the woman there appeared to be a bird, which with the tip of one wing touched the other. When I saw this, I went down on my knees and prayed right there five Pater Nosters with five Hail Marys, and after that, three Pater Nosters with three Hail Marys, all on my knees, begging God that if this were a good thing, to tell me so, and if not, to take it away. While I was doing that, the thing that I saw disappeared, and it seemed to me that I felt consoled in my heart, and so I went home and I never mentioned it to anyone.)

Prior to his visionary experience, Sánchez probably had encountered an example of the image he describes in such detail. As it turns out, the particular iconography of the Virgin Mary described by Sánchez was quite common in the fifteenth and sixteenth centuries both in church paintings and in book illustrations.[16] The image Sánchez describes—a woman flanked by two men, surmounted by a bird—appears often in various forms in surviving Spanish books of hours. In fact, in one book of hours, facing the office of the Conception of Mary, just as Sánchez said, there is a woodcut showing Mary seated in a colonnaded structure, flanked by two men. Over her head is a dove with outstretched wings. The illustration represents Pentecost, and normally appears at the beginning of the hours for the service of the Holy Spirit (*Hore dei pare virginis* . . .) In several hours, we also find woodcuts illustrating Mary being crowned Queen of Heaven: again the Virgin is flanked by two men (Jesus and God) who are in the act of crowning her, all surmounted by the Holy Spirit in the form of a dove with outstretched wings.[17]

Iconographically, the model for Sánchez's vision is easy to track down. He could have seen the image as a stained glass window, as a painting, or as a separate print, sold out of the rucksack of an itinerate salesman. Perhaps Sánchez saw the illustration in his neighbor's book before he had the vision, and forgot about it—it really doesn't matter. What is important is what happened next. The vision, its authority confirmed by its representation in a wood print, became the catalyst for Sánchez's heretical self-education. The woolcarder took a standard scene from the life of the Virgin, one which we would expect to be universally read as the Coronation, and perversely twisted it into a new version of the Trinity. He would argue in the years to come that three persons of the Trinity consisted of God the Father, the Son, and the Virgin Mary, who was simultaneously the mother and wife of God. The Holy Spirit served to bind and inform all three at once into one will, one desire, and one cause. In other words, we are not actually dealing with a trinity, but a quaternity, described by Sánchez in much the same terms as were used to explain the fifteenth-century "*cuaternidades*." Despite the teaching of the church during the Counter-Reformation era, Sánchez was not alone in his mistaken reinterpretation of the persons of the Trinity. Thirty years later Juan de Tolosa, prior of the monastery of St. Augustine in Zaragoza, told this story about his experience confessing a lady who was regarded as the crucible of religious learning in her community:

> Y preguntándole: "Señora, ¿Quántas son las personas de la S. Trinidad?," respondióme: "Por cierto, padre, que me admira el preguntarme cosas que los doctrineros las suelen preguntar a los niños de la escuela." Y porfiándole . . . en fin me dixo: "A Padre, que me trata como a criatura, yo le diré," y dixo: "Quatro son." Yo le pregunté quáles eran, y díxome: "Padre, Hijo y Espíritu Santo y la Virgen nuestra Señora." (Milhou 81)

> (And asking her, "Lady, how many persons are in the Holy Trinity?," she answered me: "Surely, father, I am amazed to be asked things which the catechism teachers usually ask school children." And pressing her . . . finally she told me: "Oh, Father, you're treating me like a baby, I'll tell you," and she said: "There are four." I

asked her which were they, and she said to me: "Father, Son, and the Holy Spirit and the Virgin Our Lady.")

Once Sánchez began to study his book of hours, the same process of reinterpretation of the canon occurred as had taken place with the vision. In the course of his reading he absorbed a good portion of the book's contents and learned how to speak with a certain amount of scriptural authority. However, just as Sánchez managed to misinterpret the iconography of the Coronation of the Virgin, he willfully refashioned the contents of his book of hours to develop a radical heresy of retribution and social action, and modified the prayers and language from his book of hours to support his ideas. The prayers were defiantly egalitarian, especially Sánchez's reworked version of the Magnificat (Luke 1, 46-55). A sixteenth-century Spanish version in part runs:

> Hizo fortaleza en el su poderío: derramó los soberbios con voluntad de su corazón. Derribó los poderosos de la silla y ensalçó los humildosos. E a los hambrientos cumplió de bienes: y a los ricos dexó vazíos. Rescibió Israel a su saluador: acordóse de la su misericordia. (*Horas*, Ayala, f. cxvi^{v}/cxvii^{r})

> ([God] made a fortress in his power: he scattered the proud with the will of his heart/ he put down the mighty from their throne,/ and exalted those of low degree;/ and he filled the hungry with good things,/ and the rich he left empty./ Israel received her savior and remembered his mercy.)

> Sánchez's version is:

> Señor mío, vos dixisteis que él que os teniese, hariades fortaleza en su poderío: ansí vos tened por bien de hazer fortaleza en mi poderío, y tened por bien de derramar los soberbios con voluntad de su corazón y de derribar los poderosos de la silla y ensalzar los humildosos y a los hanbrientos cumplillos de bienes y a los ricos dejarlos vacíos para que resçibamos el pueblo de Israel que son los legos, a dios, que es su salvador. (ADC, Inq. leg. 196, exp. 2216, f. 55^{v})

> (My Lord, thou didst say that him that thou held, thou wouldst make a fortress of his might. So Lord, please maketh a fortress of my might, and please overthrow the proud with the will of my heart, and cast down the powerful from their seat, and raise up the humble, and the hungry, fill them with goods, and the rich, leave them empty so that we, the people of Israel, who are the lay people, might receive God our savior.)

To call on God to buttress his revolutionary ideas, Sánchez made two essential, but small, changes to the Magnificat. By changing the verb tense from the third person past tense to second person vocative, Sánchez abandoned praise of past actions to underscore God's willingness to intervene in the present to achieve justice. In a bit of astonishing arrogance, Sánchez called on God to work His will through him, and made it explicit that the people of Israel were the Spanish lay people, as opposed to their priests.

This happens again in Sánchez's rendering of the Lord's Prayer. One Spanish version of the sixteenth century ran as follows:

> Padre nuestro que estás en los cielos, sanctificado sea el tu nombre. Venga a nos el tu Reyno. Hágase tu voluntad, así en la tierra como en el cielo. El pan nuestro de cada día dánoslo oy. Y perdona nos nuestras deudas, así como nos las perdonamos a nuestros deudores. Y no nos traygas en tentación: mas líbranos de mal. Amén. (*Horas*, Ayala, f. iiii^{r})

> In Sánchez's reinterpretation, the prayer now read:

> Padre myo qu'estáis en los çielos, sanctificado sea vuestro nombre. Venga en my vuestro reyno. Hágase en my vuestra voluntad así como se haze en el çielo, sea fecho en my qu'es a tierra. El pan vuestro Señor tened por byen de dármelo oy y cada día, a my y a todo el pueblo de Ysrael, y a quien vos señor tuvyere d'él por byen, y libradme de tentaçión por syempre jamás, amén. (ADC, Inq. leg. 196, exp. 2216, f. 51^{v})

> (My Father, who art in heaven, hallowed be thy name. Thy kingdom come in me. Thy will be done in me; just

as it is done in heaven, let it be done in me on earth. Give me this day my daily bread, to me and the entire people of Israel, and to whomever else thou pleaseth. And deliver me from temptation forever and ever. Amen.)

Note that in this new rendering of the Lord's Prayer, beyond Sánchez's personal exaltation, he omitted any mention of paying back debts, the bane of the life of the poor in the sixteenth century.

Sánchez was also able to create original prayers which were reminiscent of the biblical language used to address God. In the following prayer, Sánchez called on God to rescue him from the Inquisition and to exalt him.

Señor dios padre, vos sois pan; señor dios hijo, vos sois vino; virgen sancta marya, vos sois carne. [A more complete meal than just the bread and wine of the mass; with three food groups!] Señor, por vuestra sanctíssima trinydad no me dexere caer, y si cayere, vos me levantad. Señor, enseñad vuestro saber, descubrid vuestra bondad; vean todos en my las maravillas de vuestra sanctísyma claridad para que en vuestro nonbre pueda vençer y conquistar este cargo que me avéis dado con el Antechristo y con el diablo. (ADC, Ing. leg. 196, exp. 2216, f. 52^{v})

(Lord God the Father, thou art the bread. Lord God the Son, thou art the wine. Holy Virgin Mary, thou art the flesh. Lord, by thy most holy Trinity, do not let me fall. And if I should fall, thou shalt raise me up. Lord, teach me thy wisdom, reveal to me thy goodness. Let all see in me the marvels of thy most holy splendor so that in thy name I might overcome and vanquish this burden which thou hast given me with the Antichrist and the Devil.)

The most virtuoso performance came when Sánchez prophesied to the inquisitors the coming of the second Messiah, whom he linked with Elijah, and identified with himself.

Y ese Elías, junto con él que dicen Rey de los Judios, y el Mesías prometido en la ley, y el Duque que dice el Evangelio de San Mateo, dó dice, "Tú Belén tierra de

Juda, no eres pequeña, que de ti saldrá un duque que regirá el pueblo de Israel," estos cuatro son todos una persona, y trae la palabra que dijo Dios, "Bien aventurado será aquel que no me viere y me creyere," lo cual escribió San Juan, que dijo "Vendrá la luz contra las tinieblas y las tinieblas no podrán comprehender esta luz," y torna a decir San Mateo, "Tu Belén tierra de Judá etc. que de ti saldrá el duque que regirá el pueblo de Israel," y sella el evangelista San Lucas, "Reinará en la casa de Jacob y de su reino no será fin," y sobre esto habla San Marcos Evangelista, "Que aunque a este duque le den cosas matíferas no le empecerán nada." Todas estas cinco palabras, que son "Bienaventurados son los que no me vieran y creeren," están confirmadas por cuatro evangelistas, y toda cuanta maldad hay en el mundo se confundirá, y estas dichas palabras no pueden dejar de cumplirse, porque dijo San Juan en otro evangelio, "Verán en El que traspasaron mas no querrán de El otra escritura." (ADC, Inq. leg. 196, exp. 2216, f. 25[r])

(And this Elijah, together with the one that they call the King of the Jews, and the Messiah promised in the Old Testament, and the Ruler who is mentioned in the Gospel of St. Matthew, where it says, "You Bethlehem, land of Judah, are not small, for out of you will come a ruler who will rule the people of Israel" these four are all one person, and he brings the word that God said, "Blessed will be he who does not see me and believes in me" which St. John wrote, who said, "The light will come against the darkness, and the darkness will not understand that light." St. Matthew says once more, "You Bethlehem, land of Judah, are not small, for out of you will come a ruler who will rule the people of Israel," and St. Luke concludes, "He will rule in the House of Jacob and of his kingdom there will be no end," and concerning this speaks St. Mark the Evangelist, "That although they give this Ruler deadly things they will not harm him one whit." All these five words, which are, "Blessed are those who do not see me and believe," are confirmed by four evangelists, and all the evil there is in the world will be confounded, and these words will not

> fail to be fulfilled, because St. John said in another gospel, "They will see Him pierced through but they will not want of Him another scripture.")

Identification of the exact printed source for Sánchez's enlightenment is very difficult. Despite the rich printing history of books of hours, unfortunately virtually no examples of the hundreds of editions from the sixteenth century survive today. There are two copies of Spanish hours from the sixteenth century at the Hispanic Society of America, and a few more in the National Library in Madrid. The books did not survive for a variety of reasons. The cheap ones, printed on poor-quality paper in very small format, obviously were not made to last very long. The changes which came with the Council of Trent rendered many of the books obsolete, and they would have been thrown out, especially if they were not valuable. Finally, by order of the Spanish Inquisition, all books of hours in vernacular were destroyed in 1573. However, aiding in identification is the fact that there was a great deal of variation between different hours. An examination of the surviving sixteenth-century editions reveals that there was no commonly accepted translation of the Bible or even of the prayers of the catechism; nor were hours uniform in their content—all of which helps us to pin down Sánchez's particular book of hours, or at least, to eliminate which ones it *was not*. At the moment, in terms of both content, illustrations, and actual language, the closest match is the 1565 Juan de Ayala *Horas de Nuestra Señora*, which appears to be a reprinting of a book composed in the first half of the century.[18] Ayala printed many editions of hours prior to 1553; of the 959 volumes in stock in 1556, 846 were his own production in small format valued at 25 maravedis each. Given the proximity of Toledo to Cuenca and the generally large volume of Ayala's business, in all likelihood, Sánchez's copy came from that shop.

It is not the purpose of this article to follow Sánchez's adventures with the Inquisition or even to explain his ideas in their full form.[19] Sánchez's heterodox reading of his innocent-looking book of hours, however, provides us with a textbook case of the danger posed by any form of scripture reaching the lower classes. Armed only with his native intelligence and small bit of the word of God, Sánchez began to dream of a world where poor people like himself received justice, and the priests and nobility would be punished for their dishonesty and their perversion of religious truth. The church was not against all forms of religious reading; in fact, the sixteenth century witnessed the church-sponsored publication of many texts intended for use by lay people. However, the popular reading of devotional texts based directly on Scripture opened the door to the laity's interpretation of the word of God independently of priestly supervision. That freedom was one of the hallmarks of the Protestant reformers, and of the Lollards and Waldensians before them. As we have seen in the case of Sánchez, with the diffusion of vernacular hours, misinterpretation and misappropriation of Scripture ceased to be a theoretical possibility or a problem exclusively confined to learned people. In 1573, twenty years after Sánchez's arrest by the Inquisition, all books of hours in the vernacular were banned. Those in Latin were allowed to circulate, to be read by only those who, having passed the test of an expensive education, could be trusted to interpret sacred texts exactly as the church wished them to be understood.

As we know, religious authorities' distrust of certain texts began long before the banning of books of hours in 1573. Who does not remember St. Teresa's anguish when she learned that many of the books which had been central to her formation as a mystic and religious woman were placed on the Index? Thanks to the Inquisition's censorship, after 1559 the popular religious press was brought under control. The superstitious, apocryphal, and heterodox tendencies of the pamphlet literature were purged, and the experiment in making Scripture partially available in translation was terminated. While the fate of the books by the mystics has attracted much attention, less well documented is the fate of the truly cheap religious literature, which may have experienced far more radical changes than the industry in devotional texts. The *nóminas* seem to have been the first to go. In 1528 Pedro Ciruelo dedicated an entire chapter of his influential (and popularly priced) book, *Reprobación de supersticiones y hechizerías*, to a description and condemnation of these amulets, which he found were even put on animals and in the fields in a vain effort to protect them from disease.[20] Cromberger had thousands of *nóminas* in stock, but twenty years later, despite their large inventories of very cheap religious publications, neither Remón nor Ayala carried any *nóminas* in their trade. Many of the other extremely popular publications, *oraciones*, were condemned formally in the first Spanish Index prepared by Fernando de Valdés in 1559. It is interesting to note that in 1556, Ayala carried none of the "*oraciones*" which had figured so prominently in the inventories of Cromberger and Remón. As for the *farsas*, their performance was banned from the churches; in another generation the mystery play was overshadowed by the development of professional theater and the more sophisticated *autos sacramentales*.[21] Finally, in the latter half of the sixteenth century, the church attempted to assert some measure of control over the miracle stories as well. Miracles could happen, but one had to distinguish between real miracles, natural events, and out-and-out chicanery, otherwise people's gullibility would make a mockery of true religion. The result in the printing industry was a hybrid publication, a cross between the news release and the former miracle stories, like "The absolutely true account sent from the city of Alicante to Doctor Castañeda, Professor of Theology at the University of Valencia, which tells how a Genoan merchant, who carried with him a crucifix, etc., etc. . . ." (*Relación muy verdadera . . .*) Unlike earlier accounts of miracles, which appeared unadorned and without bombast, the *relaciones* clamored to be sold. They attested over and over again to their veracity and newsworthiness—the true report, hot off the press, read all about it![22] It is important to remember, however, that despite the Inquisition's control over the *content* of popular devotional books and pamphlets, their general *accessibility* in no wise was affected by the censorship. That is to say, although certain forms of religious literature came under scrutiny, other forms remained unaffected and continued to be available to the public at popular prices.

In this article, I have attempted to link a largely devalued literature to its cultural and religious milieu and place it within a certain economic framework. Anyone who has read a *cartilla* or book of hours will realize how poorly they compete for our attention when compared to the works of Spanish mystics (many of whom do not even appear in the inventories) or the imaginary literature of the day. The Spanish did not have the good sense, like the Germans did, to produce an entertaining, well-illustrated, polemical literature which several centuries later could attract the interest of cultural historians.

However, we cannot ignore the implications offered by this study of five printer-booksellers' inventories and the experiences of one extraordinary reader. Although the physical evidence has disappeared, we must wonder about the influence of this enormous popular trade in mostly orthodox religious publications. Perhaps Spanish popular religious printing has been unremarkable because in a sense it served its purpose too well: we take for granted the fact that Spain remained a profoundly Catholic country during an age of unprecedented religious strife.

How To Read The Graphs

Each step on the pyramid corresponds to a price category. The lowest step represents the cheapest category (1-9 *blancas* or 0.5 to 4.5 maravedis [mrs.] and the highest step corresponds to 154 maravedis and over, or over four and a half reales. There were 2 *blancas* to a maravedis, 34 maravedis to a real, and 375 maravedis to a ducat.

The percentage figure refers to a portion of the bookshop's inventory that falls within a particular price range. Thus, Figure 5.1, 74 percent of the 78,461 religious items in stock were valued at 1-9 *blancas*, the cheapest range.

The black portion of each step indicates what portion of the stock in this price category was destined for ecclesiastical use; the portion in white indicates devotional materials.

For Figures 5.1-5.4, the first three steps on the pyramid's price structure fall under the contemporary equivalent of a worker's daily wage, which hovered around one real between 1528 and 1556. In Figure 5.5, the bottom five steps fall under a worker's daily wage (85 maravedis). Thus, according to Figure 5.1, 94 percent of Cromberger's religious inventory was priced at or below a worker's daily wage.

Figure 5.1

CROMBERGER SHOP, SEVILLE, 1528
(Total Religious Publications in Stock: 78,461)

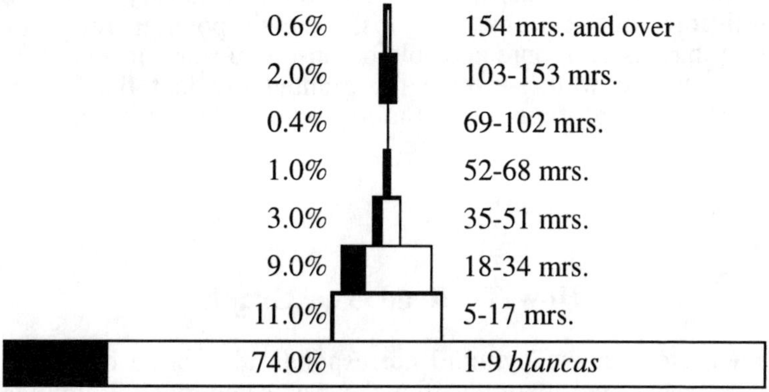

Figure 5.2

CROMBERGER SHOP, SEVILLE, 1528
(Total Value of Religious Stock: 979, 806 mrs.)

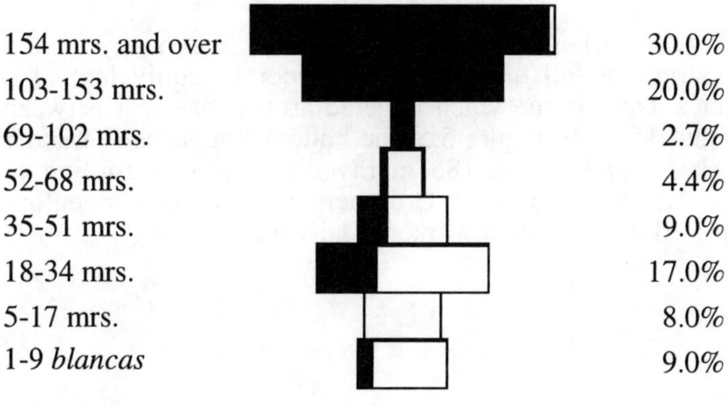

Figure 5.3

REMON SHOP, CUENCA, 1545
(Total Religious Publications in Stock: 9,184)

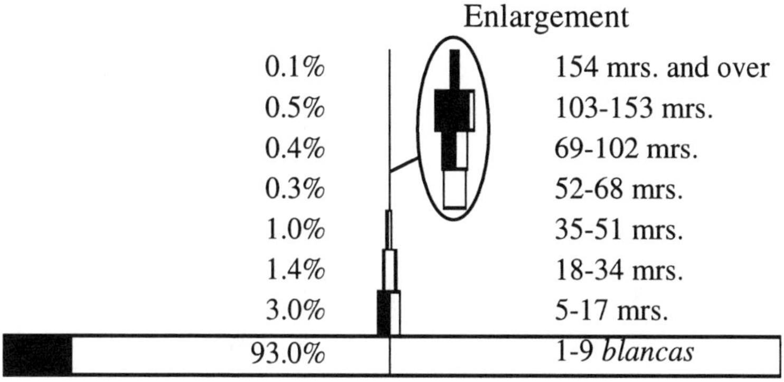

Figure 5.4

REMON SHOP, CUENCA, 1545
(Total Value of Religious Stock: 30,837 mrs.)

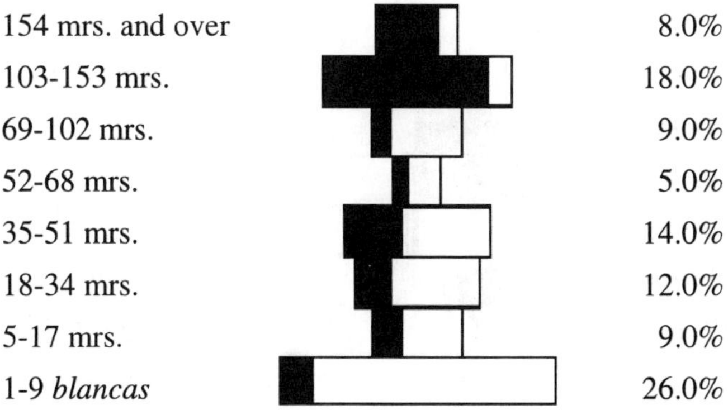

Figure 5.5

AYALA SHOP, TOLEDO, 1556
(Total Religious Publications in Stock: 89,211)

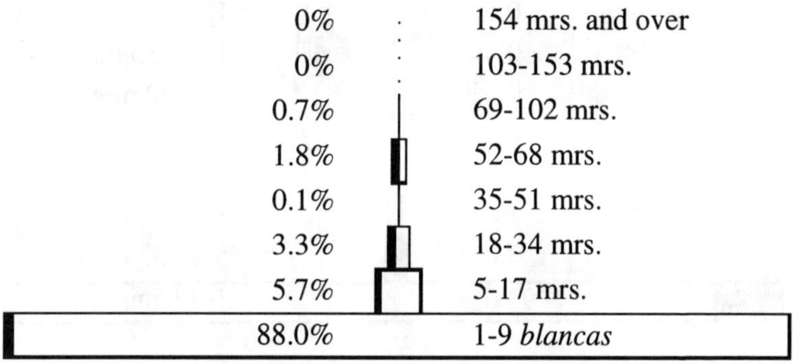

Figure 5.6

AYALA SHOP, TOLEDO, 1556
(Total Value of Religious Stock: 413, 600 mrs.)

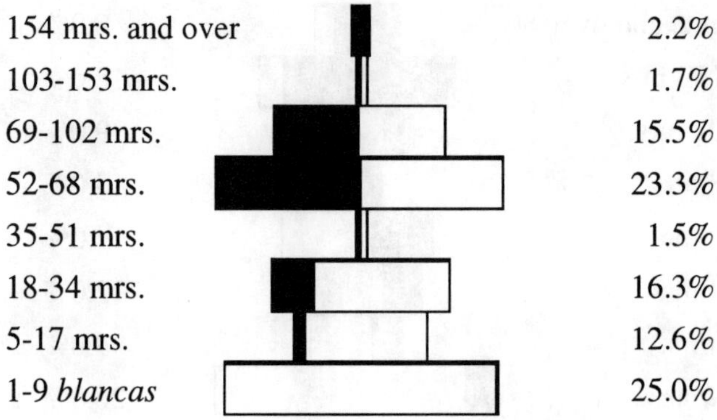

Figure 5.7

JUNTA SHOP, BURGOS, 1556
(Total Religious Publications in Stock: 6,103)

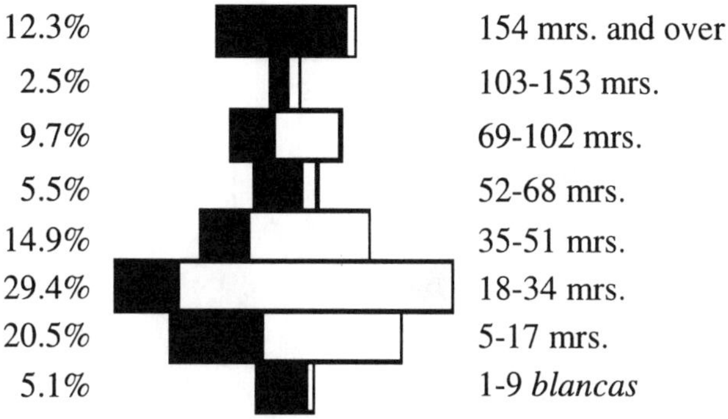

Figure 5.8

JUNTA SHOP, BURGOS, 1556
(Total Value of Religious Stock: 353,534 mrs.)

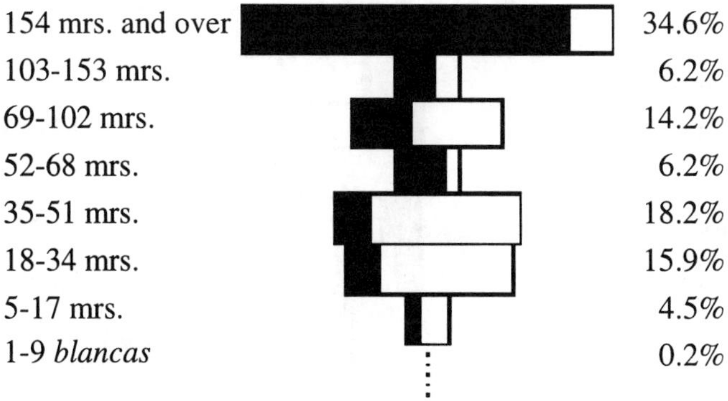

Figure 5.9

RODRÍGUEZ SHOP, TOLEDO, 1581
(Total Religious Publications in Stock: 2,725)

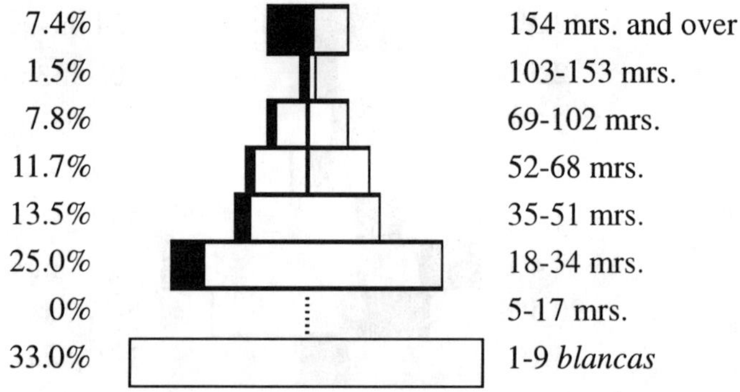

Figure 5.10

RODRÍGUEZ SHOP, TOLEDO, 1581
(Total Value of Religious Stock: 151,986 mrs.)

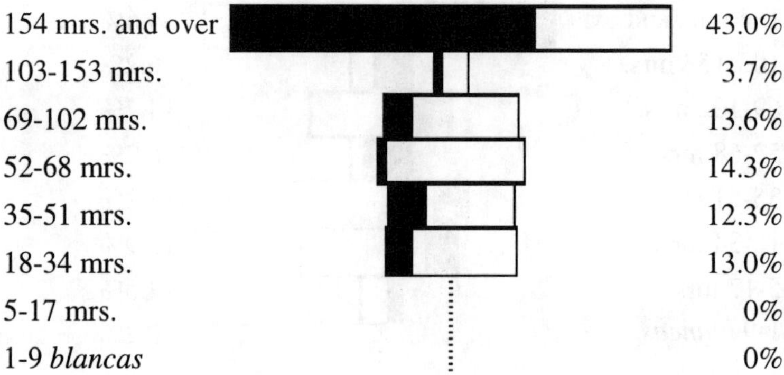

Notes

1. Perhaps the most thorough study of the book industry in one Spanish city has been P. Berger, *Libro y lectura en la Valencia del Renacimiento.*

2. I broach the subject somewhat in "Literacy and Culture in Early Modern Castile." A recent study is M. Peña Díaz, "Religiosidad y libros 'populares' en el siglo XVI." Peña's article is based on an impressive survey of Barcelona wills and inventories of bookstores, material collected for his Ph.D. thesis, *Libro y lectura en Barcelona, 1473-1600*, which I have not consulted.

3. Aside from Bataillon's work, see also Angel Alcalá, "Inquisitorial control of humanists and writers," *The Spanish Inquisition and the Inquisitorial Mind*, ed. Angel Alcalá, pp. 321-59; and Virgilio Pinto Crespo, *Inquisición y control ideológico en la España del siglo XVI.*

4. See Griffin, "Un curioso inventario de libros de 1528"; Archivo Histórico Provincial de Cuenca, leg. 226, f. 366^{r}-74^{v}; A. Blanco Sánchez, "Inventario de Juan de Ayala, gran impresor toledano, 1556"; William Pettas, *A Sixteenth-Century Spanish Bookstore: The Inventory of Juan de Junta*; and Archivo de Protocolos de Toledo, Protocolo 1758, respectively.

5. Whether or not the laborer could read is another question. Anywhere from 50 percent to 70 percent of urban males were literate in the sixteenth century (Nalle 1989, 65-96). Salaries for various occupations are available in E.J. Hamilton, *American Treasure and the Price Revolution in Spain, 1501-1650* (Cambridge: Harvard UP, 1934).

6. Cromberger listed 2,355 "little guides to plain song" (#34) for 2 maravedis each; 619 diurnals of the Dominican order for 16 maravedis each (#86); and 797 psalters (#91) for 26 maravedis each. Remón and Junta carried Díaz de Luco's *Aviso a curas* and Ciruelo's *Confesionario.*

7. *Constituciones del arçobispado de Toledo: E tabla de lo que han de enseñar a los niños*; *Doctrina cristiana*, and Luis de Salazar, *El credo el pater noster la salve . . . .*

8. Also, Hernando de Talavera, *Breve y muy prouechosa doctrina de lo que saber todo cristiano*, P.F. Grendler, *Schooling in Renaissance Italy*; and Huerga, "Sobre la catequesis . . . ." See also Sara T. Nalle, *God in La Mancha: Religious Reform and the People of Cuenca, 1500-1650*, Chapter 4.

9. See the very useful bibliography and article on religious theater by Rafael María de Hornedo in *Historia de la Iglesia en España*, vol. 4, pp. 309-58.

10. See David Coleman, *Creating Christian Granada* (unpublished Ph.D. thesis, U. of Illinois, 1995) and D. Ramírez de Villaescusa, *Constituciones synodales,* f. 41^{v}, respectively.

11. See A. Vílchez Díaz, *Autores y anónimos españoles en los índices inquisitoriales*. On the Spanish indices generally, see J.M. de Bujanda, *Index de l'Inquisition espagnole*, 2 vols.

12. The first Spanish Index was issued in 1551, but referred to foreign works. The 1559 Index included many Spanish authors and editions.

13. Both are collected by A. Rodríguez-Moñino, *Diccionario de pliegos sueltos poéticos*, nos. 395 and 396.

14. Despite their importance in devotions, books of hours have received little scholarly attention. For a general introduction, see the article on "heures" by A. Labarre in the *Dictionnaire de spiritualité ascétique et mystique, doctrine et histoire*, vol. 7, pt. 1, pp. 410-31; the collection edited by Roger S. Wieck, *The Book of Hours in Medieval Art and Life*; and Paul Saenger, "Books of Hours and the Reading Habits of the Later Middle Ages."

15. In addition to the bookshop inventories, Peña (1994) found references to books of hours in one-third of the private libraries which were inventoried on the death of their owners (92). By contrast, postmortem inventories were rarely taken in Cuenca, so that references to books are almost never encountered in testaments.

16. Alain Milhou collected many examples for his study, *Colón y su mentalidad mesiánica en el ambiente franciscanista español*.

17. These occur at complines in the following editions: *Las Horas de nuestra señora segun el vso romano: en las quales son añadidas muchas oraciones muy deuotas. Y de nueuo el rosario de nuestra señora* (Lyon: Guilliemo Rovillio, 1551); *Las horas de nuestra señora segun el uso Romano* (Lyon: Herederos de Jacobo Junti, 1560); *Horas de nuestra señora en romance: segun el vso romano muy cumplidas* (Toledo: Juan de Ayala, 1565).

18. Because Sánchez memorized his texts, differences in translations are crucial. Compare Ayala's Magnificat (f. cxvi^{v}/cxvii^{r}) with the 1569 Casiodoro de Reina translation: "Hizo valentía con su brazo, esparció los sorberbios del pensamiento de su corazón. Quitó los poderosos de los tronos y levantó a los humildes. A los hambrientos hinchió de bienes y a los ricos envió vacíos. Recibió a Israel su criado acordándose de la misericordia" (*La biblia del oso* 145).

19. For more on Sánchez, see my article, "Popular Religion in Cuenca on the Eve of the Catholic Reformation," and my forthcoming book, *Mad for God: Bartolomé Sánchez, the Elijah-Messiah of Cardenete* (Charlottesville, VA: UP of Virginia, 2000).

20. Ciruelo's book was valued at 30 maravedis in Cuenca in 1545.

21. Unfortunately, Rodríguez's business was not the type to carry *farsas*, so no conclusion may be drawn concerning their absence from his inventory. The *farsa* did not disappear altogether; early in the seventeenth century, the lowly skits still played a modest part in the popular printing industry of the city of Cuenca.

22. See Raphael Carrasco, "Milagrero siglo XVII"; on parallel development in France, see Roger Chartier, "The Hanged Woman Miraculously Saved: an *occasionnel*."

Works Cited

Alcalá, Angel. "Control inquisitorial de humanistas y escritores." *Inquisición española y mentalidad inquisitorial.* Barcelona: Ariel, 1984. 321-59.

Berger, P. *Libro y lectura en la Valencia del Renacimiento.* Valencia: Edicions Alfons el Magnànim, 1987. 2 vols.

Blanco Sánchez, A. "Inventario de Juan de Ayala, gran impresor toledano, 1556." *Boletín de la Real Academia Española de Historia* 62 (1987): 207-50.

Bujanda, J.M. de. *Index de l'Inquisition espagnole.* Geneva: Droz, 1984-93. 2 vols.

Carrasco, Raphael. "Milagrero siglo XVII." *Estudios de Historia Social* 1-2 (1986): 401-22.

Chartier, Roger. "The Hanged Woman Miraculously Saved: an *occasionnel.*" *The Culture of Print: Power and the Uses of Print in Early Modern Europe.* Ed. Roger Chartier. Princeton: Princeton UP, 1988. 59-91.

Ciruelo, Pedro. *Reprobacion de las supersticiones y hechizerias.* Ed. Alva V. Ebersole. Valencia: Albatros, 1978.

Coleman, David. *Creating Christian Granada.* Unpublished Ph.D. thesis, U. of Illinois, 1995.

Constituciones del arçobispado de Toledo. E tabla de lo que han de enseñar a los niños. Salamanca: Second Gothic Group?, 1488.

Doctrina cristiana. Sevilla: P. Brun y J. Gentil, 1493.

Grendler, P.F. *Schooling in Renaissance Italy.* Baltimore: Johns Hopkins UP, 1989.

Griffin, Clive. "Un curioso inventario de libros de 1528." *El libro antiguo español: actas del primer Coloquio internacional.* Ed. María Luisa López Vidriero and Pedro Cátedra. Madrid: Sociedad Española de Historia del Libro, 1988. 189-225.

Horas de Nuestra Señora en romance: segun el vso romano muy cumplidas segun se vera por la tabla. Toledo: Juan de Ayala, 1565.

Hore dei pare virginis marie secundum vsum Romanum plerisquae biblie figuris atque chore lethi circumcumnite Paris: Thielman-Kerver, 1523.

Hornedo, Rafael María. *Historia de la Iglesia en España.* Ed. R. García-Villoslada. Vol. 4. Madrid: Editorial Católica, 1979. 309-58.

Huerga, Alvaro. "Sobre la catequesis en España durante los siglos XV-XVI." *Analecta Scra Tarraconencia* 41 (1968): 299-345.

Labarre, A. *Dictionnaire de spiritualité ascétique et mystique, doctrine et histoire.* Vol. 7. Paris: Beauchesne, 1937-.

La biblia del oso. Nuevo testamento, según la Traducción de Casiodoro de Reina. Ed. J.M. González Ruiz. Madrid: Alfaguara,1986. 4 vols.

Lobo Cabrera, M. "Libros y lectores en Canarias en el siglo XVI." *Anuario de estudios atlánticos* 28 (1982): 643-702.

Milhou, Alain. *Colón y su mentalidad mesiánica en el ambiente franciscanista español.* Valladolid: Universidad de Valladolid, 1983.

Nalle, Sara T. "Popular Religion in Cuenca on the Eve of the Catholic Reformation." *Inquisition and Society in Early Modern Europe*. Ed. S. Haliczer. London: Croom-Helm, 1987. 67-87.

_____. "Literacy and Culture in Early Modern Castile." *Past and Present* 125 (1989): 65-96.

_____. "A Saint for All Seasons: Cuenca and the Cult of San Julián." *Culture and Control in Counter Reformation Spain*. Eds. Anne Cruz and Mary E. Perry. Minneapolis: U of Minnesota P, 1991. 25-50.

_____. *God in La Mancha: Religious Reform and the People of Cuenca, 1500-1650*. Baltimore: Johns Hopkins UP, 1992.

Peña Díaz, Manuel. "Lecturas y lectores populares en la Barcelona del siglo XVI." *Muerte, religiosidad y cultura popular*. Ed. E. Serrano Martín. Zaragoza: Instituto Fernando el Católico, 1994. 81-95.

_____. "Religiosidad y libros 'populares' en el siglo XVI." *Política, religión e inquisición en la España moderna: Homenaje a Joaquín Pérez Villanueva*. Eds. P. Fernández Albaladejo, J. Martínez Millán, and V. Pinto Crespo. Madrid: Universidad Autónoma de Madrid. 1996. 529-47.

Pérez, Miguel. *La vida y excelencias y Milagros de la Sacratisima Virgen Maria nuestra Señora nuevamente corregida y enmendada*. Toledo: Juan de Ayala, 1549.

Pettas, Williams. *A Sixteenth-Century Spanish Bookstore: The Inventory of Juan de Junta*. Philadelphia: American Philosophical Society, 1995.

Pinto Crespo, Virgilio. *Inquisición y control ideológico en la España del siglo XVI*. Madrid: Taurus, 1983.

Ramírez de Villaescusa, D. *Constituciones synodales*. Cuenca: Francisco de Alfaro, 1531.

Relacion muy verdadera embiada de la ciudad de Alicante, al Doctor Castañeda, Catedrático de Theologia en la Vniversidad de Valencia. La qual trata como a un mercader Genoues, que lleuaua consigo un Christo. . . . Cuenca: Cornelio Bodan, ca. 1600.

Rodríguez-Moñino, A. *Diccionario de pliegos sueltos poéticos*. Madrid: Castalia, 1970.

Saenger, Paul. "Books of Hours and the Reading Habits of the Later Middle Ages." *The Culture of Print: Power and the Uses of Print in Early Modern Europe*. Ed. Roger Chartier. Princeton: Princeton UP, 1988. 141-73.

Salazar, Luis de. *El credo el pater noster la salve. . . .* Toledo: 1496?

Talavera, Hernando de. *Breve y muy prouechosa doctrina de lo que saber todo cristiano*. Granada: J. Pegnitzer and M. Ungut, ca. 1496.

Venegas, Alejo. *Formula de orar, o formar meditaciones en la oracion dominica, distribuydas por las siete peticiones, en los siete dias de la semana*. Toledo: Juan de Ayala, 1555.

Vílchez Díaz, A. *Autores y anónimos españoles en los índices inquisitoriales*. Madrid: Universidad Complutense de Madrid, 1986.

Wieck, Roger S. *The Book of Hours in Medieval Art and Life*. London: Sotheby's, 1988.

◆ Chapter 6

Emblematic Representation and Guided Culture in Baroque Spain: Juan de Horozco y Covarrubias

Bradley J. Nelson

The Spanish baroque has been characterized by historians and cultural theorists alike as an age of crisis, both morally and politically (Elliot 1986; Maravall 1986).[1] In José Antonio Maravall's view, this mentality of "crisis" motivated the development of aesthetic projects which attempted to define, promote, and carry out the constantly transforming political and social interests of the so-called monarchical-seigniorial segments of Spanish society. In fact, the prevailing imperialist spirit of the time was so contrary to the historical evidence that presented itself to the Spanish populace that it prompted the economist González de Cellorigo to observe: "It seems that the desire has been only to reduce these kingdoms to a republic of bewitched individuals who live outside of the natural order" (qtd. in Maravall 1986, 214). Aesthetic projects such as *la comedia nueva* and the picaresque novel, in this view, become linked to the interests of ruling elites in order to ensure their survival in the face of obvious decadence. Thus, in order for the prevailing power structure to remain in place, subjects must in fact be estranged from their material reality—a reduced political and military presence in Europe, a state of continuous economic instability, political opportunism—in order to occupy an interpretive point of view that reads history in an allegorical instead of a literal manner. Historical events must be converted into mobile signifiers, if you will, so that they may be utilized to protect and perpetuate an existing semiotic and ideological regime. One such aesthetic phenomenon that has remained omnipresent, albeit on the margins of cultural and literary studies, is the emblem book. A cursory glance at the introductions and prologues of these multidiscursive productions reveals that the composers of emblem books were very conscious of the active role that the reader needed to play if their aesthetic project was to produce the desired effect. Just as *arbitrista* literature contains a wealth of theory on matters of culture, emblem books constitute an important theoretical and practical link between emerging theories of culture and seventeenth-century aesthetic trends (Praz, Daly, Clements, R. de la Flor).

Serious thought concerning the interaction of reader and artifice abounds in the world of emblematics, originating with Neoplatonists such as Pico della Mirandola and Emmanuele Tesauro, who privilege both the difficulty of the construction of devices, *empresas*, and emblems, as well as the pleasure and knowledge that reward the hermeneutical effort invested by the prudent reader. The emblematic mode in Spain, by contrast, is characterized by an arguably more utilitarian consciousness of how this discourse of wonder might be employed for ideological ends, as well as how its structural components might be varied in order to reach literate and non-literate "readers" alike (Ledda). It could be argued, for example, that Juan de Horozco y Covarrubias's *Emblemas Morales* (1589) articulates an emblematic method in which the consciousness of class, manifested in the distinction between erudite (readers of Latin), literate (readers of Spanish), and nonliterate subjects, guides a discussion of how emblematic discourse might be most effectively employed in the moral education of a wide range of actual and potential subjects of the Spanish Crown. In the baroque, this education in the interpretation of visual and discursive signs is equated with prudent and ingenious behavior and forms the basis for the accumulation of what Pierre Bourdieu terms cultural and symbolic capital.[2]

Horozco's collection is divided into a Prologue and three books, which can be broken down in the following manner: a theoretical treatise and philological study of the emblematic mode of discourse, including detailed definitions and historical examples of *imprese*, devices, insignias, symbols, *pegmas*, *orchestras*, hieroglyphics, as well as the emblem;[3] a second book, which is composed of a Prologue and a collection of emblems; and a third book of emblems, many of which repeat efforts from earlier in the collection. The focus of this study is Horozco's first book, which, apart from educating the reader in a hermeneutical practice of political and moral allegoresis, attempts to create a field of new possible "position-takings" both for emblematists and readers through a historical survey that takes up virtually all historical and artistic discourses as they relate to the emblem.[4] His expressed objective is to move from an elaboration of previous theories of poetic language and the visual image to a social praxis that involves Spanish subjects, literate and nonliterate alike, in the construction of a field of identities which revolves around the will to absolutism that permeates the efforts of many of his fellow *preceptistas*.[5] By conjoining the moral, the useful (*lo provechoso*), and the novel (*lo curioso*), Horozco seeks to move the reader to action, that is, toward a hermeneutical performance in which s/he participates in the construction of certain ideological truths (*enseñar verdades*). Through this interpretive practice the deceptive façade of everyday reality is unveiled as a transitory and morally dangerous theater of disguises which must be rejected in favor of a higher and more permanent reality: a doctrine more widely known as *desengaño*.[6] Put another way, the desired result of such a signifying apparatus is the estrangement of the subject from her/his own material and historical reality. Horozco's answer to the epistemological and ontological uncertainties that accompany the consciousness of *desengaño* is the emblematic interpretation of the material world. As such, the immediate goal of the first book is the simultaneous naturalization and privileging of emblematic discourse through a multipronged rhetorical strategy: a philological study of poetry which places all other rhetorical modes at the disposal of poetic language;[7] a philological study of emblematic modes of representation, which establishes the political and theological authority of hieroglyphic and heraldic images; the establishment of aesthetic and structural parallels between the emblem and perspectival painting; and a discussion concerning the wider social applicability of the emblematic mode in more public settings such as churches (religious oratory), religious and state festivals, and theater.

As part of his rhetorical strategy, Horozco takes an elliptical path toward his discussion of the emblem, waiting until the fifteenth chapter of the first book to discuss the specific rules of the emblem. His greatest concern seems to be contextualizing his understanding of the emblem within other social discourses that are more widely known and understood. He is, as Bourdieu would put it, creating a new position for emblematic discourse, a strategic move which "determines a displacement of the whole structure and that, by the logic of action and reaction, [it] leads to all sorts of changes in the position-takings of the occupants of the other positions" (58). Horozco's thesis is that the superiority of the emblematic mode is based on the fact that it is the culmination of all previous aesthetic and epistemological formations and, thus, the most effective vehicle for transmitting the accumulated wisdom of inherited rhetorical and artistic forms to the memory of heretofore culturally dispossessed subjects.[8]

Foreshadowing the prominent role that poetry will play in his emblems, Horozco dedicates the greater part of the Prologue to a panoramic and combative defense of poetic mimesis. He begins by demonstrating that the roots of poetry can be found in the songs that spurred ancient soldiers to battle, a move that immediately connects two discourses, emblematic (heraldic) and poetic: "Y esto fue con los versos que les ordenó con tanta fuerça, que los animó para aquella batalla" (6) ("and this was with the verses that he [Tirteo] commanded them with so much force, and that he encouraged them for that battle").[9] Horozco establishes a plainly utilitarian and imperial tone for his discussion of verse, placing the origin of almost all emblematic discourse, like poetry, in war.[10] In fact, *empresa*, a word which refers to individual emblematic devices used to express future intentions or actions—military, spiritual, or amorous—was commonly used in Spain to refer to the Reconquest and the subsequent establishment of Christian dominance on the Peninsula. Much as the practices of conquest and discovery move from military dominance to juridical and religious legitimation, Horozco continues his treatise with a catalogue of discourses which have at one time or another been represented in verse in order to facilitate the memorization of cultural, religious, and legal norms:[11] law, philosophy, theology, mathematics, in short, all discourse in which poetry has been used as a socially and ethically conservative mnemonic strategy:

> y assi dezian, que entre las demas Musas estaua la memoria a cargo de la que se llamó Polymnia de los muchos hymnos, y se ocupaua en celebrar las hazañas de los que viuian, por la memoria dellas referidas en sus versos, para que entre todos y en todo tiempo se cantassen, como se solia vsar entre nosotros con particular cuydado; y no sin enbidia de otras naciones, antes que se vsassen las prophanidades que en nuestro tiempo se han introduzido. (7)
>
> (and so they said, that of all the Muses memory belonged to the one who was called Polymnia of the many hymns, who busied herself celebrating the deeds of those who lived, through the memory of those referred to in her verses, so that they would be sung by everyone at all times, as was practiced by us with particular care; and not without the envy of other nations, before the practice of profanities that have been introduced in our time.)

Notice how Horozco frames his project as a return to a more heroic and pious period of Spanish history. The deeds performed by heroic individuals in great battles, which Horozco argues were the direct result of the special hortatory properties of poetry, are invoked in the celebration of current successes and then joined to poetry's potential for cultivating memory, creating a "natural" link between the glorious history of the people of a "nación" and the use of poetry for the construction and maintenance of this collective memory. Moreover, the historical remoteness of many of his examples perpetuates a rather Ciceronian understanding of how metaphorical language in general, and poetry in particular, is a "natural" and spontaneous cultural medium produced from man's struggle to make sense of, and exercise control over, his world. In this scheme it is virtually impossible to separate the founding moment of the Spanish nation, as well as its perpetuation, from poetic discourse. One might say that the Spanish nation is the reflection of the mimetic ability of poetry to create an ideologically informed *locus* which subjects then imaginatively conquer and inhabit through the recitation of verse.[12]

Moving from the establishment of a territorial empire to a juridical one, Horozco now explains how poetry facilitated the memorization of laws in ancient Crete, in ancient Spain, and in the Biblė. In this way he is able to assemble a single, self-reflexive, continuous "emblem" of history by connecting classical culture, what might be termed prehistoric Spain, and, finally, the Holy Scripture of the Israelites through a strategy of juridical metonymy. Thus, the true use of poetry and emblematic representation, the perpetuation of the Spanish state, can be found lurking—in potential—behind masks of all types in a poetic narrative or painting (*ut picta poesis*) that spans virtually all of history:

> Y para concluyr en esto bastara dezir q la autoridad y precio de la concertada poesia, se entendera claramente poniendo delante la grauedad de los santos assi Griegos como Latinos, que se ocuparon en semejantes exercicios de virtud y de ingenio, imitando los sagrados volumines, donde se hallan cinco libros enteros escritos en versos, como se conoce en su original, y lo advierten los Doctores santos; . . . y assi perdonaran los que no lo fueron si teniendo diferente parecer no fueron creydos en esto, y menos en q no auia de ser en legua vulgar el escriuirse este libro; lo qual no se escusaua por auerse escrito con intento que aprouechasse particular a los de nuestra nacion, pues seria justo ocuparse en buenas leturas los que no saben mas que nuestra lengua. (8)

> (And to conclude with this it will suffice to say that the authority and esteem of orderly poetry, will be clearly comprehended showing the seriousness of the saints both Greek and Latin, who practiced similar exercises of virtue and ingenuity, imitating the sacred volumes, where five entire books are written in verse, as is known in the original, and as the learned Saints observe; . . . and so they will excuse those which were not if having a different appearance they were not believed in this, less so if this book did not not have to be written in the common tongue; which was not excused for having been written with the intention that it be of particular profit to those of our nation, for it would be just for those who know only our own language to spend their time on good readings/lessons.)

Horozco connects the auspicious origins of poetic and pictorial mimesis to its ultimate realization in the construction of the Spanish nation by the Spanish language. Not only is this an excellent example of how a particular material necessity results in the rewriting of history—through the incorporation of all that is seen to be necessary to the construction and maintenance of the good health of the political body—it also demonstrates how an emblematic turn of discourse can convert a pagan into a saint. In his placement of the inscription "Saint" over the verbal images of ancient, classical, and biblical artists and scholars, and the meticulous organization of these within the confines of a single textual vision, Horozco is able to extend the reach of the Spanish state seemingly to the origins of known history: an origin that coincides with the origins of poetry. This rather "unnatural" configuration of names and places—to borrow Tesauro's language—acts as an emblematic image in which a new meaning is suggested through a metaphorical and metonymic conceptualization of history.[13] At the same time, by placing this meaning within the political and, more importantly, linguistic frame of the Spanish state, the reader of the *vulgar* tongue can now project her/his own identity alongside the Greek and Latin saints, thus playing a part in this historical narrative, mimetically occupying the constructed and imagined place.[14] Because the conditions of poetic interpretation are made accessible to literate subjects—literate in Spanish, not Latin—they can now participate in the emblematic project presented here and start to amass their own cultural capital.

Horozco ends the Prologue by proclaiming that the goal of his book is to extend the territorial realm of the Spanish language: "y para los de otras partes se vee q tambien aprouechara el libro por estar nuestra lengua tan estendida en el mundo, que ya viene a ser tan general como la Latina, y aun algunos les parece que lo es mas, o lo sera muy presto" (8) ("and for those from other parts one can see that the book also will profit them because our tongue extends throughout the world, and is already coming to be as common as Latin, and to some it seems that it is even more so, or will be very soon"). With this suggestion that the result of his book will be the colonization of other languages and territories—much as the Prologue has colonized ancient and classical history—Horozco sets the stage for his theoretical and historical study of the emblematic mode of discourse and thought. In a sense, this passage echoes Antonio de Nebrija's declaration upon handing his grammatical treatise on the Castilian vernacular, the first of its kind in Europe, to Ferdinand and Isabella a century before: "'What is it for?' asked Isabella when it was presented to her. 'Your Majesty,' replied the Bishop of Avila on Nebrija's behalf, 'language is the perfect instrument of empire'" (Elliot 1970, 128). Of course, when one considers that Nebrija was the royal historiographer for the Catholic kings, who enjoyed political successes at home and abroad unequaled in the history of *Hispania*, his optimism concerning the future of Spain is both immediately understandable and eventually justified. Horozco, on the other hand, is writing in the midst of Spain's century of crisis, when compromise is the rule and mere political survival is the goal. This is the era of the "favorites" who, like Olivares and Lerma, are more manipulators of image and orchestrators of behind-the-scenes maneuvering than visionaries with a concrete plan for hegemonic expansion and the means to follow through. Horozco's statement, in fact, is a direct contradiction of the material circumstances in which he lives and the prevailing spirit of the age in which he moves. One can plainly see that his invocation is a mimetic strategy that aspires to take root in the imagination of a purposefully expanded range of reader-subjects, who are led to re-create this ideal of Spanish linguistic and political hegemony by identifying with his allegorical narrative.

What the author does, in other words, is explain why this book will be a good cultural investment for the reader: if s/he learns the knowledge in this book, s/he can participate in a project that guarantees transcendental dividends. Through a particular interpretive praxis, the subject, all interested subjects in fact, can mimetically bring about the regeneration of Spanish national identity, redress the wrongs, so to speak, suffered by Spanish subjects due to the loss of faith in the unequivocal sense of mission in Spanish national destiny. Horozco not only repositions poetry in relation to other discourses; he repositions the Spanish language itself in relation to all of Europe. As for the emblem, the avidly theorized artifice, which in practice traditionally belonged to the social and cultural elites, will from this point forward configure a mode for the material production of culture, history, and, ultimately, consciousness for several classes of subjects.

Chapter 1 of *Emblemas Morales* is entitled "En que se declara que cosa son Emblemas, Empresas, Insignias, Diuisas, Symbolos, Pegmas, y Hieroglyphicos," yet the first subject refers to none of the above, but rather to painting:

> Como las cosas todas representando en si la virtud Diuina q en ellas resplandece, nos lleuan a la consideracion del Autor del vniuerso, y en esto recrean el alma; assi la pintura de las mismas cosas en la razon de semejança, tambien nos lleua y recrea, de manera, que algunas vezes lo que es natural no da tanto contento, como lo que se vee con propiedad imitado. Y en parte diremos, que la pintura tiene gran excelencia; y es que pone las cosas de suerte que se puede dezir permanecen. (9)

> (As all things representing the Divine virtue that shines forth in them, bring us to the consideration of the Author of the universe, and in this manner re-create the soul; thus painting these same things through the reason of semblance, also carries and re-creates us, in such a manner, that at times that which is natural does not give us as much satisfaction, as that which is seen with close imitation. And in part we will say, that painting has a great eminence; and it is that it puts things in such a way that one could say they endure.)

It is significant that Horozco begins his treatise with a discussion of the properties of painting, just as it is significant that the Prologue is dedicated to a discussion of poetry. Both are situated in the foreground of Platonic and Aristotelian theories of mimesis (*imitatio*), and any privileging of the emblem as an art form with the potential to create models of reality worthy of being imitated will have to pass through these two schools of artistic and historico-political theory. So it is that Horozco explains how the ability of painters to create "permanent" images or appearances imitates the all-encompassing creative powers of God. As is well known, Plato was, at best, ambivalent toward painters and poets, appreciating their powers to create worlds of pure appearance while criticizing their potential for diverting subjects from the imitation of proper models for the welfare of the republic (*decorum*).[15] For Aristotle, in the meanwhile, the goal of mimesis is to elevate and universalize certain aspects of historical reality, molding it as dictated by political necessity. Horozco uses aspects of both philosophies, placing a painterly emblematic discourse in a mimetic frame of appearances which seeks to elevate history and, by extension, the consciousness of the reader, all the while stabilizing its manifold potential by presenting its product as a God's eye view of reality. Thus, it may be said to partake of the Neoplatonic privileging of the image as cipher or referent of an immobile center of universal Ideals while, at the same time, directing the image's interpretation through poetic language, which takes precedence in Aristotelian thought due to poetry's ability to communicate elevated ideals among subjects: the image which points toward a diachronic panorama of visual truths is anchored by the synchronic language of Counter-Reformation, monarchico-seigniorial institutions, and vice versa.[16] Another way to say this is self-reflection, as the truth of the Spanish identity recognizes its origins in antiquity just as the true meaning of antiquity is reflected in the Spanish will to empire. Temporal contingencies and historical anomalies that are subjected to emblematization lose their independent and radical potential by being absorbed into a semiotic regime which translates everything in relation to an axiological schema of history.

As Horozco continues his comparative treatise on art, literature, and history, he moves from painting, which is admirable for its presentation of memorable histories, to Egyptian hieroglyphics, which, in his mind, are the only letters which teach truths:

> Y porq de todas las letras solas aquellas (hieroglyphicos) que enseñan las verdades, y el camino de la virtud, se deuen dezir letras, les dieron nombre de sagradas, a imitacion de las quales se han introduzido las q en el presente libro llamamos Emblemas, pudiendo muchas dellas llamarse, como luego veremos, empresas, y son aquellas q tienen respecto al intento particular de alguno. Mas reduzidas al bien comun en algun auiso q puede aprouechar a todos, dexan de ser empresas y son Emblemas, como se entendera de lo q luego diremos. (10)
>
> (And because of all the letters [signs] only those (hieroglyphics) that teach truths, and the way to truth,

should be called letters, which were given the name sacred, in imitation of the ones that have been introduced which in the present book we call Emblems, many of which are called, as we will see, *empresas*, and they are ones that pertain to one's individual intention. But converted to the common good in some notice which can become useful to all, they cease to be *empresas* and are Emblems, as will be seen from what we will say later.)

Horozco's argument for privileging emblems over *empresas* is that they can be employed in the education and edification of many subjects all at once; thus emblems more faithfully reflect the sacred nature of Egyptian hieroglyphics due to their potential to reach all subjects. As in the case of painting, the stakes of this mimetic game are very high, as Horozco places his project of creating emblems adjacent to God's creation of transcendental truths. The artist becomes godlike in his ability to assemble a reality that must, on the one hand, be understood typologically and, on the other, be imitated by a reader who moves toward salvation through the practice of emblematics.[17] Moreover, as the reader is invited to participate in the discovery of knowledge, the re-creation of this artistic rendering of worlds is also placed at the reader's disposal. In fact, as many studies of Renaissance perspective have demonstrated, spectator and artist exist in a relationship of dependency. This is a complex process, and, as Horozco makes clear several times, the participation of the reader in the emblem is activated by the same representational rules that drive perspectival painting.

For example, in defining what it is exactly that an emblem ought to be, he does not use examples from other emblematists, but, once again, from painting:

> Emblema es pintura q significa auiso, debaxo de alguna o muchas figuras, y tomó el nombre de la antigua labor que assi se dezia, por ser hecha de muchas partes puestas y encaxadas, como es co menudas piedras de varias colores la labor qu llaman Mosayco: y tuuo este nobre, segun dizen algunos, del autor que la renouo siendo inuencion de los Godos. . . . y tomó el nombre del verbo Griego encaxar, o embutir. (10)

> (An Emblem is a painting that indicates prudence, under any or many figures, and it took the name from the ancient labor that was expressed in this manner, because it was made of many arranged and enclosed parts, as is the work done with small stones of various colors that they call Mosaic: and it took this name some say, from the author who renewed it being the invention of the Goths. . . . and it took the name of the Greek verb to enclose, or insert.)

This idea of insertion or placement of objects is essential to understanding how the emblematic mode is constructed (Praz, Daly, R. de la Flor). Contemporary critics of the emblem (Daly), like Horozco, understand the terms *encaxar* or *embutir* as referring to Greek assemblages of mosaics and epigrams, and they suggest that the emblematists use these terms to explain how the image is inserted between the inscription and subscription. In this way, the meaning of the *pictura* is stabilized by the textual components of the artifice (Daly). Horozco, for his part, illustrates this idea by explaining how mosaics are constructed, organizing a great number of components under a single theme.

In her book *The Art of Memory,* Frances Yates notes that the placement of objects and their relation to each other, as well as to the mind's eye—including an imaginary depth of perception—are also essential to the cultivation of artificial memory. In one of her examples, she analyzes how the appearance of perspectival painting in Giotto resembles concurrent theories on artificial memory:

> And the illusion of depth depends on the intense care with which the images have been placed on their backgrounds, or, speaking mnemonically, on their *loci*. One of the most striking features of classical memory as revealed in *Ad Herennium* is the sense of space, depth, lighting in the memory suggested by the place rules; and the care to make the images stand out clearly on the *loci*, for example in the injunction that places must not be too dark, or the images will be obscured, nor too light lest the dazzle confuse the images. He (Giotto) has, I would suggest, made a supreme effort to make the images stand out against the variegated *loci*, believing that in so doing

he is following classical advice for making memorable images. (93)

In this case the insertion of objects into a mosaic-ike relationship, one that aids in the memorization of concepts and knowledge, is brought to painting, and the painter, imagining how the mind of the spectator will react to the painting, not only inserts objects into memorable locations, but virtually inserts the eye of the spectator into the painting as an absence that organizes the spatial relationships.

Similarly, in saying that the emblem is created by many "parts," and that the image itself, unlike the case of the *imprese*, should be capable of speaking its truths directly to the reader, or spectator, Horozco moves us more forcefully into the world of Albertinian perspective.[18] For Konrad Hoffmann, it is precisely this relationship between single-point perspective and the emblem which characterizes the emblem as a specifically modern representational phenomenon:

> The pictorial interpretation of surrounding reality that is constitutive of and underlies emblematics is not a more or less accidental expansion of the medieval repertoire of representation by individual motifs. Here it has more to do with the central art-historical event which led to the formation of a spatial imagery that was both distanced perspectively and related to the observing subject. The representation of an object is always connected at the same time with an interpretation that is already understandable either by the image itself through the striking combination of motifs, or only (in literary emblematics) with the help of the accompanying text; and the representation is thereby aimed at the lived reality of human relationships in historically varying intensity of its claims and applicability. (1)

Emblematics plugs into an aesthetic structure that had already radically changed the relationship between the subject and reality, opening up the representation of reality to multiple perspectives and interpretations.[19] One need only see the many works that a philosopher such as Descartes dedicated to perspective and anamorphosis to understand the gravity of the issues in question.[20] Lew Andrews, in an excellent repositioning of current theories concerning the philosophical and social significance of single-point perspective, reminds the reader that the mathematical organization of different planes of depth in early Renaissance painting allowed for a temporal organization of objects that was not possible before the rediscovery of Euclidian geometry.[21] We have already seen how Horozco organizes in a type of verbal spatialization an entire history of poetry and visual sign systems in order to lend authority to his treatise. When the artist positions the objects or scenes in Renaissance narrative paintings either in the foreground or background (*visos* and *lejos* in Spanish perspectival language), the spectator's eye may be directed through the various scenes much as in a linearly structured narrative. The visual narrative is thus reconstructed by the viewer who follows the signs of the arrangement that the artist has placed inside the frame. Ultimately the meaning of the painting only reaches fruition in the eye of the spectator, who sutures the various elements in the narrative together with his own desiring eye, creating, in effect, a mental concept that coincides with the visual organization. Mathematically rendered space thus becomes the hermeneutical condition by which the individual is interpellated into the reconstruction of temporally organized ideas which spring from the visual narrative. Moreover, as in the case of other humanistic aesthetic movements, the emerging practices of representation displace the epistemological authority of Scholasticism through their new "scientific" means.[22]

Instead of producing strict typological denotations which the representatives of the Church or ruling elites textually interpret for the viewer, the surface of a painting (or the engraving in the text) now provides the illusion of depth and allows the spectator to enter into a relationship with the image, discovering conceptual knowledge in the process.[23] Similar to the case of hieroglyphics, the more "realistic" rendering of space engages the spectator/reader in the production of meaning by drawing her or him into contact with the image by means of "that transparent plane through which we are meant to believe that we are looking into a space, even if that space is still bounded on all sides" (Panofsky 55).[24] Alberti recognized that the painter's goal was not to provide the spectator with an objective view of reality but rather "to draw with lines and paint in colors on a surface any given bodies in such a way that, at a fixed distance and with a certain, determined position of the centric ray, what you see represented appears to be in relief and just like those bodies" (cited in Carabell 5).[25] This "determined position" from which the spectator views the image, outside and in front of the painting, corresponds to the geometrical vanishing point that determines the distribution of space and bodies inside the painting. Thus, the spectator is included, represented as an absence in the painting, just as the concept or Idea is only suggested but ultimately absent from the surface of the painting: in Lacan's words "I have drawn the two triangular systems . . . the first of which is that which, in the geometral field, puts in place the subject of the representation, and the second is that which turns *me* into a picture" (105).[26] The picture gazes on the spectator, whose position has been predetermined, while the spectator gazes on the image: the spectator sees her/himself in the act of self-conscious representation, split between the eye that sees and the gaze that observes.

The key to the effectiveness of these anamorphic techniques, just as we have seen in the emblem, is the idea that the painted image is itself a cipher that is not to be taken at face value.[27] In other words, the success of this perspectival construction rests not on a recognition of what is represented, but on a calculated misrecognition and misconstruction.[28] Like the hieroglyphic sign, the image, in its very opaqueness, seems to conceal something more, an empty space into which the spectator projects a desire to reach eternal, universal realities and truths about the optical experience. In the new rationalized system of perspective, images appear to function like an independent and self-contained language, erasing the historically grounded act of their material production. The artist directs the gaze of the subject via the mediation of a mathematical system of perspective and then, effectively, disappears, leading the spectator to believe that s/he her/himself, without the intervention of an authoritative voice, has arrived at an understanding of ideal truths.[29] The artist is masked by the mathematical conventions of the mediating grid, and his historicized, self-interested eye is replaced by a dehistorizing Other who guarantees the transcendental meaning of the image.[30] Similar to the manner in which the humanist philological method attempts to reveal universal knowledge, the perspectival method seeks to provide a universal visual experience (Bryson). Moreover, the knowledgeable spectator, artistically competent in the deciphering of perspectival rules, is not so much distanced by this knowledge as that much more in control of the artifice and thus even more willing to appropriate its meaning.[31] Bourdieu writes:

> Since the work of art only exists as such to the extent that it is perceived, or, in other words, deciphered, it goes without saying that the satisfactions attached to this perception—whether it be a matter of purely aesthetic enjoyment or of more indirect gratification, such as the *effect of distinction* —are only accessible to those who are disposed to appropriate them because they *attribute a value to them*, it being understood that they can do this only if they have the means to appropriate them. (227)

The perspectival space, then, does not simply initiate the spectator into a game of meaning concerning the content of the represented object but into the game of cultural production and self-representation in general. As the spectator recognizes the gap between the image and an abstract meaning which is suggested or pointed at in another sphere, outside of time, the gaze that guarantees this other meaning also gazes on the subject, splitting it into its social representation or symbolic reality, and that which assembles said self-representation.

Another name for this specular game is narcissism, which is not, as is often thought, the acceptance of one's image as sufficient and plenary, but just the opposite. The self exceeds the limits of its visual or symbolic representation, just as the meaning of the visual image exceeds the sum total of its parts. Joan Copjec notes how this rejection of the reflection is constitutive of the subject of psychoanalysis: "All objective representations, its very own thought, will be taken by the subject not as true representations of itself or the world but as fictions: no 'impression of reality' will adhere to them. The subject will appear, even to itself, to be no more than a *hypothesis of being*" (Copjec 28, not my emphasis). According to Copjec, the subject who gazes on the representation of an objectified reality is constantly asking the question "what is being concealed from me? . . . Thus, the effect of the more modern sense of mimetic representation is not clarity but rather the suspicion that some reality is being camouflaged, that something has been left unsaid concerning the exact nature of some 'thing-in-itself' that lies behind representation" (34, 37). In referring to baroque painting, José Ortega y Gasset calls this dual characteristic "su ansia de expresar y su resolución de callar" (its anxiety to express and its determination to remain silent), which becomes the basis for his two somewhat Derridian laws of semiotic reception and production: "la ley de deficiencia y la ley de exuberancia" (60)[32] ("the law of deficiency and the law of exuberance"). The art object is one and the other simultaneously.

In terms of the emblem, the predetermined location from which the artifice speaks little and says much—Alberti's centric ray—takes on ideological proportions as the image, as well as its doctrine, only makes sense from the interpretive point of view which the emblematist constructs for the reader. If the reader steps away from this exegetical space, the emblem becomes truly polivalent (or magical), because the image and the doctrine which together suggest a higher abstract meaning or truth depend for their unity on the interested *inventio* of the reader, as well as the reader's belief that this meaning is guaranteed in another sphere. Thus, the desire of the spectator and the excess meaning produced by the interpretation of contradictory signifiers exist in a dependent relationship, which makes these types of artifices ideal for the construction and subsequent abstraction of "master signifiers" around which a hegemonic field of meaning revolves.[33] The semiotic regime of a particular historical "problem-situation," in this case artists who have a personal and professional interest in the maintenance and expansion of the values of ruling elites, may exploit this suspicion of incompleteness by linking the meaning that the spectator projects beyond the surface of the signifying apparatus to a mystified content of "national" values. In this way the desire of the spectator is lured into the artifice and momentarily frustrated by a visual construction, caught up and suspended in a search for meaning and, eventually, guided toward the discovery of this "excess" meaning. Here, "discovery" carries imperial implications, as the discoverer claims ownership of knowledge in the name of a higher authority. The individual subject brings into being the reality of the field of identities by claiming personal ownership of an ideal that by rights belongs to a projected higher authority, to the Other. In other words, as both the abstract or universal meaning of the painting or emblem and the desiring eye of the individual spectator are incorporated into this representational mode as absences—structural coordinates—the subject projects an Other on the horizon of the representation who guarantees both the transcendental meaning of this constructed reality and the place of the individual in it. Because meaning is placed outside of the artifice and outside of time, its authority also takes on an incorporeal yet ontologically more substantial characteristics. It is this materially absent but structurally indispensable Other which becomes the object of desire in the historical and aesthetic struggles to define the dominant discourses in an emerging hegemony. Moreover, as we have seen, this discovered knowledge takes on the appearance of being substantial and permanent, having "waited" for the subject to discover its meaning at the same moment as s/he recovers her or his own self-consciousness.

Horozco is consciously involved in the struggle over who will dictate the forms and content of the field of cultural production in early modernity. For this reason his project constantly hearkens back to the perceived origins of emblematic, poetical and, ultimately, historical time, and the authority that resides therein. As in the case of poetry in the Prologue, his etymological and historical survey of emblematic images (*empresas*, insignias, symbols, etc.) spans centuries of historical and literary knowledge. Chapters 2 through 14 read much like the first version of Cesare Ripa's *Iconología*, in that there are philological explanations and discussions of a virtual encyclopedia of symbols without a single visual image to aid the imagination of the reader—with one important difference: in Horozco's survey, all historical and mythological references to the emblematic mode are incorporated into a Spanish narrative of symbolic authority.[34] The historical authority of the emblematic mode, the Other who guarantees its meaning, arises from the invocation of its original practitioners: warriors, emperors, kings—in short, epic heroes. Symbolic capital and real power become an immanent legacy of the emblematic mode of discourse. The illustrious historical conditions of its development together with heroic *exempla* of emblematic social-semiotic praxis, prepare the reader to take ownership of what Horozco is going to present in Books 2 and 3 of his collection. Thus, the way through material objects and *letras* to knowledge and power traverses the emblematic artifice, which is, in a sense, deterritorialized from its original social moorings and placed in the hands of diverse subjects.

Through the emblem, Horozco seeks to convert *agudeza* and *ingenio* into an aesthetic of massive proportions, educating all prudent readers in the inner workings of representation. Moreover, he has plans for illiterate subjects as well. In this way, the emblematic mode will be transformed by Horozco into the vehicle for the massive dissemination of monarchico-seigniorial values, making all subjects potential producers and proprietors of his ideal of Spanish identity.

In the chapters in which he begins to discuss the rules for the construction of emblems, he talks about the types of *empresas* that are appropriate for public festivals and celebrations:

> mas ay empresas que hablan con otros, unas en particular con alguna persona, otras con todas. Estas vltimas son, o deuen ser las que se sacan en fiestas y regozijos publicos, donde seria impropriedad no hablar con los que juzgan y miran; aunque sea dando a entender particular intento: y vsando de figuras y letras, deue acomodarse con la claridad, porque de otra manera no dara contento, ni ay esse lugar para detenerse en pensar que querra dezir; y quando se detuuiessen, es lo mas cierto que pensaran lo peor. (46)

> (but there are *empresas* that speak with others, some in particular with a certain person, and others with everyone. These last ones are, or should be the ones that are shown in festivals and public celebrations, where it would be improper not to speak with those who judge and watch; even when leading one to understand a particular intention: and in employing figures and letters, one should do so with clarity, because done in any other way it will not give satisfaction, nor is there any place for detaining oneself to ponder its intention; for when they do wait, they most certainly will think the worst.)

He expresses this same concern for clarity in subsequent chapters, and it is clear, as in the case of painting, that the material artifice of emblematic language should not bring attention to itself but rather act as a "transparent window" through which the spectators may gaze onto the constructed meaning.[35] Moreover, it is very clear that Horozco is not equating the literate mode of reception to its illiterate counterpart, for what he is actually proposing are two distinct modes of cultural reception-production. If you are literate and most likely a member of the social elites, you not only profit culturally from the content of the emblems; you also prepare the way for a symbolic windfall by learning the aesthetic strategies of the emblematic mode of discourse. Literate subjects thus have the opportunity to participate in the material processes which result in the creation of the art object and, subsequently, produce their own symbolic capital—prestige—from their surplus of cultural capital. Illiterate subjects, on the other hand, who are lured into the artifice by public festivals and celebrations where emblematic and hieroglyphic constructions will be (in theory) much more clearly and simply constructed, will mainly consume and reproduce the emotional feelings aroused by contact with heroic ideals (*contento*).[36] In either case, reception is at the very center of Horozco's emblematic project. In fact, as can be seen in any number of Renaissance and baroque treatises on the subject, it is theories of reception which guide the aesthetic composition of the emblematic mode in general.[37] In the case of Horozco, however, the abstract ideas suggested by the emblematic mode clearly take precedence over the difficulty of its construction.

For this reason, Horozco feels compelled to compose new rules concerning the content of the emblem that will accompany and guide the more traditional ones that regulate its rhetorical composition: "La sexta regla que yo añado, y ha de ser la primera es, que el proposito y el intento sea bueno" (50) ("the sixth rule that I add, which has to be the first, is that the purpose and intention be good"). Horozco is consciously adding rules to the five that he has inherited from previous emblematists;[38] moreover, all the traditional rules concerning proportion, difficulty, the subscription, and the figures will be guided by his new emblematic theory, which privileges the dogmatic concept of the proposal at hand: "is the *costumbre* worthy of being imitated?" In the seventh rule, the manner in which the emblematic mode will attempt to guide the imaginary of readers becomes more explicit:

> La septima regla es, que de mas de ser bueno el proposito, lo que para el se escogierie se procure que sea

> de manera, que ni en la figura, ni en la letra se pueda torcer, y desto ay hartas empresas con falta notable. (51)
>
> (The seventh rule is, in addition to its purpose being good, that when it is chosen it should be of such a manner, that neither in the figure, nor in the script can it be distorted, and of this there are many *empresas* with remarkable errors.)

Horozco bemoans the lack of fixity that emblematic practices have previously introduced into the interpretation of signs. When dealing with a discursive mode that is based on visual symbols in early modern Europe, one must keep in mind that there were groups that considered certain symbols, including many that eventually became standard emblematic signs, to possess magical or, at the very least, mystical qualities. One only needs to read some of the emblems of Giordano Bruno or the Englishman John Dee to recognize that the magic and alchemistic theory suggested in the Neoplatonic writings of Marcelo Ficino or Giovanni Pico della Mirandola had its proponents in the seventeenth century. John S. Mebane has commented on the presence of these hermetic currents of thought in the Elizabethan theater of Marlowe, Jonson, and Shakespeare:[39] "the mystical cults generally drew their support from the lower social and economic classes or from other groups who, for various reasons, were denied a meaningful place in the existing hierarchy" (16). Such residual cultural elements would help explain Horozco's concern with the stability of the meaning of the emblem in the context of public festivals such as the Corpus Christi.[40]

Following up on his theories concerning the public display of emblems, Horozco demonstrates how to construct a singular meaning in the emblem by referring to the representational strategies which aid in the configuration of a central line of argument in theater:

> porque es como en las comedias, que aunque ayan de hablar dos y aun tres, la quarta ha de ser persona muda, como dezian: y assi dixo el otro Poeta, que la quarta persona no procurasse hablar, y aqui ha de hacer lo mismo la tercera. Tambien se entiende, que quando muchas cosas representan una, no importa como en el tropheo porque todo ello habla como una figura. (52)

(because it is as in the *comedias*, that although two or even three (figures) speak, the fourth must be silent, as they said: and thus said the other Poet, that the fourth person not try to speak, and here the third person must do the same. It is also understood, that when many things represent one, it matters not as in the emblem of triumph, because it all speaks as one figure.)

As in the case of theater, the main intent or meaning of the emblem is stabilized by the surrounding yet inferior components of the image. In fact, a sort of perspectival game is played in which the proportion of one object to another causes the central focus of the artifice to shine forth, luring the eye of the spectator to one area instead of another. The effect, conscious or not, of Horozco's general movement from artifice to meaning, from material signs to ideas, is to make the artifice itself give way to his simultaneously abstract and practical concerns. In the words of Octavio Paz, "The baroque Age . . . was irresistably drawn toward the dissolution of the very forms of which it was enamored" (146). The vital connection between personal interest, symbolic apparatus, and the eventual cultural production of ideology becomes a veritable blind spot in the hegemonic field, which is perceived to be self-sufficient and complete.

Raymond Williams has commented on this phenomenon in the context of certain schools of Marxist thought in which analytical tools such as "base and superstructure" become abstract and mystified structural absolutes:

> What is fundamentally lacking, in the theoretical formulations of this important period, is any adequate recognition of the indissoluble connections between material production, political and cultural institutions and activity, and consciousness. (80)

Similarly, the emblem, along with the material processes of signification which it initiates, gives way to the idea of *desengaño*, which becomes the philosophical base of the cultural superstructure of the baroque, while its existence as a social practice immanently tied to the economic and political struggles that characterize Habsburg Spain is elided. Maravall has commented on the fact that Spanish baroque culture is in essence a culture of "alienated individuals."[41] Not only are subjects alienated from each other through a type of intellectual competition to which the emblematic mode of discourse contributes—in the exercise of *agudeza* as well as due to its historical antecedents—but individuals also become alienated from their own materially grounded participation in the construction of an imagined Spanish hegemony. Such an abstraction of the relationship between the "base and superstructure" of a social reality, according to Williams (as well as Bourdieu), tends to separate the individual from her/his role as agent in the construction of reality as well as to effectively free ideological edifices from their dependence on individual desire and, ultimately, history. One concept that much literary analysis tends to obscure which a cursory understanding of the emblematic mode of discourse makes obvious, especially treatises concerning the creation of "good" emblems, is the degree to which ideas and even consciousness itself are the result of a historically grounded and active process of cultural production. In the practice of reading emblems, the mathematical grid of the perspectively rendered images, as well as the method of exegesis, may indeed act as vanishing mediators; but in emblem theory the importance of the encounter between the individual and the art object is never understated. Perhaps this is one reason that the emblem has remained a poor cousin to more privileged genres in literary institutions: it reminds one of the very real material historical dialogism and political compromise of all literary manifestations, be they conservative or subversive in nature.

Furthermore, Horozco sees no contradiction between the material artificiality of the signifying apparatus and the "naturalness" of the knowledge produced by its interaction with a reader. In fact, this knowledge, along with the artistic competence which is attained through practice and repetition, are both naturalized. Thus, we can see how the emblematic mode and Counter Reformation ideology become immanently linked, even though not all subjects will interract with emblematic artifices equally. In fact, the emblematic mode configures both a common base of cultural beliefs and the means with which subjects may differentiate themselves within the belief system. Bourdieu analyzes a homologous phenomenon in the nineteenth century when he writes:

> Culture is thus achieved only by negating itself as such, that is, as artificial and artificially acquired, so as to become second nature, a habitus, a possession turned into being; the virtuosi of the judgement of taste seem to reach an experience of aesthetic grace so completely freed from the constraints of culture and so little marked by the long, patient training of which it is the product that any reminder of the conditions and social conditioning which have rendered it possible seems to be at once obvious and scandalous. (234)

Specifically, Bourdieu is analyzing the philosophical coordinates of a post-Enlightenment understanding of cultural production in which the acquisition and manifestation of artistic competence are equated with natural charisma and brilliance: a process which Bourdieu sees as the culmination of a "self-seeking silence [which] makes it possible to legitimize a social privilege by pretending that it is a gift of nature" (234). The struggles to define the aesthetic composition as well as the social function of the emblematic mode of expression in the Spanish baroque are in many ways homologous to the aesthetic debate between the Symbolists and the Naturalists which Bourdieu uses to illustrate his analytical model. If the nineteenth-century field of cultural production can be divided into heteronomous (i.e., bourgeois) and autonomous (i.e., "art for art's sake") art, perhaps the artistic field in sixteenth- and seventeenth-century Spain can be roughly divided into homologous categories: a heteronomous art that is concerned with the mass/illiterate reception of a conservative artistic content, such as festivals, *la comedia nueva*, *el auto sacramental*; and an art that seeks an elite/literate reception, that is, *conceptista* and *culteranista* poetry, elaborate mythological plays staged at Buen Retiro, and literature that would include works by the *arbitristas*, historical narratives, and emblem books.[42]

The emblem, in essence, functions as a *speculum subjecti*, in which the subject's image is reflected alongside of the protagonists of the emblematic artifice: the Church and the monarchico-seigniorial segments of Spanish society. Moreover, the aesthetic exigencies of the emblematic mode will assist the subject in participating in other cultural phenomena that employ similar rhetorical and perspectival rules. With each new experience the subject becomes more adept at consuming the dogma that is pointed at by the emblematic mode of representation and less conscious of the perspectival techniques that lead her/him to this content (Bourdieu). The mediating structures become more and more transparent and the ideals to which they lead become more and more real. Many emblem books have as many as three hundred emblems, most of which present almost identical topics and themes, preaching the importance of prudence and honor, while emphasizing the transitory and deceptive nature of mundane reality; just as the *comedias de capa y espada* exploit the same formulae and narrative structures in an attempt to please and entertain spectators (see Lope de Vega). Both provide the means to momentarily fulfill and immediately reawaken the appetite for repeated satisfaction of a desire stimulated by their material construction.

Maravall has developed the theory of "baroque guided culture" by studying not just the literary and artistic genres that have been privileged by literary critics, but by also studying the material production of cultural and symbolic realities and consciousness as manifested in all manner of social discourses: historical narrative, *arbitrista* literature, dress, courtly behavior, philosophical writings on poverty, residual humanist thought in the Counter Reformation, epistolary literature, and so on. In his study of emblem books, for example, he does not base his analysis on a relationship between a state-centered ideological apparatus and a literary mode of expression. On the contrary, he analyzes how the emblematic artifice interacts with the individual reader in the creation of a new reality out of a very real struggle over "possible position-takings" for both artist and reader. Similarly, what I have attempted to demonstrate in this essay is that the active participation sparked by the emblematic mode of discourse, as Horozco theorized, is an alienating activity, and it is this very alienation which results in the construction of an ideological hegemony with which the reader comes to identify. In fact, the individual must be alienated from her/himself (suspended) in order to be lured into reconstructing a relationship with her/his historical circumstances by connecting a desire for completion to an imagined, mimetically rendered, field of identities. Through the symbolic and cultural practice of *desengaño* subjects no longer maintain imaginary contact and control over their material reality and, thus, actively search for that which offers to link them to the estranged world around them: ideology. As a result, that which creates and sustains the hegemonic field does not and, in fact, cannot reside in its material structures, but is projected through language by individual desire to discover a stable space for an imagined reflection of wholeness.

Notes

1. For a historical study of this phenomenon see J.H. Elliot's *The Count-Duke of Olivares. The Statesman in an Age of Decline.* José Antonio Maravall's *Culture of the Baroque: Analysis of a Historical Structure* is probably the most well-known and influential cultural analysis of this same period.

2. Randal Johnson defines cultural and symbolic capital in the following manner: "*Cultural capital* concerns forms of cultural knowledge, competences or dispositions. In *Distinction*, the work in which he elaborates the concept most fully, Bourdieu defines cultural capital as a form of knowledge, an internalized code or a cognitive acquisition which equips the social agent with empathy towards, appreciation for or competence in deciphering cultural relations and cultural artefacts. . . . *Symbolic capital* refers to a degree of accumulated prestige, celebrity, consecration or honour and is founded on a dialectic of knowledge (*connaissance*) and recognition (*reconnaissance*)" (7).

3. Horozco provides the following definitions of emblematic terminology: "Empresa se dize la figura de algun proposito, que por ser el fin de lo que se emprende, vino a llamarse empresa, y fue propia de los hechos de armas verdaderos, y a imitacion dellos vino a vsarse en los fingidos; y en particular se vsaron estas empresas en los desafios. . . . Insignias dichas entre los Romanos signa, eran las señales que los Capitanes trayan en sus estandartes, que primero fueron figuras leuantadas en alto . . . Diuisas son señales con que se diferencian los que las traen, y estas solian traer algunos esquadrones, o legiones antiguas, como se vee en la noticia del vno y otro Imperio . . . Symbolos se dizen tambien las señales, mas son aquellas, que como en cifra dan a entender alguna cosa, y son en la guerra las que se llamaron entre los Latinos Tesseras; y estas seruian de mostrar con silencio leuantadas en alto lo que auia de hazer el exercito . . . Pegmas es otro nombre que se ha dado a las Emblemas, por la semejança que tienen con aquellas, las quales eran vna representacion que se hazia con figuras mudas en vna fabrica quadrada de madera; mostrãdose primero vn suelo que a las orillas tenia estas figuras, y de en medio deste suelo se leuantaua otro quadro menor con otras figuras diferentes; y luego el tercero, y quarto, hasta disminuyren manera de torre: y esto es lo q Marcial dixo, que las altas Pegmas se leuãtauan en medio de la calle: hallase la figura destas en el reuerso de algunas medallas antiguas, en memoria de las lisonjas que alli

se dezian a los Principes y del seruicio q les hazian, por que sin duda serian de mucha costa. . . . Orchestras, que son las dãças del verbo Griego, que significa saltar, que es lo mismo que dançar; y estas se hazian con solo meneos: y porque lo principal era con las manos, llamó a las destos dançadores Casiodoro, manos habladoras, y que sus dedos tenian lenguas; cuyo silencio era clamoroso, y la exposicion callada" (10-12) ("The figure of a particular intention is called an enterpise (*empresa"*), which because it is the object of what one carries out, came to be called an enterprise, and it belonged to those made of real weapons, and the imitation of these came to be called feigned ones; and these enterprises in particular were used in challenges (duels) . . . Insignias were called signs by the Romans, they were the signs that Captains carried on their standards, that at first were images carried up high . . . Devices are signs that distinguish those who wear them, and they were carried by some squadrons, or ancient legions, as can be seen in the notice of one or another Empire . . . Symbols are also called signs, but they are those, that communicate something like a monogram, and the ones that are used in war were called "Tesseras" among the Latins; and they were used to silently indicate raised up high that which the army was supposed to do . . . *Pegmas* is another name that has been given to Emblems, because of the resemblance that they have with them, which were a representation that was constructed with still figures in a square wooden construction; first showing a surface with figures placed at the banks, and in the middle of this ground another smaller scene was raised with different figures; and then the third and the fourth, until it diminished in the manner of a tower: and this is what Martial said, that tall *Pegmas* were raised in the middle of the street: the image of these may be found on the back side of some ancient medallions, in memory of the adulation that was directed to Princes and of the service that was done on their behalf, because without a doubt they would have been very costly. . . . Orchestras, which are dances from the Greek word, that signify to jump, which is the same as to dance; and these are done only with wriggling: and because it was done mainly with the hands, Casiodoro called these dancers, speaking hands, and that their fingers had tongues; whose silence was clamorous, and the exposition silent").

4. In his introduction to Bourdieu's *Field of Cultural Production*, Randal Johnson writes: "In his discussion of the literary field in nineteenth-century France . . . Bourdieu analyses these opposing principles through the opposition between bourgeois art [notably the theatre], social art, and art for art's sake. . . . The cultural field, is furthermore, structured by the distribution of available positions . . . and by the objective characteristics of the agents occupying them. The dynamic of the field is based on the struggles between these positions, a struggle often expressed in the conflict between the orthodoxy of established traditions and the heretical challenge of new modes of cultural practice, manifested as *prises de position* or position-takings" (16-17).

5. Horozco writes on the vast differences between theorization and practice in the Prologue to the First Book: "pues seruia de poco saber vno

mucho del gouierno de los cielos, y de las medidas de la tierra, si en sus cosas no sabia medirse, ni alcançaua saber como se auia de gouernar. Por lo qual segun los Stoycos, sola esta sciencia moral se deuia llamar Philosophia, y por lo menos confessauan era auentajada a las otras sciencias naturales; por que sin ellas se podia viuir en alguna manera, y sin esta en ninguna. Y si miramos la diferencia que ay de la especulacion a la obra, essa hallaremos entre esta y las demas sciencias; pues en las otras se puede alcançar mucho dellas con la theorica, y en esta es impossible, sino se pone por obra, y se platica" (5) ("well it would be of little use to know much about the disposition of the heavens, and of the measurements of the earth, if in his own things he did not know how to measure himself, nor manage to learn how to govern himself. In which case according to the Stoics, only this moral science should be called Philosophy, and at the very least they confessed it surpassed the other natural sciences; for in the others much can be accomplished with theory, and in this one it is impossible, unless it is turned into works, and discussed").

6. Horozco y Covarrubias writes in the Prologue to the second volume, "Si es verdad lo que el otro Poeta dixo, que se lleuaua la aprouacion de todos, el que juntó lo que es gustoso, con lo que ha de ser de prouecho, no sera fuera del proposito el auer juntado con lo q es doctrina moral y prouechosa, lo que es curiosidad, ordena al gusto que conbida a leer lo demas, por estar tan estragado y aun perdido el de muchos, que no solo es menester salsa y apetito, sino engaño, que piensen es vna cosa, y hallen otra" (A 2) ("If what the other Poet said is true, which had the approval of everyone, that he who joins that which pleases, with that which is profitable benefit, it will not be out of the question to have joined with that which is moral doctrine and beneficial, that which is rare, order the delight so that it bids read the rest, because it is so depraved and even missed by many, because not only are sauce and appetite necessary, but also deceit, so that they ponder one thing, and find another").

7. This is a fairly common strategy that is repeated in any number of poetical treatises written by Horozco's contemporaries. See Porqueras Mayo.

8. Calderón takes a similar position on the importance of painting in a "defense of painters" that he wrote. See Curtius and ter Horst.

9. "Y assi vemos lo que sucedio a los Lacones con Tirteo su Capitan, dado de los Athenienses por desprecio, siendo coxo y tuerto, mas de tal ingenio que los hizo vencer a los Mesenios, de quien antes auian sido tres vezes desbaratados y vencidos. Y esto fue con los versos que les ordenó con tanta fuerça, que los animó para aquella batalla, y para las demas que despues tuuieron, quedando entre ellos la costumbre de cantar los mismos versos, que en algunos autores Griegos se hallan referidos."(6) (Thus we see what happened to the Lacons with Tirteo as their Captain, who was scorned by the Athenians, being lame and missing an eye, but of such ingenuity that he was able to cause the defeat of the Mesenios, who had destroyed and defeated them three times before. And this was accomplished with the verses that compelled them with so much power, that it incited them for that battle, and

for the others that they had after, remaining among them the custom of singing the same verses, that have been mentioned in some Greek authors.)

10. Praz, Daly, R. de la Flor, Clements, and Maravall all connect the emblem to medieval heraldic devices, family crests, and symbols.

11. Luiz Costa Lima discusses this "rationalization" of poetry in the Renaissance and baroque: "I merely point out, in opposition to purely aestheticist modes of inquiry, that the cult of reason, viewed as able to crystallize eternal norms to be obeyed by the poet, and as well the concomitant disdain for anything that transgressed its canon, were bound up with the form in which social power was organized, a form no longer grounded in medieval theocentrism" (32).

12. See Gebauer and Wulf on Platonic and Aristotelian mimesis.

13. In a note, Mario Praz discusses such unnatural configurations of images in relation to Walter Ong's work on the allegorical tableau: "According to Ong the sixteenth- and seventeenth-century addiction to the allegorical tableau is closely related to addiction to new habits of communication of thought introduced by printing, such as the development of tables of dichotomies or bracketed 'outlines' of subjects: such outlines represent a kind of ultimate in the reduction of the verbal to the spatial: words are made 'intelligible' by being diagrammatically related to one another. The allegorical tableau occupies a kind of intermediate position between the aural and the visual worlds because of its special interaction of words and design. The peculiar dependence of visual symbols on verbalization which marks the great age of allegorical tableau is testimony to the fact that it was a marginal age—an age when a verbal culture was being transmitted into a visual culture" (15).

14. Giuseppina Ledda finds a similar strategy in the Prologue to Villava's *Empresas espirituales*: "Poniéndome una vez a mirar la galana invención de las Empresas de que tanto an usado y usan estrangeros, y más en particular italianos y franceses, comencé a dar traças en mi pensamiento, en qué manera podría hazerles servir a la Christiana piedad, por ser todas las que hasta este tiempo se an estampado con diferente fin . . . Porque siempre me pareció zelo piadoso, y digno de ingenios virtuosos, el de los qualesquier invenciones, que se ha usurpado el mundo tyranicamente para su servizio, las procura reduzir a la obediencia de su dueño que es Dios; que éste ha de ser el fin y el blanco de nuestras obras . . . Tomado an algunos esta empresa, bolviendo los versos humanos en divinos, trocando la materia, y guardando la composición . . . Yo bien quisiera entrar en este número, como lo he significado en las ocasiones que se han ofrezido bolviendo algunas cosas profanas, y haziéndolas servir a Dios nuestro bien" (49-50) ("Setting myself one time to look at the invention of *Empresas* that foreigners have employed and employ so often, the Italians and French in particular, I began to make sketches in my imagination, concerning the way in which I could employ them in the service of Christian piety, since all of those that have been printed up to now are of a different object . . . Because it always seemed pious zeal to me, and worthy of virtuous talents, that these inventions, which the world has tyrannically usurped for its own service, be

reduced to the obedience of their master who is God; that this must be the object and aim of our efforts . . . Some have taken this *empresa*, exchanging human verses for divine, exchanging the substance, and maintaining the composition . . . I would well like to enter among this number, as I have indicated on the occasions that have offered themselves changing a few profane things, and making them serve God the object of our esteem").

15. On Plato's opinion concerning the mimetic properties of painting, Gebauer and Wulf write, "Painters and poets, in distinction to specialized craftsmen, are therefore in the position of creating and giving form to manifold things. In this they are more similar to God than to craftsmen. Mimesis means the *production of an appearance*. Artistic representation, however, is not the appearance of that which is or really exists but the appearance of something phenomenal. . . . The central meaning of mimesis for art, literature, and music is already apparent in Plato's works. He attributed to it the capacity of producing a world of appearances. He understood imitation as the capacity not for producing things but for producing images" (38); and on Aristotle, "At the center of painting and poetry lies mimesis; but it does not imply the mere copying of the externalities of nature and the portrayal of individual features. Art and poetry aim much more at "beautifying" and "improving" individual features, at a *universalization*. Mimesis is thus copying and changing in one. . . . Mimesis thus names neither an imitation nor a representation of a reality; it leads instead, via the arrangement of individual elements, to the creation of a literary fiction that cannot be reduced to its presuppositions" (54).

16. Speaking to this combination of Neoplatonic elevation of images with an Aristotelian ethical tone, E.H. Gombrich writes "It was the Platonists who made man feel the inadequacy of 'discursive speech' for conveying the experience of a direct apprehension of truth and the 'ineffable' intensity of the mystic vision. It was they, also, who encouraged a search for alternatives to language in symbols of sight and sound which could at least offer a simile for that immediacy of experience which language could never offer. . . . It may be argued that the Aristotelians, by contrast, kept this reaction alive by overrating the powers of language. Language, after all, is a tool, an 'organon' developed by mankind under the evolutionary pressures which favoured collaboration and communication between members of a clan or tribe. It thus became adapted to the intrasubjective worlds of facts and arguments. It could never have performed these functions if it had not categorized the world of experience and formalized the structure of statements. The way it fulfilled this task was of course first described by Aristotle, but it is notorious that the Aristotelian tradition tended to take the categories of language for the categories of the world" (190).

17. Barbara Kurtz follows Erich Auerbach's definition of typology in her book on Calderón's *autos*: "According to this so-called figural vision," every occurrence, in all its everyday reality, is simultaneously a part in a world-historical context through which each part is related to every other, and thus is likewise to be regarded as being of all times and above all time.

This analogical reading of history, historical events, and historical personages is also known, of course, as typology: "the broad study, or any particular presentation, of the quasi-symbolic relations which one event may appear to bear to another—especially, but not exclusively, when these relations are the analogical ones existing between events which are taken to be one another's 'prefiguration' and 'fulfillment.'" More specifically, typology refers, in a Christian context, to "the science of history's relations to its fulfillment in Christ" (1991, 125).

18. The list of authors who have analyzed early and (post)modern literary and historical phenomena is significant, but perhaps no critic has studied the ideological importance of perspectivalism to early modern thought more elegantly than Martin Jay, who notes that the institution of modern perspective coincides with developments in modern science and philosophy: "for a long time, Cartesian perspectivalism (Albertinian perspective) was identified with the modern scopic regime *tout court*. . . . Brunelleschi is traditionally accorded the honor of being its practical inventor or discoverer, while Alberti is almost universally acknowledged as its first theoretical interpreter. . . . Growing out of the late medieval fascination with the metaphysical implications of light, light as divine *lumen* rather than perceived *lux*, linear perspective came to symbolize a harmony between the mathematical regularities in optics and God's will" (115-16).

19. Ernst Cassirer discusses this destabilization of medieval truths by emerging trends in Renaissance thought in his book on Nicholas of Cusa: "In the cosmology of Cusanus the universe dissolved into an infinite multiplicity of infinitely different movements, each circling around its own centre, and all held together both by their relationship to a common cause and by their participation in one and the same universal order. The same is true of spiritual being. Every spiritual being has its centre within itself. And its participation in the divine consists precisely in this centring, in this indissoluble individuality. Individuality is not simply a *limitation*: rather, it represents a particular *value* that may not be eliminated or extinguished. . . . For only by virtue of this thought do the multiplicity, the difference, and the heterogeneity of these forms cease to appear to be a contradiction of the unity and universality of religion and become instead a necessary expression of that universality itself" (28).

20. See Lyle Massey's article "Anamorphosis through Descartes or Perspective Gone Awry." Also see Kurtz, "Defining Allegory, or Troping Through Calderón's *Autos*."

21. Andrews writes: "one-point perspective provides spacious settings in which action can occur—over time, as if on a stage, making room for a variety of figures involved in different episodes or activities. Indeed, perspective space gives rise to many sorts of settings, small pockets of space or vast panoramas, all having a kind of temporal resonance, demanding, in effect, to be explored or inspected over time and almost inviting, by their very emptiness, the inclusion of additional figures and events. Ultimately, the deeper and more expansive it seems, the more

readily that space can encompass an extended series of moments or scenes; in short, the more easily it can accommodate a continuous narrative" (18).

22. Panofsky writes: "The particular form of this unity once again finds its theoretical analogue in the view of space of contemporary philosophy: in the metaphysics of light of pagan and Christian neoplatonism: 'Space is nothing other than the finest light,' according to Proclus; here, just as in art, the world is conceived for the first time as continuum. It is also robbed of its solidity and rationality: space has been transformed into a homogeneous and, so to speak, homogenizing fluid, immeasurable and indeed dimensionless" (49).

23. Panofsky, once again: "Perspective subjects the artistic phenomenon to stable and even mathematically exact rules, but on the other hand, makes the phenomenon contingent upon human beings, indeed upon the individual: for these rules refer to the psychological and physical conditions of the visual impression, and the way they take effect is determined by the freely chosen position of a subjective "point of view." . . . the perspectival view, whether it is evaluated and interpreted more in the sense of rationality and the objective, or more in the sense of contingency and the subjective, rests on the will to construct pictorial space, in principle, out of the elements of, and according to the plan of, empirical visual space" (67-71).

24. The list of critics who have studied anamorphosis is too extensive to include all of the names here, but the most influential on this study include the following: Jurgis Baltrusaitis's *Anamorphic Art*; *The Curious Perspective* by Ernest Gilman; *Baroque Reason* by Christine Buci-Glucksmann; *Looking Awry. An Introduction to Jacques Lacan through Popular Culture* by Slavoj Zizek; *The Dialogic Imagination* by Mikhail Bakhtin; and *The Four Fundamental Concepts of Psychoanalysis* by Jacques Lacan.

25. What Alberti accomplishes with his conceptualization of a pyramidal scheme of space, which becomes regularized in the static monocular gaze of the viewer, is this mathematical systemization of three-dimensional space onto a two-dimensional surface, which, as Jurgis Baltrusaitis points out, is an illusion: "It is a science which fixes the exact dimensions and positions of objects in space, but it is also an art of illusion which recreates them" (4).

26. For more on the monocular point of view and its deconstructing oblique counterpart (anamorphosis), see Baltrusaitis, Panofsky, Gilman, Buci-Glicksmann, Bryson, Jay, Maravall, and Zizek.

27. In his study of Velázquez and Goya, Ortega y Gasset comments on this particular characteristic of baroque painting: "La obra es entonces un aparato de significar . . . la pintura como un diálogo entre el artista y el contemplador" (54) ("The work is thus an apparatus of signification . . . the painting like a dialogue between the artist and the contemplator").

28. Paula Carabell, in "Narcissus and the Conditions of Painting," stresses this element in an analysis of Alberti's work that takes as its point of departure Alberti's own comments concerning the origins of painting: "I

used to tell my friends that the inventor of painting, according to the poets, was Narcissus, who was turned into a flower: for, as painting is the flower of all arts, so the tale of Narcissus fits our purposes perfectly. What is painting but the act of embracing by means of art the surface of the pool?" (1). Thus, Carabell demonstrates that Alberti is fully conscious of the "tension between the planarity of the pool and the illusion of depth, between the reflecting surface and the reflection in it" (2). Upon seeing his reflection in the pool, Narcissus's first reaction is not one of recognition, but rather one of wonder and misrecognition. As the surface of the pool is two-dimensional, Narcissus at first refuses to acknowledge that he is indeed looking at an optic rendering of himself because it does not coincide with his "haptic," or corporeal, experience. Later, when he returns to the pool, he recognizes his image, but he does not accept the image as a complete representation, but rather attempts to penetrate the depths of the pool to find his own essential depth, the *other* which lies behind the visual sign. Narcissus plumbs the depths of the pool beyond his reflection looking for his true self.

29. Gracián writes, "Atiende la dialéctica a la conexión de términos, para formar un buen argumento, un silogismo, y la retórica al ornato de palabras, para componer una flor elocuente, que es un tropo, una figura" (15). The use of the word "flor" here is not coincidental. Gracián is commenting on how Narcissus raises himself out of his desperate contemplative state through self-representation.

30. Lyle Massey summarizes Bryson's view in the following terms: "Norman Bryson . . . has argued that Alberti's perspective grid and vanishing point, based on the notion of the centric ray, construct a viewing subject that imagines him/herself as the objective focus of representation. In a tripartite system that Bryson calls the "logic" of representation, perspective embodies the viewer as both the origin of and object in the gaze and at the same time posits a third metaphysical or divine viewpoint (the disembodied view) that stands outside the closed system of reference implied by the grid" (1149). Lacan explains this relationship in this way: "This is the function that is found at the heart of the institution of the subject in the visible. What determines me, at the most profound level, in the visible, is the gaze that is outside. It is through the gaze that I enter light and it is from the gaze that I receive its effects. Hence it comes about that the gaze is the instrument through which light is embodied and through which—if you will allow me to use a word, as I often do, in a fragmented form—I am *photographed*"(105-106).

31. If such knowledge of how the technical "trickery" functions seems inconsistent with a continued belief in the truth-effect of the signifying apparatus, one need only take note of the popularity of after-the-fact television shows that reveal the technological advances behind the special effects of spectacular movies in order to encounter a contemporary homologous situation. If anything these shows actually increase the truth-effect of the cinema because they treat special effects technicians like so

many modern-day magicians, while simultaneously satisfying the desiring (voyeuristic) eye's hunger to see the "real" truth.

32. Maravall writes, "It was a painting of what was incomplete, shifting, and unstable, a painting adequate for grasping the human being and life . . . the human being does not possess a being that has become, but a being becoming—a fieri, not a factum; consequently, a being incomplete and in continuous change" (260). René Jara finds a similar semiotic narcissism in literature: "El libro que leemos es sujeto y objeto a la vez. En la medida en que es objeto la lectura produce el surplus que surge de su interpretación y representación. En tanto que sujeto el libro sufre una pérdida que el lector pone voluntariamente bajo tachadura para seguir los rastros de lo que el otro ha perdido, conciente de que los resultados de su escrutinio serán siempre precarios" (14) ("The book that we read is subject and object at the same time. Insofar as it is an object reading produces the surplus that arises from its interpretation and representation. As subject the book suffers a loss that the reader voluntarily places under an erasure in order to follow the tracks of what the other has missed, conscious that the results of his/her scrutiny will always be precarious").

33. Slavoj Zizek, in his book *The Sublime Object of Ideology*, defines the Lacanian concept of master signifier, or *"point de capiton"*: "The 'quilting' performs the totalization by means of which the free floating of ideological elements is halted, fixed—that is to say, by means of which they become parts of the structured network of meaning. If we 'quilt' the floating signifiers through 'Communism,' for example, 'class struggle' confers a precise and fixed signification to all other elements: to democracy (so-called 'real democracy' as opposed to 'bourgeois formal democracy' as a legal form of exploitation)" (87-88). By the same token, the complex movement of the plots of the Spanish *comedia* become fixed around the "quilting points" of honor, purity of blood, prudence, and so on.

34. For more on the baroque fascination with compiling encyclopedic collections of all sorts, see the following: "The Aesthetics of the Marvelous: The Wondrous Work of Art in a Wondrous World," James V. Mirollo; "A World of Wonders in One Closet Shut," Joy Kenseth; "Strange New Worlds: Mapping the Heavens and Earth's Great Extent," James A. Welu; "Remarkable Humans and Singular Beasts," William B. Ashworth Jr.; "A Paradise of Plants: Exotica, Rarities and Botanical Fantasies," Elisabeth B. MacDougall; "Love, Monsters, Movement, and Machines: The Marvelous in Theaters, Festivals and Gardens," Mark S. Weil.

35. In talking about the proportion between the image and the subscription, Horozco writes: "En lo que son fiestas y regozijos publicos, suelen sacarse empresas, y el proposito se dize en vno, o mas versos, como la inuencion del demonio rodeado de llamas, y la letra: MAS PENADO Y MAS PERDIDO Y MENOS ARREPENTIDO" (49) ("In festivals and public celebrations, many times *empresas* are carried out, and the intention is said in one, or more verses, such as the artifice of the devil surrounded by flames with the script: MORE TORMENTED AND MORE LOST AND LESS REPENTANT").

36. Godzich and Spadaccini discuss three possible modes of cultural reception: mass, elite, and popular. They write, "The constitution of a mass-oriented auditive culture permits thus, by virtue of the structure of its operation, what we shall call an elite reception, in which the receiver, perceiving the manipulation, subtracts himself/herself from it, in order to identify with the goals of the manipulators. Such a receiver need not belong to the class or group doing the manipulation, but culturally s/he seeks to join them. In such a mechanism of ideological identification lie the roots of high culture, which, in our view, should not be constructed as merely the culture of the actual manipulating elite" (48). Also, "If one grants that a majority of the population receives the artifacts of such a culture in the way that they are intended, one must see this majority as being essentially manipulated . . . In other words, one must presuppose a certain amount of uncritical reception, a reception inattentive to the logical discontinuities of what is being propounded and unaware of the passivity enforced upon its subjects." Or, perhaps more succinctly stated, "Official culture consists of two distinct realms: an elite culture that is ideologically consonant with the goals of the state's ruling groups and dedicated to their promotion and realization, and a mass culture that is manipulated and purveyed on behalf of the state to a broad audience" (60). "In other words, the distinction between mass, elite, and popular that we are proposing is not based on the inherent formal properties of cultural artifacts but upon patterns of reception and usage of these artifacts. This implies that the very same artifact may be subject to at least three different usages according to our differentiation, certainly a complication that most literary historians fail to envisage" (49).

37. See Praz, Clements, Daly, and R. de la Flor.

38. Mario Praz writes: "Five requisites by Giovio: 1) that the device would have a just proportion between body (that is, the picture) and the soul (the motto); 2) that it should not be so obscure as to need the Sybil for its interpreter, nor so transparent that every mean mechanic might understand it; 3) that above all it should make a fine show, that is, represent things pleasing to the eye, such as stars, fire, water, trees, instruments, fantastic animals and birds; 4) that the human figure should not appear therein; 5) that the motto which is its soul should be in a different language from that of the author of the device, so that the sentiments should be somewhat more concealed, and that the motto should be brief but not so much so as to be obscure and misleading" (63).

39. Mebane writes "My thesis is that philosophical occultism carried to its logical extreme the humanists' affirmation of the power of human beings to control both their own personalities and the world around them. In the late sixteenth and early seventeenth centuries, magic became the most powerful manifestation of the growing conviction that humankind should act out its potential in the free exercise of its powers on the social and natural environments; moreover, those who explored 'natural magic' often asserted that the quest for truth should not be limited by traditional religious, political, or intellectual authorities" (3). Much of this alchemy or magic worked within sign systems that shared a great deal of the images of

the emblematists. See also Frances Yates, *The Art of Memory*, especially the chapter on Giordano Bruno, or Yates's book on Bruno, *Giordano Bruno and the Hermetic Tradition.*

40. Gwendolyn Barnes-Karol writes: "The manipulation of images through sermons as a vehicle for disseminating ideas that would facilitate the reconsolidation of the eroding power base of the Church, Monarchy, and nobility was ultimately tied to the preservation of the aura and authority, grandeur, and infallibility of these three institutions in order to halt the increasing autonomy of the individual and/or of new social groups" (61).

41. Maravall writes: "in attempting to resolve one of those situations that the seventeenth century considered to be without precedent, [the individual] felt thrown out of, beside himself, alienated. In such a sense baroque culture led human beings to be other than themselves, to go outside of the beaten path. . . . The basis for the baroque to be a guided culture is revealed in the fact that it was fundamentally a culture of alienation" (1986, 252).

42. For more on literature that falls somewhere between an elite reception and mass reception, see Godzich and Spadaccini's analysis of Dwight MacDonald's concept of "mid-cult" literature in relation to the phenomenon of chapbooks in Golden Age Spain. Also, Pedro F. Campa notes how many of the emblem books were written for the teaching of rhetoric in the universities in Spain and Europe, including Diego López's 1613 translation of Alciati's *Emblematum Liber.*

Works Cited

Andrews, Lew. *Story and Space in Renaissance Art. The Rebirth of Continuous Narrative.* Cambridge: Cambridge UP, 1995.

Bakhtin, M.M. *The Dialogic Imagination.* Ed. Michael Holquist, Trans. Caryl Emerson and Holquist. Austin: U of Texas P, 1981.

Baltrusaitis, Jurgis. *Anamorphic Art.* Trans. W.J. Strachan. New York: Harry N. Abrams, 1969.

Barnes-Karol, Gwendolyn. "Religious Oratory in a Culture of Control." *Culture and Control in Counter-Reformation Spain.* Eds. Anne J. Cruz and Mary Elizabeth Perry. *Hispanic Issues* 7 (1992): 51-77.

Benjamin, Walter. *The Origins of German Tragic Drama.* Trans. John Osborne. London: NCB, 1977.

Bourdieu, Pierre. *The Field of Cultural Production.* New York: Columbia UP, 1993.

Bryson, Norman. *Vision and Painting. The Logic of the Gaze.* New Haven: Yale UP, 1983.

Buci-Glucksmann, Christine. *Baroque Reason: The Aesthetics of Modernity.* Trans. Patrick Camiller, intr. Bryan S. Turner. London: Sage Publications, 1994.

Campa, Pedro F. "Diego López's *Declaración Magistral sobre las Emblemas de Alciato*: The View of a Seventeenth-Century Spanish Humanist." Hecksher and Sherman 223-48.

Carabell, Paula. "Narcissus and the Conditions of Painting." Mimeograph.

Cassirer, Ernst. *The Individual and the Cosmos in Renaissance Philosophy*. Trans. and intr. Mario Domandi. New York: Barnes and Noble, 1963.

Clements, Robert J. *PICTA POESIS. Literary and Humanistic Theory in Renaissance Emblem Books*. Roma: Edizioni di Storia e Letteratura, 1960.

Copjec. Joan. *Read My Desire: Lacan Against the Historicists*. Cambridge, Mass.: MIT P, 1995.

Costa Lima, Luiz. *Control of the Imaginary. Reason and Imagination in Modern Times*. Trans. and intr. Ronald W. Sousa, aft. Jochen Schulte-Sasse. Minneapolis: U of Minnesota P, 1988.

Curtius, E.R. *European Literature and the Latin Middle Ages*. Trans. Willard R. Trask. Princeton: Princeton UP, 1967.

Daly, Peter M. *Emblem Theory: Recent German Contributions to the Characterization of the Emblem Genre*. Nendeln: KTO Press, 1979.

_____. *Literature in Light of the Emblem: Structural Parallels Between the Emblem and Literature in the Sixteenth and Seventeenth Centuries*. Toronto: UP, 1979.

Elliot, J.H. *Imperial Spain: 1469-1716*. London: Penguin Books, 1970.

_____. *The Count-Duke of Olivares. The Statesman in an Age of Decline*. New Haven: Yale UP, 1986.

Gebauer, Gunter and Christoph Wulf. *Mimesis: Culture—Art—Society*. Trans. Don Reneau. Berkeley: U of California P, 1992.

Gilman, Ernest. *The Curious Perspective. Literary and Pictorial Wit in the Seventeenth Century*. New Haven/London: Yale UP, 1978.

Godzich, Wlad and Nicholas Spadaccini. "Popular Culture and Spanish Literary History." *Literature Among Discourses: The Spanish Golden Age*. Ed. and intr. Godzich and Spadaccini. Minneapolis: U of Minnesota P, 1986. 41-61.

Gombrich, E.H. *Symbolic Images. Studies in the Art of the Renaissance II*. Chicago: U of Chicago P, 1972.

Harms, Wolfgang. "The Authority of the Emblem." *Emblemática* 5 (1992): 3-21.

Hecksher, William S. and Agnes B. Sherman, Eds. *Emblematic Variants: Literary Echoes Alciati's Term Emblema: a Vocabulary Drawn from the Title Pages of Emblem Books*. New York: AMS P, 1995.

Hoffman, Konrad. "Alciato and the Historical Situation of Emblematics." Hecksher and Sherman 1-45.

Horozco y Covarrubias, Juan de. *Emblemas morales*. Çaragoça: Alons Rodrigues y Juan de Bonilla, 1603.

Jara, René. *Los Pliegues del Silencio: Narrativa latinoamericana en el fin del milenio*. Valencia: EUTOPÍAS, 1996.

Jay, Martin. "Scopic Regimes of Modernity." *Force Fields: Between Intellectual History and Cultural Critique.* Ed. Martin Jay. New York: Routledge, 1993. 114-33.

Johnson, Randal. "Introduction," to his edition of Pierre Bourdieu's *The Field of Cultural Production.* New York: Columbia UP, 1993. 1-28.

Kenseth, Joy, Ed. *The Age of the Marvelous.* Hanover, N.H.: Hood Museum of Art, Dartmouth College, 1991.

Kurtz, Barbara E. "Defining Allegory, or Troping Through Calderón's *Autos.*" *Hispanic Review* 58 (1990): 227-43.

_____. *The Play of Allegory in the* Autos Sacramentales *of Pedro Calderón de la Barca.* Washington, D.C.: The Catholic U of America P, 1991.

Lacan, Jacques. *The Four Fundamental Concepts of Psychoanalysis.* Ed. Jacques-Alain Miller, trans. Alan Sheridan. New York: W.W. Norton and Co., 1981.

_____. "Logical Time and the Assertion of Anticipated Certainty: A New Sophism." *Newsletter of the Freudian Field* Vol. 2, N. 2, 1988. 4-22.

Ledda, Giuseppina. *Contributto allo studio della letteratura emblematica in Spagna (1549-1613).* Pisa: Universita de Pisa, 1970.

Lope de Vega, Félix. *Arte nuevo de hacer comedias.* Madrid: Espasa-Calpe, 1948.

Massey, Lyle. "Anamorphosis Through Descartes or Perspective Gone Awry." *Renaissance Quarterly* 50 (Winter 1997): 1148-89.

Maravall, José Antonio. "La literatura de emblemas en el contexto de la sociedad barroca" *Teatro y literatura en la sociedad barroca.* Ed. José Antonio Maravall. Madrid: Seminarios y Ediciones, 1972. 149-88.

_____. *The Culture of the Baroque. Analysis of a Historical Structure.* Trans. Terry Cochran. Minneapolis: U of Minnesota P, 1986.

Mebane, John S. *Renaissance Magic and the Return of the Golden Age: The Occult. Tradition and Marlowe, Jonson, and Shakespeare.* Lincoln: U of Nebraska P, 1989.

Mignolo, Walter. *The Darker Side of the Renaissance: Literacy, Territoriality and Colonialization.* Ann Arbor: U of Michigan P, 1995.

Ong, Walter. "From Allegory to Diagram in the Renaissance Mind: A Study of the Allegorical Tableau." *The Journal of Aesthetics and Art Criticism.* Ed. Thomas Munro. 57.4 (June 1959): 423-40.

Ortega y Gasset, José. *Papeles sobre Velázquez y Goya.* Ed. Paulino Garagorri. Madrid: Revista de Occidente en Alianza Editorial, 1987.

Panofsky, Erwin. *Perspective as Symbolic Form.* Trans. Christopher S. Wood. New York: Zone Books, 1991.

Paz, Octavio. *Sor Juana or, The Traps of Faith.* Trans. Margaret Sayers Peden. Cambridge, Mass.: Harvard UP, 1988.

Porqueras Mayo, Alberto. *La teoría poética en el renacimiento y manierismo españoles.* Barcelona: Puvill Libros, 1986.

Praz, Mario. *Studies in Seventeenth-Century Imagery.* Roma: Edizioni de Storia e Letteratura, 1964.

R. de la Flor, Fernando. *Emblemas: Lectura de la imagen simbolica.* Madrid: Alianza Editorial, 1995.

ter Horst, Robert. "The Second Self: Painting and Sculpture in the Plays of Calderón." *Calderón de la Barca at the Tercentenary: Comparative Views.* Eds. Wendell M. Aycock and Sydney P. Cravens. Lubbock: Texas Tech UP, 1982. 175-92.

Williams, Raymond. *Marxism and Literature.* Oxford: Oxford UP, 1977.

Yates, Frances A. *The Art of Memory.* Chicago: U of Chicago P, 1966.

Zizek, Slavoj. *The Sublime Object of Ideology.* London/New Haven: Verso, 1989.

_____. *Looking Awry: An Introduction to Jacques Lacan Through Popular Culture.* Cambridge: MIT P, 1991.

◆ Chapter 7

Intellectuals, the State, and the Public Sphere in Spain: 1700-1840

José A. Valero

The year 1833 seems to establish definitely, after the truncated experiences of 1808-14 and 1820-23, a new stage in the publicity of social and political discourse in Spain. There is a proliferation of spaces (periodicals, coffeehouses, the Ateneo, the Liceo, etc.) that could be seen as constitutive of what Habermas has called the bourgeois public sphere. However, while not denying the importance for the transformation of the conditions for public discourse of the political revolution that follows the death of Fernando VII, I would like here to question the radical novelty of that publicity as contrasted with the eighteenth-century situation, in which public discourse was more tightly and visibly controlled from state and Church power. Recent revisionist historians (Cruz, Ringrose) have shown that the political and legal novelties of the postfernandine years can distract us from the fact of the absence of a parallel social revolution and the continuity of traditional practices of patronage, clientelism, *amiguismo,* and so on, in the process of recruitment and replacement of political elites.[1] My suggestion is that something similar occurs with the "explosion" of publicity in the 1830s: such a development seems to liberate the intellectual from state patronage, allowing him to speak as representative of "the public," but there are reasons to think of the public sphere—or at least those spaces of it cultivated by the intellectual elites—as a simulacrum of publicity in which a constant effort takes place to empty it of political antagonism. Public spaces frequented by intellectual elites also play an important function, I argue, as spaces of testing, co-optation, and training of new intellectual generations by the older intellectuals already tied to state power. These factors point to important continuities between the eighteenth century and the decades before the Revolution of 1868 in the relation of intellectual elites both with the state and with the "public."

Political revolution in Spain, according to revisionist historiography, was "not the result of the ascent of a new social class but rather the product of the acceptance of modernization on the part of the old elite that coopted some bourgeois elements" (Cruz 171). The acceptance of the need for political and cultural modernization by the governing elite is linked to the development along the eighteenth century of a symbiotic relation between the state and secular intellectuals, propelled by the awareness that Church monopoly in cultural matters is a serious hindrance to much-needed change, and that it is necessary to promote a secular national culture. There begins to emerge a kind of parity of the educated and an ideology of merit, premised on the acceptance by intellectuals of social conservatism, which, once the political revolution is set in motion, produces a general occupation of the higher positions of the state by men of letters. In this essay I search for causes of the development of that symbiotic relationship between intellectuals and the state during the eighteenth century, and I suggest that the relation should be part of the explanation of the belated rise in Spain of the political public sphere and of "public opinion" as a legitimating construct. I hope to add some perspective with a few proddings into Spain's differential dynamics vis-à-vis eighteenth-century France. Rather than the proposal of hard conclusions, my objective is to draw the attention of researchers dealing with eighteenth- and nineteenth-century Spain to the centrality of categories such as that of "intellectuals" and "publicity" to cultural and political history.

The age that inaugurates the new relation of the state and secular men of letters opens, in the wake of the War of Succession, with the transformation in state policy entailed by the renunciation to Flanders and Italy and the suppression, by the *Nueva Planta* decrees, of the particularistic institutions of the Crown of Aragón, which had supported the archduke

Carlos. The *Nueva Planta* was a decisive step toward centralization; it put an end to legal resistance from the Crown of Aragón to the will of the sovereign, it introduced there Castillian functionaries and magistrates and a strong military presence, and it suppressed internal customs. The process would continue into the reign of Carlos III with measures such as the imposition of Castillian in schools and commercial books (Molas Ribalta 219). The reorganization of the administration in a centralizing direction with the Orry plan of 1714 concentrated decision-making power in the hands of the Secretarios de Despacho (ministers), and limited the Grandees to the Consejos, which would slowly (very slowly in the case of the Consejo de Castilla) fade into nonoperativity. A means was thus established to circumvent and eventually eliminate the main obstacles to royal despotism.

According to Giovanni Stiffoni, there was a clear sense at the end of the War of Succession that the Bourbon triumph represented a cultural break with the imperial Spain of the Austrian dynasty. What was not so clear was the content of that break. Once the irredentist phase of Alberoni's foreign policy was over, the notion begins to take shape that cultural intervention could be "an important weapon for the construction of a consensus, which necessarily had to be wider and more socially open to enable reformist programs to turn from theory into reality" (Stiffoni 79). The priority task in the construction of a new cultural project could only be an exercise of historical interpretation, of definition of the present by opposition to an immediate past that had to be overcome. In this context, official historiography has to serve a variety of functions, which at times clash with one another. It must be at the same time a vehicle of knowledge, of consensus-building, and of propaganda. Historiographical veracity and the needs of power were then just as now in an uneasy tension; from official spheres preference is given to political interests, which may coincide or not with the findings of reformist historians. Antonio Mestre's studies around Gregorio Mayans show that when they do not coincide, the reformist effort is marginalized and neutralized by official action. The reaction toward critical historiography is the clearest example. The official sphere (to which figures like Feijoo and Flórez subordinated themselves) often opted to support a traditional, noncritical history of affirmation of pious nationalist superstitions and to silence in their defense the most rigorous representatives of a critical and rational historiography, such as Mayans. Often recounted by Mestre, the 1742 episode of Mayans's censure of Francisco Javier de la Huerta's officially endorsed *España Primitiva* and his subsequent relegation to ostracism by the cultural elite of the Court illustrates the limits of official reformism during the eighteenth century. According to Mestre, episodes such as this signal the beginning of a clearly despotic cultural policy. Since then "the contours of Spanish cultural policy were clearly established, at least for many years to come. Men of letters had to be compliant with power if they wanted to receive government favors" (1990, 131).

During the reign of Felipe V important institutions are created from which official culture will attempt to control traditional spaces of cultural propagation. The Royal Library in 1711, the Royal Academy of Language in 1713, the Royal Academy of History in 1735: these are the first institutions that grant literature—in the wide sense—a certain power over the whole of society. For the first time state functionaries and *criados* of the king have a function of regulation of linguistic uses, which will expand, in time, to book censorship and the creation of official social discourse. Perhaps for the first time one can speak of an official secular intelligentsia. As is the case with the army, the royal academies exercise their jurisdiction with a certain degree of independence from intermediate institutions, in direct contact with the king and his cabinet. Like the army, they will be an instrument for the rationalization and extension of state power, the hegemonic or cultural arm of the state supplementing the coercive one. What Lucie Robert says of the French academies applies as well to the Spanish: "a language that founds at the same time law and knowledge, that contributes to the territorial unification of the country, that presides over commercial exchanges, can not and should not leave room for ambiguity. The efficiency of the law and of scientific knowledge is threatened by the very nature of their main support, linguistic exchange." Works like the *Diccionario de Autoridades* can, like the normative works of the Académie (Dictionary, Rhetoric, Poetics), be considered as an attempt to "subjugate metaphor in what it represents of spontaneous, individual, private, carnivalesque . . . , to put in its place rules of clarity and order" (Robert 18).

The struggle against the baroque and popular excess of language will be a defining characteristic of the first group of reformist intellectuals working within the newly created official cultural institutions. Around the protection and leadership of Agustín de Montiano y Luyando, a team of men of letters will strive to impose in the production and in the historiography of national poetry and theater a classicist orthodoxy that favors Greco-Roman and French models while attempting at the same time to define a national classical canon. Montiano, Blas de Nasarre, Luis José Velázquez, the authors of the *Diario de los Literatos*, including Juan de Iriarte, and some reform-minded Jesuits such as Andrés Marcos Burriel and José Francisco de Isla constitute a circle of intellectuals based in the new royal academies and library, the direction of which they attempt to control. The activities of Montiano and his circle illustrate the workings of official cultural patronage, and how that patronage was dependent on compliance with official guidelines. From his earlier years as a protégé of the minister Patiño, and following the latter's policy, Montiano was the main promoter of the centralization of the cultural institutions of the nation. In 1738 he obtained the royal decree that made of the Academy of History a public institution, with its first seat in the Royal Library. Stiffoni places the reformist group that began to take shape in the Royal Library in what he calls the "Patiño-Feijoo line" (199), because they favored the programmatic centralism articulated by the Benedictine in his essay "Amor a la patria y pasión nacional." Since 1737 Montiano belongs to the Academia de la Lengua; in 1745 he is named director in perpetuity of the Academia de la Historia; he will belong to the Academia de Bellas Artes from its foundation, as well as to several foreign academies. Along with the cultural success comes the political: in 1740 he is *Oficial Mayor* of the Ministry of State (Secretaría de Estado), and in 1746 he is Minister of Grace and Justice and of State. Toward the middle of the century he is no doubt the person with more influence and decision-making power within the cultural institutions of the state, and he uses his power to grant favors to men of letters compliant with the official line. "He is the father and protector of all men of letters" ("Es el padre y protector de todos los literatos"), according to one of the interlocutors in Manuel Lanz de Casafonda's 1761 *Diálogos de Chindulza* (50). In the later years of his life, he holds a *tertulia* that seems to have played an important role as a link between the first two generations of Spanish neoclassicists. Montiano, Luzán, Juan

Trigueros, Juan de Iriarte, and Velázquez transmit their cultural ideals to a younger group that includes Cándido María Trigueros, Llaguno, Nicolás Fernández de Moratín, Huerta, and perhaps Bernardo and Tomás de Iriarte, all of them relevant intellectuals during the reign of Carlos III (Deacon 397). In his role of patron of culture, Montiano obtains royal protection for the academies of Buenas Letras of Barcelona (1751) and Sevilla (1752), but only after these institutions accept their subordination to the Academia de la Historia and to follow its statutes. By contrast, and as a new early example of the dark side of reformist absolutism, when the Academia Valenciana, founded by Mayans in 1742, rejects its subordination to the academy of which Montiano was to be perpetual director, Fernando VI denies it protection, and it can only survive until 1751.

The trajectory of Montiano provides us with a view of literary life from the upper echelons of official culture, and suggests that success was dependent on support of a strongly centralized cultural life. The counterpart, the view from those struggling to "make it" as men of letters, would immerse us in an atmosphere of suspicion, of personal resentments, of personal rather than intellectual alliances, of cliques, of hoarding and secrecy with respect to documents and materials that can be used, through publication, as means for promotion and for obtaining state favors; it would situate us in a field of struggle for pensions, prebends, and bureaucratic positions granted from a power over which one has very little influence, and which can, sometimes without clear reasons, grant sudden favors or inflict sudden punishments. It would be a general atmosphere of unstableness in which success or failure depends, rather than on personal merit, on compliance with power and on networks of friendships and personal contacts. What Mestre says of the episode of Mayans's censorship of Huerta's *España Primitiva,* that "the drama consists in that a scientific problem is resolved as a personal problem" (1970, 391), can be generalized to the relation between power and intellectual production during all the century, and the prevalence over intellectual argument of an atmosphere of personal envies and alliances between intellectuals will also continue and perhaps intensify as the century advances.[2]

In the search for security, hidalgo intellectuals without means could find their way to state favors through work for the high nobility, as preceptors, librarians, or secretaries (Deacon 395). But the most sought-after positions were in royal institutions, as librarian, academic, *cronista,* or, after the expulsion of the Jesuits, as a professor in the Reales Estudios de San Isidro. For these positions the support was needed of at least one of the high powers: the royal family, the minister of state, the royal confessor, the members of the Consejo de Castilla, and especially its president, and so on. That the writer could not earn a living from his pen alone was a frequently observed fact in eighteenth-century Spain. Presenting a project for a scientific and literary academy, and contrasting the Spanish situation with the French, Tomás de Iriarte writes that "here it is necessary for the Government to do [finance] everything, because the nobility does not feed any writer, and the public does not buy books" ("aquí es menester que por ahora el gobierno lo haga todo, porque ningún Señor da de comer a literato alguno, y el público no paga los libros") (in Alvarez Barrientos 1994, 23). Periodical journals provide the only opportunity for survival through the support of the reading public. But when a degree of economic independence is achieved through the market, it is always a precarious independence. State intervention can ruin in an instant a successful venture, and only state protection grants relative security, premised on a careful self-censorship. The dangers of and the alternatives to market-supported journalism are clearly shown in a text by Cristóbal Cladera, a journalist left in a precarious position after the suppression in 1791, out of fear of infiltration of revolutionary ideas, of all periodicals except the *Gaceta* and the *Diario de Madrid.* Cladera had invested all his means in a publication, *Espíritu de los mejores diarios literarios que se publican en Europa*, that had been received favorably by the public. When the subscribers demand the return of the advance payment for a re-edition of the journal, he finds himself in the need to address a petition to the king to permit the continuation of the publication, following whichever official guidelines were imposed on it, or, if that is not possible, to be granted an official position in the state bureaucracy (petition reproduced in Varela Hervías 70-71).

The relative initial success of Cladera's journal is one of a handful of isolated cases. Most periodicals that are successful have some degree of official support (as do *El pensador* and *El censor,* the latter until it ignores once too often the premise of self-censorship), and those without such support that try to survive through the market cannot attract a large enough readership and are short lived. The relative slowness in the growth of the reading public of course only tightens the dependency of writers on the state, and their subjection to the dynamics of personal networks. If in Montiano's time the incorporation into the intellectual elite of the Court was premised on the subordination of criticism to the interests of a power on whose patronage it depended, this does not change substantially during the reigns of Carlos III and Carlos IV, even if instead of incorporation into official institutions we think of attempts to attain market success. These factors contributed to the permanent limitation and precariousness of the public sphere in Spain, since the general reading public did not have, as it did in France, well-known intellectual figures with which it could identify and at the same time associate with specific positions in cultural and political matters. The problem was circular, since the lack of support from the public at the same time eliminated the only possibility for reformist intellectuals to free themselves from state dependency.

How does this dependency affect the capacity of reformist intellectuals to engage in rational-critical discourse? It seems that the "rationality" of Spanish reformist intellectuals has, when it comes to sociopolitical matters, little to do with the Kantian *sapere aude,* the overcoming of prejudice and inherited authority, and also little to do with the development of abstract ideas, values, and models of society. Rather, it is a regulating and instrumental rationalism, in the service of the objectives of social control and accumulation of power in the state. Such objectives themselves escape rational questioning, and public debate is sacrificed for their sake. It is a rationality aimed at the renovation of the mechanisms of social reproduction in times in which that reproduction according to established ways is becoming problematic. Perhaps its main thrust can be described as the incorporation of hegemonic mechanisms together with the spatial extension of time-honored coercive mechanisms as means for the preservation of power. What it wants from the public is not rational-critical debate but identification with the productivist and modernizing ends of the state. Or rather, it doesn't want a public at all (beyond a reduced clique of intellectuals) but good old-fashioned royal subjects.

In support of the modernizing impetus of the state on which they depend, intellectuals in Spain engage in an effort to channel moral psychology toward more ascetic and utilitarian attitudes, toward a positive disposition toward productive work, and toward identification with the interests of the Crown. Intellectuals try to promote this mental revolution from their positions in the state bureaucracy. When not yet incorporated into the paid service of the state, they turn the latter into their interlocutor with writings in which they point to the need for social change and to the role of the state and the undersigned, its most humble servant, in that task. The initial premise is generally the recognition of the state as subject of the rationalization of society and as the only public actor. Public critical discourse emanating from the royal subjects as individuals (the public sphere) must constrain itself to "customs" and "culture"; that is, it must be restricted to criticism of the habits of the subjects themselves. Public discourse on political matters is a monopoly of the state. This latter notion is well illustrated in the censorship by Jovellanos and Antonio de Alcedo, performed in their role as members of the Academia de la Historia, of a work of political *arbitrismo*:[3]

> Ninguno que la vea podrá dudar del mérito de la obra, que contiene las máximas de gobierno más sabias, los más acertados medios de corregir los males y las más justas providencias para evitarlos; pero como al mismo tiempo pinta con suma claridad, energía y viveza la infeliz constitución de nuestro gobierno, el exceso de ociosidad y de los vicios que de ella nacen, que domina a la nación; la falta de justicia en los tribunales y magistrados, como de ministros íntegros y justificados; la escasez de generales, aunque hay muchos con este nombre, y así respectivamente de todos los ramos por las letras del alfabeto, bien claro es que obras de esta naturaleza sólo se escriben para instrucción de los que tienen a su cargo la dirección del Gobierno y deben cuidar de que éste sea arreglado a las leyes divinas y humanas, pero no para que se publique ni ande en manos de todos, porque esto sería autorizar al público para censurar al gobierno y a sus ministros, y quizás causaría mayores daños. (Jovellanos 54-55)

(Nobody that reads it will doubt the merit of the work, which contains the wisest maxims of government, the most appropriate means for correcting the defects, and the fairest measures to avoid them. But because at the same time it paints with utmost clarity, energy and liveliness the unhappy constitution of our government; the excess of idleness and of the vices that are born of it; the lack of justice in courts and magistrates; the scarcity of generals, even though there are many so ranked; and so on in all branches, considered in alphabetical order, it is plain that works of this nature are written only for the instruction of those who are in charge of the direction of government and who should procure that the latter agree with divine and human laws, but not to be published and in everybody's hands, because this would mean authorizing the public to censure the government and its ministers, which would perhaps cause greater harm.)

The work is praiseworthy and replete with useful observations, but permission to print it must be denied. Political discourse is restricted to the state, and public opinion must be acted upon but not actor, object but not subject of politics. The state is immunized against rational-critical discourse, and state reform is restricted to an internal operation. The bureaucratic intellectual has no qualms in accepting that mutilation of the public sphere because he is not only a reformer, but also a servant of the state. The reforming impulse is tied, then, to the will to preserve one's own position, and to the corporative interest in the preservation and enlargement of the state bureaucracy, a priority of the means over the ends.

In *Legislators and Interpreters* Zygmunt Bauman discriminated between an ideal and a real Enlightenment: "The Enlightenment has entrenched itself in our collective memory as a powerful drive to bring knowledge to the people, to restore clear sight to those blinded by superstition, to give wisdom to the ignorant, to pave the way for the progress defined as the passage from darkness to light, ignorance to knowledge . . . And yet, under close scrutiny, the substance of enlightened radicalism is revealed as the drive to legislate, organize and regulate, rather than disseminate knowledge" (74). Historians of the European Enlightenment have traditionally had the tendency to emphasize the antiabsolutist strands of the movement, forgetting or relegating to secondary importance the consolidation of an alliance between intellectuals and the state. But without having to agree with Bauman's sweeping reduction of the Enlightenment to one of the poles of its dialectic, in eighteenth-century Spain it seems unquestionable that the dominant impulse of intellectuals engaged in social reform is not a rational-critical but a regulative rationality closely associated, in fact or in will, with the power of the absolutist state. How much this dominance separates Spain from the countries with a "higher" Enlightenment is for the moment a question mark. In Bauman's account of the rise of intellectuals in Europe, the conclusions for his European—but mostly French—scenario seem to converge with the Spanish one (with which, unsurprisingly, Bauman doesn't deal): enlightened radicalism boils down to "the drive to legislate, organize, and regulate, rather than disseminate knowledge." But although the similarities between France and Spain are worth considering, the differences are at least as significant.

In the slow passage to modernity, the horizontality of structure of the republic of letters was according to Bauman a radical alternative not to aristocratic power, which was not a power of ideas, but to the Church, with its vertical hierarchy and transcendentally founded truth. The polyvalence and resulting crisis of religious skepticism ushered in by the Reformation could only find an answer in the overcoming of verticality through consensus, the new court of appeal of the horizontal republic of letters (Bauman 35). The repression of the Reformation in Spain means the persistence, by contrast, of the "command economy of thought" represented by the Catholic Church, given the generalized acceptance of its authority. It is precisely in the eighteenth century that it becomes clear that the monopoly of the Church in matters of public morality is an impediment to the needs of enhanced social control of the state. Literature is born as an institution and men of letters are endowed with a certain amount of social power thanks to the support of a state that needs to free itself from the fixated and limiting ideological authority of the Church. The limitations of the Church in matters of social engineering, and the possibilities for enhancement through products of secular culture developed by men of letters, are spelled out by Clavijo y Fajardo in the course of his state-sponsored polemic against the *autos-sacramentales*. The vices and virtues of "civil life," he argues, can not be dealt with through the Christian polarity of theological virtues and sin:

> muchos defectos morales no tienen en el evangelio precepto que los ataque; y . . . es preciso que nos esmeremos en unir en igual grado las virtudes morales con las prácticas del Cristianismo. ¿Cuántos disgustos y molestias acarrean en el trato de la vida civil las ridiculeces de varios hombres, que por esto no dejan de ser muy honrados, y buenos Cristianos? No me señalarán las leyes, así divinas como humanas, que atacan estas ridiculeces. ¿Habrá hombre bastante insensato para pretender que no importa el que un hombre sea ridículo, con tal que sea virtuoso? (160)
>
> (many moral defects do not have in the gospels any precept that attacks them; and . . . we should strive to join in the same degree moral [civic] virtues with Christian practice. In the dealings of social life much quarreling and annoyance is caused by the ridiculousness of some men that are nevertheless very honest and good Christians. You can not point out to me the laws, divine or human, that attack that ridiculousness. Would anybody be so foolish as to claim that it does not matter if a man is ridiculous, provided that he is virtuous?)

Christian virtue and the fear of human laws must be complemented with civic virtue. The selfishness of man cannot be repressed with laws. The only weapon against it is literature, for Clavijo here specifically theater, which "with the delight of its ornaments captures our attention with gentle violence, and it mends our ways precisely because it doesn't seem to seek this purpose, but that of entertaining us" ("con el embeleso de todos sus adornos nos lleva con suave violencia la atención, y nos corrige por lo mismo que no parece proponerse este fin, sino el de divertirnos") (158).

Once the literary institution is granted a capacity to dispense autonomous norms, the state can use literature both as a means of representation and as an instrument for the moral legitimation of its power that frees it from theological legitimation. As Peter Bürger points out (8-9), the dependency of the literary institution (and we may add of secular intellectuals generally) on its utilization by the state is, paradoxical as it may seem, a necessary step toward its autonomy, since state support allows the literary institution to successfully challenge the Church as a rival institution for moral ascendance over society.

Moral condemnations of the more popular theater practices in eighteenth-century Spain were frequent both from traditional sectors of the Church and from reform-oriented men of letters. Curiously, the terms of their condemnations were for the most part quite similar. What separates clerical criticism from that of the reformers is that the former condemn the medium itself, whatever its nature, while the latter are trying to reconvert it, since, according to Nicolás Fernández de Moratín, "after the pulpit, which is the cathedra of the Holy Ghost, no school is better suited to teach us than the theater" ("[d]espués del púlpito, que es la cátedra del Espíritu Santo, no hay escuela para enseñarnos más a propósito que el teatro") (156). The difference in reality leads us to a fundamental tension, more important than the surface agreements: when theological opposition confronts the immorality of theater, it is confronting not only its content but the medium itself because it represents a menace to the monopoly of the Church in the control, through the pulpit, confession, schooling, and so on, over social morality. When the neoclassicist condemns the immorality of the stage, what he has in mind—more clearly in the reign of Carlos III—is an alternative theater that could serve to spread a new secular social morality.

It is easy to see then why the collaboration between the Jesuits and the court intellectuals of Montiano's times imposed limitations to a clear definition of a cultural program directed to the modernization of the nation and to an increased reach of the state, a program which could be properly developed only from a secular perspective. Educational reform, specifically, was seriously hindered by Jesuit control of all levels of education. If the order embraced the cause of reform, it would be only with the condition that it dictate itself the pace of change.

These limitations perhaps explain why it is not until the reign of Carlos III and the beginnings of anti-Jesuit policy that men of letters begin to promote literature in terms of its potential as a means of social engineering. In an essay in which he attempts to set precisely the chronological limits of the Enlightenment in Spain, Rinaldo Froldi offers several reasons for its restriction to the period that begins with the reign of Carlos III, and among the elements of rupture with the previous period he highlights "the idea of the need to diffuse culture, and of a basic and extended education, which supplants the elitist academicism that characterized the reigns of Felipe V and Fernando VI" (67). Of course we should be aware that "culture," as Froldi uses the term, means the culture that the intellectuals try to impose over already existing cultures, and that education was to be extended down the social hierarchy in a differential manner. But what I want to emphasize here is that intellectuals engage in the last third of the century in the promotion of the idea that social modernization can be achieved by changing the patterns of thought of all different social sectors, and that this can be done best through the cultural creations of the intellectuals themselves. With the new function of literature in the service of the moral configuration of individuals, we are entering what can properly be called, again to use Bürger's terms, the Enlightenment literary institution. With it, "[t]he process of modernization thus obtains a new quality: the character of a conscious project. In so far as this occurs in literature, literature becomes a central institution of social life" (10).

This common confrontation with the Church is then another factor that further tightens the knot between intellectuals and the state in Spain. The experience of "freedom of thought" of men of letters in countries where Church authority had been shaken long before was sometimes reinforced, as happened in France, by the fact that an important number of them where not dependent on the state. Free from social attachments and social functions, the only power they could invoke was the power of argument, of logic, of abstract reason; consensus could be the only court of appeal. According to a line of thought that stems from Tocqueville, eighteenth-century sociability produced the separation of authority and power, of politics and administration, and promoted the abandonment of practical experience and time-honored customs in favor of abstract theories on the nature of government (Tocqueville 138-48). This was in a sense a "literaturization" of politics, its subordination to the abstract and universalist normativity of classicist poetics and its dreams of "ideal worlds." In this view eighteenth-century sociability is seen as a forerunner of Jacobin revolutionary assemblyism, with its connotations of messianism, forced unanimity, and so on (see Chartier 10-17). The other view, of course, is the line of thought that runs from Kant to Habermas, which sees eighteenth-century sociability as helping to develop a public sphere composed of a free, critical, rational, egalitarian public. The fact is that such abstract theorizing on the nature of government is virtually absent from the Spanish Enlightenment. A determining factor for the limited development in eighteenth-century Spain of critical rationalism and "abstract" thought was that men of letters here were not "floating" intellectuals in the manner of the French *philosophes,* who were "encouraged to comport themselves as representatives of the whole society, and . . . were confirmed in this generalized character of their outlook by the absence of a traditional status or particular function specially appropriate to them in the society" (Krieger 174). In Spain reformist intellectuals are either state functionaries or members of the clergy, when they are not at the direct service of the aristocracy. This is an obstacle to the horizontal structuration that characterizes the republic of letters of the French *philosophes*. Which is not to say that the latter were altogether free from the need of patronage. But, as Leonard Krieger points out, the spirit of patronage had been transformed in France, and with it the general outlook of modernizing intellectuals: "the competition for *philosophes* was keen, the responsiveness of royal favorites and of nobles was apparently unlimited, and the advantage was on the side rather of the patronized than of the patron. These social ties served, then, not to constrain the ideas of the philosophes, but only to augment their effects. Although very few tried, like Diderot, to support themselves through their writing or editing, the protagonists of the French Enlightenment did in fact assume the self-appointed trusteeship for the whole society that we associate with the independent profession of letters" (174-75). There was no such seller's market in Spain, but rather a general apathy of the high nobility with regards to literature (Alvarez Barrientos 1995b, 53-61), and the social ties of intellectuals did certainly have the effect, through direct state intervention or through self-censorship, of constraining their ideas. There were all the reasons, then, for the absence in Spain of anything resembling the "high Enlightenment" that in France developed, as Keith Michael Baker notes, a progressively more critical stance toward the Crown, forcing it eventually to enter into "public" political contestation, thus surrendering the notion, central to absolutism, that the monarch is the only public person. According to Habermas, the historical origin of the institutions that constituted the bourgeois public sphere was "the attempt to restrict the power of the absolutist state," and the literary public sphere "did not serve the feudal class or the absolutist state," but was rather "the area in which the rising middle class developed moral and political self-consciousness" (Hohendahl 1989, 25). But this can hardly be said to be so in Spain, where there develops in the eighteenth century a tight interdependence between the literary field and the state, and where rational critique is displayed against whatever traditional beliefs, customs, and institutions may be perceived as a hindrance to concentration of power in the state, but which never confronts state power itself.

Do discursive spaces develop in late eighteenth-century Spain that can be characterized as constituting a literary public sphere? If it is a question of degree, then that degree is certainly a very low one. If it is a question of reaching a critical density, it is not too risky to assert that in Spain there does not develop in that century a dense network of public communication springing from the private sphere. In support of this assertion I will comment on what I perceive as limitations of a series of cultural spaces in eighteenth-century Spain that could be thought of as constituting or promoting a public sphere.

In Habermas's account of the rise of the public sphere, masonic lodges are among the most important institutions for the growth of that network. Ferrer Benimelli (1986) convincingly shows that Spain is an exception in Europe in that Freemasonry is almost absent on its soil until the War of Independence. The presence of Freemasonry is sporadic, usually in port cities and related to foreign visitors, and the vigilance of the Inquisition is relentless. Carlos III, about whom a legend has spread and been accepted by historians that he belonged to a lodge, is in fact the European eighteenth-century monarch of which we possess most testimonies of a clearly antimasonic attitude and policy, in line with the papal interdiction.

The sphere of literary discourse has its origins in courtly aristocratic circles (Hohendahl 1982, 53), but we cannot properly talk of a literary public sphere until critical argument is freed from considerations of social status. The precondition of discursive equality is undermined by the centrality of *honra* in elite institutional settings such as the royal academies, strongly vertical and based on codes of preeminence and status-display. *Honra* codes are also at work, albeit in a more attenuated way, in the Sociedades Económicas de Amigos del País (Sánchez-Blanco Parody 100-01). These institutions created during the reign of Carlos III, although more clearly modern in outlook than the academies, were mainly concerned with technological improvement. They were composed mostly by nobles and clergymen, and the provincial societies, many of them instituted not by private initiative but by royal decree, had to follow, like the academies, the official Madrid model.

Eighteenth-century private *tertulias* such as the one held in the early 1770s in the Fonda de San Sebastián in Madrid have been viewed by cultural historians as "horizontal" spaces of communication between equals, where the participants escape the "baroque" norms of communication. But to what extent can a sociability based, as the *tertulia* of the Fonda de San Sebastián was, on strong ties of friendship be considered as constitutive of a public sphere? Mutual trust made it possible to deal with topics that could not be dealt with openly, but for the same reason it closed the space of communication to the outside and contained the public diffusion of ideas. Moreover, the "forbidden matters" of preference seem to have been issues not of politics but of women, social customs, and literary rivalries, approached not through rational-critical discourse but through burlesque and satire. The Fonda de San Sebastián group seems to have viewed itself not as a reunion of citizens gathered to discuss public affairs in a spirit of citizenship, but rather as a closed group of friends who confronted society as a hostile "outside" that reinforced, as its negative image, the Arcadian nature of their own closed male society. The *tertulia* can be seen then as a "third space," a male refuge in between the rigors of occupational life and domestic life, two spheres the separation of which was accelerated, as La Vopa (115 n.76) observes, by the type of salaried bureaucratic employment characteristic of the "service elite."

Of course *tertulias* of intellectuals do not exhaust the modes of sociability of gathering spaces like coffeehouses and inns. There is no doubt that coffeehouse sociability was a growing concern of government authorities, but could it be perhaps better to talk of the development of a popular public sphere in reference to them? Our "recognized" intellectuals, again, are not precisely the ones that promote this kind of open sociability, but are rather, and Moratín's *La comedia nueva o el café* is a good example, allies of the state in its attempt to control them, if not eliminating them at least restricting their gatherings to certain sectors of society (see E. Baker).

According to Keith Michael Baker, with the religious, economic, and administrative debates of the 1750s and 1760s in France, the absolutist model of state monopoly of publicity was broken: "The reign of silence imposed by an absolutist monarch could no longer contain debates and contestations that made increasingly explicit appeal to a world of public opinion beyond the traditional circle of institutional actors" (210). While in France the understanding of "public opinion" as tending to unity, as embodying reason, and as an infallible tribunal is born toward the middle of the century and is firmly established, according to Mona Ozouf, in the 1770s, in Spain the old view of opinion as unreflexive, inherited, usually doubtful or false knowledge seems to be the only widespread one until the years of the War of Independence, precisely in a situation of practical nonexistence of the state, and of exceptional freedom of the press on political matters.

During these years, Richard Herr observes, "the press helped the traditionalists more than the Liberals, but on both sides it was drawing the common people into the public sphere" (93). The explosion of political publicity will return in an intensified way a few years later, during the also truncated constitutional experience of the Liberal Triennium. According to Gil Novales, it is during these two periods of intense public political discourse, and in particular during the second one, that Spain finally catches up with the display of social ideas and positions of the European high Enlightenment (1978, 28). Together with the eclosion of the press, a defining institution of the Liberal Triennium are the Sociedades Patrióticas, public clubs of political discussion similar to the clubs of the French Revolution, stemming directly from those coffeehouse tertulias and gatherings that Old Regime authorities—and their intellectuals—had viewed so suspiciously. For the almost four years of the Triennium, the Sociedades Patrióticas coexist with the Sociedades Económicas de Amigos del País, which serve the former as a model for the discussion of matters of economic development and education. But soon the differences are clearly established, since the Patrióticas become a public sphere of political discourse: "the birth of the Patrióticas displaces the model, the Económicas, to the right. From 1820 the supporters of the Sociedades Económicas are the *moderados,* those who are afraid of politics, the more or less shamefaced endorsers of counterrevolution. A dialectical movement comes to closure with the praise of technology, opposed to the demand for and obtainment of rights" (Gil Novales 1975a, 1, 9).

Most Sociedades Patrióticas are open to the public, and the attendance, at least in the larger cities, is numerous, so much so that the Madrid actors complain that they are left without an audience. It is in these discussion clubs that a popular public opinion is created; they are "the pulse of the Revolution," in Gil Novales's words: "The maneuvers of the king or his ministers in their attempts to return to absolutism are blocked by the Sociedades. The moderado ministers know it and hate them, although when they are the ones that feel threatened by the king, they occasionally threaten him in their turn with the Sociedades. The king, as all absolutists, fears and loathes them. The fierce persecution in 1814 and 1823 of all those who had belonged to Sociedades Patrióticas is a good proof of it" (1975a, 1, 14-15). What we witness in these years then is the coming of age of a popular public sphere of political discourse. If during the War of Independence the people are restrained by an intense religious and monarchical propaganda and by their own political inexperience, in the Triennium the contact between writers and the people that had been missing in the eighteenth century becomes a reality, and many of these writers come from the same popular classes they address. Needless to say, the "high" literary intellectuals, accustomed to a discursive environment restricted to themselves and power, do not have much sympathy for the popular public sphere. Periodicals like *El Zurriago, El Eco de Padilla, El Diario Gaditano,* and many others contribute to the spread of a democratic *(comunero)* liberalism and awaken the consciousness of their rights in important numbers of urban and suburban masses, attain a great popularity, fuel urban mobilization, and finally precipitate national and international counterrevolution (Gil Novales 1975b). With the birth of a more truly open sphere of political discourse, conservatives have to resort to the appeal to "public opinion," which they separate from what they present as a degraded and manipulated popular opinion.[4]

The differentiation of "public opinion" and "popular opinion" appears when it becomes necessary to deny political legitimacy to popular opinion, given its growing power of mobilization. In this context, La Vopa's words are most pertinent: "Precisely because the public consensus was 'invisible,' it was easily abused" (80). In the years after the death of Fernando VII the public sphere becomes again a space of contention, but the traditional alliance of "high" literary intellectuals with power continues, which explains the generalized acceptance of a conservative romantic reading of the nation's cultural past, as well as the relentlessly antidemocratic rhetoric of that liberal intelligentsia, who assume the role of spokesmen of public opinion.

During the finally successful (because socially counterrevolutionary) political and legal Liberal revolution of the years following the death of Fernando VII, institutions such as the Ateneo and the Liceo, which at first glance we would associate with the bourgeois public sphere, are of central importance for the consolidation of a political elite of *notables* supported by a Romantic and historicist reading of national culture. Garrorena Morales has pointed to the parallels between the ups and downs of the Ateneo and those of moderado rule between 1835 and 1850 and explains the moderado quasi-monopoly of the institution by the social composition of its members: the institution had an aura of elegance, distinction, *buen tono,* with a clientele of up-to-date intellectuals—meaning enthusiasts of French doctrinarism—and well-to-do bourgeois comfortable with the mesocratic regime. Through the teachings there of Donoso Cortés, Alcalá Galiano, and Pacheco, conservative liberalism will build a theoretical basis for the legitimation of its ideal of "government by the intelligent," which through the equation intelligence = education = affluence will deny the majority of the population the right to political participation.

In a good example of the way in which the discourse of publicity is deployed as a strategy of distinction, in Bourdieu's sense (Eley), Mesonero Romano's *Semanario Pintoresco Español* praises the "spirit of association" as "the most positive conquest" of the times, and the Ateneo as the perfect example of that spirit:

> Y (lo que no puede menos de estamparse en justo elogio del país) en todas estas reuniones en que han tomado parte casi todas las notabilidades políticas, científicas, literarias y artísticas de la capital, ha reinado constantemente la más cortés armonía, la abstracción más absoluta de toda pasión política, el decoro y buen tono de la más distinguida sociedad, sin que ni un solo accidente por pequeño que sea, haya venido a alterar en un punto tan grata y apacible reunión. ("Sociedades literarias . . ." 426-27)
>
> (What must be stated in just praise of the nation is that all these meetings—in which almost all the political, scientific, literary, and artistic notables of the capital have participated—have been governed at all times by the most courteous harmony, the most absolute exclusion of any political passion, the propriety and good form of the most distinguished society, without the smallest of accidents occurring to alter a bit such a pleasant gathering.)

A trait, discernible here, of conservative liberal intellectuals in their stance toward public discourse is that the praise of communication and publicity is constantly coupled with the reviling of politics as a fallen arena, taken over by a "factionalism" that has come to distinguish *popular* opinion and of which they, the intellectuals, spokesmen of true *public* opinion, are of course free.

The press, the Ateneo, and the Liceo sustain the literary institution of the 1830s and 1840s. In these spaces, the practices of literary production and criticism were performed by a minoritarian intellectual caste, and through those practices the generational replacements of that caste were infused with the cultural outlook and the rhetorical skills necessary for the continuity in the cultural legitimation of bureaucratic-oligarchic rule. In the 1838 opening issue of the periodical of the newly created Liceo, Patricio de la Escosura expects the free exchange of ideas to create a homogeneous public opinion in cultural matters, and ends up hinting at the idea that the Liceo can serve as a space of co-optation of naturally rebellious intellectual youth and of reproduction of intellectual and ruling elites:

> La reunión frecuente de los artistas en todos géneros ha de producir por necesidad entre ellos un comercio de ideas, cuyo resultado es de esperar que sea un pensamiento único y dominante, que dando á todos sus esfuerzos la dirección conveniente contribuya á acelerar la obra de la civilización del país. La juventud tiene en el Liceo una arena en que probar sus fuerzas, si presume de ellas lo bastante para no temer la lucha. (12)
>
> (The frequent gathering of artists of all genres must necessarily produce among them a commerce of ideas, which will hopefully result in a single and dominating thought which, by giving to all their efforts a convenient direction, will contribute to accelerate the task of civilizing the country. Our youth has in the Liceo an arena in which to test its strengths, if these are presumed to be such that it needn't fear the fight.)

As has been frequently noticed, there is a profusion of literary authors among the political and bureaucratic elite of the early years of conservative liberal rule. Literary training and participation in the literary public sphere seem to have worked as a springboard for incorporation into the governing elite. Anne Burdick has shown that these authors came generally from the same noble and professional backgrounds as the political elite of the Old Regime, and were launched into political careers through long-standing social networks of influence linking the provincial oligarchy with the Madrid governmental bureaucracy. What characterizes these time-honored networks from the 1830s on is the fact that a literary component seems to become institutionalized as an established stepping stone to political office, in what would seem a generalized recognition of the mutual dependency of power and literature developed in the previous century: "Our data on the Madrid authors suggests that the Romantic decade modified these established networks by adding a literary component. We can clearly trace members of traditionally important elites passing through a literary phase as they were recruited to government-related and professional careers very much like those of their parents. Madrid's literary community of the 1830's and early 1840's thus appears to have functioned as a new training ground in an otherwise long-standing system for recruiting the personnel of the political system" (Burdick 15-16).[5] As elite self-recruitment adapts to the new political ways, it assures the continuity of patronage and personal influence as the basic mechanism of reproduction. But the fact that now the new recruits are "public" figures recognized through their literary activities in a competitive literary public sphere would seem to give legitimacy to that process of reproduction in that it could claim to be based on merit and intelligence rather than on inherited status.

A true social revolution implies, as Ringrose puts it, "a pronounced change in the origin, mental universe, and objectives of the people recruited into the economic and political elite," and this doesn't seem to have happened in Spain, "although each successive generation of people recruited from traditional origins came to office acculturated to the changing values and behaviors of its own era" (363). While the liberal intelligentsia paid lip service to meritocratic and rationalist administrative ideals, it was at the same time legitimating a state of affairs in which the formal distinction between the private and the public was being constantly overridden by the informal institutions characteristic of oligarchic practice, such as local patronage, clientelism, and nepotism. Rather than constituting the spaces of a bourgeois public sphere, institutions such as the press, the Ateneo, and the Liceo functioned as a discursive simulacrum for the creation of the "public opinion" that the state needed to legitimate its task of "changing everything so that everything remained in its place," to echo the often quoted dictum from *Il Gattopardo*.

The view that I am here suggesting of an important continuity in the practices of eighteenth- and nineteenth-century intellectuals parallels, and finds support in, the thesis, developed most cogently by Jesús Cruz and David Ringrose, of the absence of a social revolution (understood as substitution of one ruling class by another) behind the political-legal revolution undergone by Spain in the first half of the nineteenth century. These historians argue that the political transformations of the 1830s can be better explained, rather than by the confrontation of a capitalist and revolutionary bourgeoisie with a feudal aristocracy, as a response of the ruling elite to the economic and moral bankruptcy of traditional estate society and monarchical absolutism. Dominant elites had to accept and push for certain modern formal institutions, no matter how sincere their commitment to them really was. Once these institutions were established, "traditional elites sought to control them, working from within but also creating new ways of neutralizing them so as to maintain the old relationship between central authority and provincial oligarchies. The outcome combined traditional family strategies, clientage, and patronage with revised societal alliances, manipulation of elections, and *caciquismo*. As a result many aspects of the old order were perpetuated even as society assimilated economic and political arrangements we think of as 'modern'" (Ringrose 386). The assimilation of modern economic and political forms, then, went hand in hand with the prolongation of many of the older mechanisms of elite reproduction, as well as with the preservation in power of a basically unaltered elite—as to its social provenance and networks, except for the co-optation into its ranks of some bourgeois elements. The acceptance of modern forms entails a certain revision of social alliances, and what Terry Eagleton says of the English scenario, that "culture" is what will help in the unifying of the ruling bloc, can be applied to the Spanish case. The institutions of the public sphere become an important means for the unification of the power elite. Through these institutions, "[a] new cultural formation is mapped on to the traditional power-structure . . . , momentarily dissolving its distinctions in order to more thoroughly buttress its hegemony" (Eagleton 13). With the rise of a political public sphere and the legitimation crisis of traditional estate society, the power elite realizes the need for political modernization, and at the same time the need to engage in hegemonic practices that will promote a convergence between actual public/popular opinions and the "public" discourse produced in the controlled public sphere of the dominant groups.

Institutions, such as the press, the Sociedades Económicas, and later the Ateneo, the Liceo, and others, provide a simulacrum of an open and accessible public sphere, which is now needed to legitimate power and to promote a "national" culture through which the interests of the ruling bloc can be presented as those of the country. Behind this simulacrum of an open public arena, there is a real blurring of the formal liberal differentiation of the public and the private, given the continuity of informal practices of clientelism and patronage as the main mechanism for the reproduction of elites. The reality is that these spaces of debate are tightly managed to prevent a truly open and democratic politics of discourse, and that spaces where this management is more difficult (coffeehouses, the Sociedades Patrióticas of the Liberal Triennium, the popular press) are stigmatized as breeding grounds of anarchy, thus justifying their repression.

I have tried to show in this essay that a continued and for the most part successful effort to suppress the political public sphere is a central characteristic of official culture during all the period considered, and that intellectuals play an instrumental role in this suppression. Specific structural causes (cultural domination of the Church, slow growth of the reading public, lack of private patronage from the aristocracy, strong censorship) impeded the potentially more critical writers—those with fewer family ties to traditional oligarchic and bureaucratic elites—from becoming "floating" intellectuals, thus tying them to the patrimonialist-clientelistic dynamics of the state bureaucracy. The ties of intellectuals to the state were reinforced by the awareness, on the part of intellectuals and reformist administrators alike, that the needed modernization of the country could by achieved only through the challenge of the intellectual and moral hegemony of the Church and the promotion of a secular social morality. A consequence of the symbiotic relation that develops between state and intellectuals, and an element of continuity in the activity of public men of letters during 1700-1850, is a certain disposition or habitus of placing oneself and one's discourse in the "locus of power," of considering politics as a question of social engineering (the task that makes them necessary to the state), and an unwillingness to take up political matters in more "abstract" terms of human rights or social equality, or to adopt antagonistic positions toward the ruling oligarchies. The contradictoriness and allegiances of "public" reformist intellectuals will be made manifest in their reactions to the phenomenon of the rise, in the early nineteenth century, of a popular political public sphere, to which they counteract with their appeal to "public opinion" as a higher authority to which all other opinions must surrender.

I do not pretend to suggest that there is a direction of causality from the specific relation of modernizing intellectuals with the state to the atrophy of the public sphere in the period considered. Rather, I understand these and other factors explored in this essay as interrelated and mutually reinforcing characteristics, that taken together may shed some light on the process (peculiar or not) of belated modernization in Spain.

Notes

1. However, the fact that there was not a surrender of power from one social class to another should not prevent us from considering the political-legal revolution of the 1830s as a fundamental stage in a longer process of "bourgeois revolution." As Paul Ginsborg observes, it is a mistake to think that the bourgeois revolution must always be carried out by the bourgeoisie: "The specificity of bourgeois revolution . . . does not depend on its leading actors but on its contribution to bourgeois society. Quite often classes other than the bourgeoisie objectively further the bourgeois revolution while pursuing their own aims. Sometimes they do this in opposition to sections of the bourgeoisie itself" (37-38). See also Eley 116-18.

2. Alvarez Barrientos comments on the end-of-the-century rivalry between the two intellectual groups that included Moratín, Forner, Estala, Melón, Arrieta, one of them, and Quintana, Cienfuegos, Munárriz, the other: "These confrontations, although usually sparked by aesthetic matters . . . were really caused by the struggle to increase one's influence in order to obtain positions, favors, prebends, and privileges, rather than by aesthetic disagreements. The writers themselves are the most direct enemies of the writers, because they compete for an academic seat, or a position in a ministry" (1995b, 54).

3. The censored work is *Lo que tiene España de más y de menos, para que sea lo que debiera ser y no lo que es,* by José del Campillo y Cosío, reformist minister of Felipe V.

4. As La Vopa observes, "Public opinion had unimpeachable moral authority because it formed out of an aggregate of morally autonomous individuals, each arriving at his (or her?) judgment in splendid isolation"; it was posed not only against the absolutist denial of the public sphere, but also, and increasingly, against the emerging arena of modern politics and the menace of democratization of access to that arena. Against, in the rhetoric of the times, the "spirit of party" or of "faction" (110). See Elorza (183-90) for examples of the latter during the Liberal Triennium.

5. "In the 1830s aspiring functionaries were 'processed' through a modified version of the old recruitment system. As before, they generally arrived in Madrid with a veneer of university education, typically in law, to pursue their familial and caciquil connections. In the capital they embarked on a period of informal testing in which they cultivated contacts while combining political advocacy with work as journalists, political writers, and professional or literary apprentices. This allowed the more astute (or better connected) to expand contacts, find patrons, and operate in the world of patronage and political influence" (Ringrose 375).

Works Cited

Alvarez Barrientos, Joaquín. "El escritor según Tomás de Iriarte: su plan de una Academia de Ciencias y Buenas Letras." *Anales de Literatura Española* 10 (1994): 9-35.

_____. "La República de las letras y sus ciudadanos." *La República de las letras en la España del siglo XVIII.* Eds. J. Alvarez Barrientos, François Lopez, and Inmaculada Urzainqui. Madrid: C.S.I.C., 1995a. 7-17.

_____. "Los hombres de letras." *La República de las letras en la España del siglo XVIII.* Eds. J. Alvarez Barrientos, François Lopez, and Inmaculada Urzainqui. Madrid: C.S.I.C., 1995b. 19-61.

Baker, Edward. "En el café de Moratín: *La comedia nueva.*" *Materiales para escribir Madrid. Literatura y espacio urbano de Moratín a Galdós.* Madrid: Siglo XIX, 1991.

Baker, Keith Michael. "Politics and Public Opinion Under the Old Regime: Some Reflections." *Press and Politics in Pre-revolutionary France.* Edited by Jack R. Censer and Jeremy D. Popkin. Berkeley: U of California P, 1987. 204-46.

Bauman, Zygmunt. *Legislators and Interpreters: On Modernity, Postmodernity and Intellectuals.* Ithaca: Cornell UP, 1987.

Burdick, Anne Victoria. *The Madrid Writer in Spanish Society: 1833-1843.* Ph.D. dissertation. U of California at San Diego, 1983.

Bürger, Peter. *The Decline of Modernism.* Trans. Nicholas Walker. University Park, Penn.: Penn. State UP, 1992.

Chartier, Roger. *The Cultural Origins of the French Revolution.* Trans. Lydia G. Cochrane. Durham: Duke UP, 1991.

Clavijo y Fajardo, José. *Antología de* El Pensador. Ed. Sebastián de la Nuez Caballero. Islas Canarias: Viceconsejería de Cultura y Deportes del Gobierno de Canarias, 1989.

Cruz, Jesús. *Gentlemen, Bourgeois, and Revolutionaries: Political Change and Cultural Persistence Among the Spanish Dominant Groups, 1750-1850.* Cambridge: Cambridge UP, 1996.

Deacon, Philip. "Vicente García de la Huerta y el círculo de Montiano: La amistad entre Huerta y Margarita Hickey." *Revista de Estudios Extremeños* 44 (1988): 395-421.

Eagleton, Terry. *The Function of Criticism: From The Spectator to Post-Structuralism.* London: Verso, 1984.

Eley, Geoff. "In Search of the Bourgeois Revolution: The Particularities of German History." *Political Power and Social Theory* 7 (1988): 105-33.

Elorza, Antonio. *La modernización política de España (Ensayos de historia del pensamineto político).* Madrid: Ediciones Endymion, 1990.

Escosura, Patricio de la. "Introducción." *Liceo Artístico y Literario* 1 (1838): 6-11. Reprinted in José Simón Díaz. *Liceo Artístico y Literario (Madrid, 1838).* Madrid: C.S I.C., 1947. 10-13.

Fernández de Moratín, Nicolás. *La petimetra: Desengaños al teatro español. Sátiras.* Eds. David T. Gies and Miguel Angel Lama. Madrid: Castalia, 1996.

Ferrer Benimelli, José A. *La masonería española en el siglo XVIII.* 2ª edición corregida. Madrid: Siglo XXI, 1986.

Froldi, Rinaldo. "Apuntaciones críticas sobre la historiografía de la cultura y de la literatura españolas del siglo XVIII." *Nueva Revista de Filología Hispánica* XXXIII (1984): 59-72.

Garrorena Morales, Angel. *El Ateneo de Madrid y la teoría de la monarquía liberal (1836-1847).* Madrid: Instituto de Estudios Políticos, 1974.

Gil Novales, Alberto. *Las Sociedades Patrióticas (1820-1823): las libertades de expresión y de reunión en el origen de los partidos políticos.* 2 vols. Madrid: Tecnos, 1975a.

_____. "La prensa en el Trienio Liberal (1820-1823)." Eds. M. Tuñón de Lara, A. Elorza, and M. Pérez Ledesma. *Prensa y sociedad en España (1820-1936).* Madrid: Cuadernos para el Diálogo, 1975b. 201-06.

_____. "Ilustración y Liberalismo en España." *Spicilegio Moderno* 10 (1978): 26-41.

Ginsborg, Paul. "Gramsci and the Era of Bourgeois Revolution in Italy." *Gramsci and Italy's Passive Revolution.* Ed. John A. Davis. London: Croom Helm, 1979. 31-66.

Glendinning, Nigel. "Cambios en el concepto de opinión pública a fines del siglo XVIII." *Nueva Revista de Filología Hispánica* 32 (1984): 157-64.

Guillory, John. *Cultural Capital: The Problem of Literary Canon Formation.* Chicago: U of Chicago P, 1993.

Habermas, Jürgen. *The Structural Transformation of the Public Sphere.* Trans. Thomas Burger. Cambridge, Mass.: MIT P, 1989.

Herr, Richard. "The Constitution of 1812 and the Spanish Road to Parliamentary Monarchy." *Revolution and the Meanings of Freedom in the Nineteenth Century.* Ed. Isser Woloch. Stanford: Stanford UP, 1996. 65-102.

Hohendahl, Peter Uwe. *The Institution of Criticism.* Ithaca: Cornell UP, 1982.

_____. *Building a National Literature: The Case of Germany, 1830-1870.* Trans. Renate Baron Franciscono. Ithaca: Cornell UP, 1989.

Jovellanos, Gaspar Melchor de. *Obras de D. Gaspar Melchor de Jovellanos.* Tomo V. Madrid: Atlas (Biblioteca de Autores Españoles), 1956.

Krieger, Leonard. *Kings and Philosophers, 1689-1789.* New York: W.W. Norton & Company, 1970.

Lanz de Casafonda, Manuel. *Diálogos de Chindulza (sobre el estado de la cultura española en el reinado de Fernando VI).* 1761. Ed. Francisco Aguilar Piñal. Oviedo: Cátedra Feijóo-Universidad de Oviedo, 1972.

La Vopa, Anthony J. "Conceiving a Public: Ideas and Society in Eighteenth-Century Europe." *Journal of Modern History* 64 (1992): 79-116.

Mestre, Antonio. *Historia, fueros y actitudes políticas: Mayans y la historiografía del XVIII.* Valencia: Publicaciones del Ayuntamiento de Oliva, 1970.

_____. *Mayans y la España de la Ilustración.* Madrid: Instituto de España-Espasa Calpe, 1990.

Molas Ribalta, Pere. "Los comienzos del centralismo en España. Una perspectiva catalana." *Actas del Simposio sobre Posibilidades y límites de una historiografía nacional.* Madrid: Instituto Germano-Español de Investigación de la Goerres-Gesellschaft, 1984. 215-24.

Ozouf, Mona. "'Public Opinion' at the End of the Old Regime." *The Rise and Fall of the French Revolution.* Ed. T.C.W. Blanning. Chicago: U of Chicago P, 1996. 90-110. [Originally in *Journal of Modern History* 60 (1988).]

Ringrose, David R. *Spain, Europe, and the 'Spanish Miracle,'" 1700-1900.* Cambridge: Cambridge UP, 1996.

Robert, Lucie. "Le fétichisme de la littérature." Dir. Clément Moisan. *L'histoire littéraire: Théories, méthodes, pratiques.* Québec: Les Presses de l'Université Laval, 1989. 17-24.

Sánchez-Blanco Parody, Francisco. "Una ética secular: la amistad entre los ilustrados." *Cuadernos de Estudios del Siglo XVIII* 2 (1992): 97-116.

Sempere y Guarinos, Juan. *Ensayo de una biblioteca de los mejores escritores del reinado de Carlos III.* Madrid: Imprenta Real, 1785-1789. 6 vols. [Edición facsímil, 3 vols., Madrid: Gredos, 1969.]

"Sociedades literarias y artísticas. El Ateneo. El Liceo." *Semanario Pintoresco Español* 94 (14 de Enero de 1838). 425-27.

Stiffoni, Giovanni. *Verità della storia e ragioni del potere nella Spagna del primo '700.* Milano: Franco Angeli, 1989.

Tocqueville, Alexis de. *The Old Régime and the French Revolution.* Trans. Stuart Gilbert. New York: Doubleday, 1955.

Varela Hervías, E. *Espíritu de los mejores diarios literarios que se publican en Europa. Madrid, 1787-1791.* Madrid: Hemeroteca Municipal, 1966.

◆ Chapter 8

Constituting the Subject: Race, Gender, and Nation in the Early Nineteenth Century

Susan Kirkpatrick

In 1836 M.J. de Larra announced to his public that Spain was entering a new era:

> [Estamos e] n momentos en que el progreso intelectual, rompiendo en todas partes antiguas cadenas, desgastando tradiciones caducas y derribando ídolos, proclama en el mundo la *libertad moral,* a la par de *la física,* porque la una no puede existir sin la otra *Libertad* en literatura, como en las artes, como en la industria, como en el comercio, como en la conciencia. He aquí la divisa de la época, he aquí la nuestra. (Larra 134)
>
> (We find ourselves at a moment when intellectual progress, everywhere breaking ancient chains, wearing away obsolete traditions and tearing down idols, proclaims moral as well as physical freedom, because one cannot exist without the other. Freedom in literature, as in the arts, as in industry, as in trade, as in consciousness. This is our motto, the emblem of our age.)[1]

These words were written at a time when Spanish liberals were confident that the new government of Juan Alvarez Mendizábal would succeed in carrying out definitive reforms. In writing about the overthrow of old regimes and authorities impeding the individual's action in the economic, political, and intellectual spheres, Larra drew on the liberal discourse that had been used for decades to justify and motivate the transformation of the absolutist state into a constitutional, representational government. Liberals like Larra used and elaborated this discourse to promise an era of greater opportunity, justice, and prosperity to those who supported their political goals, promulgating their message in the universal terms just cited—freedom in all areas of human activity, freedom for all.

Yet a decade later, a young poet threw Larra's words back in his face as it were, asking: "¡Libertad! ¿pues, / no es sarcasmo / el que nos hacen sangriento/con repetir ese grito / delante de nuestros hierros?" ("Freedom! Is it not a cruel sarcasm to shout that claim in the presence of our chains?"). The poet was a woman, Carolina Coronado, and these words come from a poem titled "Libertad," in which she speaks on behalf of her sex while watching the men of her village celebrate a new victory of liberal reform in the plaza. The men may be happy and excited, she tells her implied female interlocutors, but women's situation will not change under the new laws: "¡Libertad!, / ¿Qué nos importa?, / ¿qué ganamos, qué tendremos?, / un encierro por tribuna / y una aguja por derecho?" (389) (Freedom! What does it matter to us?/ what do we gain, what will we have? / A closed house for our tribunal / and a needle for our right?") The talk of freedom and equality, she concludes, is only for men: "Pero os digo, compañeras, / que la ley es sola de ellos,/que las hembras no se cuentan / ni hay Nación para este sexo" (390) ("But I tell you, fellow women, / that the law is only for them, / that females do not count/nor is there a nation for this sex").

This textual confrontation between Larra and Coronado sets up the question I will explore in this essay. Focusing on the liberal discourse that justified and motivated Spain's uneven journey toward a liberal state, I want to ask how it drew the lines of exclusion noted by Coronado when she declares that women were not part of the nation. A highly charged term of liberal discourse, "nation" denoted a hypothetically unified aggregate of the Spanish population, one undifferentiated by estate or class.[2] Yet differentiations among kinds of national subjects were built into the emerging discursive system through which the relationship between the liberal state and its subjects was represented. "Representation of the nation" was, of course, a key concept in the political debates of early nineteenth-century Spain, and in a broader sense it will also be central to my discussion, for I want to look at two forms of symbolic representation of the nation and ask what different kinds of subjects they imply and what roles they ascribe to these subjects. One form to be examined is to be found in legislative texts such as the Constitution of 1812 and documents associated with it. The other is the theater, seen as both an example and a mirror for its audience, the subjects of the nation.

Enrique Tierno Galván, writing about the Constitution of 1812, suggests how constitutional and theatrical representation might be connected. He argues that the deputies in Cádiz who wrote and ratified the Constitution did not represent the Spanish people in a strict political sense, but instead represented: "quizá . . . a la 'nación,' palabra que repiten bastante y definieron en la Constitución. La nación admite una representación en cierto sentido teatral; se puede representar a la nación desde una idea o arrogándose unas cualidades" (9) ("perhaps . . . the 'nation,' a word that they repeat frequently and that they defined in the Constitution. The nation admits of a representation that is theatrical in a certain sense; a nation can be represented through an idea or by assuming certain qualities"). Tierno implies that the framers of the Constitution of 1812 were performing a new idea of the nation by convening the Cortes in the absence of the monarch, but I would argue that they were at the same time writing for the nation a script that set out the roles of citizen, monarch, and state—a script that was not in fact ever performed as written, but which tells us a great deal about how such characters were taking shape in the discourse of the period. By midcentury, however, when the Constitutions of 1837 and 1845 became operational legal codes, constitutional scripting lost some of the innovative representational force it had had in Cádiz. The more revealing representations of the nation are to be found by this time in the realm of the aesthetic, including the theater itself. Therefore, in the second part of my essay I will discuss *Don Juan Tenorio*, a theatrical work that also had great scripting power, inasmuch as it projected an image of the nation that became dominant throughout the rest of the century. Before turning to the Constitution of Cádiz, I want briefly to consider some of the eighteenth-century roots of the Spanish liberal tradition, roots from which the members of the Cortes drew their understandings of nation and subject. The writings of Gaspar Melchor de Jovellanos were extremely influential in emerging ideas of the relationship between the state and its subjects. His *Memoria para el arreglo de la policía de los espectáculos y diversiones públicas*, written in the early 1790s, clearly assumes a direct, almost causal link between the form of government and the feelings, morals, and activity of those ruled. Protesting against the restrictive and oppressive ancien régime policies that in his opinion were responsible for the dreary monotony and constraint of communal life in rural Spain, Jovellanos makes his case for liberalization: "Un pueblo libre y alegre será precisamente activo y laborioso, y siéndolo, sería bien morigerado y obediente a la justicia. Cuanto más goce, tanto más amará el Gobierno en que vive" (Jovellanos 120) (" A free and happy people will necessarily be active and hard working, and in being so, will be well controlled and obedient towards the law. The more freedom a people enjoys, the more it will love the government under which it lives"). Throughout the whole treatise, Jovellanos focuses on the impact of government policy on the moral character of a people. In contrast to the what he considers weak, corrupt, impassive individuals produced by overly restrictive rule, he describes the kind of subjectivity that develops in an environment of free social intercourse:

> Unos hombres frecuentemente congregados a solazarse y divertirse en común formarían siempre un pueblo unido y afectuoso; conocerían un interés general, y estarían más distantes de sacrificarle a su interés particular. Serán de ánimo más elevado, porque serán más libres, y, por lo mismo, serán también de corazón más recto y esforzado. (121)

> (Men who frequently meet to relax and enjoy themselves together will always form a united and caring people; they will have common interests, and will be less inclined to sacrifice these to their private interests. They will have a more elevated spirit, because they will be freer, and, likewise, they will be more virtuous and stout-hearted.)

It is axiomatic for Jovellanos, then, that the free subject will develop the virtues and qualities necessary to integrate individual self-interest with the collective welfare.

In both passages cited above, the terms "pueblo" and "hombres" appear to have been used in an expansive, inclusive sense to designate the whole community of the nation. Jovellanos's blueprint for change, nevertheless, favored certain political and economic interests at the expense of others. Although he was a nobleman in alliance with members of the highest echelons of the aristocracy in a country whose bourgeoisie was small and not particularly innovative, he aspired to replace certain basic aspects of seigneurial society with the political and economic structures of modern capitalism. Writing about land reform, one of the issues that concerned him most, he provides a crucial context for his idea of freedom: "el poder político que sostiene los privilegios e impide el desarrollo espontáneo de la libertad, proviene del régimen de propiedad de la tierra. Si la tierra es libre, lo serán los hombres que viven en ella" (38) ("The political power that sustains privileges and impedes the spontaneous development of freedom proceeds from the type of land-ownership. If the land is free, the people who live on it will be free"). The "freedom" of the land here means freedom from entailment, which in turn gives the absolute freedom to sell it to its owner—who is not necessarily the man who lives and works on it, a fact obscured by Jovellanos's phrasing: "los hombres que viven en ella." The underlying model that structures Jovellanos's discourse of freedom becomes clear: "el desarrollo espontáneo de la libertad" depends on a space of economic practice liberated from traditional or governmental constraint, the free market of absolutely owned commodities.

Implicitly, then, the subject who will exercise the freedoms Jovellanos envisions for the reformed state is property-owning and masculine. The differences and hierarchy among state subjects become explicit when Jovellanos's examination of the space of diversion moves from the village square to the theatre. "The working people" (123) has neither time nor means to attend the theater, which is patronized above all by "the nobility and affluent youth" (133). The theater also has a unique power to affect the inner life of its spectators—the power "to perfect or corrupt the citizenry" (130). With this shift from particular classes to the generic term "citizen," one particular type of national subject stands in for all others, as Jovellanos demonstrates in his description of what images the theater should promote:

> ciudadanos llenos de virtud y de patriotismo, prudentes y celosos padres de familia, amigos fieles y constantes; en una palabra, hombres heroicos y esforzados, amantes del bien público, celosos de su libertad y sus derechos, y protectores de la inocencia y acérrimos perseguidores de la iniquidad. (133)
>
> (Citizens full of virtue and patriotism, prudent and protective fathers, faithful and constant friends; in a word, heroic and spirited men, lovers of the public good, zealous in regard to their freedom and rights, protective toward innocence and relentless persecutors of iniquity.)

This moral characterization of the citizen will show up again in the constitutional blueprint for the reformed nation, and so will the exclusions it implies. There is no place here for a female subject, for example, except possibly under the category of the innocent who must be protected. Members of "the working people" can only be included if they conform to the bourgeois patterns of the subject described. Versions of the assumed mirror-relationship between the representation of the nation (a theatrical one here) and the subjects who make it up will also surface in the text of the Constitution.

Shaped by a process of political conflict and compromise among the diverse sectors of the Spanish elite present in Cádiz during the Peninsular War, the Constitution of 1812 formulated a new idea, that of the Spanish nation as a unified and self-determining entity. Its first task was, as Tierno Galván observed, to define what the nation is. In stating axiomatically that "son españoles, todos los hombres libres nacidos y avecindados en los dominios de las Españas, y los hijos de estos" (Art. 5, Esteban 46) ("All free men born and living in Spain's territories and their sons are Spaniards"), Article 1 raises the question I want to address: If the nation is made up of all Spaniards, who counts as a Spaniard? Are differentiations made within that category? The first thing to note in this regard is how smoothly the constitutional text closes out any acknowledgement of a gender other than masculine: the nation is "all Spaniards," and Spaniards are "all free men born and living in Spanish territories, and their sons." The ambiguity of the masculine form "español" allows it to be understood as gender neutral in some instances, perhaps, but certainly not in Article 9, which obliges "todo español" to take up arms to defend the nation when called upon. My point is that the subordinate gender is so completely subsumed by the dominant one in this text that no distinction between them is ever drawn: women do not exist in the civic and political universe represented in the Constitution. No wonder, then, that in the discursive tradition that followed from this text Carolina Coronado could not see herself and her sex as members of the nation.

While gender remains invisible, however, other kinds of difference complicate and perturb the sleek sameness of the nation as it is characterized in the Constitution. The very first article, for example, insinuates the difference between metropolis and colonies, a difference both signaled and denied on the textual surface by the formulation "todos los españoles de ambos hemisferios" ("all Spaniards in both hemispheres"). Beneath this bland phrase lurks a tangle of opposing political interests, maneuvers, and debates of which I can only indicate a few salient strands here. By 1810, when the drafting of the Constitution began, pro-independence insurrections had arisen but failed in Quito and Alto Peru, taken root in Venezuela and the River Plate region, and caused a civil war in Mexico. To counteract the independence movements, the Cortes passed a decree on October 15, 1810, stating that "los dominios españoles en ambos hemisferios forman una sola y misma monarquía, una misma y sola nación y una sola familia, y que por lo mismo los naturales que sean originarios de dichos dominios europeos o ultramarinos son iguales en derechos a los de esta península" (Martínez Sospedra 127) ("Spanish territories of both hemispheres form a single and unified monarachy, a single and unified nation and a single family, and likewise those who are native to said European or overseas territories are equal in rights to those of this peninsula"). This formulation, which set the precedent for the juridical equality of overseas and peninsular subjects, in fact introduced an exclusion about which the American delegates as well as their Peninsular colleagues would remain sharply divided throughout the constitutional debates. Although indigenous Americans along with the descendants of Europeans were given equal rights with Spaniards, a large segment of the Spanish American population was left out—the *castas*, as free Americans with African ancestors were designated. The divergent positions adopted by delegates on the issue of race reflected multiple political tensions. Liberal Spaniards' belief in the universality of human rights was overbalanced by the fear that the American electoral census would far outnumber that of Spain if the *castas* were counted. Americans disagreed sharply on the issue: some wanted to seize the opportunity to dominate the Cortes by expanding the census as far as possible; others, *criollos* from colonies with large slave and mulatto populations, feared losing power to more populous subordinate groups. As one historian of the constitutional debates puts it: "si admitían las castas, perdían el poder en América; si las rechazaban, veían disminuida su representación y por ende su poder, en las Cortes" (Martínez Sospedra 164) ("if they admitted the "castas," they would lose power in America; if they rejected them, they would see their representation diminished and as a result their power in the Cortes"). The compromise incorporated in the Constitution stands as one of its distinct features: the differentiation, this time explicit, between two categories of national subjects, those including the *castas* who possess nationality and thus basic juridical rights and those excluding the *castas* who possess citizenship and with it voting rights. The disavowed difference between metropolis and colony, we might say, has branched out through a set of subterranean displacements into distinctions that surface in the text as questions of race. I want to examine in more detail the articles distinguishing nationality from citizenship because we know from the records of the debates that these provisions were among those regarded as the least consistent with the liberal idea of nation.

In declaring that all free men born and residing in Spain's territories are Spaniards, Article 5 may be indeterminate with regard to gender, but in dividing them into enslaved and free, it makes another sharp distinction among human beings, a distinction that in the modern world had come to be associated with race. Although most delegates accepted this exclusion without question as one based both on Roman law and on Greco-Roman models of the state, some did not. The ultraliberal José Manuel Quintana, for example, argued that slaves should be allowed to vote, though only for a nonslave to represent their interests in the Cortes (*Actas* 95). Whereas

Spanish nationality, as defined in Article 5, includes free men of all races born on Spanish territory or naturalized by legal procedures or ten years' residence, citizenship, defined in the articles of Chapter 4, includes according to Article 18 only "aquellos españoles que por ambas líneas traen su origen de los dominios españoles de ambos hemisferios" (Esteban 48) ("those Spaniards who on both sides derive their origin from the Spanish territories of either hemispheres"). The excluded category is identified explicitly in Article 22: "los españoles que por cualquier línea son habidos y reputados por originarios del Africa" (Esteban 48) ("Spaniards who are held and reputed to have African origins on either side"). The underlying tensions and contradictory interests at work in shaping the Constitution's definition of the national subject manifest themselves in the very text of this article. The clause offering to those with African origins individual remedy under certain conditions registers what is obviously an uneasy compromise in regard to the exclusion of the *castas*: "les queda abierta la puerta de la virtud y del merecimiento para ser ciudadanos: en su consecuencia las Cortes concederán carta de ciudadano a los que hicieren servicios calificados a la Patria, o a los que se distingan por su talento, aplicación y conducta" (Esteban 48-49) ("the door to becoming a citizen through virtue and merit is left open for them: consequently, the Cortes will grant citizenship to those who performed recognized service to their country, or to those who distinguish themselves through their talent, zeal, and conduct").

In the protracted and heated debate over the provisions of Articles 18 and 22, which were sent back to the Committee on the Constitution more than once for rewriting, the inconsistencies of the compromise were vehemently pointed out. Some deputies noted internal contradictions, such as the fact that the Constitution grants automatic citizenship to the Spanish-born sons of foreigners but "los españoles descendientes de Africa que pueden contar entre sus abuelos cuatro o cinco generaciones ya naturalizadas" (*Actas* 186) ("Spaniards descended from Africa who can count among their forefathers four or five already naturalized generations") can only be citizens in exceptional cases. Others, like the Mexican delegate Uria, declared that the exclusion violated the principles of justice upon which the Constitution was presumably founded: "si son españoles para contribuir a proporción de sus haberes a los gastos del Estado, lo sean igualmente para que . . . los eleve a la clase de ciudadanos llanos y comunes, que es el lugar que les corresponde como hombres buenos que son" (*Actas* 164-65) ("If they are Spaniards for the purpose of contributing proportionately of their wealth to the expenditures of the State, being Spanish should likewise . . . elevate them to the type of citizenship that as good men they deserve"). Stung by these criticisms, the Asturian Argüelles, a leading liberal and a member of the Committee on the Constitution, rose to defend himself and his colleagues: "No puedo oír con indiferencia que se trate a la comisión de iliberal y poco mirada, presentando un artículo contradictorio, inconsiguiente y lleno de . . . otros defectos más" (*Actas* 173) ("I cannot hear with indifference the commission treated as illiberal and careless, presenting an article that is contradictory, in consistent and full of . . . other defects"). His argument, which eventually prevailed because it corresponded to political realities if not to ideological consistency, was essentially that political expedience—in this case, sensitivity to the concerns of the *criollo* elite—must take precedence over principle.[3] With characteristic incisiveness, the Committee's chairman, Muñoz Torrero, clinched this line of argument by using the rhetorical tactic of *reductio ad absurdum* (the absurd in this case being the political equality of women): "si llevamos demasiado lejos estos principios de lo que se dice rigurosa justicia sin otras consideraciones, sería forzoso conceder a las mujeres con los derechos civiles los políticos y admitirlas en las juntas electorales y en las Cortes mismas" (*Actas* 248) ("If we take these principles of strict justice unmitigated by other considerations too far, it would be necessary to grant women political rights, along with civil rights and admit them to the electoral 'juntas' and even the 'Cortes'"). Thus the differentiation between the sexes, regarded as so elemental and self-evident that the Constitution does not need to explain when the masculine plural term includes women and when it does not, is trotted out to demonstrate the necessity of another distinction based on race. What I find significant here is that in the final analysis the justification of these exclusionary differentiations rested on an idea of different subjectivities that remains tacitly understood in Muñoz Torrero's reference to gender, but which receives more explicit elaboration in the debates on race.

Let me shift focus a moment here to comment on a noteworthy and rather unique feature of the Constitution of 1812: its attachment of subjective qualities to the nation, state, and citizen whose roles it defines. "Love for one's Fatherland," states Article 6, "es una de las principales obligaciones de todos los españoles, y asímismo el ser justos y benéficos" (Esteban 46) ("is one of the fundamental duties of all Spaniards, and likewise fairness and kindness"). Corresponding moral attributes are assigned to the nation by Article 4: "La Nación está obligada a conservar y proteger por leyes sabias y justas la libertad civil, la propiedad y los demás derechos legítimos de todos los individuos que la componen" (Esteban 46) ("The Nation is obligated to preserve and protect through wise and just laws civil liberty, property, and the other legitimate rights of all individuals of whom it is composed"). Thus, the nation/state and its subject were set up in a mirroring relationship with each other, so that each reflected the virtues and dispositions required by the other. The relationship is circular: as Jovellanos had intimated, the state structure, understood as benevolent, rational, and just, guarantees and makes possible the freedom, rationality, benevolence, and patriotic commitment of its subjects, whose qualities in turn guarantee the establishment and perpetuation of the constitutional state. The Constitution itself was understood as a kind of mirror, figuring forth—representing—the national subject. This is the function that Argüelles himself ascribed to the first several articles. In the *Discurso preliminar* which accompanied the publication of the Constitution and explained the thinking of its framers, he states:

> Los españoles de todas clases, de todas edades y de todas condiciones sabrían lo que son y lo que es preciso que sean para ser honrados y respetados de los propios y de los extraños. No es menos importante expresar las obligaciones de los españoles para con la nación, pues que ésta debe conservarles por medio de leyes justas y equitativas todos los derechos políticos y civiles que les corresponden como individuos de ella. Así van señaladas con individualidad aquellas obligaciones de que no puede dispensarse ningún español sin romper el vínculo que le une al Estado. (79)

> (Spaniards of all classes, ages and conditions will know what they are and what it is necessary for them to be in order to be honored and respected by one and all. It is no less important to express Spaniards' obligations to the nation, since it [nation] must guard through just and aquitable laws all the civil and political rights due to them as members of the nation. Thus, those duties from which no Spaniard can be excused without breaking the bond that links him with the State are clearly listed.)

The Constitution tells the subjects of the nation who they are; their duty to maintain their connection with the State is couched in terms of "what it is necessary for them to be" rather than of what they should do.

Such attention to a collective subjectivity was perhaps inevitable. The underlying agenda of the Constitution's makers was to establish the concept of national sovereignty in opposition to the absolutist monarchy's claim of divine right, and in this sense the document was intended to transform the passive subjects of the ancien régime monarchy into a unified, active, self-determining subject—the modern nation. But it should be noted that the mirroring relationship between national subject and nation-state could be used negatively to justify exclusions. A presumed subjective difference was thus the principal rationalization adduced in the constitutional debates by those who argued in favor of excluding the *castas* as a group from citizenship rights. The Committee on the Constitution, for instance, defended its decision on the grounds that the descendants of Africans were not yet morally or socially ready to have the political rights of citizens. The committee's position was summarized by one of its members, the Catalan delegate Espiga:

> creyó que era necesario formar nuevas inclinaciones, nuevos hábitos, nuevas afecciones; prepararlos por la educación pública y por la enseñanza . . . y por la unión recíproca de intereses y demás relaciones a ser unos dignos ciudadanos de la nación española. (7 Sept. 1812; *Actas* 256)

> ([the committee] believed that it was necessary to form new inclinations, habits, and affections; to prepare them through public education and instruction . . . and

> through a reciprocal union of interests and other relations to be worthy citizens of the Spanish nation.)

Within the text of the Constitution, the idea of the subjective disqualification of the *castas* is expressed in Article 22, which states that individuals with African ancestry must prove they have the relevant attributes to enter "la puerta de la virtud y del merecimiento para ser ciudadanos" (Esteban 48) ("the door of virtue and merit to become citizens"). This article, the product of compromise and amendment, reflects a tension between the desire, born of eighteenth-century political philosophy, to extend equal juridical rights to all those defined as Spaniards, and the sense, rooted in political and economic interests, of significant differences of race, class, and gender.

Having raised the issue of class, I should point out that it forms an important subtext of the Constitution of 1812. Article 8, for example, in stating that all Spaniards, "without any distinction whatsoever" (Esteban 48), are obliged to pay taxes to support the government is aimed at the ancien régime privileges that exempted the aristocracy from taxation. In regard to the question of class difference, the tension between inclusive and exclusive definitions of citizenship was resolved on the side of inclusiveness, producing one of the distinctive features of the Constitution of Cádiz—its provision of universal male suffrage for whites and indigenous Americans. The tipping of the balance in this direction is explained by the circumstances under which the Constitution was elaborated: popular resistance to the French invaders was crucial to the cause of national independence at home while popular support for Spanish rule was Spain's only hope of retaining its colonies. Nevertheless, concern about the popular classes' suitability to be included as part of the national subject surfaces in Article 25, which spells out the conditions under which citizenship rights can be suspended. The sixth section actually states a new restriction: "Desde el año de mil ochocientos treinta deberán saber leer y escribir los que de nuevo entren en el ejercicio de los derechos de ciudadano" (Esteban 49) ("Beginning in the year 1830 those who for the first time exercise citizenship rights should know how to read and write"). The makers of the Constitution, then, regarded literacy as fundamental to the process of forming the "new inclinations, habits, and affections" that the delegate cited earlier believed were necessary to make appropriate citizens of black Spanish subjects. Political expedience dictated the inclusion of white and indigenous American working classes despite widespread illiteracy, but the Cádiz delegates stipulated literacy—and the qualities it supposedly inculcated—as a condition of citizenship rights after 1830, for they assumed that the constitutional regime would develop a system of public education by that date.

Indeed, shortly after the Constitution was completed and ratified, Manuel José Quintana was appointed chair of a commission to develop a plan for public education. His report, submitted to the Regency in Cádiz on September 9, 1813, elucidates further the replication of social hierarchies within the constitutional discourse about the national subject. The introduction of the report focuses quite explicitly on the connection between the new Constitution and the subjects it reflects, requires, and creates:

> La Constitución ha restituido al pensamiento su libertad, a la verdad sus derechos. Debe pues el Congreso nacional, que ha restituido a los españoles al ejercicio de su voluntad, completar su obra y procurarles todos los medios de que esta voluntad sea bien y convenientemente dirigida. Estos medios están evidentemente todos bajo el influjo inmediato de la instrucción. Sin ella no puede . . . el Gobierno corresponder dignamente a los fines de su institución. . . . Ella, enseñándonos cuáles son nuestros derechos, nos manifiesta las obligaciones que debemos cumplir; su objeto es que vivamos felices para nosotros, útiles a los demás; y señalando de este modo el puesto que debemos ocupar en la sociedad, ella hace que las fuerzas particulares concurran con su acción a aumentar la fuerza común, en vez de servir a debilitarla con su divergencia o con su oposición. (176)

> (The Constitution has restored freedom of thought and the right to truth. . . . Therefore, the National Congress, which has given back to Spaniards the exercise of their will, should complete its work and provide them with the means to govern their will effectively and appropriately. These means are clearly all directly influenced by education. Without providing education, the Government cannot worthily meet the objectives for which it was

> instituted. . . . Education, by teaching us what our rights are, shows us the obligations we must fulfill; its purpose is that we should find happiness for ourselves and be useful to others; and in this way indicating the place we should occupy in society, it insure that the action of individual forces will increase collective strength instead of weakening it by divergence or opposition.)

Here, as in the Constitution, the properly constituted subject corresponds to the structuring state: national will and individual will are indistinguishable; duties and rights are balanced; happiness and usefulness are both goals and defining qualities; and—an explicit theme in Quintana—disunity and conflict, perhaps even difference, are to be avoided. The school emerges here as the location, the space of social interaction, in which the necessary correspondence can be achieved. What stands out in Quintana's report is the stress on the need for uniformity, since the unity of the state will be the product and the image of the unity of its subjects: "Debe pues ser una la doctrina en nuestras escuelas, y unos los métodos de su enseñanza, a que es consiguiente que sea también una la lengua en que se enseñe, y que ésta sea la lengua castellana" (177) ("There must be tone single doctrine in our schools, and one single method of instruction, from which it follows that instruction must be given in one single language, and that that language must be Castillian").

One difference, however, is explicitly endorsed and justified in Quintana's report—the difference of gender. Unlike the Constitution, this text finds it necessary directly to address the exclusion of women, perhaps because the specificity of the public space it delineates brings into focus the bodily concreteness of the subjects that will or will not occupy it. In one of the final paragraphs, the report explains why it has not commented on the schooling women should receive:

> La Junta entiende que, al contrario de la instrucción de los hombres, que conviene sea pública, la de las mujeres debe ser privada y doméstica; que su enseñanza tiene más relaciones con la educación que con la instrucción propiamente dicha; y que para determinar bases respecto de ella era necesario recurrir al examen y combinación de diferentes principios políticos y morales, y descender

> después a la consideración de intereses y respetos privados y de familia. (190)

> (The Junta understands that, unlike the education of men, which should be public, education for women should be private and domestic; that teaching women is more closely related to upbringing than to education properly speaking; and that to set out a plan for it [women's education], it would be necessary to examine and combine different political and moral principles, and then to get down to the consideration of private and familial interests and attitudes.)

Catherine Jagoe notes, in a study of women's education in nineteenth-century Spain, that the gendering of the distinction made here between "instrucción" ("education") and "educación" ("upbringing") sets a pattern that will persist throughout the century. Whereas Quintana's report advocates extending free, public "instrucción" to all citizens, she points out, it regards women's training as "educación," which "ha de ser discrecional, privada, doméstica, y sujeta a una agenda política diferente, no destinada a producir ciudadanos libres e independientes, sino esposas y madres" (Jagoe 50) ("Ought to be discretionary, private, domestic, and subject to a different political agenda, not aimed at producing free and independent citizens, but wives and mothers"). The distinction, furthermore, offers a key to the Constitution's exclusion of women as subjects: the private and domestic is excluded as an arena of the relationships and practices modeled in liberal discourse. Subjectivity itself is divided by this difference. The psychological and moral qualities stipulated for the subject of the national state, we might recall, are all public virtues: love of country, beneficence, a sense of justice. The subject's experience of himself and his feelings and attitudes toward intimates are simply outside the purview of this discourse. Since by a long tradition of interlocking systems of signification, women's existence had been associated with the realm of the private, the domestic, or the intimate, women's education was thus felt by Quintana and his committee to entail "different moral and political principles" from those operating in the discourse of the Cortes and the Constitution. And not simply different, but lower: to shift the focus to what would be appropriate for women would be to "descend" to considerations related to family matters. Perhaps this explains why the one occupation named in the Constitution as justifying suspension of the rights specific to a citizen was that of domestic servant.[4] Immersion in the domestic coupled with servitude—occupying the position of a woman, in other words—thrust a person below the horizon of competent subjecthood in the state.

I want to explore a bit further the system of signification that defined "public" in relation to its contrary because it is revealing in regard to the "sphere of subjectivity" projected by the discourse associated with the struggle to institute a liberal state in Spain. It is true, on the one hand, that the "private" designated an area of freedom which liberal public institutions were designed to protect from government or other forms of interference. This area of freedom was economic, of course, the market in which Jovellanos's "free land" could be disposed as its owner willed, but it also included inner life—thought, feeling, family. Yet despite the high value assigned to the "private" as the independent core made inviolable by "freedom," we have seen that the subjects assigned to function primarily in nonpublic or private space are given secondary or lower value. Quintana's report, accordingly, takes pains to specify that the space of the school be open and public: "Tambien conviene que la enseñanza sea pública, esto es, que no se dé a puertas cerradas" (177) ("It is also best for education to be public, that is to say, that it should not occur behind closed doors"). Openness to observation by the public, the report argues, will stimulate both students and teachers to do their best and insure the quality of the educational system. Given the connotations of "mujer pública" (prostitute) and the particular emphasis Spanish culture placed on containing and enclosing women, it is easy to see why the report's writers did not think such instruction was appropriate for women. Yet, as a warrant for their argument in favor of publicity, the report's writers invoke a negative view of what is closed away from public view: "son muy pocas las cosas de utilidad común a quienes convenga el secreto" (177) ("very few things of general usefulness are well served by secrecy"). Shut behind the closed doors of nonpublic space, women and domestic servants are connected with the antipublic, the secret, the dark regions of irrationality shut off from "las luces," from the public gaze of reason on which Enlightened liberals pinned the guarantees of a restructured state.

Beset during the next two decades by counterrevolutions and coups, invasions, colonial and civil wars, the Spanish nation implemented neither the structure of governance nor the educational system called for by the Constitution of Cádiz. Yet the years of the First Carlist War, whose outcome would definitively lay to rest the specter of an integral reestablishment of the ancien régime, saw renewed struggle over who fit within the sphere of national subjectivity under the liberal state. The new Constitution drawn up in 1837 revised the formulations of 1812 in the light of an emerging consensus among the governing classes, a consensus that reflected considerably altered historical circumstances. The colonies, with the exception of two Caribbean islands and the Philippines, were lost. The popular classes, no longer allied with the property-owning elite in the defense of national independence, were becoming more volatile. Not surprisingly, the Constitution of 1837 eliminated some of the more democratic provisions of the earlier charter. It divided sovereignty between the nation and the monarch, made the legislature bicameral so that the elite members of the upper house would temper the popular tendencies of the lower, and tied suffrage rights to property and income. With regard to the question that concerns me here, the definition of the subject of the constitutional state, the changes are pronounced. The articles specifying the psychological and moral attributes of the Spanish subject disappear, as does the distinction between a Spaniard and a citizen. Gone too are the distinctions made on the basis of race or slavery. This change, however, is based on a narrower, rather than a broader view of the composition of the nation, for under this Constitution the subjects of the remaining Spanish colonies are no longer given juridical equality with citizens of the metropolis. An article appended at the end of the Constitution of 1837 stipulates that "las provincias de Ultramar serían gobernadas por leyes especiales" (Esteban 117) ("the Overseas provinces will be governed by special laws"), suggesting that different provisions will determine citizenship in slave-owning colonies such as Cuba or Puerto Rico.

These changes are significant because they set patterns that persist throughout the various constitutions that followed in the course of the nineteenth century, the progressive as well as the conservative ones. The Constitution of 1837 makes no place for representation of the subjective, that realm now strictly marked off from the arena in which the state functions. The mirroring structure noted in the first constitution thus vanishes, as the subject becomes opaque, defined only according to the geographical and genealogical coordinates with which the state concerns itself. The political national subject is less characterized, more abstract, and this remains true of all the succeeding constitutions. What happened, in my view, is that Spain's idea of itself as a modern nation had taken root and begun to stabilize. Even though the rest of the century saw several different constitutions, there were no serious challenges to the basic principle of a constitutional state. Characterizing and differentiating national subjects was no longer seen as a representational task of the constitutional document itself, but was carried out by a number of institutions that promoted common habits, inclinations, and interests. The function of representing the subject as a subjectivity, a structure of feelings, desires, and self-reflection was now primarily carried out by literary or aesthetic discourse, on the rebound after suffering a relative eclipse during the disruptions of the Peninsular War and the repressive censorship imposed by Ferdinand VII.

Unlike the constitutional discourse of the early nineteenth century, which focused on race as the most troubling difference among national subjects, the difference that preoccupies midcentury literary representation is gender. With the restriction of the nation's boundaries to the peninsular metropolis, the question of race became an issue of colonial administration rather than of national identity. At the same time, a new ideology of gender difference developed, requiring that women should emerge from their previous invisibility as national subjects and be characterized, differentiated, and ultimately assigned their place in the scheme of the new bourgeois society.[5] As we might expect, literature played a key role in this process. Thus, to conclude, I want to turn to the social space I mentioned at the beginning—the space of the theater—for that was the arena of a much-repeated aesthetic representation of the paradigm of gender difference that would govern both political and literary discourse for the rest of the century. José Zorrilla's drama *Don Juan Tenorio* first staged in 1844, was destined to become one of the most popular and frequently performed plays in the Spanish-speaking world. In it we shall see a refunctioning of the nonpublic subjectivity associated with women.

The protagonist of this drama is the mythical don Juan, reincarnated by Zorrilla from a nineteenth-century perspective as a prototypically masculine figure.[6] Fundamentally, the play's action traces the process by which don Juan's masculine force, initially presented as socially disruptive in its raw aggressivity and will to dominance, is tamed and integrated into a social order structured by paternal and religious authority—a conservative image of the nation that was becoming dominant at midcentury.[7] But if this play is about masculinity, it is equally about femininity. The key factor in don Juan's transformation is a woman—doña Inés, the innocent novice whom he abducts from her convent on a dare but whose love captivates him and ultimately saves him from hell. The character of doña Inés is one of Zorrilla's most notable departures from the seventeenth-century precedent, and was in the author's own mind his most significant innovation: "Mi obra tiene una excelencia que le hará durar largo tiempo sobre la escena" ("My play has an excellence which will make it last a long time on the stage"), he wrote later, "la creación de mi doña Inés cristiana" (*Recuerdos* 2293) ("the creation of my Christian doña Inés"). Doña Inés, I would argue, could only have been created in the nineteenth century because she embodies a conception of the female subject that developed in the spaces set aside by liberal discourse. That is, she exemplifies the qualities and functions of the intimate and the domestic, the domain of women, the area excluded from consideration by the civic discourse of Jovellanos, Quintana, and the new constitutions. In doña Inés the nature and the powers of the feminine subject of postabsolutist Spanish society are set forth—not in the language of political theory or argumentation, but in the language of imagination, poetry, and symbolic performance.

In certain ways doña Inés prefigures the model of Spanish womanhood that became predominant after 1850, the model Bridget Aldaraca, following the terminology of the period, has labeled "el ángel del hogar" ("angel of the hearth"). Even though doña Inés never literally appears as a wife and mother in a home, she enacts on stage the principal subjective qualities of the domestic angel: she is pure, innocent, and pious but capable of total self-sacrificing love. She begins to love don

Juan when she first hears the words of a letter he has smuggled into her cloister, and soon feels such an all-consuming passion for him that she cannot survive the catastrophe that concludes Part 1 of the drama. In Part 2, doña Inés's capacity for love is carried to a transcendent level. Her ghost appears to don Juan to inform him that if he does not repent, she will suffer condemnation and hell along with him, for she has wagered her immortal soul on his choice. Evident here are the close links between the feminine ideal represented by doña Inés, and the Virgin Mary, a potent image of femininity in Spanish culture. Like the Virgin, Inés is man's pure, selflessly loving intercessor with God the Father. She stands thus in the symbolic position of mother in the second part, even though there is no literal domestic hearth in the scenario.

There are two aspects of doña Inés's representation of the feminine position that I want to emphasize. The first is her power. In Part 1 of the drama, doña Inés is passive, powerless even to determine her own location in the world; she is placed in the convent by her father and removed from it by don Juan. Control of her fate becomes the fulcrum of the battle between two powerful masculine wills. Despite her impotence in physical, political, or economic terms, however, in the moral and psychological realm she is able to effect a transformation that male authority has repeatedly failed to achieve. Don Juan has remained out of control, despite the best efforts of both fathers, Inés's and don Juan's, backed by the most powerful social institutions—the state, the church, and the family. Inés, however, is able to transform the renegade with her innocent declaration of love—"te adoro." He is so captivated that when Inés's father arrives to rescue her from her abductor, don Juan does exactly as both fathers originally wished: he proposes marriage and offers to repent and to reintegrate with the family through submission to the patriarch:

> Yo seré esclavo de tu hija,
> en tu casa viviré,
> tú gobernarás mi hacienda,
> diciéndome *esto ha de ser.* (1.4.9, 607-10)
>
> (I will be your daughter's slave,
> In your house I will live
> You will govern my property
> By telling me what must be done.)

Don Juan's proposal to embrace the domestic ideals of a good bourgeois son-in-law fails, not because the conversion is inauthentic, but because Inés's father is unable to recognize his daughter's power. He sees her only as a helpless victim incapable of producing a true transformation and rejects don Juan's offer as insincere.

Part 2, however, shows through the logic of theatrical representation that doña Inés does have power and agency—only in a different realm from that recognized by her father. And this leads me to the second point I want to emphasize—the social or cultural space of doña Inés's agency as a subject. Part 1 plays itself out in the places of masculine action—the tavern, the streets, the country estate—and also shows how men control and penetrate at will feminine spaces such as the convent or the sitting room. Part 2, on the other hand, takes place in another space-time frame, the space of transcendental moral and psychological realities—good and evil, salvation and perdition, self-knowledge and dream. The principal setting is the pantheon where don Juan's victims lie buried and statues of them have been erected. When don Juan wanders into this otherworldly place for the confrontation with death that will determine the meaning of his life, these statues are animated by the spirits of those they represent, who speak to him from beyond the grave.

Feminine power, obscured in the realm of everyday social and political reality, becomes visible in this moral/psychic space as Zorrilla's text organizes it. From the opening of the curtain, this other hierarchy of values and powers is visually represented in stage space. The elaborate *acotaciones* that set the stage for Part 2 specify that the tombs of don Luis and don Gonzalo and of doña Inés should dominate the foreground, arranged in the following manner: "El sepulcro de don Gonzalo a la derecha, y su estatua de rodillas; el de don Luis a la izquierda, y su estatua también de rodillas; el de doña Inés en el centro, y su estatua de pie" ("The grave of don Gonzalo is on the right and his statue is kneeling; don Luis's grave is on the left and his statue is also kneeling; doña Inés's grave is in the center and her statue is standing up"). The spatial representation of Inés's pre-eminence in the transcendental order is reinforced by the verbal text in scene 4 of the first act, where Inés's ghost issues a warning to don Juan that prescribes the action to follow: in the coming night he will face the crisis ("ardua lucha" 2.1.4, 385) of his existence, the choice that will seal his—and her—eternal fate. She does not predetermine don Juan's choice, but tells him only that it will be made for good or ill. Yet in the actual moment of crisis, the visual and spatial representation—more semiotically powerful in Part 2 than the verbal text—makes it clear that Inés does have the power to determine the outcome. At the end of scene 2 of the final act, when don Juan's fate hangs in the balance, the stage directions describe the tableau that represents the moment of judgment. While don Gonzalo's statue pulls him down by one hand: "don Juan se hinca de rodillas, tendiendo al cielo la mano que le deja libre la estatua. Las sombras, esqueletos, etc., van a abalanzarse sobre él, en cuyo momento se abre la tumba de doña Inés y aparece ésta. Doña Inés toma la mano que don Juan tiende al cielo" (2.3.2, 169) ("Don Juan falls to his knees, stretching toward heaven the hand which the statue leaves free. The ghosts, skeletons, etc., are about to seize him when the tomb of doña Inés opens and she appears. Doña Inés takes the hand that don Juan raises toward heaven"). She visibly has the ascendency, the upper hand, and swings the balance; her dramatic "¡No!" interrupts and halts the advance of death's punitive spectres upon don Juan. She declares her power in the speech that follows:

> Heme ya aquí,
> don Juan, mi mano asegura
> esta mano que a la altura
> tendió tu contrito afán,
> y Dios perdona a don Juan
> al pie de mi sepultura. (2.3.3, 171-75)
>
> (Here I am
> don Juan, my hand securing
> the hand that in contrition
> you stretched toward heaven
> and God forgives don Juan
> at the foot of my grave.)

The final triumph is hers. Neither the visual nor the verbal text leaves any doubt that it is a triumph over a version of masculine authority. The loser who holds the "lower hand" in the tableau of judgment is Inés's father, the stern representative of a social order based on the father, his name and law—on honor, in other words. Don Gonzalo stands for justice and retribution, aspects of the deity associated with the function of the father. But the aspect of God that asserts itself at the conclusion of this drama reflects the love, compassion, and forgiveness that characterize doña Inés and thus are coded as feminine. Indeed, these are the qualities epitomized in Catholicism by the Virgin Mary. When don Juan declares in the final words of the text that "don Juan Tenorio's God is the God of clemency," he confirms the predominance of feminine values in the order that brings the dramatic conflict to a happy resolution. This is not to say, of course, that Zorrilla implies a feminine deity: throughout the graveyard scenes the silent figure of don Diego has presided "in the background and in an elevated position" (2.1.1), visually representing the divine Father in whose name Inés speaks. It is through him that her powers and agency are validated.

Alicia Andreu, in her study of popular literature and Galdós, has shown how popular Spanish fiction from the 1850s to the 1870s seemed to promise women that through submission in this world and ardent, unwavering faith in the next, they could act as agents of national moral regeneration. This message, echoed in sermons, conduct books, and pedagogical texts, served the interests of the Church, an institution that had suffered considerably under liberal reforms and attempted to combat the anticlericalism of many Spanish men by intensifying the piety of their mothers and wives. Zorrilla's drama, where that theme found early and powerful expression, represented the redemptive woman as simultaneously a crucial and subordinate element in an inclusive, unifying vision of family, social, and transcendental order. Serving as a figure of the nation, this vision embraced all, from the rebelliousness of liberal youth to the old guard's resistance to change, harmonizing conflict in a hierarchy whose oppressiveness was mitigated by the feminine power of love and mercy. What we must understand, nevertheless, is that in Spain this discourse about women's spiritual and redemptive function worked in tandem with a political discourse—with liberal discourse—that wrote women out as subjects of civic or economic activity. Women might have a kind of ascendancy in the imaginary, phantasmagoric realm represented in the finale of *Don Juan Tenorio*, but, as Carolina Coronado asserted, they had no actual place in the affairs of the nation.

Along with numberless others, the texts we have examined here reflect the ongoing process through which Spanish writers, intellectuals, and politicians of the early nineteenth century attempted to represent a new ideological entity—the modern nation and its collective subject. Despite a language of universality dictated by the need to allow the broadest possible spectrum of the Spanish population to recognize itself in the image of the nation, this discourse inevitably reproduced the differentiations inscribed within the social body by inequalities among classes, races, and genders. Consequently, as theatrical as well as constitutional representations show, the national subject always broke down into a hierarchy of differentiated subjectivities. What Zorrilla's drama demonstrates is that by midcentury it had become the role of imaginative or aesthetic writing rather than of liberal discourse itself to draw these different subjects into identification with the national whole by offering each a differentiated and compensatory image of itself.

Notes

1. Quotations have been translated from Spanish by Luis Marxuach.

2. The emergence in Cádiz of the modern concept of nation from traditional Spanish legal traditions is discussed by Sánchez Agesta (84). Martínez Sospedra, another commentator on the Constitution of 1812, notes the new idea of the nation as an equal society without estates and argues that it was tightly linked to the whole system of liberal ideas (59).

3. "No obstante los rigorosos principios de justicia y libertad social, (entre los griegos y los romanos) estuvieron siempre subordinados a la conveniencia pública, que usaron como la ley suprema. La nación debe llamar a componerle a los que juzgue oportuno. Para esto no hay ni puede haber reglas de rigorosa justicia que no estén sujetas a la modificación que exija la pública utilidad. Si una numerosa clase de españoles no se halla en el día en disposición de desempeñar todos los derechos de ciudad, ¿no sería prudente y justo proporcionar el medio que progresiva y gradualmente pueda ir adquiriendo su goce sin chocar la opinión, que, por más que se diga, lo habría de repugnar?"*(Actas* 178) ("Not withstanding the strict principles of justice and social freedom [among the Greeks and Romans], these were always subordinated to public convenience, which they utilized as the supreme law. To constitute itself, the nation should call upon those it deems appropriate. For this there are not nor can there be rules of strict justice that are not subject to the modifications required for the public good. If a sizable class of Spaniards is not at this time qualified to exercise the rights of

citizenship, would it not be prudent and just to provide it with the means to gradually acquire this exercise without reject it no matter what we say?").

4. Article 25 declares that "el ejercicio de los mismos derechos (de ciudadano) se suspende: Tercero. Por el estado de sirviente doméstico" (Esteban, 49) ("the exercise of the same rights of citizenship are suspended: Third: By the condition of domestic servant").

5. I discuss this process at more length in *Las Románticas*, especially pp. 3-9, 283-92.

6. In contrast, I would argue, Tirso's seventeenth-century version of don Juan is conceived more in terms of his aristocratic class (its disruption of social harmony through abuse of power) than of his masculine gender.

7. David Gies has pointed out that the play's early success corresponded with the predominant political tendency of the "Moderate Decade" of 1844-54, in which the liberal zeal of the preceding ten years gave way to a cautious conservatism.

Works Cited

Actas de las Cortes de Cádiz. Antología. Ed. Enrique Tierno Galván. Madrid: Taurus, 1964.

Aldaraca, Bridget. "El ángel del hogar: The Cult of Domesticity in Nineteenth-Century Spain." *Theory and Practice of Feminist Literary Criticism.* Ed. Mora G. and Karen Van Hoostf. New York: Bilingual Press, 1982. 62-87.

Andreu, Alicia. *Galdós y la literatura popular.* Madrid: S.G.E.L., 1982.

Argüelles, Agustín de. *Discurso preliminar a la constitución de 1812.* Intro. Luis Sánchez Agesta. Madrid: Centro de Estudios Constitucionales, 1989.

Coronado, Carolina. *Obra poética.* Ed. Gregorio Torres Nebrera. Mérida: Editora Regional de Extremadura, 1993.

Esteban, Jorge de, Ed. *Las Constituciones de España.* Madrid: Taurus, 1982.

Gies, David. "From Myth to Pop: Don Juan, James Bond and Zelig." *The Western Pennsylvania Symposium on World Literatures. Selected Proceedings: 1974-1991. A Retrospective.* Ed. Carla E. Lucente. Greensburg, PA: Eadmer Press, 1982. 183-98.

Jagoe, Catharine. "La enseñanza femenina en la España decimonónica." *Hacia una historia de la mujer española. Textos y contextos (1850-1900).* Eds. Alda Blanco, Cristina Enríquez de Salamanca, and Catherine Jagoe. Madrid: Siglo XXI, 1999.

Jovellanos, Gaspar Melchor de. *Espectáculos y diversiones públicas. Informe sobre la ley agraria.* Ed. José Lage. Madrid: Cátedra, 1977.

Kirkpatrick, Susan. *Las Románticas: Women Writers and Subjectivity in Spain, 1835-1850.* Berkeley: U of California P, 1989.

Larra, Mariano José de. "Literatura." *Obras.* Ed. Carlos Seco Serrano. Vol. 2. B.A.E. Madrid: Atlas, 1960. 131-34.

Martínez Sospedra, Manuel. *La Constitución de 1812 y el primer liberalismo español.* Valencia: Fac. de Derecho, 1978.

Quintana, Manuel José. "Informe de la junta creada por la Regencia para proponer los medios de proceder al arreglo de los diversos ramos de instrucción pública." *Obras completas.* B.A.E. 19. Madrid: Atlas, 1946. 175-91.

Sánchez Agesta, Luis. *Historia del constitucionalismo español: 1808-1936.* Madrid: Centro de Estudios Constitucionales, 1984.

Tierno Galván, Enrique. "Introducción" to his edition of *Actas de las Cortes de Cádiz.* Madrid: Taurus, 1964.

Zorrilla, José. *Recuerdos del tiempo viejo. Obras completas.* Ed. Narciso Alonso Cortés. Valladolid: Santarén, 1944. 2 vols.

_____. *Don Juan Tenorio.* Ed. José Luis Varela. Madrid: Espasa Calpe, 1975.

◆ Chapter 9

Religious Subject-Forms: Nationalism, Literature, and the Consolidation of *Moderantismo* in Spain during the 1840s

Tom Lewis

Segundo Lucifer que se levanta
del rayo vengador la frente herida,
alma rebelde que el temor no espanta,
hollada sí, pero jamás vencida.
(Espronceda, *El estudiante de Salamanca*)

(A second Lucifer rising,
His brow wounded by the avenging thunderbolt,
A rebel soul who knows no fear,
Beaten down, yes, but never defeated.)

Between September and December 1854, the *New York Daily Tribune* published a series of articles by Karl Marx collectively entitled *Revolutionary Spain*. In these articles Marx observes that one can "trace in the Constitution of 1812 symptoms not to be mistaken of a compromise entered into between the liberal ideas of the eighteenth century and the dark traditions of priestcraft" (Marx 67). Indeed, the document which otherwise merits recognition as the most advanced statement of liberal principles prior to the Constitution of 1931 declares Spain to be "perpetually Catholic, Apostolic, and Roman, the only true religion" (Art. 12, qtd. in Marx 67). Despite its assertion that sovereignty resides in the nation, the liberal Constitution goes on to locate the Bourbon monarchy at the heart of the Spanish state by requiring the King to swear a sacred oath to defend and preserve the "Catholic, Roman, and Apostolic religion, without tolerating any other in the kingdom" (Art. 173, qtd. in Marx 68). In this way, the Constitution of 1812 positions the monarch as the guardian of the most popularly held component of an emergent Spanish national identity.

It is no wonder, therefore, that Robert Marrast considers "satanism"—especially Espronceda's version in *El estudiante de Salamanca*—to stand as the consummate expression of Spanish romantic rebellion against the *antiguo*

régimen. For a minority of *progresista* writers such as Espronceda in the mid-1830s:

> España—o Madrid—en aquellos años no es sino un cementerio poblado de fantasmas, en medio del cual un espíritu libre y vuelto hacia el porvenir es víctima del trágico conflicto con una sociedad incapaz de integrarse al mundo moderno y de superar sus contradicciones fundamentales. (Marrast 40)

> (Spain—or Madrid—in those years is nothing but a cementery populated by ghosts, in the midst of which a free and forward looking spirit is the victim of the tragic conflict with a society incapable of becoming integrated into the modern world and of overcoming its fundamental contradictions.)

Yet Marrast underestimates in this passage the degree to which Spain is already embarked on the road to modernity by 1836-37. Indeed, as Marrast argues elsewhere, Espronceda's satanism indicts emerging structures and practices of capitalist society in Spain alongside those of the *antiguo régimen*. This understanding remains crucial, for the subsequent ebb of Spanish political and cultural *progresismo* in the 1840s is often wrongly interpreted as resulting from the holdover of major components of aristocratic society within a "new" society that has only weakly, if at all, become bourgeois.

The purpose of the present essay is to demonstrate that the *moderantismo* which emerges as hegemonic both politically and culturally in Isabelline Spain arises more from real transformations in Spanish society than it does from unbroken continuities in institutions and behaviors carried over from the *antiguo régimen*. To argue this perspective is in fact to seek to restore a class dimension to our understanding of capitalist transformation in nineteeth-century Spain. Over the past two decades, this perspective has fallen out of favor in the face of approaches that emphasize institutions over classes in their explanatory practices. Recent efforts to challenge the customary equation of Spanish romanticism with Spanish liberalism have also contributed to the general trend dissociating nineteenth-century cultural forms from "bourgeois revolution." This essay seeks instead to discern a class dynamic at the heart of those cultural processes which work to bring about the political and cultural triumph of Spanish *moderantismo* in the 1840s.

Beginning in 1837 and continuing into the 1850s, literature serves as a key site of symbolic negotiations among competing political discourses in Spain as the result of various attempts within both literature and literary criticism to imagine what the nation should or would be. The particular vision of the community of national subjects which eventually wins hegemony is deeply grounded in religious forms of subjectivity. These "religious" subject-forms are no longer those of the official Church; rather, they are subject-forms that have been relocated from the cultural space of a weakened ecclesiastical institution and into the space of an emerging aesthetic institution. Hence, the cultural signficance of the 1840s for the development of Spanish literature includes the transformation of fundamentally religious sensibilities into secular sensibilities by means of the elaboration of a specific aesthetic ideology. This new aesthetic sensibility functions to support bourgeois social relations in Spain, ones which entail new relations between subjects and the nation-state.

Since we will conclude by considering literary examples of the explicit production of national subjectivity in the interest of defending bourgeois rule in Spain, it is useful to recall at the outset that the nation-state has its origin and basis in capitalist class processes. The rise of the market in Europe from the sixteenth century onward entails the spontaneous appearance of elements that later converge to form the nation-state. Along with new trading networks comes the need for increased administration as well as pressure toward standardized forms of communication. As trading networks evolve into linguistic networks, there gradually emerge states that are linguistically homogeneous—or at least predominantly so—and which are "able as none previously had been to insist on the allegiance of all those who lived within their boundaries" (Harman 7). The advantages of the new linguistically based states in Europe accrue not only to absolutist kings but also to a developing bourgeoisie. Traders and manufacturers now compete more readily in their "home" markets against rivals speaking "foreign" languages. State administrators are more easily influenced and even agree to back "national" traders in economic contests over world markets. Sections of the middle classes can parlay their knowledge of the national language into "state jobs denied to minorities at home and colonized populations abroad" (Harman 7).

Moreover, conscious nation-building elements soon reinforce spontaneous ones. Administrative reformers argue for policies aimed at furthering bureaucratic centralization and enhancing commerce. Political economists advance theories of mercantilism in an effort to identify "the interests of the state with the accumulation of trade surpluses by its merchant class" (Harman 7). Print technology is exploited both to ratify certain languages as "languages of power" as well as to permit poets, playwrights, and pamphleteers to take early steps in inventing the very stuff of what will come to be known as the "national" traditions (Anderson 48; Harman 7). Print-language in particular enables a necessarily literate bourgeoisie, clustered in cities and towns across Europe, "to visualize in a general way the existence of thousands and thousands like themselves" (Anderson 74). Hence, "in world historical terms bourgeoisies were the first classes to achieve solidarities on an essentially imagined basis . . . The convergence of capitalism and print technology on the fatal diversity of human language created the possibility of a new form of imagined community, which in its basic morphology set the stage for the modern nation" (Anderson 74, 49). It proves in no way surprising, then, that the nation-state should surface "as the typical form of capitalist rule" (Harman 42).[1]

Nationalism is indeed about the organization of capitalist society. This assertion raises a number of controversial issues, some of which must be set aside on this occasion. But it is important to examine one such controversy in some detail: namely, the methodological consequence for Hispanism that follows from the recent detachment of nationalism from the dynamic of capitalism. Over the course of the past two decades, the relaxation of causal relationships between capitalism and nationalism in Spanish historiography and literary criticism has led to the dominance of neo-Weberian or Foucauldian approaches not only to the question of state formation but also to the question of literary formation in Spain. Wlad Godzich's and Nicholas Spadaccini's important research on the institutionalization of literature in nineteenth-century Spain is arguably the most influential example of this phenomenon. And it is to their elegant but flawed perspective on Spanish romanticism that we now turn in order to lay the groundwork for analyzing some of the class dimensions of Spanish literature in the 1840s.[2]

Godzich and Spadaccini have put forward the most provocative thesis concerning Spanish romanticism since Edmund King's (erroneous) idea that romanticism does not appear in Spain until after the crisis of 1898. For Godzich and Spadaccini,

> When the ideas of Romanticism enter into Spain they do not take part in the project of constructing the Nation; they do not engage in the search for a new societal model in which the aesthetic domain has the capacity of intervening independently. Rather, they encounter a state structure that recruits and mobilizes them in its service and frames them within an institution they did not help construct. We will suggest that the course of literature in nineteenth-century Spain, as much in aesthetic questions as in the role assumed by the writers themselves, derives from this fundamental fact in Spain's history. (Godzich and Spadaccini, *Crisis* 18)

On the surface, Godzich's and Spadaccini's statement would appear ridiculous: evidence abounds of the close connection between cultural romanticism and political nationalism in Spain.[3] What Godzich and Spadaccini mean to suggest, however, is that aesthetic processes cannot perform the cultural work of signifying the "nation" in Spain because the "aesthetic" as such—having been instrumentalized by Spanish absolutism as part of its effort to create a state-directed culture—is no longer available to serve the revolutionary cause of bourgeois nationalism. "Aesthetics," that is, has already been institutionalized as part of Spanish aristocratic society. Hence, on Godzich's and Spadaccini's view, the new (relatively) autonomous practice of "aesthetics" which helps to construct ideas of the "nation" in other bourgeois societies cannot do so in Spain because it is incapable of cohering into an independent institution *rendering service to the bourgeois state*.

There are three problems with Godzich's and Spadaccini's interpretation. First, their view underestimates the extent to which the structure of the Spanish state is actually transformed between 1834 and 1837. Second, their view adopts a mechanical approach to the complex duality of the "aesthetic" domain as constituted in the late eighteenth and early nineteenth centuries in Europe. And, third, it pays little if any attention to the articulations of concrete subject positions during the period 1835-50—subject positions that are recognizably bourgeois and not aristocratic.

The Weberian/Foucauldian underpinnings of Godzich's and Spadaccini's view of Spanish romanticism are nowhere more apparent than in their persistent refusal to utter the words "feudalism" or "capitalism." The passage from Louis XVI to the July Monarchy in France, or from Ferdinand Vll to Isabel II in Spain, is conceptualized not as a transition between two modes of production but rather as a series of mutations in and among abstractly defined spheres of power:

> After the societies of orders, estates and revolutions, there appear the societies of institutions—instruments of the legal and administrative State exercising a regulative power in its area of influence. . . . Societies then emerged in which power was already more sparse and diffuse and in which the various spheres were diferentiated: the political, the social, the economic and, also, the cultural. (17, 16)

Godzich and Spadaccini specifically suggest that what makes Spain unique in the system of European nation-states remains the basic continuity in the structure of its state after the successes of the revolutions against the "societies of orders and estates": "In fact it could be affirmed that following the revolutions alluded to previously, European history is characterized, to a certain extent, by some attempts to regroup these spheres among a single entity: the State. In Spain this regrouping was unnecessary since the State had controlled these spheres for several centuries" (16-17).

Godzich's and Spadaccini's understanding of the nature and extent of the transformation of the Spanish state between 1834 and 1837 can and should be challenged. It is true, of course, that the liberal revolution of the first half of the nineteenth century is in no sense "pure."[4] Martínez de la Rosa's Estatuto Real of 1834 thus gives formal expression to an alliance (though not necessarily an identity) of interests between bourgeois groups and the landed aristocracy. In stark contrast to the radical Constitution of 1812, moreover, the Estatuto refuses to recognize popular sovereignty, stacks its bicameral Cortes in favor of the upper house of royal appointees, drastically limits the franchise to the richest property owners, and reserves to the Crown the power to convoke and dissolve the Cortes. And yet it is possible to affirm that, "pese a su carácter restringido, el régimen del Estatuto sirvió como marco donde fueron cristalizando los principios establecidos en las Cortes de Cádiz" (Arostegui Sánchez 785).

Indeed, under the regime of the Estatuto, legislative steps are taken to secure a number of the conditions necessary for a new capitalist economy with emphasis on agricultural production. Principal measures included "la libertad del comercio de granos, el proteccionismo estatal a las inversiones capitalistas, la protección a la industria, la libertad fabril y ciertas medidas liberalizadoras del comercio (mejores comunicaciones, uniformidad de pesos, medidas y monedas, fomento de las ferias y mercados, apoyo a los consulados y juntas del comercio)" (Bahamonde Magro and Toro Mérida 17). In addition, other legal and political reforms rationalize the state administration: the national territory is divided into modern provinces; the census is improved; and a new, uniform tax code is created and applied. All of these measures serve to give a boost to the ongoing elaboration of internal markets.

The *progresista* Constitution of 1837 subsequently completes the dismantlement of the *antiguo régimen* and ensures conditions that make irreversible the capitalist transformation of Spanish society. The 1837 Constitution reshapes the two houses of the Cortes to resemble a modern parliament, conceding them the right to initiate legislation. It imposes upon the monarchy the obligation to call a new Cortes within three months in the event of a dissolution, and it democratizes the organs of local government. Most importantly, the new Constitution establishes the regime of individual, private property in which all land—including those entailed by noble and ecclesiastical estates—can be freely bought and sold.[5]

Godzich's and Spadaccini's emphasis on continuities in the nature of the Spanish state from the *antiguo régimen* throughout the 1800s ultimately rests on the questionable view of the "failure" of "bourgeois" revolution in Spain during the first half of the nineteenth century. Recent scholarship by David Ringrose demonstrates instead that Spain follows "a path of gradual, accelerating economic expansion throughout the eighteenth and nineteen centuries. The dynamic sometimes shifted from one region to another, but even in the troubled first half of the nineteenth century there is evidence of expanding population, commercial activity, and per capita income" (390). Moreover, as Jesús Cruz documents for the 1830s, "the dominant social group was made up of agrarian and urban property holders, followed by administrative officials, professionals and businessmen" (272). Even prior to the major changes of the period, Cruz argues, factions of the nobility and the bourgeoisie are "already united by a community of interests that, if not social, were *definitely political and economic*" in response to the crisis of Spanish feudalism (272, my emphasis).

Ringrose and Cruz themselves, of course, stop short of endorsing the idea of a full-blown "bourgeois" revolution in Spain during the 1830s. They consider that the "liberal" revolution fails to pit a homogeneous bourgeoisie against a homogeneous aristocracy and that no immediate change in elite "habitus" takes place that might serve as an indicator of a thoroughgoing social revolution. Despite the unevenness displayed by the "liberal" revolution, however, Ringrose's and Cruz's own evidence amply justifies the view that a "capitalist" revolution—a revolution that unfetters the development of capitalist forces of production by instituting new social relations—succeeds in Spain between 1833 and 1839.[6]

Turning now to the cultural field, Godzich's and Spadaccini's claim about the inability of Spanish romanticism to intervene "independently" in the process of constructing the "nation" implies that culture under the Estatuto Real of 1834 and throughout the entire first half of the nineteenth century operates every bit as much under the yoke of state-direction as it did under Spanish absolutism. When they disqualify Spanish romanticism from participating in the project of articulating Spanish nationalism, therefore, Godzich and Spadaccini view both literature and literary criticism as ideologically homogeneous and as aloof from the fractious debates over defining the "nation" that characterize the political and economic spheres. Yet the ideologically differentiated and conflictive sphere of both literary production and literary consumption in the mid-1830s could hardly be greater. During this period, the literary field actually

mirrors the split within Spanish liberalism between moderates and progressives.

At the core of the political split between *moderados* and *progresistas* in the second half of the 1830s lie attitudes toward revolution.

> What distinguished the two groups most clearly was the Progressives' theory of the legitimacy of revolution; the Moderates rejected the radical tradition of revolution . . . The sovereign nation made, by the instrument of a Constituent Cortes, a constitution, a fundamental code; if this constitution was attacked by the conservative parliamentary majority of an Ordinary Cortes, then there was a "legal right of rebellion." (Carr 163)

And it is in this context that the key to understanding the basic configuration and permutations of Spanish romanticism can be found. Spanish romanticism itself is divided along at least two cultural trajectories that compete ideologically in the second half of the 1830s: a dominant "historico-nationalist" romanticism arising out of political *moderantismo*, but also a momentarily intense "social" romanticism arising out of *progresismo* and political ideologies further to the left. It is indeed the phenomenon of the cultural articulation and coexistence (for a time) of rival romanticisms that most vividly stands out as characteristic of Spanish cultural history from the mid-1830s through the early 1840s.

The debate among Spanish literary theorists and critics culminates in a hegemonic discrimination between, on the one hand, a "bad" aesthetics of social romanticism given to artistic and moral excess in the "revolutionary" manner of Hugo and Dumas, and, on the other hand, a "good" aesthetics of historico-nationalist romanticism "conveniently stripped of anything that might smack of spiritual uncertainty or pessimism" (Flitter 1993, 4). In 1837, for example, the year of the liberals' split into *moderados* and *progresistas*, Spanish essayist and literary critic Jacinto de Salas y Quiroga openly links the aesthetic ideology of historico-nationalist romanticism with the political ends of *moderantismo*: "Es preciso que el escritor público se revista de toda su dignidad para oponerse al torrente que lo va todo arrasando y que lejos de adular las pasiones populares se alce tremendo como sacerdote de paz que es a predicar una religión de

fraternidad" (qtd. in Flitter 5) ("It is necessary for the public writer to don all of his dignity in order to oppose himself to the torrent that is dragging down everything and, instead of praising popular passions, he should rise up like the priest of peace he is and preach a religion of fraternity"). Hence, by 1840, there evolves in Madrid a literary establishment aiming to channel the energies of contemporary writers into a national project of social "regeneration." Such a project is based, in the minds of *moderado* intellectuals such as Salas de Quiroga and Nicomedes Pastor Díaz, on the "power of literature to stimulate collective moral improvement and inspire an enhanced sense of spirituality in a society laboring under the twin burdens of materialism and irreligion" (Flitter 1993, 4).

Historico-nationalist romanticism on this definition comes to be viewed as the most suitable "literary vehicle capable of powering this idealistic mission" (Flitter, *Spanish* 4). Such a mission, in a word, involves nothing less than the management of those revolutionary energies from below that continue to circulate—albeit in more or less inchoate forms—throughout the mid-1830s and 1840s.[7] Although the debate over regenerationist aesthetics carries on for several more years, Flitter suggests with some reason that the cultural tide shifts definitively in favor of historico-nationalist romanticism after 1837. For the "regenerationists" of 1837-50, the role of literature is to contribute to forming individuals into a national community based on fellow-feeling—"predicar una religión de fraternidad" ("to preach a religion of fraternity")—in order to help to quiet popular demands for broader economic equality and social justice. Such demands, it should be recalled, are directed now against the new liberal state as opposed to the absolutist state. And the hegemonic responses in defense of the liberal state that develop within and through literature and literary criticism have correspondingly become more (relatively) autonomous than under absolutism.

Marx's observation on the Constitution of 1812 with which we began this essay can now begin to point the way toward an explanation based on social class for Flitter's insights in *Spanish Romantic Literary Theory and Criticism* in favor of recognizing the generally conservative nature of Spanish romantic ideology as opposed to maintaining the customary equation of cultural romanticism with Spanish *progresismo*.[8] By casting the religious spirit as central to the development of literary ideas during the first half of the nineteenth century in Spain, Flitter's view diminishes the quantity of social and philosophical discontent within Spanish cultural romanticism that stems from the frustration of social expectations held by progressive fractions of the bourgeoisie regarding their own revolution. Marx serves to remind us, however, that religious ideas and sentiments are not exclusive to historico-nationalist romanticism but in fact inhabit the range of Spanish liberalisms from birth. We shall soon see that, when faced with working-class revolutionary threats to bourgeois order and stability, even Spain's progressive poets and intellectuals turn to the power of religion to calm the rebellious spirits challenging the new liberal state.

For the moment, it is enough to underscore the origin within the eventually dominant *moderado* bourgeois fraction in Spain of an aesthetic project—historico-nationalist romanticism—designed to appropriate and to resignify religious sentiment in the interest of producing well-behaved political subjects through literature. The impulse behind such an aesthetic project, as we have seen, is to be found in political debates rooted in classes and class factions. The reality of aesthetic practice in the 1830s and 40s, therefore, is not one of a mechanical continuation of state-directed culture, as Godzich and Spadaccini would have it. On the contrary, already in the 1830s Spain shows signs of the more properly modern institutionalization of a relatively autonomous set of aesthetic practices fashioned to respond to the twin pressures, on the one hand, of the desires of a new hegemonic class seeking to imagine the terms under which it will constitute itself as a "community," and, on the other, of the need on the part of the new state created by this class to police a new realm of individual feelings embodied within all of its subjects, bourgeois or not.[9]

One way of conceptualizing the process undergone by literature in the 1830s and 40s is inadvertently provided by Godzich and Spadaccini themselves. Recall that Godzich and Spadaccini assert that, in the wake of the bourgeois revolutions against absolutism and feudalism, European societies—with the exception of Spanish society—experience a differentiation among spheres of power: the political, the social, the economic, and the cultural. As a result, throughout all of Europe—again with the exception of Spain—there develop "attempts to regroup these spheres under a single entity: the State. In Spain this regrouping was unnecessary since the State had controlled these spheres for several centuries" (Godzich and Spadaccini 16). Nevertheless, Godzich and Spadaccini themselves describe the effect on literature of the regrouping of spheres around the state in the following manner:

> When the different spheres are relatively independent, they need to look for ways of regulating themselves and of locating their powers—those that penetrate other spheres as well as their internal ones. This is the role assumed by the institutions. . . . In England, France, and Germany, the society of institutions that emerges in the nineteenth century allows literature to appear together with other institutions that are born in the same era, a period in which the entire society seeks a model that permits the maintenance of some appearance of order in the midst of the process of modernization that was destroying it. This is an era of opportunity for literature but it is likewise an era of trial since it is constantly obliged to negotiate its power in relation to other institutions. Literature is always present in the social sphere, advancing and receding, exploring aesthetic options in view of aesthetic possibilities and vice versa.
> "In Spain the situation is substantially different." (Godzich and Spadaccini 17)

But, as we have seen above, the situation of literature in Spain turns out not to be really so different after all. An institution of Spanish literature and literary criticism that is itself the site of inflamed ideological struggle assumes the task of helping a politics of order win hegemony in the face of profound social changes. That is, a literary institution that to a significant degree asserts its autonomy from the state rejoins on new terms the project of supporting the state. Furthermore, as we shall soon see, literature accomplishes this trajectory precisely by "locating" and "negotiating" its powers in relation to other institutions. In particular, it defines and asserts itself in relation to a weakened and somewhat transformed religious institution.

Before proceeding to examine aspects of the relation between literary and religious institutional discourses during the romantic period, a last point remains concerning

Godzich's and Spadaccini's thesis that Spanish romanticism does not participate in building the new Spanish "nation." Godzich and Spadaccini write that "when the ideas of Romanticism enter into Spain . . . they do not engage in the search for a new societal model in which the aesthetic domain has the capacity of intervening independently."[10] Yet, how else, if not on the basis of an aesthetic search for new societal models, can we explain the production of a significant number of new subject positions by Romantic writers between 1835 and 1850? In fact Godzich and Spadaccini seriously underestimate the extent to which Spanish romanticism creates a number of new images of the relations between self and society. Susan Kirkpatrick, for example, provides a critical inventory of several such subject positions: Larra and *mal du siècle*; Rivas's Don Alvaro and the dispersed self; Espronceda and the Promethean self; and the important transformations of these male paradigms of romantic subjectivity by women writers, including Gómez de Avellaneda, Coronado, and Cecilia Bohl (see Kirkpatrick). In our context, subject positions can be understood in the Althusserian sense of identifications that enable individuals to explain both to and for themselves the nature and meaning of their experiences of the world. The particular subject positions analyzed by Kirkpatrick, moreover, can be further understood as so many figurations of a new "aesthetic" self—a self in possession of and possessed by a profoundly new space of interiority.

To put the historical and textual argument which follows on a theoretical footing, we may recall here the basis of Michel Pêcheux's assertion that there is no meaning independently of a "subject-form." The subject-form does not appear in Pêcheux's work as anterior or pregiven to meaning; that is, Pêcheux does not consider the empirical subject as the "origin" of meaning. Rather, Pêcheux views the subject-form as the effect of those interdiscursive operations which he calls the "preconstructed" and "articulation" (Pêcheux 115). By the "preconstructed" Pêcheux means the representation of the world of objects and social relations in a "discursive formation" through modalities that presume an already constructed identity of the subject among such objects and within such relations. By "articulation" he means representational modalities whereby the subject's identity is newly activated and subjected, or even reactivated and resubjected, in a discursive formation as a necessary (though not sufficient) support for meaning (the process also requires the world of objects and social relations). "Articulation" for Pêcheux thus primarily involves the workings of what he calls "transverse-discourse":

> interdiscourse as transverse-discourse crosses and connects together the discursive elements constituted by interdiscourse as preconstructed, which supplies as it were the raw material in which the subject is constituted as "speaking-subject" with the discursive formation that subjects him [sic]. (117)

A comparatively easy way of understanding the distinction between the "preconstructed" and "articulation" is to recall again that for Pêcheux all meaning arises as a function of the subject-form (136-37); thus both the preconstructed and articulation entail such a form. In any concrete discursive situation or act, however, some meanings—those of the preconstructed—represent already "bound" or "embedded" relations between a subject-form and the experiential world, whereas other meanings—those effected by transverse discourse—are "in process" and require for their "construction" or "reconstruction" the new articulation or rearticulation of a subject-form as their support. Therefore, as long as one ascribes no a priori or a posteriori form of necessity to the interdiscursive process, one can think of the "preconstructed" as a discursively stabilized "center" of already articulated and secured subject-world relations in and for a given context. And one can think of "articulation" ("transverse-discourse") as a discursively destabilized "periphery" of still-to-be-articulated and secured subject-world relations in and for a given context.

The contexts which will concern us for the remainder of this discussion are those of religious discourse and literary discourse in Spain around 1848. Given the blaring religiosity of *moderado* ideology, it is easy to forget the significant changes imposed on the Spanish Church by the new liberal governments of *moderados* and *progresistas* alike:

> Although Spanish liberals were divided into factions whose commitment to reform ranged from moderate to extreme, they were agreed at least on the necessity of redefining the Church's position within a new political

> and economic order. There was no question of allowing the eighteenth-century Church to transfer its privileges intact into a society with political, economic, and intellectual assumptions so different from those that had characterized absolute monarchy. In the end the conflict between liberalism and the Church was an uneven contest, which the latter could not hope to win. By 1843 the institutional base of the Old Regime Church had been largely dismantled. (Callahan 145)

After the fall of Espartero's regency in 1843, *moderado* governments prevail in the 1840s. Their main concern is to "slow the pace of change and consolidate a regime to be dominated by a small elite . . . Above all, the *moderados* wished to enjoy the economic benefits of possessing power and to avoid a revolution demanding wider participation in the political porcess and redress of popular grievances" (Callahan 186). *Progresistas,* of course, are no less fearful of revolution, but their political strategy continues to depend on a willingness and ability to mobilize the lower classes in pursuit of *progresista* factional interests (186). *Moderados* instead seek means whereby they can permanently control, neutralize, or otherwise "pacify" the masses. In this they see the Church as "a useful ally in the struggle against radicalism and possible revolution." Their wielding of power thus creates for "the Church an opportunity to recover from the shocks it had suffered after 1834" (186).

Nevertheless, relations between the Church and the liberal state, even during the period of *moderado* hegemony, remain filled with tensions. This is especially true in light of the new ideologies of individualism and economic modernization that lie at the core of the liberal project.

> The pragmatism with which the Church adjusted to poltical reality vanished when it confronted an expansive capitalism and secular culture existing beyond the reach of clerical supervision. In the eyes of the churchmen, liberalism had created a society out of control in which individual passions were allowed to run riot at the expense of morality and religion. Whether moderados or progresistas governed the country made no difference ... During the late 1840s and 1850s, few aspects of liberal society moved the clergy to more rhetorical paroxysms

> than the economic changes that had produced wealth in abundance for the kingdom's elite. (225-26)

In fact, over and against the emerging ideologies of capitalism in Spain, the Church defends "an organic view of human society derived from a centuries-old scholastic tradition. Such a philosophy demanded that the individual curb his natural acquisitive passions for the common good . . . What churchmen saw about them was a consumer society, admittedly confined to a minority, which defied this traditional view of social organization" (226). Acknowledging the contradictory nature of its relationship even to *moderantismo*, then, the Church starts to supplement its activities with direct appeals to Spaniards by means of popular evangelization. Not only the establishment of new missions but also the publication of "religious books, simply written and cheaply produced" (236) become priorities.[11] Such activity, designed to strengthen the Church in relation to the liberal state, could not help but result in a compensatory move on the part of the state.

That move, as has already been suggested, involves the enlistment of a now relatively autonomous institution of "literature" in the project of defining the new "nation" and cementing the foundations of bourgeois rule. The process through which "literature" contributes to this project includes an interdiscursive negotiation of its new relation to religion. Thus a significant component of "imaginative writing" throughout the 1840s consists of transdiscursive operations in which "literary" texts articulate discursively preconstructed "religious" sentiments and perceptual forms into the new context of consolidating the liberal state.

All of this can be immmediately grasped if we consider representative writers who produce "literature" at the time of the great revolutionary upheavals that sweep across Europe in 1848. The Spanish rebellion of 1848, although it fails in terms of actually dethroning the monarch or winning new liberties as happens in France, conjures its own quite definite specter haunting Spain's new bourgeois society. The workers' uprising in March, which produces a pattern of barricades in Madrid that would reappear in 1854 and throughout the 1860s, is followed by a revolt of university students in April. In May, sergeants occupy Madrid's Plaza Mayor, and a classic *progresista* insurrection, with military and civilian components, spreads throughout Andalusia and Levante (Carr 232). The September rebellion in Barcelona pursues a radically democratic program, aiming at universal suffrage and an end to the military draft (Bahamonde and Martínez 295). Because the revolutionary tide in Europe for the first time includes demands directly related to bourgeois rule—shorter work days, job safety, employment, and an extension of the franchise—"el movimiento revolucionario era percebido (en España) como un atentado no sólo al orden y la estabilidad, sino al orden social edificado sobre el inviolable principio de la propriedad" (294). ("The revolutionary movement was perceived [in Spain] as an attack not only against order and stability, but also against the social order built on the inviolable principle of private property").

Even before the outbreak of revolutionary activity in Spain, the republican victory of February 1848 in France prompts Spain's archconservative prime minister Ramón María de Narváez to seek martial law powers from the Cortes. Constitutional guarantees regarding arrest, imprisonment, and unreasonable search and seizure are suspended from March to December 1848. Unsurprisingly, the special powers conceded to Narváez enable not only a violent and swift repression of revolt in Spain during 1848 but also the final consolidation of "el moderantismo como forma doctrinaria, recortada, y 'desde arriba' del liberalismo en España" (Bahamonde and Martínez 296) ("*moderantismo* as the doctrinal form, scaled back and top-down, of liberalism in Spain"). The most palpable effect of the defeat of 1848 in Spain is precisely to strengthen the politics and ideologies of the liberal project of nation-building: "El orden frente a la revolución . . . Las barricadas del 48 incitaron a un consenso defensivo entre antiguas y nuevas élites en torno al ideario liberal de corte gradualista y limitado" (293, 296) ("Order versus revolution . . . The barricades of 48 provoked a defensive consensus among old and new elites around the liberal program of gradualism and limited change").

Across the spectrum of bourgeois writers—from writers with sympathies for moderate, progressive, and even socialist politics—the events of the year 1848 provoke an astonishingly singular and highly revealing response in terms of aesthetic strategies. Whether we consider works by José Zorrilla, Carolina Coronado, or Ventura Ruiz Aguilera, in each case Spanish writers confront the specter of revolution from below by transdiscursively articulating romantic rebelliousness, social discontent, and philosophical questioning on the basis of a preconstructed discourse of religious feelings. Their literary works from 1848, in other words, appropriate and adapt religious discourse in the interests of producing subject-forms that symbolically dissolve class anatgonisms into the all-inclusive embrace of the "nation."

Vicente Llorens Castillo observes, for example, that there is no action, crime, or personal conspiracy explaining why Gabriel Espinosa, the Portuguese king defeated by Felipe II's armies at the battle of Alcazarquivir, deserves to be killed off at the end of *Traidor, inconfeso y mártir*, which Zorrilla writes during the second half of 1848 and stages in March 1849. The text itself offers only one reason—"morir debía / por la quietud del reino" ("he should die to preserve the tranquillity of the state")—indicating that Gabriel must die because he is a symbol around which others might organize insurrections. This acknowledgment of a state security reason for Gabriel's death, however, does not at the same time provide spectators or readers with a justification for his death.[12] Indeed, that justification is cued by the text on the basis of promoting spectators' more or less unconscious identification of Gabriel with Christ.

A prime candidate for casting as a romantic rebel fighting to win and to assert his own identity over and against what is clearly portrayed as an unjust social order, Gabriel is thus represented as a psychological hero—one whose heroism consists of abandoning a rightful claim to his own kingdom and submitting instead to the rationality of a Spanish "nation-state." By means of the figure of Gabriel, *Traidor* replaces the question of rebellion—no matter whether successful or unsuccessful, whether in deeds or in thoughts—with the necessity and alleged rewards of spiritual resignation and inner acquiesence. *Traidor* responds to the social turmoil of the year 1848 both in Spain and throughout Europe by seeking to produce a literary image of "peaceable" subjectivity in keeping with *moderado* ideology.

In Coronado's poem "Las tormentas de 1848" ("The Storms of 1848") emotional desperation and the search for spiritual consolation become the dominant chords struck in an interdiscursive operation that superimposes religious settings and tones on recognizably romantic tropes. The first stanza explicitly projects the emotional tumult associated with social romanticism into the spatialized discourse of religious solitude in which peace and order are violently disrupted.

> También aquí, Señor, en las entrañas
> del solitario monte a los oídos
> vienen a resonar voces extrañas,
> gritos de guerra y ecos de gemidos? (Coronado 339)
>
> (Even here, my Lord, in the depths
> of this solitary mountain, there are
> to resound in my ear foreign voices,
> battle cries and echoes of moans?)

The central portion of the poem typically proceeds to render series of images of natural disasters, which are themselves followed by stanzas eliciting a process of metaphysical questioning: "A dónde estás, clarísima ribera, en que la luz del sol no se escondía . . .?" (Coronado 340) ("Where are you, shining shore, where the light of the sun was not hidden . . . ?"). For our purposes, the ending remains especially important. Here the negative intertextual allusions to Espronceda's "A una estrella" ("To a Star") are unmistakable, while Coronado's repudiation of the metaphysical problematic at the heart of social romanticism takes the form of a willed retreat toward divine revelation in the face of revolutionary violence.[13]

> Yo no quiero su luz, recuerdo amargo
> de mi perdido bien, su luz me ofende
> y hace en la noche el padecer más largo
> cuando en vagos delirios me suspende; . . .
> no más que tu luz, Señor, deseo,
> ya a ti en la oscuridad siempre te veo.
>
> Pero que extienda sus celestes alas
> sobre el pueblo que gime moribundo;
> que esparza el resplandor que le regalas
> placando la cólera del mundo;
> sobre el estrago horrible de las balas,
> que hace de Europa el genio furibundo,
> ¡que ilumine, Señor, y que ella sea

paz en los odios, tregua en la pelea! (Coronado 343-44)

(I do not want its [the year 1848's] light, the bitter memory
of my lost happiness, its light offends me
and at night makes suffering longer
when I am suspended among vague deliriums; . . .
I desire nothing more than your light, my Lord,
I always see you in the darkness.

Let [your light's] celestial wings extend
over the dying and moaning people;
let it spread the splendor that you give it,
calming the world's anger; over the horrible destruction of the bullets,
which makes Europe's furious spirit,
let your light illuminate [us], my Lord, and let there be
peace where there is hate, truce where there is battle.)

Clearly, the political meanings of Coronado's poem involve somewhat more open sympathy for the *pueblo* than does Zorrilla's *Traidor*. Yet the two works share reigning emotions of fear, ambivalence, and tragedy, as well as the attempt to discursively manage such emotions through a formal reliance on religious constructions. And, arguably, Coronado's "Las tormentas de 1848" produces a subject-form even more infused with religiosity than Zorrilla's *Traidor*.

Ruiz Aguilera's poem, "En los últimos días de 1848" ("In the Last Days of 1848") does not explicitly affirm reaction of the sort: "better order than chaos." But this poem by an avowed "Christian socialist" also enacts a discursive retreat into religious subject-forms in the face of defeated revolutionary desires and expectations. Ruiz Aguilera subtitles his poem "Anatema" ("Anathema"), for example, and in so doing immediately flags the ideological distance that separates "En los últimos días de 1848" from his earlier expression of revolutionary optimism in "El porvenir" ("The future")—a poem which Ruiz Aguilera writes in April 1848 in response to the March uprising of workers in Madrid.

The main body of "En los últimos días de 1848" dramatizes a dialog between Liberty, identified as "el alma de Europa" ("the soul of Europe"), and a tyrannical sovereign. The curse invoked by the poem's subtitle correspondingly unfolds in part as the discursive parade of tyranny's victims before the eyes of the sovereign. But the curse is also one that Ruiz Aguilera's poetic persona hurls at the various revolutions of 1848 themselves:

> Huye . . . pasa veloz, año maldito,
> La humanidad espera tu agonía
> Como el reo el perdón de su delito . . .
> Huye a la eternidad . . . solo amargura
> Tu caliz ha tenido, y sangre y llanto:
> Cáliz que el mundo desolado apura. (Ruiz Aguilera 201)
>
> (Flee . . . quickly end, cursed year,
> Humanity awaits your death
> like a prisoner awaits a pardon for his crime . . .
> Flee for all eternity . . .
> your chalice has only held bitterness, blood, and tears:
> a chalice that a desolated world drinks to the last drop.)

Here—in what are the first and third of 67 stanzas in total—the motif of the "cáliz" introduces an explicitly religious sensibility and firmly establishes a religious framework from the outset. The "cáliz" motif resurfaces at various points throughout the poem, with its most important appearance occurring at the end of the central section, in which the oppressed have denounced and accused the sovereign. At this juncture the metonymically signified Grail enables Ruiz Aguilera to shift gears out of the mode of political denunciation and into a mode of religious sensibility on the basis of its ability to facilitate a discursive revision of romantic settings and tones.

> Busco el Templo de Dios . . . y se vislumbra
> Apenas—entre lúgubre ruina,
> Que al corazón más fuerte apesadumbra—

La humilde cruz del Redentor, divina. (Ruiz Aguilera 206)

(I search for God's temple . . . and there scarcely visible—among the lugubrious ruin, which saddens the strongest heart—
is the humble and divine cross of the Redeemer.)

Ruiz Aguilera's "En los útlimos días de 1848" culminates in the same place as Coronado's "Las tormentas de 1848": emotional exhaustion, intellectual and political confusion, and the displacement of class warfare into the desire for national reconciliation. As in the case of both Zorrilla's *Traidor* and Coronado's "Las tormentas de 1848," moreover, national reconciliation in Ruiz Aguilera's poetic view is to be made possible by means of the elaboration and assumption of religious subject-forms. Thus, in its final stanzas, "En los últimos días de 1848" interdiscursively translates the sensibilities constitutive of religious consolation into the foundation of a national harmony freed from class antagonisms:

Y tú, Dios bueno y justo, que das vida
. . .
Tú, bálsamo y aroma que consuela;
Vaso en que hartan su sed los labios rojos;
Lucero de la errante carabela;
¡Ay! cesa, pon piedad en tus enojos,
Y muéstranos la luz del arca santa
Donde en tanto peligro y sombra tanta
Europa ha de tornar los turbios ojos. (Ruiz Aguilera 208)

(And you, good and just God, who gives light
. . .
You, balm and perfume that console;
cup from which the red lips quench their thirst;
star guiding the wandering ship;
¡Oh! stop, show pity in your anger,
and show us the light of the holy arc
to where through so much danger and darkness
Europe must turn its clouded eyes.)

The poem's closing allusion to the Hebrew people marching forward in history, united in political compact behind the Arc of the Covenant, may perhaps serve as a last illustration of the reality that—contrary to the view of Godzich and Spadaccini—romantic "literature" in Spain does in fact "take part in the project of constructing the Nation" while being "constantly obliged to negotiate its power in relation to other institutions." The examples of Zorrilla's, Coronado's, and Ruiz Aguilera's writings from 1848 strikingly document the intervention of aesthetic practices into state formation during the 1840s. They demonstrate as well the centrality of class determinations in hegemonizing the *moderado* version of the liberal state in Spain.

Notes

1. Anderson makes clear in *Imagined Communities* that he would reject this last assertion, with its implicit affirmation of a constitutive link between capitalism and nationalism. Indeed, the events which prompt the writing of *Imagined Communities* are the invasion of Cambodia by Vietnam in late 1978 and early 1979, and the subsequent attack on Vietnam by the People's Republic of China. War consisting of nationalist rivalry between countries Anderson considers to be "socialist" indicate to him the inadequacy of classical Marxist theories of nationalism. Confronted by the spectacle of "socialist" nationalism, Anderson thus feels compelled to rethink nationalism's origins. In the end, he argues that nationalism emerges when social and economic changes in the late feudal period cause a breakdown in the system of cultural concepts that give meaning to everyday experiences—especially "death, loss, and servitude" (Anderson 40). "Nationalism," he claims, results from a "search . . . for a new way of linking fraternity, power and time" in a meaningful fashion (Anderson 40). As Chris Harman suggests, Anderson's perspective ultimately amounts to little more than locating the roots of nationalist ideology "in existential yearning, not capitalist development, despite the promise of much of Anderson's argument" (Harman 43). Anderson is to a real extent boxed into this explanation by his acceptance of China, Vietnam, and Cambodia as "socialist" nations. Indeed, *Imagined Communities* attempts to answer the question of why nationalism comprises a central feature not only of capitalist but also of socialist societies. Anderson in fact fails to understand the so-called "socialist" countries as themselves being dominated by the dynamic of competitive accumulation and, hence, as constituting a "state organized variant of capitalism" (Harman 43). Lacking this understanding, Anderson has no choice but to move outside the framework of capitalism

and to explain nationalism in terms of "innate psychological needs" (Harman 43).

2. For a full elaboration of Godzich's and Spadaccini's position on the rise and institutionalization of literature in Spain, see also their *Literature Among Discourses* (1986) and *The Institutionalization of Literature in Spain* (1987).

3. For a concise and recent presentation of the links between Spanish romanticism and nineteenth-century Spanish nationalism, see Philip W. Silver's *Ruin and Restitution: Reinterpreting Romanticism in Spain* (1997).

4. Under the *progresistas* as under the *moderados,* "la destrucción de la antigua red de relaciones sociales y el apuntalamiento de un Estado sobre bases distintas (fueron) el resultado de un compromiso entre los viejos grupos dominantes y las fracciones burguesas que habían entrado en colisión con el sistema feudal" (Arostegui Sánchez 789) ("the destruction of the old network of social relations and the setting up of a State on different foundations [were] the result of a compromise between old dominant groups and bourgeois factions that had entered on a collison course with the feudal system").

5. That Mendizábal's desamortización fails in its aim to create a substantial class of land-owning peasants does not diminish its role in establishing a regime based on private property in Spain.

6. An aside is useful here. Much is often made of the propensity of members of the nineteenth-century Spanish bourgeoisie to try to assimilate as swiftly as possible into the aristocracy, once having made their fortunes. Presumably, this phenomenon justifies characterizing the Spanish bourgeoisie as "weak" and "incapable of fulfilling its historic mission" in contrast with other European bourgeoisies. But, as Immanuel Wallerstein and others have remarked, this behavior is common among the European bourgeoisie from the eleventh century on. The willingness on the part of the Spanish bourgeoisie and the modernizing wing of the aristocracy in the 1830s to fight the Carlist War, moreover, indicates their clear recognition of the necessity of transforming the Spanish economy in capitalist directions. The violent struggle to counterpose the interests of capitalist transformation over and against the defenders of the *antiguo régimen* is generally ignored by those who downplay the power of bourgeois ideas and influence.

7. At least one uprising or rebellion of some significant variety takes place virtually every year between 1833 and 1848 in Spain.

8. While acknowledging that an earlier formulation such as "se es romántico en la medida en que se es liberal" erroneously implies an identification of Spanish romanticism with *progresista* writers, it is still important to affirm along with Ricardo Navas Ruiz that Spanish romanticism can still be identified with the broad family of Spanish liberals, including *moderados* and *progesistas*: "Cabe concluir que el romanticismo español nunca fue reaccionario. Pudo ser, eso sí, conservador, pero dentro de tendencias liberales" (Navas Ruiz 48) ("We can conclude

Spanish romanticism was never reactionary. It could have been, it is true, conservative, but within liberal tendencies").

9. Terry Eagleton explains well the character of the aesthetic in this period: "The aesthetic . . . is from the beginning a contradictory, double-edged concept. On the one hand, it figures as a genuinely emancipatory force—as a community subjects now linked by sensuous impulse and fellow-feeling rather than heteronomous law, each safeguarded in its unique particularity while bound at the same time into social harmony. The aesthetic offers the middle class a superbly versatile model of their political aspirations, exemplifying new forms of autonomy and self-determination, transforming the relations between law and desire, morality and knowledge, recasting the links between individual and totality, and revising social relations on the basis of custom, affection, and sympathy. On the other hand, the aesthetic signifies what Max Horkheimer has called a kind of 'internalized repression,' inserting social power more deeply into the very bodies of those it subjugates, and so operating as a supremely effective mode of political hegemony" (Eagleton 28).

10. I am not convinced that the "aesthetic" ever intervenes "independently." I do believe that the processes of cultural signification that we have come to call "aesthetic" since the second half of the eighteenth century can be said to enjoy a "relative autonomy." But I must confess that I do not know what it means to say that the "aesthetic intervenes independently."

11. To give an idea of the scale of the publication of evangelical propaganda, Callahan documents that "between 1848 and 1866 the publishing house (Antonio) Claret established printed 2,811,100 books; 1,509,600 pamphlets; and nearly 5,000,000 posters and broadsheets" (236).

12. I offer a much fuller discussion of Zorrilla's play in "Zorrilla and 1848: Contradictions of Historico-Nationalist Romanticism in *Traidor, inconfeso* y *mártir*" (1998).

13. For a discussion of metaphysical discontent in Spanish romanticism, see my "Contradictory Explanatory Systems in Espronceda's Poetry: The Social Genesis and Structure of *El diablo mundo*" (1983).

Works Cited

Anderson, Benedict. *Imagined Communites*. London: Verso, 1991.

Arostegui Sánchez, Julio. "Un nuevo sistema político." *Historia de España*. Madrid: Historia 16, 1986. 764-800.

Bahamonde, A., and J.A. Martínez. *Historia de España. Siglo XIX*. Madrid: Cátedra, 1994.

Bahamonde Magro, A., and J. Toro Mérida. *Burguesía, especulación y cuestión social en el Madrid del siglo XIX*. Barcelona: Siglo XXI, 1994.

Callahan, William J. *Church, Politics, and Society in Spain, 1750-1874*. Cambridge, Mass.: Harvard UP, 1984.

Carr, Raymond. *Spain 1808-1939*. Oxford: Oxford UP, 1966.
Coronado, Carolina. *Poesías*. Edición, Introducción y notas por Noël Valis. Madrid: Castalia, 1991.
Cruz, Jesús, *Gentlemen, Bourgeois, and Revolutionaries: Political Change and Cultural Persistence Among the Spanish Dominant Groups, 1750-1850*. Cambridge: Cambridge UP, 1996.
Eagleton, Terry. *The Ideology of the Aesthetic*. London: Blackwell, 1990.
Espronceda, José de. *El estudiante de Salamanca: El diablo mundo*. Madrid: Castalia, 1978.
Flitter, Derek. *Spanish Romantic Literary Theory and Criticism*. Cambridge: Cambridge UP, 1992.
_____. "Zorrilla, the Critics, and the Direction of Spanish Romanticism." *José Zorrilla (1893-1993). Centennial Readings*. Eds. Richard A. Cardwell and Ricardo Landeira. Nottingham, UK: U Nottingham P, 1993.
Godzich, Wlad, and Nicholas Spadaccini. *The Crisis of Institutionalized Literature in Spain*. Minneapolis: The Prisma Institute, 1986.
Harman, Chris. "The Return of the National Question." *International Socialism* 56.2: 3-61.
King, Edmund L. "What Is Spanish Romanticism?" *Studies in Romanticism* 2 (1962): 1-11.
Kirkpatrick, Susan. *Las románticas: Women Writers and Subjectivity in Spain, 1835-1850*. Berkeley: U of California P, 1989.
Lewis, Thomas E. "Contradictory Explanatory Systems in Espronceda's Poetry: The Social Genesis and Structure of *El diablo mundo*." *Ideologies and Literature* 17 (1983): 11-45.
Lewis, Tom. "Zorrilla and 1848: Contradictions of Historico-Nationalist Romanticism in *Traidor, inconfeso y mártir*." *Hispania* 81 (1998): 818-29.
Llorens Castillo, Vicente. *El romanticismo español*. 2nd ed. Madrid: Fundación Juan March and Editorial Castalia, 1979.
Marrast, Robert. Introducción. *El estudiante de Salamanca: El diablo mundo*. By José de Espronceda. Madrid: Castalia, 1978.
Marx, Karl, and Frederick Engels. *Revolution in Spain*. New York: International Publishers, 1939.
Navas Ruiz, Ricardo. El romanricismo español. 4th ed. Madrid: Cátedra, 1990.
Pêcheux, Michel. *Language, Semantics, Ideology*. London: Verso, 1975.
Ringrose, David. *Spain, Europe, and the Spanish "Miracle," 1700-1900*. Cambridge: Cambridge UP, 1996.
Ruiz Aguilera, Ventura. *Ecos nacionales*. Alicante: Pedro Ibarra, 1849.
Silver, Philip. *Ruin and Restitution: Reinterpreting Romanticism in Spain*. Nashville, Tenn.: Vanderbilt UP, 1997.
Zorrilla, José. *Traidor, inconfeso y mártir*. Introduction and notes by Ricardo Senabre. Madrid: Anaya, 1970.

◆ Afterword

Back to the Future: Spain, Past and Present

David R. Castillo and Nicholas Spadaccini

The emergence of the modern concept of nation is often linked to the Romantics' activation of the past in search of a communal essence, while the Spanish Golden Age is said to have held a privileged position in this discussion as it became a locus for reflection on issues of literary history and national construction.[1] In fact, concepts such as "nation," "literary history," and "Spanish Golden Age" are bonded in surprising ways around the same time period in the nineteenth century. The present volume attests to the continued resonance of those concepts as it explores the problematic question of culture and the state in Spain, beginning with the mid-sixteenth century and the strengthening of the absolutist monarchy and ending with a discussion of romanticism and the constitution of the nation-state.

Germane to the present book are issues of subjectivity and subject formation for, after all, it is difficult to think of kings without subjects and nations without citizens. Thus, in connection with the early modern period Malcolm Read deals primarily with the role of language, education, and grammatical homogenization within the context of the emergence of the Absolutist State, drawing from the writings of Cristóbal de Villalón (1505-58); Mary Elizabeth Perry speaks to the construction of a national identity that suppresses ethnic, gender, and sexual difference; Francisco

Sánchez focuses on early modern discourses on wealth through a reading of *arbitrista* literature and picaresque narratives, particularly the best seller of the latter genre, *Guzmán de Alfarache* (1599-1604); Edward Baker focuses on Cervantes's *Don Quijote* to address questions of patronage, authorship, and the changes brought about by the emerging literary market; Sara Nalle studies the popular religious press of Spanish sixteenth century, its accessibility to a semiliterate readership, and the unpredictability of use or reception of the same; Bradley Nelson examines the emblematic mode of thought in Spain around 1600, concentrating on its appropriation by theorists and well-known writers for purposes of education or indoctrination, projecting a type of subjectivity that is dependent upon dominant values; José Valero inquires into the reasons for the failure of "rationalization," which he attributes to the weak development of civil society from the end of the eighteenth century to the mid-1800s; Susan Kirkpatrick examines the constitutions of 1812 and 1837, respectively, and the play *Don Juan Tenorio* by José Zorrilla to explore legal and literary modes of representation of the nation and its citizens; Tom Lewis argues that midway through the nineteenth century literature becomes a sight of symbolic negotiation among political discourses in the process of envisioning the present and future of the Spanish nation.

These essays tend to show that, in the case of Spain, there is a long history of intellectual and political debate on the notions of state and nation. We might also add that in our days these debates find continuity in the discussions surrounding the validity of the constitution of 1978 and the political frame that emerged from it. Some of the most interesting exchanges on this topic have been taking place recently in the Spanish media apropos the teaching of history and the validity of centralized conceptions of Spain. The spark for these polemics was the draft of a decree published by the Ministry of Education and Culture that sought to revitalize the humanities by redefining its role in a liberal education. The draft elicited reactions from intellectuals from various disciplines and political persuasions.

What follows is a sample of recent reflections on this subject gathered from November 1997 to January 1998 from the op ed and cultural pages of the Spanish newspaper *El País digital*: Thus, Javier Varela, a historian of political thought at

UNED university, saw in the decree the manifestation of "an exquisite respect for the cultural and political variety of the historical communities" highlighting its recognition of Spain's linguistic and multicultural diversity. He observes further that in it Spain is viewed as a historically constructed reality rather than as an essential entity: "the draft [of the decree] runs against the grain of *casticismo*, the exaltation of imperial glories, Castilianist myths, and the myths of Visigothic origin . . . The word Spain only surfaces in the section dedicated to the sixteenth century; that is, Spain is not presented as an essence with a lack of temporality but as a political and cultural reality that has a date" (1-2).

While Josep Fontana, a historian from the Pompeu Fabra University in Catalonia, questions the very need of the state to intervene in the teaching of history and warns against the danger of going back "to the bugle and drum and to submit kids to protomilitary exercises" (2), José Alvarez Junco, a historian of history of ideas and social movements at Madrid's Universidad Complutense, reflects upon the question of collective memories which, for him, are "mere ideological reconstructions of the past at the service of present political ends" (2). Alvarez Junco sees these patterns in centralist nationalist histories as well as in the myths activated by contemporary forms of regional nationalism such as those of Catalonia and the Basque Country whose political elites seek to construct their own states by advancing "histories that are no less fictional about a Catalonia whose democratic and mercantile tendencies [according to these politicians] would have been in evidence from the time of Ampurias's ruins, or about a Basque Country of millenarian independence with a purity of blood tested by invasions." For Alvarez Junco, these "alternative histories . . . are characterized not only by deformation but by victimization as well" (2-3).

Camilo Nogueira, a nationalist politician from Galicia, illustrates precisely the type of argument advanced by Alvarez Junco when he contends that the decree negates the plurinational character of the Spanish territory. Nogueira can make this assertion by tracing the Galician nation back to the Middle Ages and coming to the conclusion that "the historical reality of Galicia puts into question the idea of a predestined Spanish State in its current territorial configuration" (2). This position is challenged by the novelist Rafael Sánchez Ferlosio, who argues that the "fetishism of identity" is in the end "a common delirium . . . which is both an imposition and an imposture" (1) regardless of its provenance, whether it comes from a centralist or a nationalist position. This argument is echoed by the novelist Juan Goytisolo, who bemoans the increasing balkanization of Spanish politics and the attempt by nationalist segments of Spanish society to rewrite history to suit their respective agendas. Speaking against radical Catalonian nationalists he argues that the idea that the Spanish civil war "was a war by Franco against the Catalans is the surest form of entering the slippery road of exclusionary and differentiating nationalist mythologies, which in a more propitious economic and political context have fed the most recent ethnic conflicts of the ex Yugoslav federation" (2). Perhaps one of the strongest pronouncements on the dangers of manipulating history to advance sectarian political ends comes from novelist Antonio Muñoz Molina, who maintains that while the Franco dictatorship "hid and falsified the history of Spain, democracy . . . has confirmed its prohibitions. In Francoist schools the civil war was taught as a communist aggression of international communism against Catholic and eternal Spain; today in Catalonian and Basque schools the civil war is taught as a Spanish aggression against Catalonia and Euskadi" (4).

These debates regarding the teaching of history, language, and literature underscore the potential volatility of the current political situation in Spain. A good example is the statement made recently by the head of Catalonia's Generalitat, Jordi Pujol, that Spain is not a nation, a statement which has triggered another wave of discussions on the constitution of 1978. In the end, it becomes clear that there are those who believe that the constitution provides a valid frame for the Spain of the future, that is, a European, democratic, plurinational state, and those who wish to further modify the constitution in order to allow a greater degree of devolution to the historical regions and nationalities. In this context it is interesting to note the results of the recent elections in the Basque Country which, to the surprise of many politicians reflected the traditional split between nationalists and nonnationalists, despite the cease-fire declared by the ETA—the terrorist organization that seeks total independence from Spain—shortly before the election of October 1998. The reading of the results of these elections by Imanol Zubero, a professor of sociology at the University of the Basque

Country, is significant for he establishes a distinction between the Basque Country as a historical reality made up of political and cultural pluralism and as a political project that is yet to be realized: "it may never have been as clear as today that the Basque nation is in any case a political project to be constructed, but not a historical reality to be discovered. The political pluralism of Basque society, a reflection of its deepest cultural and cosmovisional plurality, has burst forth with neither fear nor shame in these elections" (*El País digital*, 28 October 1998). This view has also been expressed by Jon Juaristi in an award-winning book, *El bucle melancólico,* in which he underscores the notion of symbolic construction in relation to the Basque Country. As Miguel Angel Villena observes in his recent review (*El País digital,* Cultura, 20 October 1998), the Basque essayist suggests that nationalists call for the "reparation of non-existent offenses" in the name of "a Basque nation-state that has never existed" ("la reparación de unas ofensas que no existen en nombre de una patria vasca que nunca existió").

Josep A. Duran I Lleida, a politician from the Unió Democrática de Catalunya, provides another interesting reading of the polarized political atmosphere in Spain today when he calls attention to the fact that a nation is ultimately a symbolic construction which contributes to the vertebration of the state: "the fact that in Spain or Catalonia plurality or unity affect sensibilities shows the importance of the symbolic in the construction of the state and ratifies the need to find an adequate response to the vertebration of the State" (*El País digital*, 29 October 1998).

Let us recall here that the idea of nation evokes the notion of community with an emphasis on commonality of past, mission, values, beliefs, and even enemies. The activation of the past to create national symbols is a common practice, for example, among certain writers of the Spanish baroque. One thinks of the plays of Lope de Vega, particularly those that emphasize historical themes (*Fuenteovejuna; Peribáñez; El mejor alcalde, el rey; El villano en su rincón;* and others), plays which construct myths of origin while they legitimize the Spanish absolutist monarchy and the system of values and authority that sustains it.[2] *Fuenteovejuna* is a paradigmatic case in this respect, for the spectator or reader of the play is called upon to celebrate the process of construction and consolidation of the state in the person of the king and witness his communion with the people. Such consolidation is effected through an epic drive which has several dimensions: the obliteration or absorption of other sources of power (whether they be other kings, noblemen, or local chieftains); the exclusion of difference, especially of non-Christian elements;[3] and the moral regeneration of the social body through an assertion of order over chaos, which finds an essential corollary in the sexual economy of the play in its idealization of marriage and family. The king becomes the guarantor of social order—the glue that binds the state together. Plays such as *Fuenteovejuna* invite the spectator/reader to accept as his/her own a model of subjectivity which emphasizes loyalty and obedience to the king and a general adherence to the values and beliefs which sustain the monarcho-seigniorial system of authority—what Maravall aptly calls a *religion of obedience.* This type of theatrical spectacle may be said to aid the process of symbolic identification of individuals with the king's body by propagating an all-inclusive notion of honor, one which links the moral (intimate) realm with the private sphere (the economic sphere of the family) and, ultimately, with the domain of public authority. The spectator/reader is thus called upon to invest in the new structuring of society; to become part of the king's honorable body: the state.

Later in the seventeenth century, with the increased bureaucratization of the absolutist court, there appears a new model of subjectivity which responds to the need for legitimization of the newly established power elites.[4] To some extent those elites succeed in absorbing bourgeois subject positions which had emerged earlier in the sixteenth century in connection with the increased circulation of money and mercantile activities.[5] This model will find its purest expression in the writings of the Jesuit moralist Baltasar Gracián, who distinguishes between a "sujeto" or a biological subject, and "persona", that is, a public subject, defined by his ability to represent himself effectively in the public sphere. The idea here is to control appearances to meet public expectations and thus enhance one's own public image or reputation. This model of subjectivity hinges, on one hand, upon a notion of self-worth that allows for the exclusion of those whose titles are not supported by wealth and, on the other, the inclusion of new moneyed groups and bureaucratic elites who participate in the management of state affairs at the highest levels.

This type of subjectivity organized around the notion of self-worth also finds expression in the emblematic mode of representation which appears everywhere in the literature of the seventeenth century. Although the emblem is an imported genre and its cultivation in Spain originates within high-culture circles, its theorization by intellectuals such as Juan Borja and Juan de Orozco y Covarrubias suggests an awareness of its potential as a vehicle for indoctrination and sociopolitical and religious propaganda.[6] Thus the emblem becomes a mode of representation which mediates between aristocratic conceptions of wit, notions of self-worth, and the indoctrinating needs of the incipient modern state.

The models of subjectivity just outlined coexist in early modern Spain with the more traditional nobiliary and religious forms of social identification. The latter play a key role in the sanctification of the king's body, so that the Church becomes the monarch's best ally as it condemns all traces of moral, cultural, and political deviancy, thus contributing to the homogenization of society and the solidification of the state. Religious spectacle such as sacramental plays, processions, the staging of sermons, the propagation of saints' cults, and so on clearly contribute to the identification of the individual with the established system of authority.[7]

We wish to caution here that while we are emphasizing the institutional view of a process of national construction, we are cognizant of the complexities of popular reception of official culture. In fact, the omnipresence of symbolic manifestations of power in both Spain and the New World signals a deepening doubt about the effectiveness of state control over its subjects. At the same time there is ample evidence that the addressees of this array of cultural artifacts are not necessarily passive and, furthermore, may come to countercultural or even heretical interpretations.[8]

As in several other European countries, in Spain the program of the enlightened state envisions greater participation and control in the realm of cultural policy. Whereas in the 1600s the state acted as arbiter in the realm of culture and as adjudicator in a field of competing discourses, in the late 1700s, the processes of cultural appropriation result in a program that seeks the nationalization of the cultural sphere. It is a culture of the state for the state. In the name of rationalization there is ultimately an attempt to exclude those practices that do not further the interests of the ruling elites. The enlightened program places great emphasis on certain educational objectives which aim toward the creation of a new citizen and a new political ideal: the modern nation. This explains the insistence on the utilitarian aspects of literature and, especially, theater, which is often referred to as "escuela del pueblo" ("a school for the people"). But this "school" is envisioned as being under the control of the state, which is responsible for its functioning on different levels—from architectural planning, to seating configuration, the price of tickets, and the content of particular productions.

Such was also the case with the discussion surrounding the school curriculum as seen, for example, from the writings of Meléndez Valdés, who laments the poverty of coherent teaching programs and textbooks and argues for state intervention through an appointed official whose mission would be to impose "order" and "vigilance" and to develop a master plan for the direction of "all schools" (cited by Maravall 1987, 82). The state is thus placed at the center of cultural and social life in the context of a trickle-down economy that at the political level is realized through the division of the citizenry into two basic groups: the decision-making elites and those who are interpellated as passive recipients of enlightened state policies. This division will endure throughout the nineteenth century in various forms, one of which relates to the issue of representation as envisioned in the texts of the constitutions of 1812 and 1837 respectively.[9] In fact, some of the most controversial political debates which will take place in the second half of the nineteenth century and at the beginning of the twentieth revolve precisely around this problem of political representation; the puzzle to solve is how to create an appearance of greater direct participation and political pluralism without diminishing the effective control exercised by the governing elites.[10]

The Isabelline period (1845-68) which follows the drafting of the constitution of 1845 aimed—as the historian José Varela Ortega observes—to "rationalize the mechanisms of power, concentrating it and centralizing it by means of an administrative machinery of pyramidal geometry . . . the result was a classic liberal regime—parliamentary yes, but with badly shared power relations, strongly unbalanced and dependent upon executive power" (50). This oligarchic system is refined during the so-called Restoration period, which saw a mandatory rotation to power of the two major political platforms—the conservatives and progressives. While such practice allowed for political peace that aimed to do away with all-too-common military coups, the practical result was the foreclosure of real political debate and electoral participation. Furthermore, according to Joaquín Costa, the "natural institution which emanated from the sovereignty of the nation was converted into an exchange that traded power among the oligarchs" (cited by Varela Ortega 58).

Much has been written on the instrumentalization of literature for political and educational purposes in the nineteenth century in relation to Romantic aesthetics. As we have argued earlier, in the case of Spain the debate has its roots in the Golden Age activation of a mythical past within the context of the absolutist monarchy. An analysis of Spanish romanticism in connection with the ongoing discourse on the construction of the nation reveals an array of positions, some of which may not fit into neat categories or paradigms. Several Romantic intellectuals partake of the national project, among them Agustín Durán, who speaks of great literature as "an expression of national character" (Donald Shaw, "Introduction" to *Discurso de Agustín Durán*, xviii-xix). Yet, there are well-known representatives of the Spanish Romantic movement such as José de Espronceda who do not seem as interested in the debate.

One could say that it is not even a question of whether or not there are two romanticisms in Spain but, rather, to what extent Spanish romanticism is a coherent movement from a political perspective. For even the notion of "pueblo," so dear to Romantics, is not without contradictions. One might ask, therefore, what "pueblo" are they invoking? Is it an essential entity that precedes the very constitution of the modern state and finds its purest expression in the Spain of the *Cortes* (as Friedrich Schlagel and his followers in Spain would have it); or is it the one invoked in a certain strain of *costumbrismo* —that of Mesonero Romanos, for example— which locates the notion of "pueblo" not in a remote past but in the reality of mid-nineteenth-century Spain; or is it something else entirely?

Francisco Villacorta Baños has recently concluded that at the end of the nineteenth century the new "pueblo" was in fact a proteic and threatening presence which needed to be stylized and petrified before it could be integrated into the normative liberal project: "this new pueblo was composed of those multiple and heterogeneous elements which ideological reason, political praxis and juridical norm systematically situated outside or on the border of the dominant order. It was the threatening pueblo of proletarian organizations which was separating itself from liberal values . . . To assimilate that pueblo it was necessary to stylize it with the make-up of an aesthetic nationalism or to petrify it in an idealized and scientific conceptualization of nation-people" (137). Significantly, Villacorta situates the process of stylization and assimilation of the notion of pueblo not in the Romantic period but in the twentieth century. Thus, he sees the Generation of 1898 and its followers as cultural catalysts that will enable the liberal appropriation of the notion of "pueblo" for a nationalist program of Enlightened origins. According to Villacorta, the "men of `98" played a crucial role "in re-creating a new form of national patriotism and in designing its basic symbolic referents" (138). Indeed, in Spain the appropriation of the notion of "pueblo" for nationalist ends has more to do with the complex and often politically contradictory patriotism of the `98 Generation and its followers than with Romantic aesthetics. From this perspective one may well say that the project of national construction in Spain is not a "romantic" one, even if some of the Romantic writers advanced notions that could be assimilated into different nationalist programs.

In this Afterword we have tried to follow two complementary lines of argumentation, one that emphasizes institutional developments centered on the evolution of the Spanish state from absolutist models to constitutional frameworks; another which focuses on the changing relations between culture and state. We have further observed that the movement from state to nation finds its mirror image in the transition from subject to citizen. The mechanisms deployed to advance the consolidation of the state also evolved, from the overseeing role of monarchical authority in the early modern period, to the enlightened programs of education and nationalization of culture, to the more recent appropriation of the notion of pueblo for nationalist programs.

The first two decades of the twentieth century witnessed a continuation of the debates on political representation, which involved new mediation agencies such as professional organizations and labor unions. These debates were to be interrupted by the dictatorship of Primo de Rivera and, after the short interval of the Second Republic, by the dictatorship of Francisco Franco. It is only in the last quarter of our century that these issues have reentered the public sphere, albeit with a change of focus. Presently, emphasis is placed on the question of regional representation in the constitutional nation-state that is Spain. As we saw in the beginning of our discussion, this situation has substantial repercussions in the sphere of culture as intellectuals from diverse political and institutional affiliation argue over the curriculum and the function of history, literature, and education in a country that is stretched simultaneously by the centripetal forces which drive it toward Europe and by centrifugal tendencies which threaten its very existence in its current form. For, after all, as Lope de Vega and his contemporaries knew very well, we write the past ("our past") from the perspective of the future that "we" want to be. The present volume examines many of these questions in light of the role played by literature and culture in the articulation of notions of "state," "nation," "subject," and "citizen" from a historicist perspective, one that underscores the inseparability of practices of subject representation and state formation.

Notes

1. For a discussion of this question, see Wlad Godzich and Nicholas Spadaccini in *Literature among Discourses* (9-38).

2. See José Antonio Maravall, *La cultura del barroco* and *Teatro y literatura en la sociedad barroca.*

3. See Mary Elizabeth Perry in this volume for an overview of exclusionary practices in early modern Spain. See also Américo Castro's classic study *De la edad conflictiva: Crisis de la cultura española en el siglo XVII.*

4. See José Antonio Maravall, *Poder, honor y élites en el siglo XVII.*

5. See Francisco Sánchez in this volume. See also Maravall's comments in *Las comunidades de Castilla: una primera revolución moderna* on the uprising of mercantile elements in Valladolid, Segovia, Toledo, and other Spanish cities against the centralizing drive of Charles V.

6. See Bradley Nelson in this volume. See also José Antonio Maravall, *Teatro y literatura en la sociedad barroca.*

7. See José Antonio Maravall, *La cultura del barroco.* See also Gwendolyn Barnes and Sara Nalle in *Culture and Control in Counterreformation Spain.* We have dealt with subjectivity in the Golden Age in our essay, "Models of Subjectivity in Early Modern Spain," where we explore different subject positions in the context of Renaissance and baroque representation.

8. See Sara Nalle's discussion of Sánchez's reading of popular liturgical literature in this volume. See also in the case of Italy the classic study by Ginszburg, *The Cheese and the Worms: The Cosmos of a Sixteenth-Century Miller.*

9. See Susan Kirkpatrick in this volume.

10. See the conclusion of Francisco Villacorta Baños in his essay "Fin de siglo: Crisis del liberalismo y nuevos procesos de mediación social."

Works Cited

Alvarez Junco, José. "De historia y amnesia." *El País digital. Debates. La enseñanza de la historia.* November 1997-January 1998.

Barnes, Gwendolyn. "Religious Oratory in a Culture of Control." *Culture and Control in Counterreformation Spain.* Ed. Anne Cruz and Mary Elizabeth Perry. Minneapolis: U of Minnesota P, 1992. 51-77.

Castillo, David, and Nicholas Spadaccini. "Models of Subjectivity in Early Modern Spain." *Subjectivity in Early Modern Spain.* Ed. Oscar Pereira Zazo. *Journal of Interdisciplinary Literary Studies* 6.2. Lincoln: U of Nebraska-Lincoln, 1994. 185-204.

Castro, Américo. *De la edad conflictiva: Crisis de la cultura española en el siglo XVII.* Madrid: Taurus, 1972.

Duran I Lleida, Josep. "Lealtad a la lectura democrática de la constitución." *El País digital,* 29 October 1998.

Fontana, Josep. "Enseñar Historia de España." *El País digital. Debates. La enseñanza de la historia:* November 1997-January 1998.

Ginszburg, Carlo. *The Cheese and the Worms: The Cosmos of a Sixteenth-Century Miller.* Trans. John and Anne Tedeschi. Baltimore: Johns Hopkins P, 1980.

Godzich, Wlad, and Nicholas Spadaccini, "Introduction: Toward a History of 'Literature.'" *Literature among Discourses. The Spanish Golden Age.* Minneapolis: U of Minnesota P, 1986. ix-xv.

_____."Popular Culture and Spanish Literary History." *Literature Among Discourses. The Spanish Golden Age.* 41-61.

_____. "Introduction: From Discourse to Institution." *The Institutionalization of Literature in Spain.* Minneapolis: The Prisma Institute, 1987. 9-38.

_____. "Introduction: The Course of Literature in Nineteenth-Century Spain." *The Crisis of Institutionalized Literature in Spain.* Minneapolis: The Prisma Institute, 1988. 9-34.

Goytisolo, Juan. "Historias, historietas e historia." *El País digital. Debates. La enseñanza de la historia:* November 1997-January 1998.

Juaristi, Jon. *El bucle melancólico: Historias de nacionalistas vascos.* Madrid: Espasa Calpe, 1997.

Lope de Vega, Félix. *El villano en su rincón.* Ed. Alonso Zamora Vicente. Madrid: Espasa-Calpe, 1963.

_____. *Peribañez y el comendador de Ocaña.* Ed. Alonso Zamora Vicente. Madrid: Espasa-Calpe, 1963.

_____. *El mejor alcalde, el rey.* Ed. José María Díez Borque. Madrid: Ediciones Istmo, 1974.

_____. *Fuenteovejuna.* Ed. Maria Grazia Profeti. Madrid: Cupsa, 1978.

Maravall, José Antonio. *Las comunidades de castilla: una primera revolución moderna.* Madrid: Revista de Occidente, 1963.

_____. *Teatro y literatura en la sociedad barroca.* Madrid: Seminarios y ediciones, 1972.

_____. *La cultura del barroco.* Barcelona: Ariel, 1975.

_____. *Poder, honor y élites en el siglo XVII.* Madrid: Siglo XXI, 1979.

_____. "The Idea and Function of Education in Enlightenment Thought." *The Institutionalization of Literature in Spain.* Ed. Wlad Godzich and Nicholas Spadaccini. Minneapolis: The Prisma Institute, 1987. 39-99.

Muñoz Molina, Antonio. "La historia y el olvido." *El País digital. Debates. La enseñanza de la historia:* November 1997-January 1998.

Nalle, Sara. "A Saint for All Seasons: The Cult of San Julián." *Culture and Control in Counterreformation Spain.* Ed. Anne Cruz and Mary Elizabeth Perry. U of Minnesota P, 1992. 25-50.

Nogueira, Camilo. "Qué historia común." *El País digital. Debates. La enseñanza de la historia:* November 1997-January 1998.

Sánchez Ferlosio, Rafael. "Historia e 'identidad'." *El País digital. Debates. La enseñanza de la historia:* November 1997-January 1998.

Shaw, Donald L. "Introduction." *Discurso de Agustín Durán.* Exeter: U of Exeter, 1973. xviii-xix.

Varela, Javier. "La enseñanza de la historia." *El País digital. Debates. La enseñanza de la historia:* November 1997-January 1998.

Varela Ortega, José. "La España política de fin de siglo." *Revista de Occidente* 202-203 (March 1998): 43-77.

Villacorta Baños, Francisco. "Fin de siglo: Crisis del liberalismo y nuevos procesos de mediación social." *Revista de Occidente,* 202-03 (March 1998): 131-48.

Villena, Miguel Angel. "Jon Juaristi gana el Premio Nacional de Ensayo por su crítica del nacionalismo vasco." *El País digital* (Cultura), 20 October 1998.

Zubero, Imanol. "Paisaje después de la batalla (electoral)." *El País digital,* 28 October 1998.

◆ Contributors

Edward Baker is Associate Professor of Spanish Literature at the University of Florida, Gainesville. Among his numerous studies on Spanish literature and historiography, he has published two books, *Texto y sociedad: Problemas de historia literaria española* (1990) and *Materiales para escribir Madrid. Literatura y espacio urbano de Moratín a Galdós* (1991).

David R. Castillo is Assistant Professor of Spanish Literature at the University of Oregon. Interested in literary theory and cultural criticism, he has published numerous essays on Spanish Golden Age texts.

Susan Kirkpatrick is Professor of Spanish Literature at the University of California, San Diego. In addition to a book on Larra (1977) and articles on nineteenth- and twentieth-century Spanish fiction, she has published *Las románticas: Women Writers and Subjectivity in Spain, 1835-1850* (1989; Spanish translation, 1991) and *Antología poética de escritoras del siglo XIX* (1992). She served on the Executive Council of the Modern Language Association from 1993 to 1996. Currently, she is preparing a study of women as aesthetic subjects of Spanish modernism.

Tom Lewis is Associate Professor of Spanish and Comparative Literature at the University of Iowa. He is the author of two monographs, *La transformación de la teoría* (1997) and *Notas para una teoría del referente* (1993), and articles on nineteenth-century Spanish literature and culture.

Sara T. Nalle is Associate Professor of History at the William Paterson University of New Jersey. Her publications include "Literacy and Culture in Early Modern Castile," *Past and Present* 125 (1989) and *God in La Mancha: Religious Reform and the People of Cuenca, 1500-1650* (1992).

Bradley J. Nelson is a doctoral candidate in Spanish literature and culture at the University of Minnesota. His dissertation focuses on the emblematic mode of thought in late sixteenth- and seventeenth-century Spain and considers both the manner in which emblems are theorized as well as specific uses in the context of different kinds of writing.

Mary Elizabeth Perry is Adjunct Professor of History at Occidental College and Research Associate at the UCLA Center for Medieval and Renaissance Studies. She has published four books and many articles on marginal groups in early modern Spain. Her books, *Crime and Society in Early Modern Seville* (1980), and *Gender and Disorder in Early Modern Seville* (1990), each won the Sierra Book Award. She has received a Fulbright Fellowship and grants from the American Council of Learned Societies, the Comité Conjunto Hispano-Norteamericano, the Del Almo Foundation, and the National Endowment for the Humanities.

Malcolm K. Read is Professor of Spanish Literature at the State University of New York-Stony Brook. He is the author of six books: *Juan de Huarte de San Juan*; *The Birth and Death of Language*; *Visions in Exile*; *Language, Text, Subject*; and *Borges and His Predecessors* and *Transitional Discourses*.

Francisco J. Sánchez is Associate Professor of Spanish Literature at the University of Iowa. He has published a book on Cervantes's *Novelas ejemplares* (1993) and numerous essays on literary and cultural criticism on *La Celestina*, picaresque literature, Gracián, and Jovellanos. He is currently writing a book on the representation of the early modern subject in relation to a discourse on wealth in Golden Age Spain.

Nicholas Spadaccini is Professor of Hispanic studies and Comparative Literature at the University of Minnesota. He has written on early modern Spain and colonial Latin America, edited a number of Spanish classics, and coedited several volumes of literary theory and criticism. His most recent publications are a coauthored book, *Through the Shattering Glass: Cervantes and the Self-Made World*, and a coedited volume, *Rhetoric and Politics: Baltasar Gracián and the New World Order.*

José A. Valero is Assistant Professor of Spanish Literature at the University of Wisconsin-Eau Claire. He has published several essays on literary and cultural criticism and on the emergence of the Spanish historiography. He is currently working on a book on the relations between modernization and the conformation of the literary institution in eighteenth- and nineteenth-century Spain.

subject in relation to a discourse on wealth in [illegible] Golden Age Spain.

Nicholas Spadaccini is Professor of Hispanic Studies and Comparative Literature at the University of Minnesota. He has written on early modern Spain and on [illegible] and has co-edited a number of ... Spanish literature and ... and ... of literary theory and criticism. He ... [illegible] [illegible]

[illegible]

... is Assistant Professor of Spanish ... at the University of Wisconsin-Eau Claire. He has published several essays on literary and cultural ... and ... on discourses of the Spanish ... He is currently working on ... and ... the relations ... of ... and the configuration of the literary ... in early modern ... and ... Spain.

Index

Compiled by Michael W. Joy

INDEX

[illegible]